Western Ukraine in Conflict with Poland and Bolshevism, 1918–1923

The Peter Jacyk Centre
for
Ukrainian Historical Research

Monograph Series
Number four

Western Ukraine in Conflict with Poland and Bolshevism, 1918–1923

Vasyl Kuchabsky

Translated from the German
by Gus Fagan

Canadian Institute of Ukrainian Studies Press
Edmonton 2009 Toronto
Published in cooperation with the Wirth Institute for Austrian and Central European Studies, University of Alberta

Canadian Institute of Ukrainian Studies Press

University of Alberta
Edmonton, Alberta
Canada T6G 2H8

University of Toronto
Toronto, Ontario
Canada M5T 1N7

ISBN 978-1-894865-12-8 (bound).—ISBN 978-1-894865-13-5 (pbk.)

Library and Archives Canada Cataloguing in Publication

Kuchabs'kyi, Vasyl', b. 1895

Western Ukraine in conflict with Poland and Bolshevism, 1918-1923 / Vasyl Kuchabsky; translated from the German by Gus Fagan.

Translation of: Die Westukraine im Kampfe mit Polen und dem Bolschewismus in den Jahren 1918-1923.
"Published in cooperation with the Wirth Institute for Austrian and Central European Studies, University of Alberta".
Includes bibliographical references and index.
ISBN 978-1-894865-12-8 (bound).--ISBN 978-1-894865-13-5 (pbk.)

1. Ukraine—History—1917-. 2. Ukraine—History—Revolution, 1917-1921. 3. Ukraine—Foreign relations—Poland. 4. Poland—Foreign relations—Ukraine. I. Fagan, Gus II. Wirth Institute for Austrian and Central European Studies III. Title.

DK508.9.U37K8313 2009 947.7'0841 C2008-906349-X

This book has been published in cooperation with the Wirth Institute for Austrian and Central European Studies, University of Alberta. A generous grant toward this publication has been provided by the W. K. Lypynsky East European Research Institute (Philadelphia).

Cover photo: members of the Supreme Command and officer staff of the Ukrainian Galician Army, photographed in Khodoriv, Galicia, in February 1919. (Photo courtesy of Oleh Pavlyshyn, Institute for Historical Research, Lviv National University.)

Printed in Canada

To Hans Eberl

Contents

Foreword

Margaret MacMillan's bestselling and widely admired *Paris 1919: Six Months That Changed the World* (2002) has recently turned the attention of scholars and the wider public to the reshaping of the world by the Versailles peace settlement and the rise of nationalism after World War I. Even though the author devotes a chapter to the restitution of Poland and its frontier questions, she pays little attention to the Western Ukrainian People's Republic. One surmises that the relative paucity of literature in Western languages may explain this omission. Indeed, one of the few contributions in a Western language, Vasyl Kuchabsky's *Die Westukraine im Kampfe mit Polen und dem Bolschewismus in den Jahren 1918-1923* (1934), is a relatively rare volume published in a pre-World War II German-language seminar series.

By publishing this translation of Kuchabsky's work in its monograph series, the Peter Jacyk Centre for Ukrainian Historical Research seeks to give greater access to this classic volume on the fate of the Western Ukrainian People's Republic and its impact on the Versailles settlement, Ukrainian state-building and diplomacy, and Polish-Ukrainian relations. As Oleksandr Pavlyuk demonstrates in his lucid introduction, despite the more than seventy years that have passed since its publication, *Western Ukraine in Conflict with Poland and Bolshevism, 1918-1923* remains critical to the study of these topics. It is also essential to understanding the views of a leading Western Ukrainian political activist and thinker, himself a participant in that struggle, and, through him, the generation that shaped Ukrainian politics in the first half of the twentieth century.

Gus Fagan, senior lecturer in international relations at London Metropolitan University, has done an admirable job of rendering Kuchabsky's text in English. Myroslav Yurkevich has edited the text and standardized personal and geographic names. Marko R. Stech and Tania Plawuszczak-Stech compiled the index. Wendy Johnson of Johnson Cartographics (Edmonton, Alberta) has meticulously redrawn the six maps of the original edition and produced color versions of them. Oleksandr Pavlyuk, who has published extensively on problems of Ukrainian diplomatic history and on the Western Ukrainian People's Republic, has skillfully placed the work in the context of historiography on the Polish-Ukrainian war and the diplomatic situation in 1918–23. The Centre is grateful to Vasyl Kuchabsky's son, Dr. Leo Kutschabsky, for providing hitherto unavailable biographical information about his father, who was thought to have disappeared without trace at the end of World War II. We are also pleased to cooperate with the Wirth Institute for Austrian and Central European Studies at the University of Alberta in the publication of this volume and are grateful to its director, Professor Franz A. J. Szabo. We also greatly appreciate a generous financial subsidy for the preparation and publication of this volume from the W. K. Lypynsky East European Research Institute (Philadelphia).

Frank E. Sysyn

Introduction

Oleksandr Pavlyuk

Vasyl Kuchabsky's study of *Western Ukraine in Conflict with Poland and Bolshevism, 1918–1923,* originally published in Berlin in 1934, has not been reprinted or translated until now, but it has gained a following among students of modern Ukrainian history. Ivan Lysiak-Rudnytsky (1919–84), a prominent Galician historian who worked in the United States and Canada, referred to Kuchabsky as "the most interesting historian of the Ukrainian revolution."[1] Two conferences devoted to Kuchabsky's intellectual legacy, sponsored by the W. K. Lypynsky East European Research Institute (Philadelphia) and a number of Lviv scholarly institutions, were held in Lviv in 1995 and 1996, and publications about Kuchabsky appeared in subsequent years.[2]

Kuchabsky's book is devoted to one of the most complex periods of twentieth-century East European history. The defeat of Germany and Austria-Hungary in World War I and the collapse of the Russian Empire made it possible for the "non-historical nations" of that region to undertake the creation of independent states. In 1917–19, a number of new nation-states emerged in the region or regained their independence: Poland, Finland, Estonia, Latvia, Lithuania, Armenia, Azerbaijan, Georgia, and others. Ukrainians, too, seized the opportunity. In November 1917, the Ukrainian People's Republic (Ukraïns'ka Narodna Respublika, UNR) was proclaimed in Kyiv. It encompassed Ukrainian territories that had previously been part of the Russian Empire. A year later, in November 1918, the Western Ukrainian People's Republic (Zakhidno-Ukraïns'ka Narodna Respublika, ZUNR), comprising the Ukrainian ethnic territories (Eastern Galicia, northern Bukovyna, and Transcarpathia) of the Austro-Hungarian Monarchy, was proclaimed in Lviv. As Kuchabsky observes in his book, "the reemergence of Ukraine has completely altered the perspective in which we are accustomed to regard the situation in Eastern Europe." Unlike the Poles, Finns, Lithuanians, Latvians, and

---

1 Ivan L. Rudnytsky, *Essays in Modern Ukrainian History* (Edmonton, 1987), p. 444. Cf. the index to vol. 2 of Rudnytsky's *Istorychni ese,* 2 vols., ed. Iaroslav Hrytsak (Kyiv, 1994) for references to further comments on Kuchabsky.

2 For the most comprehensive account of Kuchabsky's life and writings, see Stepan Helei and Iurii Kuchabs'kyi, *Vasyl' Kuchabs'kyi: Naukova spadshchyna. Storinky zhyttia* (Lviv, 1998). Cf. Christina Pelenski, "W. K. Lypynsky Institute continues to promote Ukrainian, East European studies," *Ukrainian Weekly* (Jersey City, N.J.), 30 May 1999.

Estonians, however, the Ukrainians failed to consolidate and maintain their independent statehood.

In his insightful study, Kuchabsky provided the first comprehensive account of the political, military, and diplomatic aspects of the Western Ukrainian struggle against Poland and Bolshevik Russia. He examined the process of state-building in Western (and, to some extent, also in Eastern) Ukraine, as well as relations between the two republics. Kuchabsky analyzed his subject in the broader context of European politics, considering the proceedings of the Paris Peace Conference, the interests of the major Allied powers, and the Russian attitude toward Ukrainian independence. Central to his study were Ukrainian-Polish relations and the war fought by the ZUNR and the Second Polish Republic over Eastern Galicia in 1918–19.

Vasyl Kuchabsky was born on 4 November 1895 in a village near Lviv, the capital of the Austrian crownland of Galicia and Lodomeria. In 1913 he enrolled at Lviv University as a student of law, but the outbreak of World War I put an end to his studies. The next several years were formative for Kuchabsky. That period saw an explosion of national sentiment that culminated in the Ukrainian Revolution of 1917–21, with its attempt to establish an independent nation-state.

When the war broke out, the nineteen-year-old Kuchabsky joined the Ukrainian Sich Riflemen. Created at the initiative of the Supreme Ukrainian Council in August 1914, this was the first Ukrainian military legion of modern times and one of the best-disciplined elite formations of the Austrian army. Thousands of patriotic young Ukrainians in Eastern Galicia volunteered to join the Sich Riflemen, which they regarded as the nucleus of a future army of independent Ukraine. Kuchabsky, who gained notice as an intelligent and talented junior officer, fought on various fronts and was awarded an Austrian military decoration. He was captured by the Russians and, after spending more than a year in prison, escaped in December 1917.

Kuchabsky wholeheartedly welcomed the establishment of the Central Rada as Ukraine's government in Kyiv on 17 March 1917. He became an active participant in the national revolution and the building of a Ukrainian state. Along with his Western Ukrainian fellow officers, Kuchabsky took part in the creation of the Sich Riflemen unit that defended Kyiv against the Bolshevik invasion of early 1918 and soon became one of the most capable regular units in the Ukrainian army, playing a significant role in the Ukrainian Revolution. Kuchabsky was a member of the Riflemen's Council, the unit's governing body. In the autumn of 1918, the Sich Riflemen supported democratic forces in their uprising against the conservative regime of Hetman Pavlo Skoropadsky. Together with the victorious Directory, Kuchabsky entered Kyiv in December 1918, after the defeat of Skoropadsky's forces. On 22 January 1919, Kuchabsky, now the commander of the first division of the Sich Riflemen, witnessed the solemn unification of the UNR and the ZUNR in Kyiv. Later that year, he reportedly served for a brief period in the Ukrainian diplomatic mission to Sweden.

Kuchabsky's rewarding experience with the Sich Riflemen explains his general sympathy and respect for the military and its ethos of discipline and order. Kuchabsky believed that the Sich Riflemen embodied the best characteristics of the Ukrainian people.[3] As the Riflemen saw it, the struggle for independence depended on the nation's will and military strength.

By the end of 1919, both the UNR and the ZUNR had suffered defeats: the UNR fell victim to the aggression of Bolshevik Russia, while Eastern Galicia, the core of the ZUNR, was conquered by Poland. In early 1920 Kuchabsky made brief visits to Czechoslovakia and Austria but returned to Lviv in the summer. The Western Ukrainians treated Polish rule as that of an occupying power and continued their struggle. The president of the ZUNR, Yevhen Petrushevych, established a Western Ukrainian government in exile, based in Vienna, and launched a massive diplomatic effort on its behalf. In Eastern Galicia proper, a group of officers of the Sich Riflemen and the Ukrainian Galician Army, Kuchabsky among them, established the clandestine Ukrainian Military Organization (Ukraïns'ka Viis'kova Orhanizatsiia, UVO), which continued the struggle for independence by revolutionary means. At the same time, Kuchabsky began studies at the Lviv (Underground) Ukrainian University. In the autumn of 1921, the UVO attempted to assassinate the Polish head of state, Józef Piłsudski. Together with a dozen fellow UVO members, Kuchabsky was arrested and spent more than ten months in a Polish prison.

In late 1922 Kuchabsky emigrated to Germany. The Council of Allied Ambassadors to the Paris Peace Conference officially recognized Polish rule in Eastern Galicia in March 1923. Kuchabsky enrolled at the University of Berlin, obtaining a doctorate in history and Slavic philology in 1930. In 1932 he married Anna Zaluzhna, and they had a son, Leo. During his residence in Germany Kuchabsky devoted himself to scholarship, writing more than one hundred fifty works and becoming

3 Helei and Kuchabs'kyi, *Vasyl' Kuchabs'kyi*, p. 142.

known as a historian, publicist, and journalist.[4] The present monograph stands as his most solid and thorough investigation.

The central theme of Kuchabsky's writings was Ukraine's struggle for independence and the reasons for its defeat. In choosing to concentrate on this subject, Kuchabsky did not differ from other émigré Ukrainians, especially the leading figures of the national-liberation movement. In the 1920s and 1930s, they all were searching for answers to one central question: Why had an independent Ukrainian state failed to establish itself on the political map of Europe? By the time Kuchabsky's monograph was published, many memoirs and studies on this theme had already appeared and found their readers.[5] What differentiated Kuchabsky's work from the writings of many Ukrainian and other authors was his comprehensive and analytical approach.

His book is still worth reading for two reasons. First, this is an eyewitness account, rather emotional in places, of an active participant in many of the events described. Kuchabsky was personally acquainted with most of the political and military leaders of the Ukrainian Revolution, and he did not shy away from rendering frank assessments of them. Second, while Kuchabsky's pain at Ukraine's failure to secure its independence is apparent in his book, it is no mere regretful memoir but a synthetic scholarly analysis of its subject. Indeed, Kuchabsky's book was the first Ukrainian monograph devoted to the national revolution—a study by a scholar with a good education, a sharp analytical mind, and fluency in several European languages.

At the time of writing, only a decade after the events themselves, Kuchabsky could not rely on archival documents. He drew on the first published memoirs and collections of documents, secondary literature, and his own memory. Subsequent studies have added more details, improved our knowledge of certain facts, and offered some

---

4 See the bibliography ibid., pp. 689–96.

5 See especially Volodymyr Vynnychenko, *Vidrodzhennia natsiï*, 3 vols. (Vienna, 1920); Dmytro Doroshenko, *Istoriia Ukraïny 1917–1923*, 2 vols. (Uzhhorod, 1930–32); Oleksander Dotsenko, *Litopys ukraïns'koï revoliutsiï. Materiialy i dokumenty do istoriï ukraïns'koï revoliutsiï, 1917–1923* (Lviv, 1923–24); Pavlo Khrystiuk, *Zamitky i materiialy do istoriï ukraïns'koï revoliutsiï, 1917–1920 rr.*, 4 vols. (Vienna, 1921); Mykhailo Lozyns'kyi, *Halychyna v rr. 1918–1920* (Vienna, 1922); Osyp Nazaruk, *Rik na Velykii Ukraïni: Spomyny z ukraïns'koï revoliutsiï* (Vienna, 1920); Mykyta Shapoval, *Velyka revoliutsiia i ukraïns'ka vyzvol'na prohrama* (Prague, 1927). Among early studies of the Polish-Ukrainian war in Eastern Galicia, the following are notable: Antin Krezub [Osyp Dumin], *Narys istoriï ukraïns'ko-pol's'koï viiny* (Lviv, 1933); Oleksa Kuz'ma, *Lystopadovi dni 1918 r.* (Lviv, 1931); and Mykhailo Omelianovych-Pavlenko, *Ukraïns'ko-pol's'ka viina 1918–1919 rr.* (Prague, 1929). For Polish accounts of the war, see Michał Bobrzyński, *Wskrzeszenie państwa polskiego. Szkic historyczny*, 2 vols. (Cracow, 1920–25); Czesław Mączyński, *Boje lwowskie*, 2 vols. (Warsaw, 1921); Witold Hupert, *Walki o Lwów (Od 1 listopada 1918 do 1 maja 1919)* (Warsaw, 1933); Józef Sopotnicki, *Kampania polsko-ukraińska: Doświadczenia operacyjne i bojowe* (Lviv, 1921).

new interpretations. With the recent revival of interest in the Ukrainian struggle for independence generally and the history of the ZUNR in particular, both Ukrainian and Polish authors have made noteworthy efforts to produce more balanced and impartial analyses of Ukrainian-Polish relations in the years 1918–20.[6] Even so, many of Kuchabsky's views and conclusions expressed in this monograph have stood the test of time and are now supported by new evidence. His book offers the contemporary reader a spirited and highly readable account of the "forgotten" Polish-Ukrainian war for Eastern Galicia, as it was aptly termed by the modern Polish historian Maciej Kozłowski. Furthermore, despite the greater amount of knowledge we now possess, many of the dilemmas facing Kuchabsky and his contemporaries continue to puzzle modern historians. The question of why the Ukrainian Revolution and the national-liberation movement of 1917–21 failed to establish an independent state remains one of the most debatable in twentieth-century Ukrainian history.

During Kuchabsky's years in Germany, his views evolved under the influence of the prominent Ukrainian historian and political philosopher Viacheslav Lypynsky, the major ideologue of the conservative or "statist" (*derzhavnyts'ka*) school of Ukrainian historiography. State- and nation-building was at the heart of this current of thought. In the conservative view, national development depended on the state: only within its own state could a nation successfully pursue its political, economic, social, and cultural goals. There was no mature nation without a nation-state. The process of state-building was based on the individual political experience and historical traditions of each nation. Contrary to the populists, who placed their faith in the common folk, conservatives emphasized the role of elites and leaders in the state-building process. They stressed the importance of an efficient state apparatus, strong military forces, and reliance on the nation's own powers.

For Ukrainian conservatives, then, independent statehood was both the main political goal and an absolute value. Reflecting on the failure of the Ukrainian state-building process in the struggle of 1917–21, they emphasized the internal weakness of the Ukrainian national movement,

6 For the most recent studies on this subject, see: Rafał Galuba, *"Niech nas rozsądzi miecz i krew..."Konflikt polsko-ukraiński o Galicję Wschodnią w latach 1918–1919* (Poznań, 2004); Michał Klimecki, *Polsko-ukraińska wojna o Lwów i Galicję Wschodnią 1918–1919* (Warsaw, 2000); Maciej Kozłowski, *Między Sanem a Zbruczem: Walki o Lwów i Galicję Wschodnią 1918–1919* (Cracow, 1990); Mykola Lytvyn and Kim Naumenko, *Istoriia ZUNR* (Lviv, 1995); Mykola Lytvyn, *Ukraïns'ko-pol's'ka viina 1918–1919 rr.* (Lviv, 1998); Oleksandr Pavliuk, "Ukrainian-Polish Relations in Galicia in 1918–1919," *Journal of Ukrainian Studies* 23, no. 1 (summer 1998): 1–23. See also Torsten Wehrhahn, *Die Westukrainische Volksrepublik* (Berlin, 2004).

lack of unity between Eastern and Western Ukraine, and infighting between various political forces. But the paramount reason for the failure of the Ukrainian struggle, in the conservative view, was the weakness of the elite, which proved incapable of leading the nation at that critical juncture. According to conservative critics, the leaders of the Ukrainian Central Rada and the Directory were too revolutionary, socialist, democratic, and republican. Conversely, they were generally positive about the brief rule of the conservative hetman Pavlo Skoropadsky.

Conservatives in general and Kuchabsky in particular paid a great deal of attention to geopolitics and international relations. In foreign policy, they thought in terms of *Realpolitik*: states were guided by national interests, and international relations were based on power rather than on international law, justice, and humanity. Kuchabsky was in fact the first student of the Ukrainian struggle for independence to analyze it in the broader context of European politics and the interests of the great powers and the victorious Allies (England, France, and the United States), as well as key regional actors such as Poland and Russia. The subject of Ukrainian-Polish relations figured very prominently in the thinking and writing of Ukrainian conservatives.

Until very recently, little was known about Kuchabsky's life from the mid–1930s on. In 1935 he moved with his family to the old German port city of Kiel and worked as a reference librarian at the Institute of the World Economy, becoming director of the Eastern Europe department. In early 1941 the Kuchabskys moved to Lublin, then a major center of Ukrainian activity in German-occupied Poland, and Vasyl Kuchabsky served as director of the Lublin state library (*Staatsbibliothek*) until July 1944, when the Red Army took the city. Since the Kuchabsky residence in Kiel had been destroyed in the course of the war, the family moved to the town of Blankenburg in the Harz Mountains, where they stayed with acquaintances. It was generally believed that they disappeared without trace at the end of World War II.[7] Not until 2007 did it come to light that after the war Vasyl Kuchabsky worked as an interpreter at various enterprises and then as chief interpreter (from Russian) and statistician in the Blankenburg regional administration (1947–49). The town was in the Soviet-occupied zone of Germany, which was constituted as the German Democratic Republic in 1949. In that year Kuchabsky became a teacher of Russian, history, and Latin at the secondary school in Blankenburg, continuing in that position until his retirement in 1960. He died on 28 June 1971 and was buried in Blankenburg.

7 *Encyclopedia of Ukraine*, vol. 2, ed. Volodymyr Kubijovyč (Toronto, 1988), p. 697. See also Helei and Kuchabs'kyi, *Vasyl' Kuchabs'kyi*, p. 597.

Kuchabsky's book consists of an introduction and five chapters. It begins with an examination of Ukrainian-Polish relations in Galicia in the late nineteenth and early twentieth centuries—a period of rising Ukrainian national consciousness. As Ukrainian organizations proliferated in Eastern Galicia, it became a stronghold of the national movement. Polish political parties, especially the National Democrats, were resolutely opposed to Ukrainian national aspirations in Eastern Galicia. Consequently, when the Central Powers collapsed in the autumn of 1918, Polish-Ukrainian relations in Eastern Galicia were characterized by mutual suspicion, distrust, and fear. Both sides claimed Eastern Galicia and its capital, Lviv (Lwów, Lemberg), and both prepared for a takeover. The Ukrainians were the first to act. In a surprise move by a small military unit under the command of Major Dmytro Vitovsky, they took over the city of Lviv on the night of 31 October–1 November 1918.

Thus began the organization of the Western Ukrainian state, which Kuchabsky examines in chapters 1 and 2. From the very first day, this process was complicated by the Polish military insurrection in Lviv. Kuchabsky criticizes the Western Ukrainians for not having a clear plan of action and relying instead on "revolutionary improvisation." In his view, later shared by many military historians, the fate of the Western Ukrainian capital was decided not so much in Lviv itself but in Przemyśl (Peremyshl), from which the Poles supported their countrymen fighting in the capital, taking advantage of the railway bridge across the Sian (San) River. In the end, the Ukrainians retreated from Lviv on 22 November, and the Polish-Ukrainian battle for the city escalated into a full-fledged war over Eastern Galicia between the newly established Polish state and the ZUNR, whose existence was officially proclaimed on 13 November.

Despite extreme wartime conditions, by the end of 1918 the Western Ukrainians managed (as Kuchabsky describes) the peaceful and efficient establishment of state institutions, including a cabinet in Stanyslaviv (now Ivano-Frankivsk), and ensured political stability and public order throughout the territory under their control. In this connection, Kuchabsky challenges Polish accounts of looting and chaos in Eastern Galicia. He also highly praises the successful Western Ukrainian mobilization, which made it possible for a government with no regular armed forces to recruit the Ukrainian Galician Army (Ukraïns'ka Halyts'ka Armiia, UHA), consisting of more than a hundred thousand men. This achievement contradicts Polish studies, including some of the most recent ones, which claim that mobilization in Western

Ukraine was a failure and that the UHA had poor morale and large numbers of deserters.[8]

Kuchabsky also argues that in establishing law and order and consolidating their statehood, the Western Ukrainians were more advanced than others in the region, including the Poles, who were politically divided at the end of the world war and mired in warfare with almost all their neighbors. Kuchabsky therefore concludes that "the historical significance of the Polish-Ukrainian war lies in the fact that Poland suppressed that potential." Nevertheless, Kuchabsky is highly critical of the Western Ukrainian political and military leadership, including President Petrushevych. He condemns what he believes to be their lack of statesmanship and strategic vision, provincialism and political incompetence, poor diplomatic skills and knowledge of world politics, and resulting inability to represent and defend the Ukrainian national cause effectively in the international arena.

While the ZUNR managed internal consolidation successfully, its external situation was most unfavorable from the outset. As early as November-December 1918, Romania occupied northern Bukovyna, while Hungary took over Transcarpathia, which was later incorporated into Czechoslovakia. The Western Ukrainian state was reduced to Eastern Galicia, which was relatively small in territory (about 50–55,000 sq. km) and population (about 5.3 million, with ethnic Ukrainians constituting more than 70 percent), but rich in oil resources (in 1914, it accounted for more than 3 percent of world and 9 percent of European oil production). Eastern Galicia became the epicenter of the Polish-Ukrainian war. Once Józef Piłsudski achieved the consolidation of the Polish state, 3.5 million Western Ukrainians found themselves obliged to fight all of Poland, with its population of 18 million. For Kuchabsky, fighting capacity was a key factor in establishing national statehood. Given the huge disparity of population and resources, Eastern Galicia had little chance against Poland. In Kuchabsky's opinion, "what confronted the Ukrainians from the outset was the question of whether they would lose not only Lviv or the Drohobych–Boryslav oil basin but their whole country to Poland.... But neither then nor later did the Western Ukrainian leadership see the question in this light."

As for the Poles, Kuchabsky pointed out that they had two competing eastern policies: the National Democratic camp, led by Roman Dmowski, favored a unitary state, while Piłsudski and the socialist parties supported a Polish-Lithuanian-Belarusian-Ukrainian federation. Both concepts

---

8 Galuba, *"Niech nas rozsądzi miecz i krew..."* For a Ukrainian account, see Lev Shankovs'kyi, *Ukraïns'ka Halyts'ka Armiia. Voienno-istorychna studiia* (Winnipeg, 1974).

were meant to create a strong Poland and, to that end, both envisaged the incorporation of Eastern Galicia. Dmowski, however, wanted all of Eastern Galicia, with the Ukrainian lands partitioned between Poland and Russia along the Dnipro River, while Piłsudski seemed ready to settle for the annexation of Lviv and the oil region, leaving the rest of Eastern Galicia to Ukraine in exchange for a Polish-Ukrainian alliance against the Bolsheviks. Given the prevailing political atmosphere, it was Dmowski's better-articulated maximalist concept that prevailed.

An important aspect of Ukrainian state-building was the relationship between the ZUNR and the UNR, to which Kuchabsky devotes considerable attention. The future of Western Ukraine was closely linked to the fate of the UNR. Kuchabsky rightly observes that "the failure of the Eastern Ukrainians was seen as proof of the political inability of the Ukrainian movement as a whole and, as such, was used against the Western Ukrainians." He lists several factors that account for the weakness of the Central Rada and the Directory of the UNR. The key, in his opinion, was their excessive radicalism and inability to combine elements of "revolution and counterrevolution," that is, to forge a new leadership combining young, energetic revolutionary leaders from the "lower strata," still lacking political experience, with "an element of the counterrevolution still capable of leading the nation." The Western Ukrainians, by contrast, "were generally correct in their mixture of revolution and counterrevolution." On this question, Kuchabsky shared the view of Lypynsky and other conservative historians, who believed that the broadest possible strata, including loyal nobles, officials, and specialists of the old regime ("an element of the counterrevolution") willing to cooperate with the revolution and possessing the requisite experience and managerial skills, should have been brought into the process of state-building. According to the conservatives, the only Ukrainian government that had made an effort to restore "domestic equilibrium" (so "essential to the successful establishment of the Eastern Ukrainian state") was that of Hetman Pavlo Skoropadsky. It is interesting that, unlike other conservative historians, Kuchabsky was less positive about Skoropadsky. For him, Skoropadsky was not "the kind of hetman that Ukraine needed," as he allowed all of Ukraine to become a base for the Russian counterrevolution. Indeed, Kuchabsky himself took part in the Directory's uprising against the hetman.

Among the factors that contributed to the decline of the Central Rada and the Directory, Kuchabsky pointed out their idealism and youth politics ("radical pediocracy," as he called it), which "hardly differed from [those of] the Bolsheviks"; the disintegration of the state apparatus and the spread of chaos and anarchy, which the government was unable to control; the absence of reliable and battle-ready troops; limited understanding of foreign policy; the Rada's protracted adherence to the idea of Ukraine's autonomy within Russia; the Directory's lack of a clear strategy when it "vacillated between the development of the revolution" in agreement with the Bolsheviks in Moscow, even as it concurred with the Entente in promoting counterrevolution; and the lack of genuine unity between the UNR and the ZUNR.

The Directory's initial triumph over Skoropadsky created great enthusiasm for the unification of the two Ukrainian republics, which was proclaimed in Kyiv on 22 January 1919. Nevertheless, as Kuchabsky observes in his work, they actually remained two separate states built on different principles, pursuing dissimilar interests, and conducting uncoordinated foreign policies. In Kuchabsky's view, this led to the failure of both republics, and he did not hesitate to criticize the Ukrainian leaders harshly for failing to settle the issues that divided them. The two states were preoccupied with different enemies: for Eastern Ukraine, the main problem was the aggression of Bolshevik Russia, while Western Ukraine was at war with Poland and counted on the UNR for support. Kuchabsky was convinced that "it was essential to end the war on one of those fronts" in order to establish a stable Ukrainian state. He saw only one solution: as the stronger partner, Western Ukraine should have "intervened in Eastern Ukraine" and taken over the leadership, imposing its own political culture and establishing order. To that end, Western Ukraine should have concluded peace with Poland, even at the cost of losing Lviv and the Drohobych–Boryslav oil region. Having joined forces, the Ukrainians could have established a state of their own in the east and then resumed the armed conflict with Poland in order to regain their lost territory. In practice, however, the two Ukrainian states failed to work together, and the breach between them soon became "almost an unbridgeable chasm."

Agreement with the Poles was even more pressing, in Kuchabsky's opinion, because peace with the Bolsheviks was impossible. As he wrote, "unlike the Poles, the Bolsheviks were not interested in the acquisition of some part of Ukrainian territory. They wanted complete control of Ukraine at all costs." For Kuchabsky, the "world-historical effect and significance" of the Ukrainian liberation struggle consisted in fighting the Bolsheviks and protecting Europe against them. That view was not shared by Europe itself.

In the 1980s and 1990s, several historians stressed the need to pay more attention to the international context of the Ukrainian struggle for independence.[9] Kuchabsky was the first Ukrainian historian to appreciate the significance of the external factor in deciding the fate of Ukrainian statehood after World War I. The longest section of his monograph (chapter 3) is devoted to an analysis of the deliberations and decisions of the Paris Peace Conference, the attitudes of the victorious Allied powers, and the course of Polish and Ukrainian diplomacy. As Kuchabsky points out, "the course of developments was not determined solely by… internal conditions. External factors played an equally important role." Indeed, some recent studies argue that the external factor was decisive in preventing Ukrainians from gaining their independence in the years 1917–21.[10] It was Ukraine's tragedy that none of the victorious Allied powers was prepared to support or even recognize its independence, while its immediate neighbors, especially Russia and Poland, claimed parts of Ukraine or even denied its very existence as a distinct nation.

Both the Ukrainians and the Poles placed their hopes in the Entente and the United States. The Ukrainians trusted that their cause would prevail because it was a legitimate quest for freedom based on the principle of self-determination of nations proclaimed by President Woodrow Wilson. In Kuchabsky's estimation, this naïve trust was "a serious error." The Poles, for their part, enjoyed the solid support of the Entente, having been recognized as one of the allied and associated powers and possessing long-established contacts with Western leaders cultivated by such prominent politicians as Roman Dmowski and Ignacy Paderewski. As Kuchabsky rightly observed, in the diplomatic struggle between the Ukrainians and the Poles at the Peace Conference, the former were much the weaker party. No Ukrainian since the generation of Mykhailo Drahomanov "had really concerned himself with the big questions of world politics." Lacking international support for their cause and divided among themselves, the Ukrainians had no chance of success. Kuchabsky concluded that Ukrainian diplomatic activity in Paris had been "largely a cry in the wilderness"—a judgment that appears too categorical in retrospect, as the work of Ukrainian diplomats contributed greatly to publicizing the idea of their country's independence.

9 Roman Szporluk, review of Taras Hunczak, ed., *The Ukraine, 1917–1921: A Study in Revolution* (Cambridge, Mass., 1977) in *Annals of the Ukrainian Academy of Arts and Sciences in the United States* 14, nos. 37–38 (1978–80): 269; Mark von Hagen, "The Dilemmas of Ukrainian Independence and Statehood, 1917–1921," *Harriman Institute Forum* 7, no. 5 (1995): 7–11.

10 This approach was summarized by Orest Subtelny in his popular *Ukraine: A History* (Toronto, 1988), p. 378. See also an insightful analysis by Alexander Motyl, *Sovietology, Rationality, Nationality: Coming to Grips with Nationalism in the USSR* (New York, 1990), pp. 103–18. For an alternative view, see Paul R. Magocsi, *A History of Ukraine* (Toronto, 1996), p. 520. The Ukrainian historian Yaroslav Hrytsak combines these two approaches in his *Narys istoriï Ukraïny. Formuvannia modernoï ukraïns'koï natsiï XIX–XX stolittia*, 2d ed. (Kyiv, 2000), pp. 159–65.

Kuchabsky analyzed in detail the interests of the major victors—England, France, and the United States—and their approaches to the Ukrainian question, especially its Eastern Galician/Western Ukrainian aspect. These powers had different interests and visions of the post-World War I European order, but, as Kuchabsky observes, none of them supported the all-Ukrainian or Western Ukrainian claim to independence, seeing Ukraine as a "provisional entity" and an "object of barter." The Entente and the United States considered Ukraine in the context of their broader interests in Europe, linking it with the Polish question and the problem of their relations with Russia, which was greatly complicated by Bolshevism and the civil war. The West had little knowledge of Ukraine and its aspirations, while Polish and Russian propaganda presented the Ukrainian question as nothing more than a German intrigue designed to weaken the Entente.

Kuchabsky was particularly critical of the "Anglo-Saxon" handling of the Ukrainian and Eastern Galician/Western Ukrainian questions, placing a great deal of blame on England and the United States. In the case of Eastern Galicia, Kuchabsky's position was hardly justified, for in reality it was London and, at a certain stage, Washington that constrained Polish military action and refused to support the incorporation of Eastern Galicia into Poland.[11] Kuchabsky considered the French—notably the officers who promoted the creation of a *cordon sanitaire* around Bolshevik Russia—more open with regard to the Ukrainian question. He argued that "had Ukraine been a stable state clear about its own goals and methods," it could have been drawn into the *cordon sanitaire*. In that context, Kuchabsky blamed Symon Petliura, the head of the Directory, and the Eastern Ukrainian leadership for acting "like rebels, not statesmen" and losing a chance to obtain French support during the Franco-Ukrainian negotiations in Odesa in early 1919.

At the same time, Kuchabsky recognized that "what really decided the fate" of Eastern Galicia was not the Paris Peace Conference but the war with Poland. He therefore examined the course of the war and its major military operations. His book shows that while the Ukrainian Galician Army dominated the front until mid-March 1919 and controlled almost all of Eastern Galicia, except Lviv and the Lviv–Przemyśl railway

11 On American and British attitudes, see Kay Lundgreen-Nielsen, *The Polish Problem at the Paris Peace Conference: A Study of the Politics of the Great Powers and the Poles, 1918–1919* (Odense, 1979); and Oleksandr Pavliuk, *Borot'ba Ukraïny za nezalezhnist' i polityka SShA (1917–1923)* (Kyiv, 1996). On the personal influence of the historian Lewis Namier, an expert in the Political Intelligence Department of the British Foreign Office, see Taras Hunczak, "Sir Lewis Namier and the Struggle for Eastern Galicia, 1918–1920," *Harvard Ukrainian Studies* 1, no. 2 (June 1977): 198–210.

line, it was unable to take full advantage of its initial superiority because of the lack of officers, poor coordination between military units, and the errors of the supreme command. The Poles managed to turn the conflict into a war of position and then stage a counteroffensive.

The Allies in Paris were unanimous in regarding the Polish-Ukrainian war as an undesired disruption of their efforts to contain Bolshevism and therefore sought to reconcile the belligerents. In February 1919 the Paris Peace Conference dispatched a mission led by the French general Joseph Berthélemy to Poland and Eastern Galicia. The mission proposed an armistice with a demarcation line (the so-called Berthélemy line) that gave Poland one-third of Eastern Galicia, including Lviv and the oil region: the ZUNR government declined it. In his book, Kuchabsky strongly maintains that despite the "extremely unfavorable…conditions" of the Allied proposal, the Ukrainian side should have accepted it as "the only opportunity" offered during the Peace Conference "to establish an independent Ukrainian state with the support of the Entente, that is, France." In his view, "it was a major step forward for a stateless people to be able to set up a rump state if the choice was between this and complete subjection."

Whether the rejection of the Berthélemy line was justified remains a highly debatable question, and opinions are divided to this day. Kuchabsky's view was shared by many Polish historians and some Ukrainian ones,[12] who saw it as an opportunity to put an end to the Polish-Ukrainian conflict and concentrate all Ukrainian forces against the Bolsheviks. On the other hand, it is not clear how the Ukrainians of Eastern Galicia would have responded to such a settlement or how it would have affected the morale of the UHA.[13] Nor is it certain whether the Poles would have respected the peace once their armed forces grew stronger, given that the National Democrats and Polish leaders in Galicia were adamant in their demand to incorporate all of Eastern Galicia into Poland. Kuchabsky was probably right in arguing that the inexperience of the Western Ukrainian leaders in foreign policy worked to their detriment. In their defense, it should be said that the rapidly shifting political situation made it difficult to navigate the

---

12 See, e.g., Kozłowski, *Między Sanem a Zbruczem*; Ivan L. Rudnytsky, "Polish-Ukrainian Relations: The Burden of History," in *Poland and Ukraine: Past and Present*, ed. Peter J. Potichnyj (Edmonton, 1980), pp. 3–31.

13 In his *Spomyny z Ukraïns'koï Halyts'koï Armiï (1918–1920)*, vol. 1 (Lviv, 1929), pp. 140–41, Stepan Shukhevych claimed that "no one even wanted to think about giving up any, even the smallest, scrap of land east of the Sian…. Had the Supreme Command agreed at that time to the proposed demarcation line, this would have led even then to total catastrophe at the front. There was a threat that [the soldiers along] the entire front would discard their rifles and go home."

turbulent diplomatic waters. We now know that the earlier Allied mission to the region, led by Colonel H. H. Wade and Captain T. F. Johnston of the British Army, proposed a truce in January 1919 that was more favorable to the Ukrainians but was rejected by the Poles.[14] The Ukrainian Galician leadership attributed the less advantageous Berthélemy terms exclusively to the general's pro-Polish sympathies and believed that there was nothing urgent about his conditions, which could be accepted at any time. All in all, at that moment of their history the two nations seemed unprepared for compromise. Mutual prejudices molded by decades of bitter conflict could not be overcome so quickly.

Once the Ukrainians rejected the Berthélemy proposal, "the stage was…set for a massive Polish victory." By May 1919, with the arrival of a large, well-equipped army commanded by General Józef Haller, the Poles had established military superiority over the UHA and regained the strategic initiative. They launched a full-fledged offensive, feeling strong enough to ignore appeals and pressure from England and the United States and to decline new Allied peace proposals. By the end of May, Polish troops had taken the oil fields and established a common border with Romania east of Stanyslaviv. This accomplished fact, as well as the Bolshevik advance in Eastern Ukraine and the socialist revolutions in Hungary and Germany, ultimately changed British and American attitudes. In the new situation, the Western Ukrainians came to be seen as troublemakers. On 25 June the Supreme Council of the Paris Peace Conference authorized the Polish military occupation of Eastern Galicia, and by mid-July Polish troops controlled most of it.

In chapter 4, titled "The Downfall of Ukrainian Statehood," Kuchabsky analyzes the last months of the Ukrainian armed struggle in 1919. He argues that as of early June the Ukrainians still had a chance, had they been willing to suspend the war against the Bolsheviks and wage a joint UNR-ZUNR struggle against Poland for Eastern Galicia. Kuchabsky believes that such a joint Ukrainian effort could have forced Poland to sign a peace more or less along the Berthélemy line and that a liberated Eastern Galicia could have become a base from which to "continue the struggle against the Bolsheviks," perhaps resulting in the establishment of a "Ukrainian rump state." He criticizes the leaders of the two Ukrainian states for failing to unite under a single government and for pursuing policies that "profoundly contradicted" each other. Kuchabsky concludes that no real unification of the Ukrainian governments was possible "because Eastern Ukraine was unable to bring it about, and Western Ukraine was unwilling to do so."

14 Pavliuk, "Ukrainian-Polish Relations in Galicia in 1918–1919," pp. 8–10. See also Galuba, *"Niech nas rozsądzi miecz i krew…,"* pp. 90–98.

The advantage of a united effort was proved in the summer of 1919, when after much hesitation President Petrushevych of the ZUNR, who had just proclaimed himself dictator, ordered the UHA on 16 July to cross the Zbruch and join Petliura's troops. The combined Ukrainian forces launched a rather successful offensive against the Bolsheviks, resulting in the short-lived liberation of Kyiv at the end of the summer.

In Kyiv, the Ukrainian troops encountered the Russian White army of General Anton Denikin, which had entered the city by another approach. Relations between independent Ukraine and the "all-Russian" counterrevolution, as well as the role of the ethnic factor in the fight against Bolshevism, constitute the second major theme of Kuchabsky's study. He argues that there were two driving forces in the struggle against Bolshevism: the separatist movement of the non-Russian nationalities and the "all-Russian" counterrevolution. In Kuchabsky's opinion, it was not the latter's appeal to restore the monarchy but the idea of self-determination ("the regional desire to separate") that was as capable as Bolshevism of winning mass support and countering the appeal of Bolshevik propaganda. Recent studies have shown that the White movement's ultimate goal was not so much the restoration of the Russian monarchy as of "Russia, one and indivisible."[15] Not surprisingly, as Kuchabsky demonstrates, the "all-Russian" reaction was as hostile to the national movements as to the Bolsheviks and categorically refused to negotiate with them. In the end, that policy led to the defeat of both the Ukrainians and the Russian counterrevolution.

The Entente was also unable to recognize the power of national aspirations in the former Russian Empire. Instead, it placed all its hopes in Denikin, who mobilized his forces in southern Russia, and insisted that the Ukrainian movement subordinate itself to him. This demand was unacceptable to the Ukrainians, given Denikin's repeatedly asserted hostility not only to Ukrainian independence but even to the idea of a Russo-Ukrainian federation. Denikin flatly rejected proposals by the Entente to compromise with the Ukrainian movement. This made it impossible to reach agreement during the Franco-Ukrainian negotiations in Odesa in early 1919. Ultimately, it was not so much the Entente that influenced Denikin as Denikin who shaped the Entente's attitude to the Ukrainian movement. He would negotiate only with the UHA, which he considered "extraterritorial."

Unable to fight simultaneously on four fronts (against the Bolsheviks, the Russian counterrevolutionaries, the Poles, and the Romanians) and

15 Anna Procyk, *Russian Nationalism and Ukraine: The Nationality Policy of the Volunteer Army during the Civil War* (Edmonton and Toronto, 1995).

weakened by growing internal strife and self-destructive party politics, the Ukrainians were in retreat throughout the autumn of 1919. In the end, each government decided to go its own way and entered separate negotiations, Petliura with Poland and the Western Ukrainians with Denikin, each side accusing the other of treason. By the last months of 1919, "the Ukrainian statehood of 1918–19 had come to its final hour."

The last chapter of the book examines the diplomatic activities of the Ukrainian governments in the emigration and the incorporation of Eastern Galicia into Poland. The author's hopelessness about the immediate prospects of the Ukrainian national cause is quite apparent. He writes: "there was no longer any possibility of renewing the struggle. This, were it ever to happen, would be a task for future generations."

Kuchabsky identifies four attitudes or policies in the Ukrainian national movement after the end of the armed struggle. The first was the belief that "instead of looking for some solution in the international arena, the main task now should be a rebuilding of the nation from within." As a member of the UVO, Kuchabsky himself supported this policy. Two other tendencies, in his view, opposed the first: Western Ukrainians in the emigration counted on the reunification of the country under Soviet rule,[16] while the Eastern Ukrainian group "set all its hopes on Poland." In Kuchabsky's opinion, "both these groups believed that the Ukrainian nation itself was incapable of resisting the occupying powers.... Both groups failed to see that the future of Ukraine would be secure only when this security was founded on the nation's own ability to resist and not on the support of one enemy against the other." The fourth faction, as described by Kuchabsky, was the "most disastrous group…made up of the wild anarchists."

Like all conservative Ukrainian historians, Kuchabsky was highly critical of the Ukrainian-Polish alliance concluded by Petliura and Piłsudski in the spring of 1920. In Kuchabsky's view, the alliance was "almost a mockery," while Petliura became a "tool of Polish policy." His "guilt lay much more in the fact that he invited a foreign power into his country of his own free will, a foreign country that was essentially hostile to Ukraine…." Indeed, almost all Ukrainian leaders and political forces of the day reacted negatively to Petliura's decision, as did many Ukrainian historians. It is only in recent years that Ukrainian scholarship has taken a more balanced approach to the alliance.[17] For Petliura, this was the last

16 This is a considerable oversimplification of the policies pursued by Petrushevych and his government in the emigration. For a more comprehensive account, see Oleksandr Pavliuk, "Zovnishnia polityka ZUNR," *Kyïvs'ka starovyna* (Kyiv), 1997, nos. 3–4: 114–39.

17 Michael Palij, *The Ukrainian-Polish Defensive Alliance, 1919–1921: An Aspect of the Ukrainian*

chance to continue the struggle. He believed that an independent Ukrainian state could be established, even at the price of territorial concessions in Eastern Galicia. Piłsudski's intentions are less clear. Many Polish scholars have interpreted his alliance with Petliura as an attempt to implement his federative program.[18] Yet Piłsudski's Ukrainian policy was doomed to failure from the beginning. By occupying Eastern Galicia, the stronghold of the Ukrainian national movement, Piłsudski not only nullified its potential role in the struggle against Soviet Russia but also weakened the UNR and its capacity to resist Bolshevism. By and large, then, the Treaty of Warsaw remained a personal alliance between Piłsudski and Petliura.

Kuchabsky was equally merciless in his assessment of the émigré activity of the Petrushevych government. He considered its diplomatic campaign "pointless," although in a self-contradiction he then admitted that "in fact, they won a certain amount of international recognition as a result of this propaganda campaign." True, the intense diplomatic effort mounted by Petrushevych and his government did not prevent the incorporation of Eastern Galicia into Poland. Nevertheless, it kept the Eastern Galician question alive in the international arena for three more years (1920–23), drew attention to the Ukrainian cause and, in concert with the continued Ukrainian struggle in Eastern Galicia itself, forced Poland at least formally to concede the principle of Eastern Galician autonomy.

On 14 March 1923, the Council of Allied Ambassadors in Paris took the final decision that formally recognized the Polish borders as laid down in the Treaty of Riga, ending the struggle waged by Western Ukraine in the aftermath of World War I. The Ukrainian Revolution was over. However, in the words of the historian Ivan Lysiak-Rudnytsky, "it would be an error to speak of the defeat of the Ukrainian Revolution. It did not attain its ultimate goal, but it transformed Ukrainian society from within; it created Ukraine as a modern political nation. All subsequent Ukrainian life has been developing on this basis since that time."[19] Kuchabsky was one of the first to grasp and articulate the historical and geopolitical significance of the emergence of an independent Ukrainian state. Despite the bitter defeat of the Ukrainian national cause after World War I, Kuchabsky was convinced that "Ukraine, to all appearances, will become the central problem of the Eastern Europe of the future."

Revolution (Edmonton and Toronto, 1995).

18 M. K. Dziewanowski, *Joseph Pilsudski: A European Federalist, 1918–1922* (Stanford, 1969); Piotr S. Wandycz, *Soviet-Polish Relations, 1917–1921* (Cambridge, Mass., 1969).

19 Ivan Lysiak-Rudnyts'kyi, "Ukraïns'ka revolutsiia z perspektyvy soroklittia," in his *Istorychni ese*, vol. 2 (Kyiv, 1994), p. 50.

A Note on the Text and Maps

Vasyl Kuchabsky's monograph, *Die Westukraine im Kampfe mit Polen und dem Bolschewismus in den Jahren 1918–1923*, was published in Berlin by Junker und Dünnhaupt in 1934. It appeared as volume 8 in the general series issued by the Military History Section of the History Seminar of the Friedrich Wilhelm University in Berlin. The author's name appears on the title page as "Dr. W. Kutschabsky."

In this translation, the full first names of individuals whom Kuchabsky identifies only by initial and surname are given on first mention in the text (in a few cases, first names could not be established).

Kuchabsky does not use the official names of the Western and Eastern Ukrainian armed forces, respectively the Ukrainian Galician Army and the Army of the Ukrainian People's Republic, referring instead to the Western and Eastern Ukrainian armies. This usage, probably based on a desire to avoid burdening the text with unwieldy titles and to produce an account that foreign readers could easily follow, has been preserved in the present translation.

On first mention of place-names that have changed since Kuchabsky wrote his work, present-day names are supplied in parentheses. In a few instances, historical place-names (e.g., Khvastiv, Kiev, Lemberg) are also mentioned parenthetically. Cities and towns on historically Ukrainian ethnic territory that are now in Poland are identified by their Polish names, with the Ukrainian name supplied in parentheses on first mention, e.g., Chełm (Kholm), Jarosław (Yaroslav), Przemyśl (Peremyshl). In direct quotations from Polish sources, Polish versions of Ukrainian toponyms are used; similarly, in direct quotations from Ukrainian sources, Ukrainian versions of Polish toponyms are used. Bracketed interpolations in the text and notes are Kuchabsky's unless identified as those of the editor.

In order to facilitate reference to the German original, Kuchabsky's numbering of endnotes (consecutive throughout the volume) has been retained in this translation. Because Kuchabsky inserted an endnote numbered 274a in the German edition, while the endnotes of this edition are numbered consecutively, there is a discrepancy of one digit between endnotes 275–454 of the original and the translation.

The spelling of titles of Polish and Ukrainian publications cited by Kuchabsky has not been modernized, as this would complicate bibliographic searches for such material. In the endnotes, works are identified by the author's surname and a short title; complete information appears in the bibliography.

Quotations from Kuchabsky's English-language sources are cited according to the original texts, not retranslated from the German.

In discussing Woodrow Wilson and documenting Entente policies, Kuchabsky refers frequently to Curt Thesing's German translation of Ray Stannard Baker's three-volume work *Woodrow Wilson and World Settlement: Written from His Unpublished and Personal Material* (Garden City, N.Y., 1922). In the endnotes to this translation, Kuchabsky's page references to the Thesing version are supplemented by references to the corresponding pages of the American original, identified as "U.S. ed.," in parentheses.

Stanisław Kozicki's *Sprawa granic Polski na konferencji pokojowej w Paryżu* (Warsaw, 1921), which was inadvertently omitted from Kuchabsky's original bibliography, has been added to the "Monographs" section.

The six black-and-white maps appended to the original edition of Kuchabsky's work have been redrawn and produced in color for this translation by Wendy Johnson of Johnson Cartographics Inc. (Edmonton). Kuchabsky's references in the map legends to the "present-day borders" of Poland and the Ukrainian SSR have been changed to "1934" (the year of the book's publication). References in the text of chapters 4 and 5 to "present-day borders" pertain to the same year.

Preface

The revolutions of 1917–20 in Eastern Europe yielded three principal results: Bolshevism, which took up the historical legacy of Muscovy and Russia; the reestablishment of Poland; and the reemergence of Ukraine as the third-largest national and political power in Eastern Europe alongside Russia and Poland. It is in this context that we must consider the situation in Eastern Europe today. Another perspective emerges from the outcome of the world war. Four nationalities were most severely affected by the consequences of the war: the Germans, the Bulgarians, the Hungarians—and the Ukrainians. Of these, it was the Ukrainians who, because of their extremely unfavorable historical development, were the weakest, and so it was they who were the hardest hit. They were the only nationality in Europe that did not manage to achieve national statehood in the course of the revolutionary upheavals of 1918–19—this despite the fact that, as this work will show, they made greater sacrifices for their national independence than any of the nationalities that established states of their own in that period.

As a result, the Ukrainian people today lies shattered and defeated. The spoils, in keeping with the rules of war, are shared above all by Poland and the Soviet Union and, less consequentially, by Czechoslovakia and Romania. Meanwhile, the national strength of the Ukrainian people was crushed with the greatest cruelty by the Moscow Bolsheviks in Soviet Ukraine, the Don region and the Caucasus. Thus, between 1918 and 1923, some three million Ukrainians were wiped out, partly by armed conflict, partly by the Red and White terror, and partly by epidemic disease and famine. Those in Poland, especially in Eastern Galicia, did not suffer so much, but here, too, the superior strength of the Poles, the measures of the victorious powers intended expressly to bring about the destruction of Ukraine, disappointment and despair in their own ranks, and the collapse of their own social structure as a result of the defeat brought the Ukrainian people to the brink of an incalculable national collapse.

But the national consciousness of the Ukrainian people and their basic aspiration to freedom can no longer be destroyed. They number some thirty million in their compact area of settlement between the Carpathians and the Don. Their consciousness and their aspirations are the result not only of an arduous effort of national enlightenment but also of blood spilled in many battles. To be sure, the severe breakdown from which this people is still suffering may politically paralyze those aspirations for decades. But as soon as a new national leadership emerges from the great suffering of this nation—a leadership both daring and spiritually mature enough to face the extremely difficult external situation—Ukraine, to all appearances, will become the central problem of the Eastern Europe of the future.

Thus the reemergence of Ukraine has completely altered the perspective in which we are accustomed to regard the situation in Eastern Europe. It is no longer two powers, Muscovy and Poland—as was the case in the eighteenth and nineteenth centuries—that determined this situation between 1917 and 1920 and will determine it henceforth, but, as in the seventeenth century, three elements, admittedly unequal in strength—Muscovy, Poland, and Ukraine.

What is the strength of this third force in the general East European balance of power? In what general framework is it situated? What influence did it have, during the years 1918 to 1920, in giving rise to the current situation in Eastern Europe, and what influence may one expect of it in the future? In view of the changes in the basic structure of Eastern Europe, these are no idle questions: they are important enough to merit a thorough investigation.

In order to answer these questions, there is perhaps no better way to begin than by describing the struggle in which Ukraine engaged during the years 1918–20 with its two opponents, Poland and Russia, after a pause of two centuries. That is the task of the present work, which should by no means render it a merely localized or narrowly restricted historical investigation. Although a particular country, Ukraine, lies at the heart of this project, its scope extends to the history of the whole of Europe. True, this book concentrates mainly on the internal political and military situation and developments in Ukraine but, at the same time, it strives constantly to situate those developments in a universal context: both the external factors that helped determine the fate of Ukraine and Ukraine's influence in determining developments in neighboring countries, as well as the interaction of those factors and influences in the larger, shifting play of forces. Poland and Russia; Bolshevism and the counterrevolution; the tendency toward reestablishing the unity of the Russian Empire as well as the tendency toward the collapse of that unity; the situation in Central Europe and the great decision of the German Reich to accept or reject the Treaty of Versailles; world capitalism and the world social revolution; the Paris Peace Conference and the East European policies of the individual Western powers—the great drama of forces and decisions for which Europe was the stage during those years is drawn into this study insofar as it forms part of the context, no matter how remote, of the Ukrainian question. A constant effort is made to keep in view the momentary as well as the more fundamental balance of forces among the contending nations, the changing situation and the decisive turns that it took. Above all, the great achievements of this epoch are given due recognition, regardless of which party to the conflict gave rise to them.

This work pays frequent and detailed attention not only to the actual course of events but also to the opinions about their consequences generally expressed in the historical writings of the peoples directly involved—the Poles and the Ukrainians. Material on the origins of the present situation in Europe that is for the most part entirely unknown to German historiography is here made available to it. But no great value has been placed on the exclusive use of original sources: the author has quite happily availed himself of the results of existing and valid research. Controversial and dubious questions, however, have been carefully checked. Above all, this study attempts to create for the first time a total picture of the overall context of political, diplomatic and military factors by bringing together and comparing diverse source material.

The adversity of the times has hitherto delayed the publication of this work, which was completed in 1929 and is published here almost unaltered. For helpful suggestions and friendly support I would like to thank Dr. Otto Hoetzsch and Dr. Max Vasmer of Berlin University. Special thanks are due to Dr. Walter Elze of Berlin University for his interest and help with this study over many years and for including it in the series issued by the Military History Section. Thanks to Mr. Conrad Braun of Magdeburg for his generous support and to Dr. Hans Eberl, Dr. Hans Braun, Dr. Rudolf Steinmetz, Dr. Wilhelm Richter, and Dr. Max Brünn of Berlin for their friendly participation.

V. K.

Berlin, February 1934

Introduction

The outbreak of the world war found Ukraine politically divided into two major land areas. Galicia, with a population of somewhat more than three and a half million Ukrainians and an equal number of Poles in 1910, had belonged to Austria since 1772 (Map 1). The language of the western half was Polish, while that of the eastern half was Ukrainian, with the Sian (San) River constituting an approximate dividing line between the two. The remaining nine-tenths of Ukraine and its people on both sides of the Dnipro (Dnieper) River were subject to the Russian Empire. By that time, the Ukrainian national, cultural and political revival had been under way for more than a century. This was a process that Ukraine shared with the other "non-historic nations" of Europe, in other words, those that had been defeated in the great national struggles of earlier centuries and denationalized in their upper strata by the end of the eighteenth century, such as the Czechs and the South Slavs. This all-European national revival, whose origin was everywhere to be found in romanticism, while its driving force lay in the general European process of democratization, reached different stages in the two sections of Ukraine during the decades before the world war.

Its beginnings date from the late eighteenth and early nineteenth centuries in the Dnipro region, especially in Ukraine on the Left Bank of the Dnipro, where a large part of the social and political upper stratum had retained its Ukrainian ethos, had always favored political independence for Ukraine and, as late as the end of the eighteenth century, had conspired with foreign powers against Russia. Since that time Dnipro Ukraine had constantly taken the intellectual lead in the all-Ukrainian national movement, which also reached Eastern Galicia in the course of the nineteenth century. In national scholarship, where history held first place, as it did generally throughout this period of national revival, and in national literature, wherein the national poet Taras Shevchenko, active in the first half of the nineteenth century, played a leading role, Dnipro Ukraine had impressive achievements to its credit. But Russia, unlike Austria, did not undergo a process of democratization, and because of this, as well as the severe persecution of the Ukrainian movement in Russia since the 1870s, that movement did not manage to penetrate the popular masses, with the result that until 1917 those masses, though not entirely unconscious of their nationality, were certainly by and large indifferent to it. Thus, in the decades before 1917, the Ukrainians of the

Dnipro region were represented only by a very small educated stratum. They therefore presented no great danger to Russia for the time being, although the first Russian Revolution of 1905 already brought about an extraordinary advance in numerical support. This was an indication of what was to come—the years 1917–18. Fateful for the later history of Dnipro Ukraine was the fact that this educated stratum, enraptured by Mykhailo Drahomanov, did not hold to its democratic convictions and develop them into the postulate of its own national statehood, as was the case with the other "revived" nations. Rather, influenced by the development of intellectual life among the Russian intelligentsia in the late nineteenth century, that stratum attached itself to socialist internationalism in the expectation that Ukrainian national culture and political self-administration would be achieved in the future socialist commonwealth of Russia. This was another pointer to the future—Bolshevism. Thus, in the decades before the war, Dnipro Ukraine lost the opportunity to win over the sociopolitical upper strata to the Ukrainian movement by means of the idea of independent statehood for Ukraine. On the contrary, fearing social upheaval, this stratum became all the more alienated from its people and was driven into the arms of reactionary "all-Russian" nationalism. This led, in addition, to a primitivization of the Ukrainian national movement, its intellectual degeneration, and its decline into mass demagogy.

Things were different in Eastern Galicia. At the end of the eighteenth century, when the great national revival began, the Ukrainian population here no longer possessed any sociopolitical upper strata. They had long been Polonized, and between them and the ordinary people of their land there was not only a linguistic but also an ecclesiastical and religious divide: the Poles were Roman Catholic, but the Ukrainians were thoroughly Greek Catholic, in other words, united with Rome while retaining their East Slavic rite. The people here, no more than a badly neglected peasantry in historical Poland at the beginning of the Austrian period, found themselves under the leadership, during the Polish period, of a no less neglected church that could not be compared in any respect with the Roman Catholic Church. It was only the legal and socioeconomic improvement in the situation of the peasantry, which reached its climax with their liberation in 1848, as well as the elevation of the Greek Catholic hierarchy by enlightened Austrian absolutism to equal status with the other church of that territory, that created conditions favorable to the reemergence of the Ukrainian people. Given its clerical and thoroughly popular origins, the Ukrainian movement in Eastern Galicia later showed no great level of intellectual achievement; it took its cultural nourishment from Dnipro Ukraine. It benefited, however, from the constitutional regime in Austria from the 1860s on and from the general democratization of the Danube Monarchy from the beginning of the 1900s. As a result of this, Ukrainian national consciousness penetrated the whole population: if not in intellectual, then certainly in organizational terms the Ukrainian movement in Galicia became the leading force in all Ukraine from the 1890s.

Neither the Russians nor the Poles had any understanding of the gradual reemergence of Ukraine. As everywhere else during the nineteenth century, the ruling nations considered the national revival of the "non-historic" nations artificial because they underestimated the latter's inexplicable, elemental impulse toward independent national existence. The Russians, who attached no particular significance to the Ukrainian movement until the 1860s, were thereafter of the opinion that it was being stirred up in Dnipro Ukraine by the Eastern Galicians and ultimately even suspected that it was a form of Polish or Austrian intrigue, lacking any real foundation. Similarly, the Poles were so accustomed to taking for granted the Polonization of the upper stratum of the Ukrainian population and its service under Polish supremacy that in the growing rejection of Polish hegemony in Eastern Galicia gradually manifested by that population they could discern nothing other than an Austrian, then a Russian and, finally, a German intrigue aimed at the destruction of the Polish nation. Those changes in Polish opinion mark three stages of Polish-Ukrainian relations in Galicia.

The change from the untrammeled rule of the gentry in historical Poland to the enlightened Austrian absolutist state and the benefits that accrued to the lower classes as a result of this change won over the whole Galician peasantry to the side of Austria. The Greek Catholic hierarchy was equally loyal to the state because of the efforts made by Austria on behalf of its church. This social and ecclesiastical interest that bound Galicia to Austria was further strengthened, from the first decades of the nineteenth century, by a new element—national consciousness—as first the hierarchy and then ever greater numbers of Ruthenians (the historical national name used exclusively at the time to designate the Ukrainian people) gradually became aware of their own national distinctiveness, as opposed to Polish identity. Although for decades thereafter they maintained their ties with traditional Polish culture, they saw in Austria the guarantee of their national interests—at first in religious affairs and later in the cultivation of their literary language and vernacular—as well as of their very gradually developing new national culture. Mindful of their national decline in historical Poland, they quite naturally turned against Polish irredentism as early as the first decades of the nineteenth century, especially as the Polish gentry and bourgeois democrats, who were the main representatives of the anti-Austrian revolution in this country, expressed immediate and extreme hostility to these beginnings of the revival of the Ukrainian nationality and insisted that the Eastern Galician-Ukrainian population was only a branch of the Polish nation that was guilty of treason against its own national cause—that of Poland.

This led to the renewal of the historical Polish-Ukrainian conflict in this country that had ceased in the eighteenth century as a result of the Polonization of the upper strata of the Ukrainian population. That conflict found expression in the Revolution of 1848. Since this revolution in Austria was the work of the socially more or less fully developed nations—the Germans, Hungarians, Italians, Czechs, and Poles—the crown, quite naturally, sought support among the more or less peasant nationalities. Thus the Ruthenians found themselves in the camp of the counterrevolution along with the Croats, Slovenes and Slovaks. In this way the Ruthenians achieved one thing: their recognition by Austria as a second distinct nationality in this country along with the Poles. The level of their national development, which was still much too low, prevented them from achieving more, to wit, the partition of Galicia into two crownlands, one Polish, the other Ruthenian-Ukrainian. But even this modest achievement aroused strong opposition in Poland. Confusing cause and effect, the Poles became convinced that this other national movement in the country was a creation of Austria, and so the myth of Ruthenia as an Austrian intrigue made its way into the twentieth century as Ukraine began to benefit from the general democratization of Austria. Polish National Democracy, by contrast, saw Poland's national interest in the collapse of Austria-Hungary, the defeat of the German Reich, and the unification of Polish territories in Russia that would result from the coming war.

If in 1848 Austrian state interests coincided with those of the Ruthenian nation, in the 1860s the unity of interest was between Austria and Poland. The decades-long constitutional conflict in Austria, in which it was threatened by pressure from its developed nationalities for their own independent statehood, was ended by means of the *Ausgleich* (compromise) with the Hungarians and the Poles. The Hungarians were pacified in 1867 by the establishment of the Austro-Hungarian dual monarchy. The Poles, by contrast, were propitiated in two ways. They were given the hope of the reestablishment of a Polish state dependent on the Habsburgs after a possible war between Austria and Russia, and they were compensated in advance with a substitute for their national statehood by having all of Galicia, and thus also the Ruthenians, subjected to the mercy of the Polish gentry. Those were the so-called "guaranteed" and "unguaranteed" Polish rights in Galicia. The "guaranteed" rights were: the autonomy of Galicia, represented by a Diet elected on the basis of a curial electoral system that gave the Poles an overwhelming majority; the executive organs of the Diet—a whole network of administration and bureaucracy for autonomous Galicia; and the active cultivation of Polish national culture, with the whole system of higher education and almost all secondary education becoming Polish, while the Ruthenian share was virtually reduced to a certain level of support for elementary schools. The most important of the "unguaranteed" Polish rights was the principle that the Austrian viceroy in Lviv (Lemberg, Lwów), endowed with extensive powers, had to be a Pole. In this way the Poles gained control not only of Galician autonomy but also of the state administration in that country. The second "unguaranteed right" was Polish influence in the Vienna cabinet, which now included a Polish minister without portfolio for Galicia. Those "unguaranteed" rights reached their height in the 1890s when, at times, the Poles held five ministries in the Vienna cabinet—foreign affairs, interior, and finance, as well as the office of prime minister and the ministry for Galicia.

The Ruthenians found this system bearable, inasmuch as the ruling Polish gentry sought only the Polonization of the Ukrainian upper stratum and did not set itself the goal of denationalizing the popular masses themselves, or at least placed no great emphasis on it. What was unbearable, however, was the stubborn refusal to satisfy all the higher national needs of the Ruthenians, including even the denial of an adequate system of secondary education, and the fact that the ruling stratum grossly abused its power in the interests of the large latifundia, not only opposing improvements for the peasantry but also seeking to limit the emergence of industry, trade and commerce, and a native bourgeoisie.

The overwhelming dominance that the Poles achieved by means of their *Ausgleich* with Austria dealt a very serious setback to Ruthenian-Ukrainian national development. Too weak for the time being to challenge Poland in a direct confrontation, the Ruthenians believed that they had found their salvation in Russia. By the end of the 1860s they were, in their majority, Russophile. They abandoned their idea of 1848 that they constituted a Ruthenian-Ukrainian nationality distinct from both the Polish and the Russian and identified themselves with the concept of "all-Russian" nationality, namely, the idea of a triune Russian nation whose culture and common—Russian—language united three Russian branches: the Great Russians, the Ruthenian-Ukrainian Little Russians, and the White Russians.

Once again confusing cause and effect, the Poles concluded, contrary to all the experience of historical Poland, that the Ruthenian movement was a Russian intrigue. In actual fact, the Russophile capitulation of the Ruthenian movement opened up extraordinary prospects for Polish intellectual culture and the Polish political idea in Ukraine. In view of the severe Russian persecution of the national movement in Dnipro Ukraine from the 1870s and of the progress of Russification, which reached into Galicia itself, the Galician Ukrainian minority, which had remained faithful to its national identity and greatly surpassed the stagnating Russophile Old Ruthenian movement in intellectual development, put forward the idea in the 1880s of a Ukrainian-Polish community of interests and comradeship in the struggle against Russia, especially as the Poles in the Russian Empire were severely oppressed and the whole Polish nation saw Russia as its main enemy. The idea was to establish in Eastern Galicia a basis for the struggle of all Ukraine against Russia by means of an understanding with Poland; a national, cultural and political "Piedmont" of Ukraine. Concurrently with this attempted rapprochement between conservative elements in the Ukrainian movement and circles of the ruling Polish gentry, there emerged a very close community of interests between the lower proletarian and peasant strata of Poles and Ukrainians. From the 1870s and especially from the 1880s, the socialist movement grew rapidly among the two peoples. Since the peasantry and the small urban proletariat of both nationalities was ruthlessly exploited and kept down by the same ruling Polish gentry, the friendship between them was a close one, especially as it was founded on the same ideological internationalism. The Ukrainians of Galicia thus became extremely Polonophile in both their upper and lower strata, with the result that in the 1890s a Polish-Ukrainian agreement was on the political agenda for both peoples. This made it possible for the Poles, whose intellectual and political culture greatly surpassed that of the Ukrainian national movement, to draw lasting strength from the national and political development of the as yet underdeveloped Ukrainian population. This obviously entailed the explicit recognition of Ukraine as a cultural nation equal in principle to Poland and the amalgamation of the Polish and Ukrainian political movements around the idea of a future Polish-Ukrainian commonwealth as a union of two constitutionally equal nation-states.

This, however, would have meant considerable concessions on the part of the Polish movement in favor of the Ukrainians because of

Polish cultural dominance in the country at the time, and it would have involved further concessions as the Ukrainian movement developed. The outcome of such a development was uncertain. Everything depended on whether or not the intellectual and cultural level of the Poles was indeed high enough to keep the Ukrainians under its sway in the long run, even assisted by the circumstance that the Russian threat was constantly driving the Ukrainians into the embrace of the Poles. Meanwhile in Poland there was no clear recognition of the fact that the renaissance of Ukraine was inevitable, nor was there any willingness to make immediate and freely chosen concessions in order to eliminate the possibility of later forced ones. For the Poles, Ukraine was just an upstart. It went against the grain to recognize this people as equal in principle. The Poles hoped to keep the Ukrainians in a state of permanent subjection and even, if possible—as in the eighteenth century—to Polonize them. The 1890s also happened to witness the lowest ebb of hopes for the renewal of Polish statehood, and the prevailing doctrine in the Polish movement was that of "triple loyalty" to the three powers that divided the country. Thus, while the Ukrainians awaited "great deeds" from the Poles in the generous spirit of the Austro-Hungarian or Hungarian-Croatian *Ausgleich,* in Poland conditions were such that this offer of friendship from the Ukrainians lost all meaning.

Direct conflict between the Poles and the Ukrainians began only when the Ukrainian movement appealed to the popular masses themselves. A particular strength of the Ukrainians was that they had an almost fully developed two-party system. The majority party, and thus the actual leadership, was the moderate, liberal, in many respects almost conservative Ukrainian National Democratic Party, led by Yuliian Romanchuk. The minority opposition was the highly demagogic and somewhat socialist Ukrainian Radical Party. Other groups were too small to make any difference. In a short time the whole country was covered with a dense network of popular political and cultural organizations whose origins actually dated back to the 1860s. With a powerful impetus from Ivan Franko, a respectable level of national scholarly and literary activity also developed in Lviv, especially around the Shevchenko Scientific Society, while the Greek Catholic metropolitan, Count Andrei Sheptytsky, generously promoted Ukrainian national art. A private school system flourished. The Ukrainians proceeded to improve the lot of the peasantry by establishing cooperatives and credit institutions of their own, breaking up large estates, and organizing seasonal labor emigration to Germany. In the short space of twenty years before the outbreak of the world war, Eastern Galicia underwent an extraordinary transformation: in place of a destitute peasant mass there now existed a nationally conscious rural population.

The Poles tried to hold back this development by allying themselves with the Ruthenian Russophiles. But the Ukrainian national idea proved stronger: except for a tiny minority of Russophiles, the overwhelming majority of the educated strata and of the peasantry were won to the Ukrainian movement by 1914. Only with the considerable help of resources supplied by Russia was this minority able to hold its own in certain of the most backward parts of the country. Their extremely active agitation on behalf of Russia and Russian Orthodoxy made these forlorn remnants of the Russophiles seem incomparably stronger than they actually were.

The general democratization of Austria was good for the Ukrainians, especially the parliamentary electoral reform of 1907, which made possible a large Ukrainian representation in Vienna. By then the prestige of the Ukrainian leaders, to whom the peasantry owed its relatively large advance in culture and welfare, was so great, and the national discipline of the masses so strong, that when direct and universal parliamentary suffrage was introduced in 1907 the Ukrainian political leaders, to the great surprise of the Poles, were in a position, in those electoral districts where Ukrainians did not have a majority, to direct tens of thousands of Ukrainian votes, almost at will, toward the Zionists, for example, in order to prevent the Poles from winning the mandate. Thus it came about, in the course of the two decades before the war, that in Galicia, although the Polish upper stratum was considerably superior in culture and material strength to the Ukrainian leaders, the Ukrainian peasants surpassed their Polish counterparts in national consciousness, civic responsibility, national discipline, and even in culture and manners. The progress of the Ukrainian movement brought the division of Galicia into separate Polish and Ukrainian crownlands ever more into the realm of inevitable necessity, as the growing weight of the Ukrainian fact made it increasingly difficult for Austria to govern the country against the will of the Ukrainian people.

If these advances of the Ukrainian movement, which increasingly pushed back Poland's national dominance in Galicia year by year, were apt to sharpen the Polish-Ukrainian conflict, it was raised to its highest pitch by the development, from the 1890s, of Polish National Democracy, soon to be led by Roman Dmowski. Having developed out of the traditions of Polish revolutionary democracy of the 1830s and 1840s, that movement remained faithful from the outset to two tendencies: it strove to become an actual, if conspiratorial, national government of all Poland and did not limit its activity to any one section of the country but extended it across the borders drawn by the partitioning powers to all three sections of divided Poland, thereby becoming an "all-Polish" movement. From the very beginning, Polish revolutionary democracy was characterized by a fanatical nationalism. This allowed it, for instance, to deny the existence of the Ukrainian nationality in Eastern Galicia in 1848, as already mentioned. Now, in the National Democratic movement, this nationalism developed from a fanatical attitude into a rationalistically thought out political system. Poland's striving for power was not necessarily to find fulfillment in the restoration, as soon as possible, of the Polish state but, for the time being, in the improvement of the political, cultural and economic status of the Polish national element and in Polish national expansion into neighboring territories inhabited by non-Poles. This goal was to be attained not only by the activation of their own peasant masses but also by the creation of a Polish bourgeoisie, the latter to be achieved by driving the Jews out of the towns, out of industry and trade. In non-Polish territories such as Eastern Galicia, it would be achieved by the Polonization not only of the upper strata, which was the goal of the Polish conservatives, but also of the non-Polish popular masses. Through the skillful use of every legal and illegal opportunity that arose, the weight of the Polish national element as a political factor would gradually increase, and in this way an "all-Polish" nation as a unified organism would emerge beyond the reach, as it were, of the state structures of the partitioning powers, thus gradually reestablishing the Polish question as part of the agenda of European politics. The main support for this "all-Polish" concept was to be the nationalist fanaticism of every individual Pole. The immediate organizational goal, however, was the penetration by the National Democrats, wherever possible, of existing Polish national organizations and the struggle for exclusive control over them. Their tactic vis-à-vis the partitioning powers was expedient adaptation to circumstances and deception of the enemy. The National Democrats thus combined all the advantages of an oligarchic conspiratorial coterie with the brute force of blindly obedient mass organization. Their means to that end was the virtuoso handling of mass propaganda. The fundamental principle of their propaganda system was the mobilization of popular feeling for the national-democratic cause by means of a simplistic moralism in terms of which all that the Poles themselves did, or that corresponded to Polish national interests, was proclaimed morally good, whereas all that ran counter to those interests was morally reprehensible. Accompanying this simplistic morality was an unceasing and rigorous arousal of mass hatred by the systematic and boundless slandering and denunciation of their opponents—horror stories, false representation of facts; the obstinate holding on to false assertions that served their purpose in spite of all corrections, in spite of reality itself. The Polish masses were aroused to a fever pitch, and their capacity for action was thus raised far above the ordinary. And this did, in fact, ultimately enable the National Democrats to achieve their political goals. Whether or not this unscrupulous rabble-rousing undermined the substance of the Polish nation itself remains to be seen.

The emergence of the Socialist and National Democratic movements in Poland at the same time as the democratization of Austria broke the power of the Polish gentry in Galicia. From the turn of the century, under the influence of the National Democratic movement, the fundamental goal of Polish national policy was the Polonization and, where that was impossible, the impoverishment and destruction of the Eastern Galician Ukrainian population. The Polish bureaucracy in Galicia, as well as the majority of the clergy and the large landowners, supported this policy. The means by which this goal was to be achieved were: on the religious level, the conversion of the Ukrainians to Roman Catholicism, in which process all kinds of pressure were brought to bear and the church became an instrument of Polish national power; on the cultural level, the Polonization of the Ukrainian school system and the active promotion of private Polish schools; on the socioeconomic level, an attempt to colonize Eastern Galicia through the settlement of Polish peasants. Polish-Ukrainian relations, which until then had been characterized largely by human decency, even by some measure of nobility and mutual respect, now took on something of a vulgar aspect from the Polish side as a result of the incitement of the Polish masses. This also resulted in the growth among the Ukrainians of a bitter hatred of the Poles that found expression, for instance, in the murder in 1908 of the viceroy of Galicia by a Ukrainian student and in gunfights between Ukrainian and Polish students at Lviv University in 1910. Another consequence was that Polish socialism, adapting to the mood of the masses, became somewhat nationalist in this national-democratic sense. The bridges between the two peoples were thus destroyed.

Worst of all, the already mentioned Polish National Democratic propaganda system not only poisoned existing conditions but completely obscured them. Thus the fact that the Ukrainians encouraged and organized seasonal work in Germany in order to improve the lot of their peasants was sufficient for the Poles to claim that the Ukrainian resistance in Eastern Galicia was organized and led from Berlin, a claim that the Poles later stubbornly and systematically maintained before the

Entente powers. In view of the approaching war with Russia, the Vienna government badly wanted a Polish-Ukrainian agreement but could not, as fifty years earlier, turn over the Ukrainians, now much stronger as a national group, to the unfettered despotism of the Poles. It therefore impressed upon the Poles the need for moderation. The Austrian state administration in Galicia, however, was in the hands of a Polish bureaucracy and remained a Polish instrument in the struggle against the Ukrainians. But in spite of these facts the Polish National Democrats, who themselves had raised antagonism between the two peoples to the highest pitch, now claimed that this hostility had been deliberately created by Austria. In this way they achieved two distinct goals. They made the Ukrainian movement appear contemptible in the eyes of the Polish masses; at the same time, the anti-Ukrainian feeling of the masses was directed against the Austrians, thereby undermining Poland's pro-Austrian orientation, since the National Democrats themselves, in view of the approaching war, represented a Russophile policy and looked to a defeat of the Central Powers by the Entente. Also, in Poland's dealings with the Entente powers, the claim that the hostility between Ukrainians and Poles was an artificial creation of Austria would later be used against the Ukrainian movement. The constant repetition of this claim at the Paris Peace Conference would inflict the greatest harm on the Ukrainian cause. Thus, as a consequence of the activity of the National Democrats, the Polish masses once again confused cause and effect. From that time on, the myth of the Ukrainian movement as a creation of German and Austrian intrigue became a generally accepted part of both Polish historical writing and Polish national and state policy.

In this state of incitement and mutual hatred the two peoples entered the world war.

II.

The various nationalities awaited the war with growing apprehension. For some the final goal, be it national liberation or expansion of existing small states, was to be attained through the victory of the Central Powers; for others its achievement lay with the triumph of the Entente. In Galicia it was the Poles who were the first to act. As early as 1908 Józef Piłsudski had begun to organize military units in Cracow for the approaching war with Russia. Out of those developed the Polish Legion, which fought on the side of the Central Powers. The idea of national independence for Ukraine began to grow among the Ukrainians of Eastern Galicia. They also began to organize themselves militarily, at first secretly, then openly from 1912. A Ukrainian Legion developed out of these military units and fought in the world war as part of the Austrian army.

In spite of the Russophile policy of the National Democrats, the Poles sided initially with the Central Powers, as did the Ukrainians. The Poles had good reason to do so, as Austria was giving serious consideration to the reestablishment of a Polish state. The Ukrainians, however, deceived themselves, since Austria was far from having any such plans for Ukraine. Dnipro Ukraine remained passive. Only a few émigrés from there saw the need to carry on active Ukrainian propaganda in the German Reich during the war, and their activity was not without success, for in time it gained a favorable response from the German public and among the Austrian military leaders. Admittedly, these leaders did not come around to favoring the establishment of a Ukrainian national state, but they began to realize that Austrian interests by no means fully coincided with Polish ones, and that it served their own military interests to respect the wishes not only of the Polish but also of the Ukrainian population in the war zone. Apart from this, neither the Austrian politicians nor the military leaders had any clear idea of how Eastern Europe was to be ruled after the war and the expected victory of the Central Powers. Individual views were contradictory, expressing themselves in the most diverse plans that changed from moment to moment, according to the situation, and vacillated between two contradictory concepts: the decidedly prevailing readiness to hand over the whole of Galicia to the future Poland, if necessary, and the theoretical consideration, of no decisive significance, of creating a separate Eastern Galician Ukrainian crownland. Thus Austria remained basically pro-Polish, even if this met with some opposition, especially in military circles. The mere existence of this opposition met with the greatest aversion on the part of the Poles. They were so accustomed to regarding Eastern Galicia as an exclusively Polish possession and to ignoring the demands of the Ukrainian population for their natural rights in that country that their belief in the myth of Austrian support for the Ukrainians became even more unshakable. But in the absence of any final decision about the fate of Galicia, it was impossible for the Austrians, with the war in full swing, to treat Eastern Galicia as a mere province of Poland and ignore the existence of the Ukrainian population, whose regiments were among the best in the Austrian army—this in spite of recent official histories of the world war, published in Vienna, that still promote the legend of "Ruthenian treason." Since the Polish government's way of treating the Ukrainians was well known, Austria, under pressure from the military leaders, reneged for the first time on one of Poland's "unguaranteed rights" and in 1915 appointed in Galicia not a Polish viceroy but a nonpartisan military governor, General Hermann von Colard, followed later by the pro-Polish General Karl Georg von Huyn.

But this wartime administrative practice in Galicia had no immediate effect. The war had hardly begun when the Polish bureaucracy in Galicia, heavily influenced by the National Democrats, seized the opportunity, allegedly in the interests of the Austrian state, and proceeded, under cover of combating Russophilism, which they themselves had supported only shortly before as an anti-Ukrainian measure, to settle accounts with the Eastern Galician Ukrainians. Mass arrests were carried out, and among the victims were many Ukrainians whom the authorities knew to be loyal to the Austrian state. In this manner a whole people that was decidedly on the side of Austria was branded "treasonous" on account of a few hundred genuine Russophiles who could easily have been rendered innocuous before the war began. Thousands of Ukrainians were deported to internment camps. The foreign troops, especially the Hungarians, were in the grip of a spy hysteria as a result of their own failures and the many transports of so-called traitors, and the country was witness to innumerable executions of completely innocent victims—one of the darkest and most inglorious chapters in the history of the war. Naturally, the fury unleashed by the Polish bureaucracy in Eastern Galicia was not limited to the Ukrainians. In 1914, when the Russians advanced almost as far as Cracow, many Polish peasants in Western Galicia had to expiate with their lives the introduction of this new method into the Polish-Ukrainian struggle. Not until 1916 did this gruesome episode come to an end.

Meanwhile, in the years 1914–15, Ukrainian policy in Austria was completely paralyzed as a result of the mistrust thus engendered among the Austrians toward the Ukrainians. Only in a careful and meticulous manner could that mistrust be overcome. Thousands of refugees from Eastern Galicia had to be cared for. In the internment camps, infinite care had to be taken not to attract suspicion in eliminating at least the worst forms of mistreatment and gradually arranging the release of the internees. By the end of 1915, Ukrainian prospects in Austria had improved, and there were even attempts to pacify the Ukrainian politicians with vague promises. In reality, however, the pro-Polish trend maintained the upper hand in Austrian policy. On 5 November 1916, under strong pressure from Austria, the Central Powers proclaimed the independence of Congress Poland, and at the same time Emperor Franz Josef I, a long-time supporter of the Polish cause, announced the fulfillment of an old desire of the Austrian Poles—autonomy for Galicia, in other words, an extension of Polish rights in Galicia, maintaining only a loose connection with the Danube Monarchy.

A reversal of this Austrian support for Poland was brought about only in 1917 by developments in Dnipro Ukraine. This achieved nothing for Austria, as the Poles demanded the immediate annexation of all Galicia to Poland. Immediately after the outbreak of the revolution in Russia in March 1917, the Ukrainian Central Rada [Council—Ed.] (Ukraïns'ka Tsentral'na Rada), headed by Professor Mykhailo Hrushevsky, was formed in Kyiv (Kiev) as the leadership and representative body of Dnipro Ukraine. At the mere news of the formation of their own national government, the national sentiment of the Ukrainian people emerged with strikingly elemental force. People who only yesterday had felt themselves to be Russians suddenly became conscious of their Ukrainian identity and, almost overnight, Dnipro Ukraine became the scene of a radical Ukrainian national revolution. Spontaneously, Ukrainian soldiers in the Russian army began to organize themselves in separate units and placed themselves at the disposal of the Rada. Soon the Rada was in a position to claim one and a half, even two million "Ukrainized" troops, in addition to other mass organizations. Russian patriots feared increasingly for the fate of Russia: everyone assumed that the Rada would immediately proclaim Ukraine an independent state, make peace with the Central Powers, and march against Russia. It would certainly have come to that if Dnipro Ukraine had had a proper leading stratum, for at the time the social-revolutionary tendency in Ukraine was insignificant, and the masses were everywhere in the grip of a strongly anti-Russian and separatist Ukrainian nationalism.

Meanwhile, the Rada was under the spell of Russian socialist internationalism. It stood for preserving the political unity of Ukraine with Russia and the "deepening of the revolution" in fraternal unity with Russian "revolutionary democracy," in other words, for the transformation of the revolution into a socialist coup and, linked to this, for the continuation of the war against the Central Powers, which it proclaimed as a struggle for the future of the revolution.

Thus the democratic movement of Dnipro Ukraine, together with the Russian democratic movement—which, after all, justified its revolution with the claim that the tsarist regime was incapable of pursuing the war "to final victory"—found itself, contrary to all the talk about supposed German intrigue in Ukraine, completely in the sphere of Entente policy. All that divided the Kyiv Rada from the St. Petersburg Provisional Government was the Ukrainian demand that the autonomy of Ukraine should be implemented immediately. The Provisional Government, by contrast, wanted to have this question resolved by the future Russian Constituent Assembly. In this conflict the Ukrainians were initially victorious. On 23 June 1917, they proclaimed the autonomy of Ukraine with its own parliament—the same Central Rada—and its own government, the General Secretariat (Heneral'nyi Sekretariiat) at the head, and by July 1917 the Provisional Government already found itself obliged to recognize this revolutionary fait accompli, given the massive support for the Rada among the population and the military.

In the aftermath of these events, many voices were raised among the Galician Ukrainians for union with Dnipro Ukraine. In fact, at the end of 1917 a Galician Ukrainian Legion was formed in Kyiv that was later to become very well known—the Ukrainian Sich Riflemen, a numerically small but, despite the general revolutionary disintegration, highly disciplined and battle-ready unit that soon became the guard of the Central Rada.

Only now did the Ukrainian question become a reality for the Central Powers. True, Austria, greatly exhausted by the war and sensing its approaching collapse, remained firmly on the side of the Poles, but, given the complete victory of the pro-Entente orientation in Poland, Ukrainian propaganda began to have some effect on German policy after the outbreak of the Russian Revolution in 1917. Germany welcomed the resurgence of Ukraine, in which it saw a future counterweight to pro-Entente Poland.

The pressure of these events impelled the Central Powers to intervene in Ukraine. In November 1917 the Provisional Government in St. Petersburg and Moscow was overthrown by the Bolsheviks, and Russia disintegrated completely. The Ukrainian Central Rada declared itself opposed to this coup and proclaimed the Ukrainian People's Republic (Ukraïns'ka Narodna Respublika, UNR), which was to return to a political association with democratic Russia only after the defeat of Bolshevism in Great Russia. It seemed that Ukraine was about to become a new power center, replacing a collapsed and disintegrating Russia. It was in fact the Ukrainian troops that had maintained their battle-readiness the longest and withstood the disintegrative pull. The Entente, not the Central Powers, was the first to recognize the new Dnipro Ukrainian state formation in the turmoil of revolution. France sent its official representatives to the Ukrainian government in Kyiv as early as the end of December 1917, as did England at the beginning of January 1918.

The apparent power of the Rada, however, was already a thing of the past by the end of 1917. The Rada itself had done everything, on the one hand, to dampen Ukrainian nationalism, which could later have resisted Bolshevism, and, on the other hand, by means of its own social-revolutionary propaganda and activity, to prepare the ground for the emergence of Bolshevism in Ukraine itself. As a result, the initial national enthusiasm of the masses dissipated very quickly: indeed, it was so disappointed and destroyed by social-revolutionary agitation that it never reemerged in Dnipro Ukraine with the strength and vitality it had shown on its appearance in 1917. The "Bolshevized" as well as the "Ukrainized" troops left the front and returned home. An enormous agrarian revolution shook the country. The mood of the masses lent even greater strength to Bolshevism. In January 1918, as the mass of armed Bolsheviks began to penetrate Ukraine from Moscow, the Bolshevik revolution against the Rada broke out all over Ukraine, as it had done previously against the Provisional Government in Russia. On 22 January 1918, the Rada proclaimed the independence of the Ukrainian People's Republic in the hope that this would inspire a national defense, but by now no one hastened to respond to the call. In Kyiv itself a general Bolshevik uprising broke out. The Rada was surrounded by insurgents. The massacre of all its members—who represented, so to speak, the finest flowering of all Dnipro Ukraine at the time—seemed inevitable. But the valiant companies of Eastern Galician Sich Riflemen, engaging incessantly in assaults and hand-to-hand street fighting that lasted five days and nights, managed to put down the uprising and, at the last minute, saved the Rada. However, in view of the large number of Bolsheviks approaching the capital, the Rada and its hard-pressed defenders had to evacuate Kyiv at the beginning of February 1918.

While the street fighting was in progress in Kyiv, representatives of the just proclaimed sovereign Ukrainian state presented themselves in Brest-Litovsk, where the Central Powers were engaged in protracted peace negotiations with the Bolsheviks. The Bolsheviks denied the delegation the right to sign a separate peace in the name of Ukraine, basing their own right to do so on the fact that their troops had just taken Kyiv. But it was just at this time that the Ukrainian Sich Riflemen retook the city. Having demonstrated that the Rada was still in control of Kyiv, the Ukrainian delegation was admitted to the talks and, in this way, the Brest-Litovsk peace was made possible by a company of Eastern Galician Ukrainian fighters.

The Central Powers, especially Austria, were still unaware that the power of the Rada had collapsed completely. They therefore believed, as the Entente had previously, that the forces of Dnipro Ukraine were much greater than they actually were at that moment. On the other hand,

Vienna was threatened with famine, and the Austrians—especially the Austrian foreign minister, Count Ottokar Czernin—felt themselves constrained to conclude a peace treaty at any price, and therefore to approve all Ukrainian demands, in order to obtain foodstuffs for Austria immediately from Ukraine. Hence the Brest-Litovsk peace of 9 February 1918, which was exceedingly favorable to Ukraine. All the Ukrainian territories captured by the Central Powers from Russia, including the Chełm (Kholm) region, were recognized as part of Ukraine. At the same time, in a secret treaty with Ukraine, Austria committed itself to establish a separate crownland of Eastern Galicia and Bukovyna by 20 July 1918 at the latest. In return Ukraine made a commitment, in another treaty, to deliver a million tonnes of grain to the Central Powers for appropriate recompense. By Count Czernin's reckoning, it later delivered two or three times that much.

In the meantime, whether through a Ukrainian indiscretion or a Hungarian leak—the Hungarians did not want an Eastern Galician precedent—the Poles found out about the secret treaty. A storm of indignation broke out in Poland. Under pressure, raising trivial objections as a pretext, Austria declared the secret treaty null and void on 4 July 1918. By this time, the weakness of Dnipro Ukraine had become clear to the Central Powers. In the Chełm region, boundary corrections in Poland's favor were imposed on Ukraine. Thus, for Austria, the Treaty of Brest-Litovsk was just a brief episode. It returned to its original plan of winning Poland by handing over all of Galicia, and it remained faithful to this project until its own collapse, without having won anything from the Poles.

Thus the last favorable opportunity passed for the Eastern Galicians. At the behest of the Rada, the armies of the Central Powers occupied Dnipro Ukraine from March 1918 in order to rid the country of the Bolsheviks. At the time those foreign troops entered Ukraine, the whole of the former Russian Empire was in Bolshevik hands since, in the midst of the general collapse, not only Ukraine but every other territory of the former Russia—even the Cossack areas, with their long history of military organization—had failed to stem the Bolshevik tide with its own forces.

Even during the occupation, the Rada did not give up its social-revolutionary activity. This fact, as well as the belief that a social-revolutionary Ukraine would not be capable of using all the country's resources to the full and making the agreed grain deliveries to the Central Powers, convinced the leaders of the German occupation troops of the need to bring down the Rada. On 29 April 1918 the monarchic regime of

Hetman Pavlo Skoropadsky was established, supported by a handful of Dnipro Ukrainian landowners, and, in this manner, the sociopolitical and legal order of prerevolutionary Ukraine was temporarily reestablished.

Such was the general situation in Eastern Galicia and in Dnipro Ukraine at the moment of the collapse of the Central Powers.

Chapter 1

The Rise of the Western Ukrainian State in Eastern Galicia

1. The Collapse of Austria and the Ukrainian Takeover of Eastern Galicia

The clumsiness in Austria's dealings with Poland from the beginning of the war;[1] the major disagreements between Austria and the German Reich concerning the Polish question after the victory over Russia in 1915;[2] the actions of the Polish National Democrats, who took advantage of every opportunity created by these circumstances to weaken Austrophilism among the Galician Poles[3]—all these contributed to the fact that Austria lost its Polish gamble. It was a hopeless gamble in any case, for Congress Poland had nothing in common with the Central Powers, nor did it expect of them any kind of "liberation," but rather, having become organically linked to the Russian Empire, remained unshakably attached to Russia and the Entente.[4]

The proclamation of Polish independence by the Central Powers on 5 November 1916 therefore came to nothing. The Polish Austrophiles were dissatisfied because Galicia was not included in the Polish state, and the Russophiles were similarly disenchanted because Polish areas of the German Reich, as well as other northwestern border areas of Congress Poland, also were not included. In Warsaw, on 14 January 1917 (or 22 June 1918), the Council of State (Rada Stanu) and, on 12 September 1917 (or 15 October 1917), the Regency Council (Rada Regencyjna) were inaugurated as the supreme organs of the new state,[*] but the Congress Poles refused to create an army under German command, and these institutions became instruments of opposition that the Central Powers could no longer satisfy in any way.

Since Congress Poland declined to create a Polish state dependent on the Central Powers and waited for this state to emerge automatically out of the course of the war and the victory of the Entente, Galician-Polish Austrophilism lost its raison d'être, unless Austria could be induced to

---

* The Interim Council of State, a consultative body of 25 members, was inaugurated under the auspices of the Central Powers on 14 January 1917; its members resigned on 25 August 1917 after Józef Piłsudski, the commander of the Polish Legions, switched his allegiance to the Entente. The establishment of the Regency Council, a three-man governing body with limited jurisdiction, was announced by representatives of the Central Powers on 12 September 1917, and the council was inaugurated on 15 October 1917. A new Council of State consisting of 110 members (55 elected, 43 appointed by the Regency Council, and 12 ex officio) was later formed to prepare for the establishment of a Diet; the council's inaugural session took place on 21 June 1918. [Editor's note]

continue its Polonophile policy. As long as the automatic emergence of the Polish state was still uncertain, this Austrophilism had some basis for continued existence. It collapsed, however, as soon as Russia, on 30 March 1917, declared itself in favor of Polish independence.[5] The tendency to regard Austria as a defender of the Polish cause continued to echo in Galicia for a time. But when Austria, under pressure of famine, signed the Brest-Litovsk treaty with Ukraine on 9 February 1918, recognized the Chełm region as part of Ukraine, and committed itself to the autonomy of Eastern Galicia, the echo went dead—the Galician Poles joined the Congress Poles in declaring themselves unconditionally for the Entente. The remnants of the Galician Polish Legion, which until then had survived the Poles' dissatisfaction with the Central Powers, now left their allies and went to Ukraine on 15–16 February 1918 under the command of General Józef Haller. On 10 May 1918, at Kaniv on the Dnipro, they were captured and disarmed by German troops. General Haller, with a small number of companions, escaped by way of Murmansk in northern Russia to France.[6]

In 1918, for the first time in fifty years, the Poles in the Vienna parliament went over to the opposition in spite of the fact that, at their insistence, Austria had immediately withdrawn its commitment given at Brest-Litovsk. Although their only goal now was the defeat of the Central Powers, they neither pushed their parliamentary opposition to the limit nor openly promoted the collapse of Austria, as the Czechs did. The Poles feared that, at the last moment, Austria might separate Eastern Galicia and hand it over to the Ukrainians.[7] This fear was unfounded, for until the very end Austria stuck to its policy of increasing Habsburg power by means of a Polish kingdom; nevertheless, it paralyzed Polish policy right up to the collapse of Austria.

The Galician Ukrainians' fear was perhaps even greater. The inevitable collapse of Austria became even more obvious in 1918, but the Ukrainian parliamentarians, under the leadership of Dr. Yevhen Petrushevych, refused to take seriously the possibility of the collapse of the Danube Monarchy.[8] They had become so integrated into Austrian parliamentarism and so accustomed to regarding politics as a series of "principled" declarations by the Ukrainians, followed by an occasional concession from the government, that they could not imagine a situation in which Austria no longer existed and they would have to act on their own. But those Ukrainian circles for whom the collapse of Austria was obvious also did nothing. After the Treaty of Brest-Litovsk, Austria suspected the Galician Ukrainians of wanting to join Eastern Ukraine—which was partly true—and took an unfriendly attitude. The Ukrainians did not want to cause trouble or express their dissatisfaction because they were afraid of playing into the hands of the Poles, who, as in 1914, might use the pretext of Austrian state interest to combat them.[9] The Polish nightmare was the possibility that the Ukrainians might conspire with the Austrian military command against them.[10] But the Galician Ukrainian leaders did not attempt, as a cautionary measure against a possible Polish coup attempt in Galicia, to persuade the Austrian military command to station Ukrainian garrisons in Eastern Galicia. The death agony of Austria thus paralyzed the nationalities, and the greater their loyalty to the Austrian state, the greater was this paralysis.

In the meantime, the Central Powers approached their fate. In September 1918 Bulgaria collapsed, and on 4 October Austria accepted President Woodrow Wilson's peace conditions of 8 January 1918, which included loss of territory to Italy, autonomy for the peoples of Austria-Hungary, and the reestablishment of an independent Polish state comprising all undisputed Polish territory. On 12 October 1918, however, the Austrian emperor Charles I rejected the partition of Galicia. As late as 19 October 1918, in full agreement with the Austro-Hungarian prime minister, Max Hussarek, the Austrian foreign minister, Count Julius Andrássy, Jr. (who emulated his predecessors, Count Ottokar Czernin and Baron István Burián, in this respect), offered the incorporation of an undivided Galicia into the Polish state as the price for a Polish union with Austria—a suggestion that the Poles rejected in view of the victory of the Entente.[11]

These frantic attempts to save Austria finally roused the Ukrainian parliamentarians. On 10 October 1918 they decided no longer to limit themselves to protest but to form their own Ukrainian National Rada (Ukraïns'ka Natsional'na Rada) that would proclaim the right of all Ukrainian territories of the Austro-Hungarian Empire—Eastern Galicia, northwestern Bukovyna, and Carpatho-Ruthenia—to self-determination. This decision was legalized, so to speak, by one of the last attempts to save the Habsburg Monarchy, Emperor Charles's manifesto of 16 October 1918, which proclaimed the transformation of Austria—not Hungary—into a federal state in which each of the Austrian nationalities would be granted its own state organization.[12]

The manifesto satisfied the official Galician Ukrainian leadership, as against the more radical minority of all the parties that insisted unconditionally on the incorporation of Eastern Galicia into Dnipro Ukraine. Ukrainian representatives in the Vienna parliament and the Diets of Galicia and Bukovyna, along with representatives of the different parties, met in Lviv on 18 October 1918 to form the heralded

Ukrainian National Rada. On the following day, the Rada proclaimed the union of all Ukrainian ethnic territories of Austria-Hungary into a state formation known as the "Ukrainian territory." The proclamation was supported by delegates summoned to Lviv from the whole country. This proclamation of independent statehood, entailing an association with Austria-Hungary that was not more closely defined, was prompted by the consideration that in the event the Entente should decide to maintain the Habsburg Monarchy, the union of Eastern Galicia with Dnipro Ukraine would not be feasible. Given the lack of clarity about the situation in Dnipro Ukraine, such a union would have an uncertain future. Another consideration was that the peoples of Austria-Hungary could definitely count on having their representatives admitted to the peace negotiations by the Entente, whereas Dnipro Ukraine, as a result of the Treaty of Brest-Litovsk, would incur the Entente's hostility.[13]

The logical thing to do would have been to form a secret government to prepare the political organization of the "Ukrainian territory," especially as Poland was also laying claim to it. But this was a time in which all the nationalities vanquished in the world war were enthusiastic about the so-called Wilsonian principle, believing in the dawning of a new world era in which the fate of individual countries would no longer be decided by force but by the "democratic principles" of liberty, equality and fraternity of the "self-determining" nations. Among all such nationalities, the most unlikely strata were beginning to govern. Thus it seemed sufficient to the Ukrainian parliamentarians merely to announce their desire for "self-determination" in order to achieve it, especially as Austria had been obliged by the Entente to grant "self-determination" to its nationalities.

They saw the means to this end in negotiations with the constantly changing Austrian government. Not even the note of the American secretary of state, Robert Lansing, published after long delay on 21 October 1918, succeeded in shaking this Ukrainian democratic legitimism. In this note Austria was informed that, since Czechoslovakia and Yugoslavia were still de facto in a state of war with Austria-Hungary, national autonomy was no longer a suitable basis for peace negotiations, and it was up to those nationalities themselves to determine what measures to demand from Austria-Hungary. Since the continued existence of the Habsburg Monarchy was made to depend on the decisions of the Czechs and the Yugoslavs, this was, to all intents and purposes, the death sentence of the empire, and the Lansing note was the signal for the general revolutionary self-organization of these national states, openly aiming at the collapse of Austria and ignoring the formal legalities of that process.

To the very end, however, the Ukrainians placed the greatest emphasis on a formal transfer of state power over the "Ukrainian territory" by the Austrian government and completely neglected preparations for an independent seizure of power. The negotiations were fruitless. The Austrian cabinet, led first by Hussarek and then by Professor Heinrich Lammasch, whose only task now was to organize the more or less orderly transition from the old empire to the new nation-state order, was in an extremely difficult situation with respect to Eastern Galicia. Whether they awarded Eastern Galicia to the Poles or the Ukrainians, there would inevitably be large-scale unrest in the country. So the situation remained unresolved. On 31 October 1918 the Council of Ministers recognized both the right of the Galician Poles to be incorporated into the Polish state and take over the state administration of Polish Galicia in advance and the right of the Ukrainians to their independent national state in Eastern Galicia. It decided, however—as if this were a time for formal niceties—simply to direct the Galician viceroy, in consultation with the Ukrainian National Rada, to turn over local government and finance in the mainly Ukrainian-populated areas of the country to Ukrainian officials. The functions of the viceroy of Eastern Galicia were later to be transferred to one of the local Ukrainian leaders.[14] This order never reached the Galician viceroy, General Huyn, and even if it had, he would not have been able to carry it out: a few hours after this session of the Council of Ministers, on the night of 31 October–1 November 1918, the Eastern Galician Ukrainian troops took over the city of Lviv and Eastern Galicia in a surprise coup on their own initiative.

While the Ukrainian National Rada stood idly by, the Poles moved to take over all of Galicia. As early as 7 October 1918, on hearing news of the peace offer of the Central Powers, the Warsaw Regency Council proclaimed the union of all Polish territories in an independent state with access to the sea. In view of the fact that Congress Poland was still occupied by Germany and Austria, this was a coup d'état, but no one reckoned with the Central Powers any longer. The Galician Poles in the Vienna parliament therefore promptly declared on 9 October 1918 that it was their goal to incorporate all territories in which the Polish people were historically and culturally dominant into the Polish state. On the basis of this formula they laid claim to Eastern Galicia and consoled the Galician Ukrainians with the prospect that in a democratic Poland they would easily reach an understanding with the Poles. All Polish parties were decidedly opposed to the aspirations of the Eastern Galician Ukrainians for their own national state. A few days later, on 15 October 1918, the Polish deputies in the Vienna parliament, acting as "subjects and citizens of a free and united Polish state," called for the formation of Polish-Austrian-Hungarian and Polish-German liquidation commissions whose task would be the transfer to the Polish state of the territories claimed by Poland.[15]

While the Austrian cabinet hesitated to give the Ukrainians a free hand, the war ministry bowed to the inevitable and issued an order, not made public until 2 November 1918, that as the national states on Austrian territory would be organizing their own national armies, the Austrian military command was to turn over authority to the various national governments, and it was left to the discretion of the returning troops to register with the command of their national army and take the oath of allegiance to their national state. This order, of whose existence the Ukrainians were entirely unaware, was not made known to them but to the president of the Polish parliamentary club, Dr. Tadeusz Tertil. Acting on this, on 27 October 1918 the Poles proceeded to establish in Cracow the Polish Liquidation Commission (Polska Komisja Likwidacyjna) that they had had in view for two weeks. It was led by a presidium to which the National Democrat Count Aleksander Skarbek, the socialist leader Ignacy Daszyński, the leader of the peasant party, Wincenty Witos, and the president of the Vienna Polish club, Dr. Tertil, were elected. The commission immediately issued an order to all officials in Galicia to continue their functions as subjects of the Polish state. The commission did not, however, subordinate itself to the Warsaw Regency Council and thus constituted a separate Polish government of Galicia. On 30 October 1918, with no serious difficulties, the Austrian military authorities in Cracow turned over their command to the Liquidation Commission, which immediately appointed Brigadier Bolesław Roja of the Polish Legion as military commander in Cracow. The commission had no reason to proceed with undue haste or by revolutionary means: its rule began in Cracow on 31 October 1918 and in Western Galicia during the course of the next few days.[16]

With a certain amount of support from the Austro-Hungarian military authorities, the Poles were already in virtual control of the state administration in Western Galicia and had already begun the creation of their own armed forces in Cracow, recruiting one-time members of the Polish Legion and the Austrian army. In Eastern Galicia, however, all the Austrian civil and military authorities were still in place, and the Ukrainians were still carrying on their fruitless negotiations with the Vienna government. Meanwhile, two Polish bodies simultaneously claimed authority over Galicia. The Liquidation Commission decided to move its seat to Lviv as soon as possible, perhaps on 1 November 1918, and take over the functions of the Austrian viceroy, General Huyn. At the same time, the Warsaw Regency Council appointed Prince Witold Czartoryski as the Polish government commissioner for Galicia, with authority to take over from General Huyn on 1 November.[17] In contrast to the Ukrainians, who wanted to come to a friendly agreement with the Polish minority and even planned to have in the Ukrainian government of Eastern Galicia a Polish minister with the right of veto in all affairs pertaining to the Polish minority,[18] neither the Warsaw nor the Cracow authorities paid any attention to the Ukrainian majority in Eastern Galicia as they prepared to take it over.

The Poles felt confident. Even in 1915, when the Austrians had appointed a non-Polish general as viceroy (he was in fact extremely pro-Polish and remained so to the end),[19] the whole Eastern Galician administration remained in the hands of a Polish bureaucracy. The Eastern Galician towns, especially Lviv, had an overwhelming Polish-Jewish majority; the large landowners were Polish without exception; and throughout the countryside there was a Polish village population. Since, in addition to this, the Poles had a strong underground military organization in Eastern Galicia that underestimated the strength of the Ukrainian national movement in the honest conviction that it had been artificially stirred up by Austria or Germany, the takeover of Eastern Galicia did not strike them as a particularly difficult task. They evidently assumed that a fast and furious takeover would create confusion in the enemy camp and hoped to be able to suppress local unrest with ease.[20]

The measures of the Cracow Liquidation Commission, as well as those of the Warsaw government, were predicated on armed force, represented in Eastern Galicia, especially in Lviv, by the underground Polish military organizations and the Polish soldiers in the Austro-Hungarian garrisons. These were the core of the Polish forces in Eastern Galicia that would have to hold the Ukrainians in check. Of all these secret military organizations, only one had any knowledge of Ukrainian military preparations and was preparing for battle: this was the Polish Military Organization (Polska Organizacja Wojskowa, POW), led from Cracow by the Piłsudski representative and Legion commander Edward Rydz-Śmigły. The others, influenced by the view that the National Democrats had been busily propagating for more than a decade, according to which Austria was supporting the Ukrainians against the Poles, saw no direct threat from the Ukrainians themselves but rather from the Austro-Hungarian army, which might stand by the Ukrainians in the event that Austria were to hand over Eastern Galicia to them. For there were still non-Galician troops in Lviv and in the other Eastern Galician provincial towns, although small in number, and in southern Ukraine there was a whole Austro-Hungarian army of occupation. Although militarily this army no longer counted for much, it had not yet collapsed, and it appeared that, as compared with the Polish underground military organizations, this army was powerful enough, in the event of a formal transfer of Eastern Galicia to the Ukrainians, to maintain public order and guarantee Ukrainian control of Lviv and the rest of Eastern Galicia until sufficient Ukrainian troops could be brought in from the Austro-Hungarian front. Thus the only danger confronting the Poles, as they believed, was the possibility of what they called a "Ukrainian-Austrian coup"—the establishment by Austria, with all the forces seemingly at its command, of a Ukrainian government in Eastern Galicia.[21]

As early as 31 October 1918, the Polish Military Organization carried out a general mobilization of its members in Lviv. Weapons and munitions were distributed, and the Lviv schools and student hostels were turned into armed camps. On the afternoon of 31 October, the Polish Military Organization joined with the other Polish military organizations under Captain Czesław Mączyński, who was elected their leader. On the following day, he led an uprising in Lviv against the Ukrainians. Thus, to anticipate events somewhat, this uprising was not a spontaneous act of desperation on the part of "Polish women and children," as it is so effusively described by Polish historians, but rather a planned action of militarily organized Polish soldiers with the experience of the world war behind them, whose numbers were only slightly smaller than those of the Ukrainian forces in Lviv. On the evening of 31 October, the takeover of Lviv and the rest of Eastern Galicia by the Poles seemed imminent in every respect, political as well as military.[22]

The reversal of this situation was brought about by a small group of Ukrainian soldiers. The initiative in forming such a group had already been taken in August 1918 by some of the best minds in the Ukrainian National Democratic Party, although they had no position in the party leadership: Dr. Volodymyr Bachynsky, Dr. Vasyl Paneiko, Dr. Stepan Baran, Ivan Kyveliuk, and Dr. Lonhyn Tsehelsky. In view of the approaching collapse of Austria, it was clear that it would be easy for the Poles, with the support of their bureaucracy and the Polish population of the towns, with or without Vienna's assent, to take over state power in Galicia and overcome the Eastern Galician Ukrainians by force while those Ukrainians capable of bearing arms were far away on the front lines with the Austrian army. It was also widely rumored that the Poles had long been making secret military preparations for a coup in Galicia. Under these circumstances, a number of officers of the Ukrainian Legion, which was stationed in Bukovyna and consisted of only two battalions, bound themselves by a secret oath to undertake, if necessary, the military defense of the Ukrainians. They made their resolution in September 1918, long before the creation of the Ukrainian National Rada, and their leader was Dmytro Vitovsky, a major in the Ukrainian Legion. Although there were very few Ukrainian officers among the Austrian troops stationed in Galicia, none of whom ranked higher than subaltern, by the end of October 1918 this military league managed to win over the majority of Ukrainian officers and troops garrisoned in Eastern Galicia, including those in Lviv, and in the amazingly short period of less than two months it was in a position militarily to secure a Ukrainian seizure of power.[23]

When the appeal of the Polish Liquidation Commission to the Galician authorities was announced, and when, on 31 October, the Ukrainians heard that the Vienna government had instructed the viceroy in Lviv to hand over authority to whichever party could guarantee the maintenance of public order, and that on 1 November a deputation would arrive in Lviv on behalf of the Polish Liquidation Commission to take over from the viceroy, the moment for action had arrived. On the morning of 31 October, only a few hours before the Polish Military Organization mobilized, there was a meeting in Lviv between several Ukrainian political figures who happened to be in the city and the leaders of the secret military league. In response to pressure from Major Dmytro Vitovsky, the meeting decided to instruct the clandestine Ukrainian organization to take power in Eastern Galicia in the name of the Ukrainian National Rada that night (31 October–1 November). Couriers were dispatched immediately to all the garrisons in Eastern Galicia with instructions concerning the seizure of power: the takeover was under way. Those few hours were decisive in determining who would take over Eastern Galicia, the Poles or the Ukrainians. It was the Ukrainians who won.[24]

The Ukrainian takeover on the night of 31 October–1 November 1918 was a complete success in Lviv as well as in the provincial towns of Eastern Galicia. In perfect tranquillity, and without the slightest hitch, they succeeded in disarming the non-Ukrainian troops and taking military control of the city of Lviv according to plan. The viceroy, General Huyn, and the military commander of Lviv, General Rudolf Pfeffer, had no idea of what was going on when the Ukrainians came to intern them on the morning of 1 November. The Poles in Lviv were taken so completely by surprise that they knew nothing of the takeover until, on the morning of 1 November, they saw the Ukrainian flag flying from the city hall and government buildings.[25]

The Ukrainian takeover of Eastern Galicia succeeded without any help from the Austrian central government, the Lviv viceroy, or the Austro-

Hungarian military leadership.[26] This claim is valid even though the entire Polish literature on the subject claims the opposite. There are a number of reasons for this: they know no other way to explain this surprising success of the Ukrainians and are not acquainted with the exhaustive Ukrainian publications on the subject; it allows them to make the heroism of the Polish resistance appear greater than it actually was; and in publications that appeared before 1923, it was a way of minimizing the national and political significance of the Ukrainians, compromising them in the eyes of the Entente as favorites of Austria and the German Reich.[27]

2. Ukrainian Constitutional Measures in Eastern Galicia

The effortless capture of Lviv by a branch of a clandestine Ukrainian society with only some 1,500 members was an achievement that surprised the conspirators themselves, who had rather anticipated an unfavorable outcome. Although the Ukrainians were good conspirators, they were bad as military leaders. The head of the secret society, and now leader of the Ukrainian troops, was Major Dmytro Vitovsky. An ardent patriot, he was neither a soldier nor a statesman, and his whole effort was directed toward the military success of the takeover and the seizure of state power by the Ukrainians. They made no preparations for the creation of their own armed forces under a unified command for the whole country immediately after the seizure of power. Nor did they make any preparations for planned, comprehensive military action in Lviv and on the Sian River to thwart the expected Polish insurrection. Although war with Poland was inevitable, they made no preparations for it by stationing troops on the Sian. They had made the revolution, and now they expected that everything else would follow of its own accord; that, in some mystical way, everything would come "from the people." This situation called for unusual leadership abilities and a tremendous capacity for action on the part of the mass of the people. But among all the nations drawn into this revolution, the leaders showed no particular ability, and the masses, badly exhausted by the war, were not prepared for any truly great achievements. The Eastern Galician Ukrainian regiments were all on the Italian front, and it would take weeks for them to return. After such a long war, the overriding desire of the soldiers was for demobilization. There were very few officers, and the country had no more men of fighting age. There were only a few reserve formations, consisting mostly of older members of the home guard; like any reserve formations after a four-year war, they had largely disintegrated. At first, events followed their natural course, as they were wont to do among the peoples vanquished in the world war in that period of general revolutionary disintegration. Since the fighters available to the Ukrainians in Lviv, numbering no more than 1,500, were too few to control a large city of 200,000 extremely hostile inhabitants, and since security in the city, as well as communications and cooperation among the military barracks, had been badly neglected, there was a Polish military insurrection in the city on the very first day of the Ukrainian seizure of power, 1 November 1918.[28]

Under the vigorous leadership of Captain Czesław Mączyński, the Polish fighters, reinforced by the hourly influx of patriotic Polish youth and ex-soldiers, took over the southwestern part of Lviv, successfully drove back the Ukrainian military patrols and, constantly on the attack in prolonged street fighting, gradually made their way into the rest of the city. In those parts of the city still controlled by the Ukrainians, individual Ukrainian fighters and smaller patrols were murdered and lynched by the "women and children" of Polish historical legend.[29] While all this was going on, the Ukrainian National Rada met in Lviv as the supreme organ of the newly created Eastern Galician Ukrainian state. The lack of preparation for this seizure of power was now abundantly clear. On 19 October 1918 the Ukrainian National Rada had decided to establish three committees: an executive committee, as well as "delegations of the Ukrainian National Rada" for Galicia and Bukovyna. The executive committee was to be the government, with the other two conceived as its organs. But the executive was not formed until 25 October—in Vienna, to boot—under the leadership of Petrushevych. The other two "delegations," one in Lviv led by Kost Levytsky, and one in Chernivtsi led by Omelian Popovych, were formed even later, on 27 and 29 October. Thus it came about that, while the insurrection was under way in Lviv, the responsible political leadership was in Vienna. The Lviv branch of the Ukrainian National Rada thus found itself obliged to act as the first national government of the Ukrainians in Galicia. It began by issuing proclamations "To the People of Lviv" and "To the Ukrainian People" and by taking over government functions from the Austrian viceroy on 1 November 1918.[30]

The first proclamation essentially constituted nothing more than an announcement that on 1 November 1918, according to the will of the Ukrainian people, the newly created Ukrainian state, through its supreme organ, the Ukrainian National Rada, had taken over the government in the Ukrainian territories of the former Austro-Hungarian Monarchy. The second proclamation was more significant in that it contained the first measures for the organization of the new state.

Since the Poles controlled the entire state machinery of Galicia, they could quite easily prepare the political and military takeover of the country. The Ukrainians, however, were in an incomparably more difficult situation, for they were faced with the task of replacing almost an entire hostile bureaucracy. As the Ukrainian National Rada had made no preparations for this, the first measures of the new government were inevitably in the nature of pure revolutionary improvisation. Entirely in the style of the period (numerous commissions and universal appeals) the second proclamation called on unspecified "Ukrainian organizations in the towns, districts and villages"—in other words, any kind of Ukrainian organization that existed—to exercise national, regional and local authority until such time as the organs of the new Ukrainian state had been legally established, and to carry out those functions in the name of the Ukrainian National Rada. All functionaries hostile to the Ukrainian state who had not been removed from office by the coup of 1 November were to be dismissed immediately. The measures to create a Ukrainian national army were likewise improvised. The proclamation declared that all Ukrainian soldiers in the Austrian army were now subject to the authority of the Ukrainian National Rada and its appointed military officials. The soldiers on the Austrian front were called home to defend the Ukrainian state. However, as no organizational framework for a national army had been created beforehand, this appeal again left everything to general initiative. According to the proclamation, the whole Ukrainian population capable of bearing arms was to come together to form military units that would later be incorporated into the Ukrainian army or take over guard or police duties in the districts and communities. The proclamation guaranteed civil, national and religious equality to all citizens of the Ukrainian state, regardless of nationality or religious belief, and—once again, in the spirit of the time—it called on the Poles, Jews and Germans, who were recognized as national minorities, to elect their representatives to the Ukrainian National Rada. The proclamation declared the validity of existing Austrian law and announced the convocation of a Constitutional Assembly (Ustanovchi Zbory) on the basis of a universal, equal, direct, proportional, and secret franchise as soon as the existence of the Ukrainian state was secured. That assembly was to decide on the further fate of the Ukrainian state. This reference to the state's "further fate" pertained to the decision that it would have to make whether to remain independent or unite with Dnipro Ukraine. Finally, the proclamation promised an early announcement of the composition and program of the first cabinet of the Ukrainian state, which was a stopgap measure, since no such cabinet had in fact been agreed on.

On that same afternoon of 1 November, when the battle with the Polish insurrectionists was already in full swing, a delegation of the Ukrainian National Rada under the leadership of Kost Levytsky went to the viceroy, General Huyn, to demand a formal transfer of power. Huyn rejected the demand on the grounds that he was unable to carry out any constitutional function while under arrest. He did, however, transfer his authority in writing to his deputy, the Ukrainian Volodymyr Detsykevych. The latter carried out the demand of the delegation by declaring in the name of Austria, on the basis of the emperor's manifesto of 16 October 1918 and the unanimously expressed will of the Ukrainian people, that he was handing over state power to the Ukrainian National Rada. A protocol to that effect was drawn up and signed, and so the leaders of the Ukrainian people in Eastern Galicia acquired a document—now worthless—that one day earlier had represented the summit of their political ambitions.[31]

Although the proclamation of the Ukrainian National Rada, with its revolutionary appeal "to all," might have been expected to unleash total chaos in the country, the transition from the Austrian-Polish to the Ukrainian state order took place quite peacefully, for the most part, and without significant disturbance of public security. Throughout the districts and communities, the public proceeded to improvise Ukrainian administrative bodies, and police and guard units were organized. The discipline of those provisional troops may have been somewhat loose, but they effectively protected the lives and property of citizens nevertheless. Thus the Eastern Galician Ukrainian peasantry showed a much higher level of national discipline and civic responsibility than did its counterparts in Western Galicia, to say nothing of Congress Poland. Neither then nor later did Eastern Galicia experience the tide of looting, banditry and social revolt that swept Western Galicia and Congress Poland at the time.[32]

Meanwhile the Ukrainian leadership in Lviv had very little idea of how to govern the new state. At first they were completely paralyzed by the Polish insurrection. They looked on helplessly as turmoil swept the city and squandered their time in fruitless negotiations with the Lviv Poles. Only on 9 November did they recover from their confusion somewhat and begin to organize the distribution of power within the state, thus bringing to an end the situation of collective irresponsibility. The Ukrainian National Rada took on the parliamentary functions of legislation and control. Its chief executive organ was to be a coalition cabinet made up of representatives of all Ukrainian parties—the Provisional State Secretariat (Tymchasovyi Derzhavnyi Sekretariiat) under the leadership of Kost Levytsky. As the term "provisional" indicates, it was to be a temporary cabinet whose composition was in large measure purely accidental. In any case, it represented an attempt to establish order in the midst of the confusion in which the new state found itself.[33]

The appointment of a cabinet led the Ukrainian National Rada to make another important decision. Since an independent Eastern Galician Ukrainian state was unpopular among the troops, especially among the members of the former Ukrainian Legion, who had played such a major role in the takeover of Eastern Galicia and were decidedly in favor of the incorporation of Eastern Galicia into the Dnipro Ukrainian state, the Provisional State Secretariat was instructed, on 10 November 1918, "to take the necessary steps to unite all Ukrainian territories in a single state." The significance of this decision was at first purely ideological, a matter of principle. The internal situation in Dnipro Ukraine was so uncertain that there could be no question, at that time, of an all-Ukrainian central government in Kyiv leading the struggle against the Poles in Eastern Galicia. But this decision was the first of a number of such measures uniting Eastern Galicia and Dnipro Ukraine. It thus began the amalgamation of the Eastern Galician and the Dnipro Ukrainian question—a fact of the greatest importance for the subsequent fate of Ukraine.[34]

The leadership of the Eastern Galician Ukrainian state began now, for the first time, to function in a more orderly manner. The prelude to this was the promulgation on 13 November 1918 of the "provisional constitution of the Ukrainian state." It referred to the right of self-determination of peoples as the legal basis for the founding of the new state and established its name as the Western Ukrainian People's Republic (Zakhidn'o-Ukraïns'ka Narodna Respublika). The designation "Western Ukrainian" replaced "Galician Ukrainian," as it will do henceforth in the present text. Instead of "Dnipro Ukraine," we shall now speak of "Eastern Ukraine." Decisive for the form of the new state was not only the general collapse of the monarchic order in Eastern and Central Europe or the undoubted republicanism of the Ukrainian democratic movement. There were also reports from Eastern Ukraine, where on 29 April 1918 a monarchy had been established under Hetman Pavlo Skoropadsky, that the Eastern Ukrainian parties were preparing an insurrection to reestablish a republic. The Western Ukrainians wanted to establish a state form similar to that of Eastern Ukraine as a prelude to their later unification. The territory of the new state would include all the ethnically Ukrainian territories of the former Galicia, northern Hungary and Bukovyna (Map 1). Thus the Western Ukrainian People's

Republic undertook to satisfy its territorial claims—admittedly, only on the ideological level—by means of a conflict not only with the Poles but also with the Romanians and Hungarians. Western Ukraine promulgated its constitution as a sovereign state—a source of subsequent friction with Eastern Ukraine, in spite of the later unification measures that Western Ukraine undertook. The exercise of sovereign jurisdiction within the state was entrusted to parliament as the collective leadership of Western Ukraine—the weakest variety of republican constitution. For the time being, until the convocation of the Constituent Assembly chosen on the basis of an internationally valid "universal, equal, direct, proportional, and secret" franchise, power would be exercised by the Ukrainian National Rada and the State Secretariat. Thus the new state, like those in the rest of revolutionary Central Europe, committed itself entirely to the framework of radical Western democracy, which was so poorly adapted to social and cultural conditions in Eastern Galicia. Finally, the constitution established the state's coat of arms (soon to be superseded by the Eastern Ukrainian trident): a golden lion on a blue field, the coat of arms of the Galician-Volhynian Principality of the thirteenth and fourteenth centuries. The flag of the state was to be blue and gold.[35]

The creation of a de facto Western Ukrainian state, with a legal system inherited from Austria, was thus an accomplished fact.[36] The state was not in control of the whole territory to which it laid claim, but the overwhelming majority of the population within this territory, with the exception of the Carpatho-Ruthenians, fully recognized the authority of the Ukrainian National Rada. Through its civil and military institutions, this state authority, independent of any foreign power, ruled effectively and directly over the greater part of that national territory, whose size and population were sufficiently large to validate its claim to sovereignty. It also effectively secured law and order on that territory.[37] Furthermore, the new de facto state could claim legitimacy on the basis of two precedents in international law: President Wilson's declaration committing the Entente powers to recognize the right of national self-determination as the basis of the new state order in Europe and the formal transfer of state power by the Austrian authorities according to the manifesto of Emperor Charles I.

3. The Outbreak of the Polish-Ukrainian War for Eastern Galicia

Meanwhile, the victorious course of the Polish insurrection prepared an end to the activity of the Ukrainians in Lviv. The insurrection broke out in the early morning hours of 1 November 1918. First of all, a handful of insurgents established a stronghold in the extreme southwestern end of the city, forced back the Ukrainian patrols and, by noon, considerably expanded the area under their control. The number of insurgents continued to increase dramatically. They were joined by every Pole who was at all capable of bearing arms—legionnaires, ex-soldiers of the Austrian army, university and high-school students, and city rowdies. They were undisciplined and given to plundering but extremely battle-worthy. In the midst of the fighting, the insurgents organized themselves into units and sections led by whatever officers were available. At the same time Captain Mączyński organized a supreme command (Komenda Naczelna), set up a communications and information service, created a coherent fighting front out of the confusion, and provided the fighters with a goal and a plan. On 2 November, according to a predetermined plan, the insurgents captured the barracks in the adjoining southwestern suburb of the city, which gave them a large haul of weapons and ammunition. In purposeful fighting on 2 and 3 November, they finally captured the central freight and railway station just to the north, which gave them access to fairly large stores of weapons, ammunition, food, and clothing. They concentrated their fighting forces on this section of the front, where they established a virtually unassailable position against which the desperate assaults of the Ukrainians were quite futile. This was the decisive military success of the Poles. The insurgents had established a firm base: by the second day of the uprising, the number of fighters had already grown to a thousand and continued to grow thereafter. Only with the addition of a considerable number of fresh troops could the Ukrainians hope to overcome the insurgents, as both sides were now more or less equal in strength. For the Poles, this was a brilliant military achievement. The individual fighters' defiance of death, the impetuous aggressiveness of the individual units, the brilliant organizational capacity of the supreme command, and the effectiveness of their military action all combined to give them the victory.[38]

Of course, the Poles were also helped by the circumstances prevailing on the other side. The insurgents were volunteers, whereas the Ukrainian soldiers, forcibly conscripted into the Austrian army, were somewhat war-weary and unreliable. Kept together only with difficulty by their officers, more and more of them deserted. Thus the strength of the Ukrainians diminished, while that of the Poles increased. The Ukrainian troops were few in number from the very beginning, hardly more than 1,500 fighters. Most of them were older members of the home guard unfit for fighting at the front. They fought well, however, and in many cases, under the circumstances, quite brilliantly. They did their best, tenacious in attack and defense. But they were no match for the youthful impetuousness of the Polish insurgents. As peasants, they felt insecure in a particularly hostile urban environment with which they were little acquainted. The Polish insurgents, who were familiar with the city, found refuge and assistance everywhere, while the Ukrainians were attacked and shot from behind by the inhabitants from their houses. Still, the Ukrainians had been in a position on 1 November to surround and defeat the Polish insurgents; in any case, they need not have lost the freight and railway station. But their supreme command was confused; their communications and information service was deficient; the leadership of the individual units was unable to organize properly planned maneuvers and, in addition, there was a severe lack of Ukrainian officers. Among the Poles, by contrast, even the smallest unit was led by an officer. While the Poles concentrated all their forces for an attack, the Ukrainians fought without a central plan, each unit for itself.[39]

The Polish-Ukrainian battle for Eastern Galicia broke out not only in Lviv but also, at the same time or shortly thereafter, in the fortress of Przemyśl (Peremyshl) and in the oil region of Drohobych and Boryslav. Wherever the Poles had numerically significant enclaves, the Polish military groups responded quickly to the Ukrainian action. All their feelings rebelled against subjection to a Ukrainian state and, without waiting for orders from their political leaders, they took up the fight. This response of Polish national temperament took place without a great deal of forethought.[40]

Similarly, for the Ukrainians, the thought of becoming part of Poland was unbearable. They had a deep hatred for their opponents, a hatred that grew tremendously as events unfolded. But those were the feelings of an essentially passive people, held in check by their own national ideology, which was based on the old democratic conceptions of justice and fraternity between peoples. They felt oppressed in their own country by the rule of the Polish minority and, in rebelling against this oppression, they were prepared to grant that minority the maximum of national freedom in a Ukrainian state. They saw their state goal simply as the achievement of freedom from foreign rule and not as the exercise of their own power. Hence the attitude of the Ukrainians toward the Poles as an entity was entirely passive. If the Poles wished to erect their own state, no matter how powerful, in those areas where they constituted a majority, this was not seen as a problem by the Ukrainians. Indeed, they welcomed it, as it was in keeping with the abstract principle of national freedom. What mattered was that the Poles should relinquish their rule over those areas that were ethnically Ukrainian. It was inconceivable to the Ukrainians that in some situations the flourishing of one nation could lead inevitably to the injury or destruction of another, and the inevitable struggle for existence between the Poles and Ukrainians seemed to them merely the result of Polish maliciousness. They even lacked the fundamental precondition for any heroic national war: the strong sense that the fate of nations is decided for decades, even for centuries, in great moments of the most intense exertion, and that the armed conflict between Poles and Ukrainians in general, and that in Lviv in particular, constituted such a great moment for Ukraine.

It was different for the Poles. They felt themselves to be a historic and ruling nation. The reestablishment of Poland meant for them, above all else, rule and power. At one time this rule had extended over the greater part of Ukraine, so that even now the Poles did not regard the Ukrainians as equals but rather as an alien population destined for submission to them. True, they had accustomed themselves to the thought—however unwillingly—that the reestablishment of Polish rule on the Dnipro would probably be impossible, as that Polish tradition had been broken abruptly by Russia in the eighteenth and nineteenth centuries. But here in Galicia, where Austria had allowed the Poles to rule up to the last minute, that tradition remained strong, and the Poles simply could not imagine a Polish state without Lviv and the rest of Eastern Galicia. From the Polish point of view, the Western Ukrainian national liberation movement was nothing but a rebellion that had to be broken with the use of all available force. They also had a visual image of this "rebellion" in the work of the Nobel Prize-winning novelist, Henryk Sienkiewicz, whose masterpiece of national incitement,[41] the novel *Ogniem i mieczem* (With Fire and Sword), masterfully describes the seventeenth-century uprising of the Ukrainian Cossack hetman, Bohdan Khmelnytsky. From the "wild fields" of the Ukrainian steppe comes a terrible bloodthirsty horde, destroying, burning and killing everything in its path. The basest rabble is completely overcome by a lust for destruction, and the ruling stratum, the bearers of all human culture and civilization—the Poles—are buried in the deluge. For the Eastern Galician Poles, profoundly influenced by Sienkiewicz, a war with the Austrians, the Prussians or the Russians was an abstraction. But armed struggle against the superior might of the "Ukrainian hydra" was something familiar that they could vividly imagine and become enthusiastic about. The Ukrainian troops were referred to only as "gangs," even though the Polish troops at that time were very similar in makeup. The Poles identified themselves with Sienkiewicz's heroes, who, in the name of the "majesty of the Polish state," assaulted, burned, executed, and turned whole areas of the countryside into deserts "with fire and sword" in order to wipe out, once and for all, the rebellious Ukrainian *haidamaky* ("robbers"). There was hardly a Polish insurgent in Lviv who, in a variety of situations, did not feel himself to be playing the role of one or another of Sienkiewicz's heroes,[42] and it was no accident that the insurrection had its origins at the Sienkiewicz School in Lviv. The hatred of the Poles for the Ukrainians, all in the name of the "majesty of Poland," was imbued with such aversion that any recognition of the right of the Western Ukrainians to their own state, or even to some form of special political autonomy, was impossible. This hatred, combined with a contempt for their opponents, was the hatred of an allegedly higher form of humanity for a lower colonial race.

Although the heightened Polish national sentiment already sufficed to lead to armed struggle between the Poles and Ukrainians in Eastern Galicia and to encourage a host of fanatical fighters among the Poles, the endurance of those fighters was reinforced by the influence of the Polish National Democrats, which turned that exalted national sentiment into the foundation of the whole system of political thinking of the Eastern Galician Poles. Political considerations also played a role. The Poles thought of themselves as part of the victorious Entente. They knew very well that the Western Ukrainians were at a disadvantage because they had remained to the end, for better or for worse, with the Central Powers. And they were certain of the total support of the Polish state that was coming into existence, although they greatly overestimated its strength. Under those circumstances they thought that ultimate victory was guaranteed if only they were to attack ruthlessly, and this they did. There were no skeptics among the Poles who recognized some right of the Ukrainians to Lviv and Eastern Galicia. On 1 November, as the first shots of the Polish insurrection were being fired, a congress of student representatives from all over Poland was already taking place in Lviv. Only one student, an independent socialist from Warsaw, recognized in principle the right of the Ukrainians to Eastern Galicia, but even he remained in solidarity with the insurgents, and so the congress resolved unanimously to fight the Ukrainians and immediately took up arms.[43] The Poles had faith in the Entente, a faith that all salvation was to be had from France and from the peace negotiations, which often paralyzed their immediate efforts. In the course of the conflict they often found themselves overcome by a profound spiritual depression in which they came close to total collapse. But the Poles had much stronger willpower than the Ukrainians, a willpower to overcome the Ukrainians with their own might even if the whole world should be against them. This willpower drove them on to the greatest achievements and, in the moments of greatest defeat, it enabled them to hold themselves with pride against the Ukrainians. In bravery it was the Poles who absolutely excelled, not the Ukrainians.

The attitude that one's fate is decided by one's own will, an attitude familiar to powerful and dominant nations, was completely alien to the Ukrainian National Rada. In the leading Ukrainian political circles there was not a single relatively prominent personality who was capable, in this difficult situation, of taking the reins in his own hands and directing events. On 2 or 3 November, when it became clear that it was no longer possible to subdue the insurgents with the forces available in Lviv, the next logical step would have been to leave Lviv to the military authorities, move the political leadership out of the capital to some provincial center, establish a government to conduct the war, and assemble all possible national forces to subdue the Poles in Lviv. But the weak leadership did what most weak people do: lacking the inner strength to follow a determined course of action, they tried to keep up appearances. Frightened for their reputation, and fearing the "mood of the army and of the masses," they held up their staying in Lviv as proof of their determination.[44]

In reality, the success of the Polish uprising shattered the Ukrainian leadership, although, in planning the seizure of power, they must have taken into account that the Poles would not submit without resistance. In the atmosphere of legality and security in which the Ukrainian parliamentarians in Austria had carried on their conflict with the Poles, they had never really learned that war is an instrument—in fact, the most refined instrument—of politics, and now that the Poles were no longer a negotiating partner equally subject to the verdict of Vienna, but an independent warring power, they were at a loss as to what to do in such an unusual situation. They sent their messengers into the countryside to call on the masses for support and hoped every day that new forces would arrive from "the people." On 5 November they even made a special appeal for assistance from the hetman in Kyiv, but they did nothing further and, in fact, their whole way of acting was completely inappropriate to the war situation in which they found themselves.[45]

Accustomed to the fact that in Austria their conflict with the Poles proceeded, and could only proceed, within the framework of formal legality, and accustomed to the belief that the Vienna arbitrator, under certain circumstances, could be pressured into deciding in their favor if only they insisted firmly enough on their legal viewpoint, since he was also, after all, bound by the Austrian constitution, they now imagined that international relations were also based, in some fashion, on formal legality. In their imagination the Entente resembled the Vienna court of arbitration, and the Wilson peace conditions had the same status as the Austrian constitution. From this point of view, shared at the time by the whole of war-weary Europe, they were certainly right, for their country was overwhelmingly Ukrainian, a fact that seemed to them to be their greatest strength. The Western Ukrainians could not understand how the Poles could have the audacity to try to take Eastern Galicia after Wilson's clear formulation of the "right of national self-determination" and the "creation of a Polish state on undisputed Polish territory." They did not realize that the Polish insurrection in Lviv, if not put down as quickly as possible, would be the beginning of a long-drawn-out war between Western Ukraine and the whole of Poland in which the three and a half million Western Ukrainians, unless they were really a nation of heroes—which, in the midst of this revolutionary chaos, they were not—could not possibly hold out against the seventeen or eighteen million Poles. None of the Ukrainian political leaders had a comprehensive view of what was happening. Isolated events were not seen as part of a general context—and without this comprehensive view there can be no statesmanlike leadership—and therefore they regarded the life-and-death struggle of the Polish insurgents as, fundamentally, only a misunderstanding, an unfortunate incident.[46] It seemed to them an outbreak of severe unrest whose significance was purely local; a form of opposition that could be pacified by concessions of some kind—even if large ones—to the Polish minority. To appease the Lviv Poles in some way; to convince them that they had nothing to fear from a Ukrainian state; to reach a settlement with them and then wait patiently for the judgment of the Entente: this, they thought, was the task of the hour.[47]

The Polish insurrectionists were inspired by the clear awareness that now or never the reemerging Poland could become great, but only if the Polish people were capable of great achievements. They knew they had undertaken a life-or-death struggle that could not end in compromise but only with the complete destruction of one side or the other. This awareness demanded and made possible the greatest exertion. The Ukrainians did not have this drive, this instinct to demand the utmost of themselves. They did their duty, but what they lacked was the aggressive impulse that takes one far beyond the realm of duty and is the characteristic feature of every act of heroism. This difference in momentum of both sides was perfectly reflected in the military leadership: on the Polish side a ruthless, daring warhorse, Captain Mączyński, who could rouse his troops to the attack time and time again; on the side of the Western Ukrainians, a whole series of commanders, each worse than the last, all of them men who, at best, could lead a passive defense in the trenches, whereas only a rapid, impetuous forward push could have resolved the conflict in their favor. From every point of view, it was the Ukrainians who showed the greatest passivity and the least inner strength: it was they who had the lower level of national sentiment, the narrower political horizon, the weaker military leadership. They differed even in the age of their soldiers: an old Ukrainian home guard against Poland's youth.[48]

In spite of all this, at the beginning, on 1 November, it was the Poles who seemed destined to lose. Apart from the fact that the insurgents numbered only a handful, the response of the Polish population was initially one of panic. They overestimated the strength of the Ukrainian troops and the ability of the Ukrainian leadership to marshal the country's military resources. The Poles expected the same rapid attack and the same ruthless suppression of unrest in Lviv that they themselves would have carried out had they been in the place of the Ukrainians. The Ukrainians had the whole country behind them, while the Poles had, for the moment, only the city of Lviv: although large, it was an island in the midst of a hostile sea. The Poles responded in a politically rational manner when, in spite of the armed conflict that had already begun, they entered into diplomatic negotiations with the Ukrainians. For, were the insurrection to fail, it would be the task of the Polish leaders to protect the Polish population from the unconditional rule, or even vengeance, of the Ukrainians. They could do this without giving up their claim to Eastern Galicia because, if the insurrection were to succeed, or if the Polish state itself were to enter the conflict against the Ukrainians and defeat them, any Polish concessions to the Ukrainians would lose all validity.[49]

With great skill—although not without conflict in their own camp—the Polish political leaders in Lviv played out the difficult game of diplomacy and warfare. On the evening of 1 November, when it appeared that the Ukrainians were in a position to suppress the insurrection within hours, a delegation of moderate Polish politicians was sent to speak to the Ukrainian National Rada. They declared that the uprising had been the action of a few "hotheads" for which the Polish population of Eastern Galicia was not responsible and, without recognizing the Ukrainian state, they proposed negotiations as a way of coming to some agreement until such time as the victorious Entente reached a decision on Polish and Ukrainian claims in Eastern Galicia. The Ukrainians, whose every inclination was to look for a peaceful way out, immediately latched onto this Polish proposal. This decision was in keeping with their tradition of negotiating with the Poles, their fear of the Entente, their awareness of their own weakness and inability, their wish to pacify the Poles and convince them that they need fear no injustice and thus to move them toward recognizing the Ukrainian state and giving up any armed resistance. This, however, completely undermined their own political will. By not insisting on the recognition of the Western Ukrainian state as a precondition for negotiations, they were accepting the Polish population of Eastern Galicia as an independent power on the same level as the Ukrainian state. The very fact of the negotiations themselves created hopes for peace among their own troops and weakened their will to fight in the decisive first few days of the conflict, whereas the self-confidence of the Poles was thereby only strengthened since, for them, these negotiations were only a means of deceiving their opponents or a way of getting from them an admission that Lviv was a special case, which would later be useful in obtaining an Entente decision favorable to the Poles. But worst of all for the Ukrainians was the fact that while the negotiations dragged on, Ukrainian hopes for an agreement with the Poles delayed the formation of a strong government and caused them to neglect the mobilization of the country for the war effort.[50]

During the night of 1–2 November, the military situation of the Poles in Lviv already seemed more secure than at the start of the conflict, and the panic among the Polish population began to subside. Moreover, the lack of leadership, defeatism and intimidation of the Ukrainian political and, above all, military leaders was soon apparent. This had an immediate effect on the Polish-Ukrainian negotiations, which were significant to the Poles only in the event of impending defeat, not of success. Representatives of the Polish National Democratic Party now also appeared in the Polish delegation—Dr. Ernest Adam, Dr. Leonard Stahl, and Professor Marceli Chlamtacz—and from this point on, they did not let the management of the negotiations out of their hands. The negotiators now adopted a superior tone: they declared that they did not represent the entire Polish population of Eastern Galicia, which only the government in Warsaw could do, but that they were personally willing to constitute a Polish-Ukrainian commission that would temporarily administer all of Galicia in place of the Austrian viceroy. They virtually played with their helpless opponents. Their greatest concession, which then became the subject of negotiations that lasted for weeks, was their proposal to put to one side the question of the official status of Eastern Galicia and simply restrict themselves to the organization of a truce in Lviv. The whole point of the truce was to allow time for either the Entente or the Polish state to intervene in Eastern Galicia, at which time any local agreement reached in Lviv would be irrelevant. But Captain Mączyński went even further. He felt so secure that he denied the politicians any right to make decisions concerning his "Polish army": he was prepared to accept a truce only after direct negotiations with the Ukrainian military commanders. Negotiations between Mączyński and the Ukrainian commander, Dmytro Vitovsky (now promoted to colonel for organizing the Ukrainian seizure of power in Lviv), were in fact arranged, and on the night of 2–3 November a twelve-hour truce was declared. Both commanders saw the truce as an opportunity to rest their troops and bring in reinforcements. The conflict was then renewed and went on for weeks while politicians on both sides engaged in fruitless negotiations.[51]

In the meantime, the situation of the Lviv Ukrainians began to worsen. The Poles had taken almost half the city, and the Ukrainians had almost no reserves to draw on. The return of the Western Ukrainian troops from Austria's distant southern front did not begin until much later. There were no Western Ukrainian front troops in the much closer Austro-Hungarian army of occupation in southern Ukraine. The Western Ukrainian soldiers spread out in the rear of this army were largely demoralized by their service behind the lines, aside from all the other evils they suffered, and knew nothing of the Ukrainian seizure of power in Lviv. The Austrian supreme command in southern Ukraine had suppressed the news of it, as well as of the abdication in Vienna on 1 November of Emperor Charles I. News of these events seeped through only very slowly, and it was weeks before Western Ukrainians in the army of occupation began to return to their homeland. A Western Ukrainian army began to be formed throughout the country by groups of soldiers and unpracticed young volunteers, but this army had no organized central leadership. Western Ukraine as a whole did not have the slightest idea of the scope of the events in Lviv. Every area believed that the few troops it possessed were needed for its own purposes, and no central leadership provided effective organization in that regard. The spontaneous assistance that the country sent to Lviv little by little was inadequate. The strength of the Polish insurgents increased at a much faster rate: soon after 3 November they numbered three to four thousand fighters. Later, by 20 November, the number of battle-ready men had risen to five thousand.[52]

The numerical balance of forces was just about equalized by the arrival of fresh Ukrainian troops, but between 3 and 9 November the Ukrainians were forced onto the defensive not only by the failure of their own leadership, as before, but also by the fact that the Poles had the preponderance of strength on their side. Although the political and military leadership of the Ukrainians was constantly inept throughout the Polish-Ukrainian conflict, at the time of the Lviv uprising as well as later in the war with Poland, the question of leadership was less important during those days of bitter street fighting, for the fighting in Lviv was now an elemental conflict between the two communities. In the strife that now unfolded in the city of Lviv, in the play of attack and counterattack, with the courage of the defenders pitted against the bravery of the attackers, the battlefield became for the first time the arena of conflict of nation with nation. And aside from all their differences in leadership, national ideology and national development, which guaranteed the victory of one of the opponents—the Poles—here, where the elemental forces of the two nations confronted each other, represented by their small armies, each side matched the other in strength.

The core of the Ukrainian fighting force were the crack assault troops that arrived in Lviv on 3 November. These were the two battalions, previously stationed in Chernivtsi in Bukovyna, of the old Ukrainian Legion of the Austrian army, the Ukrainian Sich Riflemen (Ukraïns'ki Sichovi Stril'tsi). These battalions in Western Ukraine, as well as the Kyiv Sich Riflemen in Eastern Ukraine, both formed out of the same Ukrainian Legion, both volunteer formations hardened by the experience of the world war, were the ideal representatives of the military will of Ukraine as a whole and constituted the advance guard of the Ukrainian armies. These were the troops that now confronted the Polish forces. The first assault of the Sich Riflemen on 3 November shattered the Polish advance and broke their lines wide apart, bringing the Polish cause to the brink of defeat. It is clear that a unification, at that time or shortly thereafter, of the Western Ukrainian and Kyiv Riflemen would certainly have put an end to the Polish uprising in Lviv. With this one blow they could probably have forestalled the subsequent war between Western Ukraine and all of Poland and resolved the question of a Ukrainian national state in Eastern Europe in favor of Ukraine. A week later the Kyiv hetman, Pavlo Skoropadsky, made an offer to a Western Ukrainian delegation to transfer the Kyiv Riflemen, who stood in the way of his goal of reuniting Eastern Ukraine with counterrevolutionary Russia. But the Sich Riflemen, made up for the most part of Western Ukrainian volunteers, numerically small* but militarily competent in the highest degree, especially in street fighting, felt themselves obliged to reject the hetman's rather artful proposal. A no less important battle awaited them on 15 November: the revolt in Kyiv against the Russian counterrevolution,

* They comprised only four infantry companies, one field guard battery, one unit of twelve heavy machine guns, and half a cavalry squadron. But these core troops were always prepared to expand promptly into a regiment (cf. Davnyi, *Pro Sichovykh Stril'tsiv*, p. 39; V. K., *Sichovi Stril'tsi*, p. 23).

which was preparing, on the basis of the hetman's official declaration of a federative union of Ukraine with Russia, to end the independence of Eastern Ukraine. On their own, even assault troops of the quality of the Sich Riflemen could no longer end the Polish insurrection in Lviv with a decisive blow. The assault of 3 November, as well as the Riflemen's attack of 4 November, were blocked by the Poles in a desperate defense. Now the Poles went onto the attack, and the Ukrainian front was severely shaken. However, the determined Riflemen beat off the Polish assault. Once again, the Poles pulled themselves together for a last desperate advance: on 9 November, with diversionary attacks on both flanks, they made a concentrated assault aimed at breaking through the Ukrainian lines and driving the Ukrainian troops out of the city. In the bloody battle that ensued, the attack was repulsed and the advance of the insurgents decisively shattered.[53]

Between 10 and 18 November, events in Lviv took a different turn. Both sides were exhausted. The war was at a standstill. A firmly established line, secured with barbed wire, now divided the city. Besides rifles, machine guns and hand grenades, cannon began to be used in the intense local battles for space. Now the Ukrainians went over to the offensive. On their left flank they achieved very little, but on their right they made daily advances, taking one strongpoint after another on the Polish front line. Now the courage of the Poles began to ebb. At the beginning of the insurrection they had called on Warsaw for aid. But central Poland, as will be shown in greater detail below, was collapsing into complete anarchy. The Poles there were in no position to rush to the assistance of their fellow countrymen in Lviv. Now that the Lviv insurrection had become a drawn-out war of attrition, in which the weight of the Ukrainian rural population slowly but surely began to tip the scales against the completely surrounded insurgents, the latter begged desperately for relief, not only from Warsaw but also from Cracow, and emissaries pleaded the Lviv cause at numerous mass meetings throughout Poland. But their pleas were in vain, for the Poles were now more concerned with their own internal discord than with the events in Lviv. At this moment the Lviv insurgents, awaiting events at their stations in profound despondency, represented the equivalent of the fighting strength of the Polish nation of seventeen or eighteen million. So there was nothing for the Lviv Poles to do but return with special emphasis to the truce negotiations with the Ukrainians. Once again, they survived. Without giving up their claim to Lviv, they played for time in the hope that Poland would soon overcome its own internal crisis and save the day for them. With this in mind, they proposed, as a basis for negotiation, turning Lviv into a free city. Their hidden purpose was to make Lviv the base, at a more favorable time in the future, for a Polish attempt to recapture the whole of Eastern Galicia.[54]

Neither the military nor the political leadership of the Ukrainians, given their limited political horizons with regard to foreign policy, understood the true situation. The military leadership did nothing to strengthen Ukrainian positions on the Sian crossings at Przemyśl and Jarosław (Yaroslav) in order to block relief routes to Lviv from central Poland. On 18 November, the political leadership approved a three-day truce with the Poles without meeting any determined resistance from the military leaders. Neither the political nor the military leaders were aware that the Ukrainian line on the Sian had already been breached some days previously and that preparations for large-scale relief for Lviv were already under way in central Poland.[55]

Thus the fate of the Western Ukrainian capital was decided not in Lviv itself but in Przemyśl. Earlier, on 2–3 November, the Ukrainians had taken Przemyśl after a few skirmishes. A truce was arranged here also, "pending the final decision of the Entente," and captured Polish officers and soldiers were released on condition that they cease to take part in the war against the Ukrainians—a promise they immediately broke. The Sian River was agreed as the demarcation line. Meanwhile in Cracow, in response to the desperate appeal for help from the Poles in Lviv, an excellent unit of Western Galician Polish assault troops was being organized, the core of which was the extraordinarily capable Fifth Legion Regiment. On 10 November these troops arrived in Przemyśl. Supported by tanks and artillery, they immediately launched an attack on the Ukrainians. The city and the bridges across the Sian were soon in Polish hands. On 12 November the route to Lviv was open for the transport of the special units from Cracow, as well as a number of units formed in Przemyśl itself. Altogether there were 140 officers, 1,228 soldiers, and eight field guns. Given the small size of the armies available in countries then in the throes of serious social upheavals, this was a highly significant addition to the Polish side. Although there were occasional skirmishes on the way, those troops were now able to avail themselves of the railway line linking Przemyśl with Lviv. On 20 November they broke through the Ukrainian encirclement of Lviv, which was now linked with central Poland. The Polish-Ukrainian battlefront, which had been very thinly manned for the time being, now extended about 150–200 km along a line south of the Przemyśl–Lviv railway, then around Lviv and in a northwesterly direction toward Jarosław. The newly established Polish state now became involved in the struggle through its advance guard, and the Polish insurrection in Lviv turned into a Polish-Ukrainian war (Map 1).[56]

There now began a profound change in the more or less civilized manner in which the Polish-Ukrainian struggle had been carried on. The Ukrainians had treated their opponents with respect, as combatants and not as rebels. In spite of the murder of Ukrainian soldiers in ambushes carried out by the Polish civil population, the Ukrainian soldiers behaved in very humane fashion (evidence of this civilized behavior of the Ukrainian soldiers during the fighting in Lviv is given by a Ukrainian eyewitness and historian).[57] In the area of Lviv administered by the Ukrainians there was no lynch law, no excesses, no looting. The Polish population in that area suffered no burdens other than those that were part and parcel of the war itself. Death sentences in the Ukrainian military courts were extremely rare, and only in the most extreme cases did the Ukrainians avail themselves of special war measures. There were no instances of mass arrest, although this would have been amply justified by the behavior of the Polish population in certain areas. No hostages were taken by the Ukrainians, either at the beginning of the fighting or later, when the Polish insurgents captured the residence of the Ukrainian metropolitan, Count Andrei Sheptytsky, and made hostages of all its inhabitants. The Polish press that appeared in the Ukrainian section of the city was prohibited only when it published the call to arms of the insurgent Polish commanders, but none of the Polish editors was prosecuted even for this.

A completely different set of standards characterized the behavior of the Poles toward the Ukrainian population. Immediately after the capture of Przemyśl the victorious Poles sacked Ukrainian national institutions and even destroyed some of the buildings themselves. The private homes of Ukrainian residents were looted. All prominent Ukrainians, even those of middle rank that they could get their hands on, were arrested and taken to the notorious internment camp in Dąbie, near Cracow, where they were very badly treated for years and finally died of hunger, want and disease. The war of the Polish nation against the Ukrainians thus took on the character of a colonial war: the victors mistreated their opponents as rebels, and those who were mistreated retaliated.[58]

With the arrival of the relief troops, which represented the beginning of Poland's colonial war in Ukraine, the Lviv Poles attained decisive superiority over the Ukrainians, not only from the viewpoint of military competence but also numerically. The Poles no longer had any interest in carrying on with the negotiations. They brusquely ended the talks on

20 November; not, however, before they had expressed their pro-Entente sympathies to a Romanian member of the Entente mission, a certain Lieutenant Henri Villaime of the French secret service, whom the Poles had invited to the talks. The Entente, whose true attitudes the Ukrainians now got to know for the first time, although its only representative in Lviv was this Lieutenant Villaime, subscribed completely to the Polish viewpoint and insisted that the Ukrainians accept the Polish demands, since Poland had already been recognized by the Entente powers, whereas Ukraine could not expect to be recognized now or at any time in the future.[59]

With this intervention on the part of the Entente powers, the period of direct negotiations between the Poles and the Ukrainians came to an end. The truce in Lviv was not extended, and the battle for the city entered its concluding phase. In the early morning of 21 November fighting resumed, and now the Ukrainians realized for the first time that they were no longer dealing simply with the Lviv insurgents but also with a strong Western Galician Polish relief force. The battle went on for another day and, although the Ukrainians were holding out well on their right flank, having lost some territory only on their left, the danger of being outflanked and surrounded by the Poles convinced the Ukrainian commander of the need to vacate the city. During the night of 21–22 November the Ukrainians began a hasty retreat eastward.[60]

On the morning of 22 November, amid the general rejoicing of the Polish inhabitants, the Polish troops occupied the areas of the city vacated by the Ukrainian troops. Immediately, as in Przemyśl, Ukrainians were interned and all Ukrainian national institutions were looted. Since the Jews in Lviv had remained neutral in the fighting, although more inclined toward the Ukrainians, the Jewish quarters of the city were immediately subjected to a three-day pogrom in which entire housing blocks were burned to the ground and numerous Jews murdered without regard to age or sex. After this the supreme command reestablished order, but from that point on the Jewish population of Eastern Galicia as a whole supported the Ukrainian side in the Polish-Ukrainian war.[61]

The loss of Lviv represented the beginning of the war between the newly established Polish state and Western Ukraine. Only now did the population of Western Ukraine realize the true significance of what had happened in Lviv, and it was only the war with all of Poland that forced them to invest energy in the creation of a state and military organization. Although this investment was by no means complete, it was pursued much more forcefully than in the days of the battle for Lviv.

Chapter 2

The Western Ukrainian State

1. The State Organization of Western Ukraine

The organization of the Western Ukrainian state began under highly unfavorable circumstances. The situation was incomparably worse for the Ukrainians than it was for the other newly emerging or newly established small states of Central and Eastern Europe. True, the Polish insurrection in the Drohobych–Boryslav oil basin was put down in a few days, but the battlefront between Przemyśl and Lviv pushed into Western Ukrainian territory like a wedge, and this was the greatest burden that a state in the process of being established could be expected to bear. But beyond the Zbruch River, the eastern boundary of Eastern Galicia, complete anarchy reigned from mid-November 1918, and, in view of the war with Poland, it was a remarkable achievement of Western Ukraine that this chaos was prevented from encroaching on its own territory (Maps 1 and 2).

Although a mood of defeatism prevailed among the leaders of the Western Ukrainian state after the loss of Lviv, by the end of November 1918 the political self-organization of the Western Ukrainians had attained a considerable degree of stability and effectiveness. The structure of Western Ukrainian civil, judicial and military organization was the same as that of the old Austrian order. The Western Ukrainians appointed their own nationals to all these offices, but the powers of the new functionaries, who were mostly confirmed in office by the State Secretariat, remained the same. The reconstruction of an effective state organization was largely the accomplishment of these energetic new functionaries, but the Secretariat's instructions soon began to penetrate effectively to the lowest strata of this whole improvised civil and military apparatus. Still, communications between the government and the subordinate authorities were very difficult. The northwestern areas of the country were completely cut off from the southwestern ones by the battlefront, and the Polish occupation of the rail center in Lviv greatly impaired communications between those areas and the rest of the country (Map 1). There were also difficulties of telephone and telegraph communication to be overcome. The greatest problem, however, was that rail traffic was held up because the stock of locomotives and carriages available to the Ukrainians was too small to handle the mass of returning Austro-Hungarian troops from southern Ukraine and the hundreds of thousands of Russian prisoners of war returning from Austria-Hungary and from the German Reich, to say nothing of local transport and the servicing of the front. The lack of coal and sabotage by Polish railway workers added to the difficulty. Many of the Polish railway workers carried out their duties honestly and did not join the anti-Ukrainian movement, but it was only much later that essential assistance became available from the Eastern Ukrainian railway workers.[62]

In spite of all this, public order in most parts of Western Ukraine was much more a reality than in the neighboring countries. Even the courts, which are the most difficult to organize, were soon functioning again. Reports of robbery or murder were few or nonexistent. The Polish residents were unmolested. There were no peasant revolts against the large landowners in spite of the unsound agrarian relations. Anti-Jewish pogroms, a prominent feature in Eastern Ukraine and, to a much lesser extent, in Poland, were completely unheard of here. Admittedly, there was not a complete absence of bureaucratic arbitrariness and abuse, or of unruliness among the mass of the population, but the general desire was that the government exercise firm control, and the masses were willing to submit to the will of the state. This was even more the case after the loss of Lviv, which had a profound effect on the Western Ukrainian masses: everyone, the educated strata as well as the peasants, was willing to make any sacrifice demanded by the government in the interests of the state.[63]

Thus the state leadership had an uncommonly tractable population at its disposal. But the Western Ukrainians did not have among their leaders men who could bring great energy and ability to bear on the problems of the country, men with the capacity to lead a tenacious struggle against unfavorable circumstances. In time the mechanism of state and military organization fell into place, but it was not permeated by any living spirit, and gradually there was an increase of bureaucratic arbitrariness and abuse, as well as an increasing breakdown of order among the population.

Thus Western Ukraine was ahead of its neighbors in the reconstitution of a state order. Had it not been for the war with Poland, there is no doubt that Western Ukraine would have been one of the first countries of Central and Eastern Europe to reestablish a firm and stable order out of the conditions of postwar chaos. The people of Western Ukraine thus demonstrated a capacity to develop into a decisive force, which, although limited to the rather small territory of Eastern Galicia and surrounded by dissolution and chaos, was capable, alongside the Bolsheviks, of exercising a strong influence on the development of all Ukraine and, thereby, on the whole of Eastern Europe. The historical significance of the Polish-Ukrainian war lies in the fact that Poland suppressed that potential, and it is this aspect of the war that makes our study of it both important and rewarding.

The breakdown resulting from the war with Poland gradually spread out from two areas of Western Ukraine: the territory along the Zbruch River, the border with Eastern Ukraine, and that of the Drohobych–Boryslav oil basin (Map 1). Beyond the Zbruch, amid the struggle of the Eastern Ukrainian parties, there was a terrible revolt against the government of the hetman in Kyiv. In this territory, adjacent to the border with Western Ukraine, well-organized and armed peasant bands made the small towns and railways highly insecure and disrupted the transport of the Austro-Hungarian army of occupation from southern Ukraine. This army, completely dissolved and moving westward since the second half of November, was attacked and plundered by those peasant bands. This chaos gradually spread into the border area of Western Ukraine. The spirit of unruliness and disorder gripped not only the masses but also the local authorities. It was only the Western Ukrainian troops, posted in very small numbers throughout that territory, who showed impressive achievements. They disarmed the masses of Austro-Hungarian troops fleeing westward. Despite the almost unanimous claim of Polish historians, it was this, rather than the delivery of arms from Austria or even Germany, that was long the only source of weapons for the Western Ukrainians, making it possible for them to continue the war with Poland.* These Western Ukrainian troops cared for the disarmed masses of soldiers, fed them and transported them as quickly as possible through Eastern Galicia. Inspired by humanitarian motives, they established hostels and food stations to care for the hundreds of thousands of Russian prisoners of war who were returning to their homeland and dying of incredible misery and hunger. They repeatedly had to engage in hard fighting with Polish troops from Western Galicia who were returning from southern Ukraine. These had to be forced to give up their arms. Finally, in order to halt the spread of anarchy, they even had to occupy towns bordering on Eastern Ukraine that had long been dens of dangerous smugglers.[64]

Apart from the breakdown along the Zbruch River, it was the corruption in the "Eastern Galician California," the oil basin of Drohobych–Boryslav, that was the greatest evil in Western Ukraine.

---

* Thus in November and December 1918 the Pidvolochyske border station alone, led by Major Stepan Shukhevych, supplied more than eighty field guns, more than three hundred heavy machine guns, some twenty thousand rifles, six searchlights, large quantities of infantry and artillery ammunition, almost all the field kitchens of the Western Ukrainian army, and untold numbers of blankets, uniforms, and shoes (Shukhevych, *Spomyny*, 1: 32).

Among the very poorly paid Western Ukrainian officials, oil speculation gave rise to dishonesty; rumor exaggerated the abuse. Distrust and discontent in the army and among the population was the result, and the government lacked the courage and strength to take vigorous action.[65]

If the internal situation in Western Ukraine was not so bad, compared with that of the neighboring countries, especially the Polish heartland, the external situation facing the newly created state was most unfavorable. The basis of the Western Ukrainian People's Republic was the "right of nations to self-determination," but it soon became clear how futile were the territorial claims of the Ukrainian National Rada's proclamation of 19 October 1918 and the Constitution of the Republic, proclaimed on 13 November, given the lack of power to back them up. These claims were disputed not only in Eastern Galicia. The ethnically Ukrainian section of Bukovyna and Carpatho-Ruthenia never in fact became part of the Western Ukrainian People's Republic. As early as 11 November 1918, on the basis of a secret treaty between Romania and the Entente (18 August 1916), the Romanian army occupied northwestern Ukrainian Bukovyna, where, on 3 November, the Bukovynian Delegation of the Ukrainian National Rada had already taken control of the state apparatus in Chernivtsi and the surrounding area. This Romanian occupation took place in spite of the willingness of the Romanian National Council of Bukovyna to cede the four western purely Ukrainian districts without Chernivtsi and in spite of Ukrainian protest. The Romanians immediately initiated a barbarous policy of denationalization with respect to the Ukrainians that is still being carried out. The Ukrainians were certainly in no position to begin an armed conflict with Romania over this small territory, and so it remains part of greater Romania, in spite of the later Ukrainian protests at the Paris Peace Conference.[66]

The Western Ukrainian proclamations of statehood were completely illusory with respect to the Carpatho-Ruthenians, the most backward branch of the Ukrainian people, who in 1918 were only in a position to attain the national and political level achieved by the Galician Ukrainians in 1848. The Ruthenian National Rada (Rus'ka Narodna Rada), formed on 8 November 1918, did not even demand incorporation into the rest of Ukraine; in December 1918 it obtained autonomy from Hungary for the "Ruthenian Land" (Rus'ka Kraïna), consisting of four komitats. It was not until 21 January 1919 that a congress of delegates from all of Carpatho-Ruthenia, meeting in Khust, proclaimed the incorporation of Carpatho-Ruthenia into the Western Ukrainian People's Republic and called on Western Ukraine to occupy it. This proclamation was of course influenced by the collapse of Hungary, the success of the Western

Ukrainians in creating their own state, and, finally, the famine in their own country. The Western Ukrainians militarily occupied the whole territory from Syhit Marmaroskyi (Sighetul Marmaţiei) to Uzhhorod but soon had to withdraw under pressure from the Hungarians and Romanians. As a result of the agreements signed at the Paris Peace Conference, a small part of Carpatho-Ruthenia was incorporated into Romania, while the larger part, on condition that it be an autonomous territory, was given to Czechoslovakia despite Ukrainian protests. The autonomy clause was never respected by Czechoslovakia.[67]

Thus the Western Ukrainian People's Republic was in fact limited to the territory of the former Eastern Galicia. But the Western Ukrainian government had almost all of this territory under its effective control. Of the forty-nine districts claimed by the People's Republic, only four in the west were occupied by the Poles, and only in six others was the exercise of government authority partly disrupted by wartime events. In the considerable remaining territory, extending over more than forty thousand sq. km and with a population of four million, of whom more than three million were Ukrainians, the overwhelming majority of the people willingly did their duty to their state, recognizing the authority of the Western Ukrainian political and military leadership in spite of the latter's weaknesses and shortcomings, and fought, arms in hand, for their freedom. They thus demonstrated with ample clarity, in the spirit of the Wilsonian principles, their desire for national statehood and their ability to rule themselves.[68]

After the evacuation of Lviv, Stanyslaviv (Ivano-Frankivsk) became the effective capital of the new republic, and it was here, in January 1919, that the final organization of the supreme government bodies was undertaken. As a result of supplementary elections held between 22 and 26 November throughout the whole country, except for towns and regions in the battle zone, the Ukrainian National Rada, the parliament of Western Ukraine, now consisted of one hundred fifty members. The Poles boycotted the new state, and neither the Jews nor the Germans made use of their right to elect delegates, since they feared the revenge of the Poles in the event that the latter conquered Eastern Galicia. The parliament therefore remained a purely Ukrainian institution. From the viewpoint of social composition, most of the delegates were middle peasants, the next most important group being the clergy, followed by representatives of the educated stratum. In party-political terms, the strongest were the National Democrats, with the Radical Party in second and the Social Democrats in third place. The extreme left, distinguished from the other parties more by its demagogical behavior than by its program, formed the Peasant Radical Group (Selians'ko-radykal'na hrupa), a split-off from the Radicals. The National Rada was therefore antisocialist in character. As an exception to the social-revolutionary ferment that dominated Europe at the time, this assembly was simply radically democratic and liberal. Even the Peasant Radicals under Dr. Kyrylo Tryliovsky were more nationalist than social-revolutionary. The struggle of Western Ukraine against Poland was thus not a social but a wholly national political revolution.[69]

The question of state leadership was resolved by the National Rada on 4 January 1919. The leading body was to be a nine-member executive of the National Rada (Vydil Ukraïns'koï Natsional'noï Rady), elected for the same term of office as the Rada itself and chaired by the president of the National Rada. The highest representative honor in the new state went therefore to the president, Petrushevych,* who remained in office until the end of the republic.

The Provisional State Secretariat was now replaced by a regular cabinet, led by Sydir Holubovych, which stayed in place, with few changes, until the end of the republic.** It was a cabinet of National Democrats and Radicals with a strong presence of nonparty experts.

The parliamentary legislative achievements of the Ukrainian National Rada were quite significant, although here we shall be able to mention only the most important ones. Already in Lviv it had established a general administration and legal system. The model was the old Austrian state order. The revolution in Russia and in Eastern Ukraine had absolutely no

* The members of the executive were as follows: Dr. Yevhen Petrushevych (National Democrat), president of the National Rada; Dr. Lev Bachynsky (Radical), Semen Vityk (Social Democrat), Dr. Antin Horbachevsky (National Democrat), Hryts Duviriak (Radical), Dr. Mykhailo Novakovsky (independent), Dr. Teofil Okunevsky (National Democrat), Omelian Popovych (National Democrat), Andrii Shmihelsky (Radical), and the Reverend Dr. Stepan Yuryk (National Democrat). The secretaries of the National Rada were Dr. Stepan Vytvytsky, Stepan Siletsky, and Osyp Ustyianovych (Lozyns'kyi, *Halychyna*, p. 63).

** Dr. Sydir Holubovych (National Democrat) was president and state secretary for trade and industry; foreign affairs: Dr. Vasyl Paneiko (National Democrat); minister without portfolio and acting state secretary for foreign affairs (in place of Dr. Paneiko, who was delegated to the Paris Peace Conference): Dr. Lonhyn Tsehelsky (National Democrat); internal affairs: Dr. Ivan Makukh (Radical); war: Colonel Dmytro Vitovsky (Radical); justice: Osyp Burachynsky (National Democrat); education and the arts: Dr. Ahenor Artymovych; transport, post and telegraph: Ivan Myron; agriculture: Mykhailo Martynets; public works: Mariian Kozanevych—the latter four were all politically independent former senior civil servants in the Austrian administration (Lozyns'kyi, *Halychyna*, p. 64). Subsequent cabinet changes were as follows: On 13 February 1919, Viktor Kurmanovych, formerly a colonel of the Austrian general staff, was appointed state secretary of war and simultaneously head of the general staff. Since he was engaged at headquarters, Major Petro Bubela took his place as head of this state secretariat. On 10 March 1919, Dr. Mykhailo Lozynsky replaced Dr. Lonhyn Tsehelsky (Lozyns'kyi, *Halychyna*, pp. 64–65).

influence. The most necessary reforms were accomplished with great care. The very moderation with which the Western Ukrainians approached the transformation of the old tried and tested political system showed that they possessed a higher degree of political statecraft than their Eastern Ukrainian counterparts. A school system was also established. The school law of 13 February and the law on official languages of 15 February 1919 both protected minority language rights. In spite of their hostile or neutral attitude at the time, the later political influence of the minorities was guaranteed. The constitutional law of 15 April 1919 on the future parliamentary assembly (Seim), which was to be elected in the usual radical-democratic manner on the basis of a general, equal, secret, direct, and proportional franchise by citizens of both sexes, protected the minorities from Ukrainian majority rule by establishing national curias for them. The parliament was to be made up of 226 representatives, of whom 160 were to be Ukrainians (70.8 percent), 33 were to be Poles (14.6 percent), 27 Jews (11.9 percent), and 6 Germans (2.7 percent). It was the standing policy of the State Secretariat to bring Polish officials and experts into the Western Ukrainian state service. And this policy was not without success, for later, when the Poles conquered Eastern Galicia, quite a number of Poles had to pay the price for having been coopted into the service of the Western Ukrainian state.[70]

The Ukrainian National Rada lacked the political ability to create a constitutional and legal order that was original and adapted to the specific character and needs of the nation. It followed the schematic conceptions of international radical democracy in every respect. As a result, the whole form of the Western Ukrainian state was internally weak and unable to avoid the kind of constitutional crisis that was to affect all the national states established in 1919. For the time being, however, the Western Ukrainian radical-democratic order remained stable.

It was within the framework of its radical-democratic politics that the Ukrainian National Rada carried out its most unfortunate and questionable action—the agrarian law of 14 April 1919. It took account of a variety of circumstances. Agrarian relations in Western Ukraine were indeed extremely unsound: for the most part, the peasants were without adequate land. The harshness of the new law was influenced, however, not only by the agrarian revolution in Eastern Ukraine but also by the fact that the large estates were almost exclusively in Polish hands, which meant, in the given circumstances, that they were hostile to the state. The law was also meant to serve the highly dubious purpose of goading the peasants into battle with the prospect of agrarian reform. It provided for the dispossession of the large landowners and the partition of their estates among the landless and poor peasants, who would take them over as their property. The dispossession was to take legal effect immediately, but partition of the land was to begin only after the conclusion of the war with Poland. The law was quite radical with regard to dispossession: it put the compensation of the large landowners into question by leaving the issue to be decided by the new parliament. As far as the partition of the large estates was concerned, this was prompted by humanitarian rather than political or economic motives: first in line for the land would be invalids and surviving dependents from the Polish-Ukrainian and Russo-Ukrainian wars, as well as from the world war, who would otherwise have had to be compensated in some different fashion. This law, however, was questionable in various respects. Even though the large Polish landowners were at that moment hostile to the Ukrainians, one could certainly have assumed that in the event of a Ukrainian victory they would abandon their historically Polish political traditions and show readiness to place themselves at the service of the Ukrainian state. The true interests of the Ukrainian nation and state required that this culturally, politically and materially most valuable element of the population be won over, not eliminated. If this law had been carried through, it would have established the spiritual and political culture of Western Ukraine at a very low and primitive level. It would also have damaged the country economically by bringing about the collapse of its main source of financial sustenance—the whole agricultural economy. Its gravest consequence, however, was that in the midst of war it aroused a revolutionary agrarian spirit among the peasantry, which weakened rather than strengthened the military effort of Western Ukraine.[71]

We have described the condition of the people of Western Ukraine, the territorial extent of the new state, and the nature of its governmental activity. But the course of developments was not determined solely by those internal conditions. External factors played an equally important role, especially in relation to the outcome of the war with Poland. These external factors were the balance of forces between Poland and Western Ukraine; the situation in Western Ukraine in relation to what was happening in Eastern Ukraine; and, finally, the attitude of Western Ukraine to the Moscow Bolsheviks.

2. *The Polish State and Western Ukraine*

With the expulsion of the Western Ukrainians from Lviv, the Polish insurrection developed into a war between Western Ukraine and the newly arising Polish state. In this conflict the Polish troops had a firm hold on two strongholds, Przemyśl and Lviv. From December 1918, the battlefront ran along a stretch of more than 250 km from the middle Carpathians south of Przemyśl, then in an easterly direction past that fortress, continuing south of the railway line toward Lviv and, finally, passing that city to the south and east, in a northwesterly direction (Map 1). The question now arises: how much of a strain could the Western Ukrainians take? Could the Western Ukrainians win such a war and establish their claim to the whole of Eastern Galicia, including Lviv, by means of armed force? First we must look at the situation in Poland at the beginning of 1919.

If Western Ukraine confronted the collapse of Austria as a united nation, Poland presented a substantially different picture at that time. In October 1917 the Central Powers established the Regency Council in Warsaw, a body that could have become the provisional political center of the nation until the consolidation of the situation made it possible to create a new state authority to supplant it. The Regency Council already disposed of its own legal and educational system, as well as of a small military force in Congress Poland.[72] The whole Austrian state apparatus in Western Galicia had long been in Polish hands. Poland therefore had a definite advantage over Western Ukraine. It already had a foundation on which to base its new state order. In this spirit, as early as 7 October 1918, the Regency Council took on the task of politically unifying the whole nation with its proclamation of a united Poland. Meanwhile the nation was divided by very deep conflicts that stood in the way of such unification. The conservative stratum now represented by the Regency Council was universally hated. This was the same stratum that had previously followed a policy of negotiating with the occupying powers, seeking at one time an "Austro-Polish solution"—the reconstitution of Poland as a dependency of Austria-Hungary—or, at another time, attempting to persuade Russia to give up its repressive policy toward Poland. The earlier achievements of this stratum were forgotten. The general mood was now national-revolutionary, and people were excited by the slogan of "matching intentions with strength." With the simultaneous collapse of the three occupying powers, Poland was no longer threatened in any way. The existence of the Polish state would be disputed by no other country. In such a situation there was ample opportunity to put forward and attempt to implement practically any program of domestic or foreign policy—a remarkably fruitful soil for the development of doctrinaire views. Two mutually opposed political conceptions now confronted each other: the national-democratic and the socialist. The Polish National Democratic Party had always considered itself the true core of the whole nation and was firmly intent on ruling alone, even if it meant the suppression of all other political forces. There could hardly have been a greater antithesis to the concept of the Social Democrats, who sought the true voice of the people among the masses. On questions of foreign policy, the differences were also unbridgeable. For years, in fact for decades, the National Democrats had been concerned with the expansion of the Polish state. They had decided that the eastern border of the Polish state lay between the historical boundaries of 1771 and those of 1793, in other words, extending almost to the Dnipro. This whole territory was to become a unitary state whose goal would be the Polonization of the Lithuanians, Belarusians and Ukrainians in the eastern regions. On this question the socialists did not have a comparably worked-out program. From time to time they spoke of a Polish-Lithuanian-Belarusian-Ukrainian federation, an alliance of nations, but this was not developed properly. In fact, their program was a fantastic mixture of international slogans of popular liberty, the right of nations to self-determination, world peace, and an idealization of historical Poland. Accordingly, many socialists shared the unitary conceptions of the National Democrats. If it was now possible to "match intentions with strength" in a secure territory, then it was naturally of the greatest importance which party would be the first to take state power in order to implement its program. Thus the alternative Polish doctrines had been bitterly opposed for decades, and the world war had greatly deepened the divisions through the clash of orientations on the Central Powers and on the Entente. There was consequently boundless spite between these conflicting orientations, and the collapse of the Central Powers was not, for Poland, an opportunity to unite but, on the contrary, the starting signal for a party-political struggle for power.[73]

The greatest exertion in this general struggle for power was made by the central leadership of the National Democrats, the Paris-based Polish National Committee (Komitet Narodowy Polski), which had been diplomatically active in relations with the Entente powers. This committee was led by Roman Dmowski, who obtained from the Entente the specification in clause 12 of the truce conditions with Germany that the Germans would withdraw from the territories they occupied in Eastern Europe only at the behest of the Entente. The committee's plan was that it would be established as the government in Poland by the Entente troops and the Polish army organized in France by General Józef Haller, which were to replace the departing Germans.[74]

Within the country itself, the situation was even worse. As early as 17 October 1918 the Regency Council called a meeting of all the Polish parties in Warsaw in order to reach some general agreement. But the meeting turned out to be a chaotic gathering of about thirty different factions, groups and coteries, all fiercely combating one another, and ended without having achieved anything. Thus the Regency Council's efforts to establish a coalition government failed. Support for the council was limited to the most unpopular conservative circles, especially the Cracow conservatives, who had been compromised by their pro-Austrian policy. The council was therefore obliged to give way to the pro-Entente factions, in particular, the National Democrats and the Realists. The latter were more than willing to take the power offered them, and on 23 October 1918 they formed a cabinet under the leadership of Józef Świerzyński. Now the battle of demagogy really began. On 29 October the cabinet appointed the commissioners of the Regency Council who were to take over the administration of southern Congress Poland in Lublin and that of Galicia in Cracow and Lviv from the Austrian occupation authorities. They also published their program, which included an end to occupation, the creation of a state administration, a domestic bond issue, the recruitment of a volunteer army, and the convocation of a constituent assembly. To this extent, their aims and actions were quite appropriate. Being aware, however, of the low level of national consciousness among the masses, they did not believe in demanding nothing but sacrifices to begin with; on the contrary, they thought that the only way to win mass favor was to make social promises. It was this same element of policy that plunged Eastern Ukraine into Bolshevism; in Western Ukraine, however, at least in the beginning, there was no trace of it, which helps explain the relatively large sacrifices that the Western Ukrainians made for their state. But this attitude also corresponded to the basic character of the Polish National Democrats and their striving for popularity. The Świerzyński cabinet tried to take the wind out of the socialist sails by means of social enticements. It was with this in mind that the post of war minister was reserved for the very popular Józef Piłsudski, who was still being interned by the Germans in Magdeburg at the time. An agrarian reform was announced, as well as measures to improve the security of the working class. A highly radical electoral law was worked out for the coming elections to the proposed constituent assembly. With these measures the Poles found themselves on a slippery slope that could only lead, as it did in the rest of Eastern Europe, to social revolution.[75]

At the same time, the left made its appearance and attempted to outbid the hated National Democrats. On 30 October 1918 the Western Galician peasant leader Wincenty Witos organized a conference of his party's delegates in Cracow. On the basis of the size of the peasant population in Poland, this party demanded almost half the cabinet portfolios for itself.

The state machine was clearly seen as spoils for the taking, and so the congress of the Peasant Party held in Warsaw on 1 November came out most resolutely in opposition to the Świerzyński cabinet. The socialists, with the support of the Polish Military Organization, went even further, protesting the creation of a national army before the constituent assembly had been convoked. They hoped to take power through a radical majority in the assembly. In Cracow the Polish Liquidation Commission refused to subordinate itself to the Regency Council and its cabinet, and the Galician commissioner dispatched from Warsaw, Count Witold Czartoryski, was obliged to return to Warsaw after fruitless negotiations with the commission.[76]

The socialists now condemned the Regency Council, saying that it was disgraceful to submit to this placeholder for a monarchy that was dependent on the Central Powers and constituted a fortress of reaction established by them. The National Democrats immediately took up the same demagogic slogan—indeed, the two sides tried to outdo each other in every respect. On 4 November 1918 the Świerzyński cabinet, under the slogan of a "Polish People's State" (Polska Ludowa), attempted a coup against the Regency Council. The cabinet proclaimed that "the interests of the privileged strata must yield to the good of the fatherland" and insisted that the government should "represent the Polish working masses." The Regency Council dismissed the cabinet, thereby losing its last base of support. Central authority had now disintegrated, and Poland was given over to the unbridled demagogy of the contending parties.[77]

Everything was now pushing in the direction of social and political civil war. On the one side, the National Democrats railed against the Regency Council, and they had long been consummate masters of the art of popular incitement. On the other side, the Galician Polish socialists, led by Ignacy Daszyński, met in Lublin on 8 November 1918, on territory just vacated by the Austrian army of occupation, and proclaimed a people's government. The small military units of the Regency Council in Lublin were disarmed and local workers and peasants called to arms. At the same time, the socialists issued an appeal to the Polish working masses that called, in the name of "peace and freedom for suffering humanity," for "the destruction of the rule of capitalists, industrialists, landowners, and militarists," proclaimed the dissolution of the Regency Council, and threatened the "enemies of democracy" with the harshest punishment, indeed outlawed them if they attempted to resist. This same appeal declared estates and forests to be state property, proclaimed the eight-hour day, and promised the expropriation of the large and middle landowners, the nationalization of most industrial enterprises, the creation of workers' factory councils, and the confiscation of capital acquired during the world war. It called on the Poles to assist in the reconstitution of the Lithuanian-Belarusian Commonwealth in its historical borders and to seek peace with the Ukrainians in Eastern Galicia and in Ukraine. Finally, it called on the people to join the ranks of the Polish people's army.[78]

It seemed inevitable, therefore, that the social furies unleashed by the nationalist and socialist sorcerer's apprentices would destroy both groups and bring Poland under the rule of the true master magicians, the communists, casting it into the same misery of civil war in which Russia and, a few days later, Eastern Ukraine had already found themselves. Not only did Poland now have four governments—the Regency Council, the Lublin government, the ersatz government of the Liquidation Commission in Cracow, and ("in the lands of the unbelievers") the Paris-based National Committee—but it was also being divided into haves and have-nots. If there was anything preventing complete disintegration, it was only the hated presence of the German army of occupation in Warsaw and in the greater part of Congress Poland north of Lublin.

This disintegration was not limited to the political leadership. The situation of the Polish masses was no less favorable a breeding ground for social revolution than that in Russia and Eastern Ukraine. "The Polish territories were a place of banditry, pogroms and dissolution," as an eminent Polish conservative historian described the situation.

> The worst manifestations were in Western Galicia. The politicians who took power in Cracow under the name of the Liquidation Commission and unfurled the banner of provincial separatism did not do so because it would be simpler and more efficient to carry out the tasks of government on a smaller territory. They did not care for the Polish regiments that were returning from the shattered Austrian army. They did not make so bold as to organize a recruitment drive for the national army. They did not impose and collect taxes or rush to the aid of Lwów, threatened and occupied by the Ukrainians. On the contrary, they saw it as their main task to get rid of the "Austrian" regime in Western Galicia, over which their rule extended, without taking into consideration that the national interest required maintaining the existing administration, which was, after all, in Polish hands, until it could be replaced by something better. The Peasant Party decided to put peasants in positions of authority in every area, as it had long been yearning to do. Because of

> the demands of unrepresentative local groups, many officials were fired and replaced by people whose only qualification was, in many cases, that they were tools of some local coterie. Above all, the Austrian police was dissolved. During the war the local population had suffered much at the hands of this force, but at least it had kept order and guaranteed public safety. Among the lower social strata this "reform" did nothing to generate respect for the government. Robber bands, made up mainly of deserters, began to be formed in the towns and villages, and Jews especially were victims of their looting. The goods trains were not spared, and even traffic on the Cracow–Lwów railway line was often brought to a halt by attacks. The crudest expression of this anarchic current was the formation of a people's government in Tarnobrzeg by peasants egged on by two radical clerical deputies, Okoń and Dąbal. A popular assembly in the region dismissed all officials, replacing them with its own people, and was so convinced that the era of popular rule had at last begun that it asked the Liquidation Commission, at the head of which stood the Peasant Party leader, Witos, for official ratification of its decisions. These anarchist forces were not easily suppressed, and in fact they once even routed a military unit. Other units prepared themselves better and made large-scale use of corporal punishment as a means of stopping the looting, without too much concern for the law, but with evident success.
>
> The same thing happened in Congress Poland. There anarchy gave rise to regular attacks by armed gangs on small towns like Działoszyce and Wodzisław, where, once the police had been disarmed, stores were thoroughly looted, especially those belonging to Jews. Toward the end of November 1918 workers' and peasants' councils took power in the province of Lublin; laborers began to take over their masters' estates, thereby seeking to break up and distribute large landholdings. There were also quite a few attempts to organize people's governments similar to the one in Tarnobrzeg. At that time a certain Lisowski established a people's republic in Pinczów that was inaugurated with looting in the city. But the worst expression of anarchy in Congress Poland was the organization of armed units at the service of sociopolitical parties—the Socialists on the one hand and the Bolsheviks on the other. Such fighting units organized themselves almost openly, even in Warsaw.[79]

This was the state of affairs among the popular masses at the end of November and in December 1918, when the arrival of Józef Piłsudski finally resolved the governmental crisis and the widespread anarchy was tackled. It was very similar to the period of general disintegration that preceded the Bolshevik Revolution in Russia, and there can be little doubt that, had it come to armed conflict between Warsaw and Lublin, which was avoided only by a hair's breadth, Poland would inevitably have been plunged into social revolution. There was also one other factor at work. Poland's best protection against the development of social revolution was its geographical location. The Moscow Bolsheviks, fully occupied with the struggle against counterrevolution in Russia and against Eastern Ukraine, did not attack Poland directly because of the continued presence of the German army of occupation in Belarus. If in November-December 1918 Poland had been subjected to an invasion of Bolshevik hordes from outside the country, linked with a massive Bolshevik organization and propaganda drive within, as happened in Eastern Ukraine, then it is highly unlikely that the Poles, in spite of the much greater strength of their bourgeois and educated stratum, would have proved themselves politically more competent than the Eastern Ukrainians. Under such circumstances Poland, too, would have succumbed to Bolshevism.[80]

It was the appearance of one man, Józef Piłsudski, that brought this development to an abrupt halt. His influence in November 1918 was decisive. In this most dangerous moment of crisis the nation recognized this man as its leader and submitted completely to his authority. Piłsudski knew how to make party conflicts less of a threat to the state. He was able to bypass the boiling, poisonous tumult of interparty strife and, with unerring judgment, do what was necessary for the establishment of the Polish state. When Piłsudski arrived in Warsaw on 10 November 1918, the Regency Council greeted him as a savior in its hour of greatest need and, on 11 November, gave him full military authority. The Lublin government was thus denied the opportunity to form a revolutionary people's army. Piłsudski's authority among the Polish masses, especially among the socialists, was unquestioned. The enthusiastic masses in Warsaw and in the provinces now took up arms, and it was an easy matter to disarm the German occupation troops and send them home. The latter were extremely war-weary and confused by the reports of revolution in Germany; they wished only to return to their homeland. The whole of Congress Poland was now in Polish hands. The occupying regime of a foreign power, which could only have acted as an obstacle to the construction of an independent state, was thus eliminated. Getting rid of the Regency Council proved just as easy. Confronted with tumultuous street demonstrations, the council resigned as early as 14 November and handed over all its powers to Piłsudski. The danger of civil war was thus eliminated. With uncommonly sure political instinct, Piłsudski now entrusted the Lublin leader Ignacy Daszyński with the task of forming a cabinet. Only one condition was laid down: experts were to be engaged in the work of state-building, and no major social changes were to be undertaken. This was a truly masterful act. In view of the revolutionary mood of the masses, there could be no question of bourgeois, let alone conservative, participation in a coalition government. But nothing suited the Lublin subversives so poorly as their revolutionary role. Nothing filled them with greater dread than the prospect of going down the same revolutionary road as Aleksandr Kerensky, and they had no greater longing than to be allowed, under cover of socialist slogans, to carry out bourgeois policies. With a feeling of relief they dissolved the Lublin government and submitted to Piłsudski, pleased that their return to Warsaw gave their submission the appearance of victory. As early as 18 November, street demonstrations organized by the National Democrats (everything was decided by street demonstrations in those days) forced Daszyński to resign and make way for the less unpopular socialist Andrzej Moraczewski. Daszyński's resignation eased the way for the later inclusion of bourgeois elements, especially National Democrats, in the government. The governmental crisis finally came to an end on 22 November 1918 with Piłsudski's decree naming himself provisional head of state until the convocation of a constituent assembly. This laid the foundations for Piłsudski's dictatorship. Party conflicts were not eliminated; National Democratic demonstrations and socialist counterdemonstrations continued to roil the streets. The screaming masses even broke up cabinet meetings on occasion. Demagogic slogans, denunciations, and extreme accusations poured from the pages of the press, flew around mass meetings and agitated the whole country, although there was nothing behind all this frenetic activity but the lust of individuals and parties for power. But Piłsudski's key achievement was that the various parties carried on this struggle without recourse to arms.[81]

However makeshift this stabilization of the situation in Poland may have been, for the Western Ukrainians it was disastrous, for the opportunity of avoiding a war with Poland over Eastern Galicia was now definitely lost. Assuming that they had managed to suppress the Polish insurrection in Lviv and march on to the Sian, and that their leaders had possessed sufficient initiative, after winning this military victory, to enter into direct negotiations with Warsaw, engaging in conciliatory diplomacy and offering, for instance, a united front against the Bolsheviks in return for recognition of Western Ukraine, such a proposal would merely have amounted to one more element of confusion in the seething caldron of Polish politics. In such a situation, however, it is extremely likely that the Poles, disorganized and unready for war, would have reconciled themselves to the loss of Lviv and the rest of Eastern Galicia without risking a military campaign against Western Ukraine. But now these conditions no longer held. From the end of November 1918, in addition to Piłsudski's authority, another factor added to the stabilization and growing strength of Poland: the successful defense of Lviv against the Ukrainians. This was the only truly great act to initiate the renewal of the Polish state, the sole luminous model of courage and sacrifice amid the gloom of national disintegration. Of course the National Democrats immediately took up the rewarding slogan of assistance to the Polish fighters in Lviv, successfully denouncing Piłsudski and the socialist cabinet for their alleged willingness to yield Lviv to the Ukrainians.[82] This demagogic slogan brought nationalist fanaticism among the Polish masses to a fever pitch, and the influence of the National Democrats, extremely hostile to the Ukrainians, went from strength to strength. Any thought of peace with the Ukrainians, such as found expression in the proclamation of the Lublin government, was silenced. Among the Poles the desire for war leading to total victory over Western Ukraine became more unshakable by the day, and the whole of the Polish population, regardless of party allegiance, was united in at least one thing: its desire to destroy the Western Ukrainians. The courage with which the Lviv Poles fought off the Ukrainians awakened feelings of national duty in every Pole. They abandoned their internal conflicts, turned their attention to the armed forces, and hastened to the front, where Polish weapons were to stake out the borders of the newly established Polish state. It is safe to say that the indolence with which the Western Ukrainians were led in Lviv gave special impetus to the formation of the Polish army at the end of 1918. The military strengthening of Poland would have proceeded much more slowly had it not been for the gaping wound of Lviv and the prospect of conquering Western Ukraine. The historical significance of the Lviv uprising lies not in its outcome, for the conquest of Eastern Galicia was a questionable achievement for the Polish state, but rather in the positive influence of the battle itself on the internal consolidation of the Polish people.

If time is to be regarded as a factor in warfare, then it must be said that on 22 November 1918, when the Western Ukrainians evacuated Lviv and began to make preparations to undertake their war with Poland in earnest, that war was already lost for them, although they were unaware of the fact. For this nation of three and a half million people now confronted a task that it was incapable of carrying out. To engage in a long-drawn-out war against the Polish nation of eighteen million people was a completely hopeless task unless, of course, the ingenuity of the Western Ukrainian leadership and the courage of their troops were overwhelmingly superior, which they were not. From now on, the resistance of the Western Ukrainians and the threat to Lviv only served to whip up the fury of the whole Polish nation and strengthen the resolve of those eighteen million to crush the three and a half million Ukrainians. Under these circumstances, even a Ukrainian victory in Lviv would have brought them no victorious peace settlement. It would have required a miracle for the Ukrainians to hold on to Lviv against the far greater strength and supreme and final effort of Poland to retake it. At the end of November 1918, what confronted the Ukrainians from the outset was the question of whether they would lose not only Lviv or the Drohobych–Boryslav oil basin but their whole country to Poland.

But neither then nor later did the Western Ukrainian leadership see the question in this light. If the Polish national movement in 1918–19, with its great political experience, was characterized by an almost complete lack of political know-how and prey to unlimited dogmatism, the situation of the Western Ukrainians was far worse. And those were confusing times. Everyone believed that the stateless nations had just achieved their freedom, "claimed on the basis of principle," and that even the Bolsheviks were rigidly implementing such a policy. But people failed to understand that these nations had achieved their "self-determination" not under their own power but because of the victory of the Entente. The Ukrainians were the only nation confronted with the task of winning their own freedom and establishing such physical boundaries for their state as their own forces could manage to wrest from their neighbors. It was just as poorly understood that the Bolsheviks had not achieved success by rigidly holding to some "principled" doctrine but rather by their capacity to fight for that doctrine with whatever means were most appropriate. Thus the Western Ukrainian leaders believed, and led their own people to believe, that it was enough to hold to the "principled" demand for all ethnically Ukrainian territory in Eastern Galicia and not weaken it by any diplomatic dealings with Poland. In this way the Western Ukrainians lost all freedom of maneuver with regard to Poland and every opportunity offered by the interplay of arms and diplomacy. Through the doctrinaire rigidity of their political position vis-à-vis Poland they put themselves in a situation whose only outcome could be total victory or total defeat.

But it was not just this general situation in Europe that helped disorient the Western Ukrainians. They also underestimated the scope of the threat from Poland. In December 1918–January 1919 all indications were that Poland was not in a position to conquer Western Ukraine militarily. The Western Ukrainian leaders were incapable of seeing how the situation would develop in the long run. Polish military strength grew numerically much more slowly than that of Western Ukraine. Until January 1919 it was almost the case that the Western Ukrainians, on their small territory, had a numerically greater military capacity than the Polish state of that day, with its much larger territory and greater population. The military situation in Western Ukraine was far from perfect, but the mass of the population had responded magnificently to the general mobilization. They joined their army, and by December 1918 Western Ukraine already had a people's army of many tens of thousands. Under a suitable leadership such a force could easily have taken Lviv and perhaps even have crossed the Sian River into Western Galicia. In Poland, although to a much lesser extent, there were similar problems of leadership, organization and equipment; much more seriously, there was a general unwillingness among the masses to do their military duty. The Western Ukrainians could order a call-up, and the troops would generally report for duty.* In Poland, however, especially in Congress Poland, the leaders were reluctant to do so, not only because the supply of weapons was inadequate but also because they feared the rise of Bolshevism among the mobilized masses. In December 1918 it was finally decided to order a mobilization in Western Galicia in order to form an army against the Western Ukrainians, but practically no one responded to the call except those who would have joined in any case, without the general call-up. The attempted mobilization proved an abysmal failure. They were therefore basically obliged to depend on volunteers, with the result that for a long time the strength of the Polish armed forces was relatively small. In December 1918 Poland had at its disposal a mere 19,065 troops on all fronts, of whom 12,508 were on the Western Ukrainian front. At this time the strength of the whole Polish army was much smaller than that which the Western Ukrainians were able to assign to the Polish front alone, not counting the Western Ukrainians who were fighting the Bolsheviks in Eastern Ukraine. The Polish army grew very

* Even much later, in February 1919, when signs of dissolution became apparent among the masses of the Western Ukrainian army because the war was going badly for it, the parliamentary deputy Oleksander Tershakovets could report to the Ukrainian National Rada that many districts, such as Komarno and Shchyrets, were voluntarily mobilizing men up to the age of forty, even though the official age limit was thirty-five (*Republyka* [Stanyslaviv], no. 4, 6 February 1919).

slowly. By mid-January 1919 the whole army numbered barely 110,532 enlisted men, of whom 23,000 were on duty at the front. The Western Ukrainians probably disposed of an equal number, counting troops at the front, those in reserve, and those fighting in Eastern Ukraine.[83]

The small number of Polish troops and the slow rate of growth of the Polish army allowed the Western Ukrainians to forget that this was only the advance guard of the massive army that the Poles were in a position to recruit. Bolstered by a sense of their own superiority, the Western Ukrainians misjudged their actual capacities and later failed to recognize the increasing inevitability of the loss of Lviv and of a significant part of their territory.*

But the growing might of Poland was not the only problem for the Western Ukrainians. Of equal importance was the problem of Eastern Ukraine.

3. *Relations between Western and Eastern Ukraine*

As early as 10 November 1918, the Ukrainian National Rada had instructed the Provisional State Secretariat to make preparations for the unification of Western and Eastern Ukraine in a single state. This decision was considered mainly a declaration of principle, and no time was specified for its implementation. But events in Eastern Ukraine soon made it a very practical question.

While the battle between the Poles and the Ukrainians was going on in Lviv, the Eastern Ukrainian socialist and democratic parties, supported by the above-mentioned Sich Riflemen, organized an uprising against the Kyiv hetman, Pavlo Skoropadsky, on 14–15 November. The outward cause of this uprising was the hetman's proclamation of 15 November announcing a federation of Eastern Ukraine with Russia. Since the Russia with which the hetman wished to federate did not yet exist as long as the Bolsheviks held Moscow and St. Petersburg, the hetman made his arrangements for the time being with the Russian counterrevolution. His goal was to organize the struggle against the Bolsheviks from Ukraine, with the support of the Entente, and establish a Russo-Ukrainian federation after the victory of the counterrevolution. The uprising against the hetman was therefore carried out under the slogan of preserving Ukrainian independence, but its fundamental causes lay deeper.

---

* By 13 February 1919 the Polish army already had 156,057 enlisted men, while those posted on all fronts numbered 56,753 (as opposed to 20,885 Western Ukrainian troops); by 15 August 1919, there were already (counting the Haller army, which had arrived from France) 300,097 enlisted men, of whom 152,307 were battle-ready (Hupert, *Zajęcie Małopolski Wschodniej*, pp. 13, 15).

The Hetman regime was an attempt, with the help of the German army of occupation, to establish a Ukrainian state on the basis of the social and legal order that had existed in Ukraine before the Revolution of 1917. Since the revolutionary democracy in Eastern Ukraine under the Central Rada, abolished on 29 April 1918 by the Hetman government, had shown itself incapable of actually establishing an independent Ukrainian state in 1917–18, the hetman's attempt to construct such a state with the support of the conservative social strata was, in principle, the only remaining option. In reality, however, it was a highly contradictory attempt. This was because the internal state of the Ukrainian nation itself, with its sociopolitical divisions, made it unfit for the task of establishing an Eastern Ukrainian state. In the art of politics it showed itself too weak to build any kind of state, whether democratic or conservative.

The major factor working against the Eastern Ukrainians was what would normally have been considered their pride and strength, namely, that they had a large country with a massive population. The national leadership would perhaps have measured up to the task of building an independent state in a country the size of Lithuania. But Eastern Ukraine was as large as the German Reich, and it had a population of thirty million. To have accomplished such an enormous task Eastern Ukraine would have required a leading stratum capable of creating a great power almost as strong as the Russian Empire had been in Eastern Europe. Such a task greatly exceeded the intellectual, political and material strength of the Eastern Ukrainian national movement, and that was its misfortune.

Although, in an age of great mass movements such as were seen in 1918–19, the existence of a strong national consciousness among the popular masses is an absolute precondition for the establishment of a national state, there is an immutable historical and political law that asserts itself over the reestablishment of state order following the disintegrative process of revolutions and coups. This law states that a nation in the throes of the collapse of an old order can create its own state order only if the revolutionary libertarian momentum of the people, which gives it the strength to achieve victory over external forces, is combined with another tendency within the nation itself that maintains stability when things are in flux and binds together the achievements and accomplishments of revolutionary energy into a secure and stable order with firm new ties. This means that a nation hoping to achieve its freedom by means of revolution must forge a new leadership in the midst of the revolutionary process. That new leadership must unite two different strata: on the one hand, the young new element—energetic, militant, revolutionary, and unprejudiced—that has emerged from the lower strata and is without political experience; on the other hand, an element of the counterrevolution still capable of leading the nation, not affected by the moral and political disintegration of the previous ruling stratum that the revolution has overthrown.* Even the Bolsheviks, with Lenin and a leadership of high intellectual rank, could not have managed without the help of the old "specialists" of every description. The Western Ukrainians were generally correct in their mixture of revolution and counterrevolution: this was, indeed, the basis of their success in the task of establishing the new state. It was also just such a mixture that Józef Piłsudski imposed on the Polish nation, which led, in the subsequent course of events, to the rise of the Polish state. In this sense, then, one can say that the founding of a state is the work of the counterrevolution, not of the revolution. It is not in revolution that nations distinguish themselves from each other but rather in counterrevolution. Revolutions always manifest themselves uniformly as a pure dynamic of explosion and disintegration. It is in the ethos of counterrevolution that differences of national spirit are expressed, for the lasting principles and values of a nation are manifested in the way in which the counterrevolution once again binds together a population that has been caught up in flux. It is the immutable ethos of nations, which continues through the centuries, that makes a nation unique amid the great diversity of the world of nations.

The radically democratic and socialist Central Rada of 1917–18 was wholly incapable of ending the revolution in Ukraine and bringing together the revolutionary and counterrevolutionary elements to form a new Eastern Ukrainian leading stratum around the idea of Ukrainian statehood. This body could do nothing other than lead the country toward a complete social-revolutionary collapse in which Eastern Ukraine would inevitably have fallen to the Moscow Bolsheviks. That process was already setting in before the German occupation of Ukraine in January-February 1918. It was only the sociopolitical restoration carried through by the Hetman government that halted the revolutionary process in Ukraine for a time. By asserting once again the authority of the counterrevolutionary strata, the Hetman government restored the domestic equilibrium that was essential to the successful establishment of the Eastern Ukrainian

* Reference should be made here to the writings of the outstanding Ukrainian historian and politician Viacheslav Lypynsky (1882–1931). Of prime importance here is one of the most comprehensive and penetrating expositions of conservative political theory that is to be found in world political literature (written to promote Ukrainian political renewal)—an exposition that includes, among other things, a sociological investigation of the relations between revolution and counterrevolution, between progress and stability or regression. This work is entitled *Lysty do brativ-khliborobiv. Pro ideiu i orhanizatsiiu ukraïns'koho monarkhizmu* (Letters to Fellow Landowners: On the Idea and Organization of Ukrainian Monarchism [Vienna, 1926]).

state. But the revolutionary and counterrevolutionary elements did not unite under the Hetman government: they went their separate ways, and so the Hetman government was a failure from the start.

The restoration would have made sense as a state-creating act if the ruling stratum in Eastern Ukraine before 1917 had been nationally oriented, either completely or predominantly, and actively committed to the idea of an independent Ukrainian state. But among conservative circles in Ukraine, nationally oriented individuals committed to separation from Russia were few and far between—so much so that even within the narrow confines of the national movement they had no weight at all. Intellectually, as well as politically and economically, the nationally minded large estate owners and the well-to-do medium-sized landowners representing the principal component of the Ukrainian national counterrevolution were not remotely comparable to the other reactionary and conservative forces in the country. And these forces, all of which benefited from the Hetmanite restoration—the large estate owners above all, industrialists, merchants, and finance capitalists almost without exception, the whole of the old bureaucracy and almost all of the old officer corps—were "all-Russian," that is to say, either Russian or Russified. They hated the idea of Ukrainian independence and dreamed incessantly of the restoration of the Russian Empire. This was the greatest contradiction underlying the Hetman government as a conservative Ukrainian state order.

Moreover, the social weight of the counterrevolution in Eastern Ukraine, both Russian and Ukrainian, was insufficient as compared with the revolutionary turmoil of the period, and the general intellectual and cultural level of the counterrevolution was too low to make it possible for the ruling stratum brought to power by the restoration to gain the respect of the masses. In the eyes of the latter, they did not appear as a stratum destined by nature to rule. In an open struggle with revolutionary democracy, there could have been no question of the Hetman government's coming to power: it had been installed not through the efforts of the counterrevolution itself but by the German army of occupation. It was a further contradiction that the social order from which, in principle, independent statehood was supposed to emerge did not develop organically from within the nation but was imposed and sustained by a foreign power. With some well-known exceptions, the political culture of the counterrevolution was given over to the comforts of power, with no sense of duty toward the country or the population. Thus, in place of revolutionary arbitrariness and unruliness, a counterrevolutionary version of the same vices spread throughout the land. But the latter was worse than the former: whereas the revolutionaries had at least justified themselves with the slogan of the people's welfare, the counterrevolutionaries blithely abjured any attempt to put a good face on their greed. There was a lack of patriotism, without which it is impossible, in present-day circumstances, to establish and maintain a national state. Most of the large landowners and the old restored bureaucracy of the Hetman government even lacked the common sense to make it as easy as possible for the revolutionary masses to return to a stable social order. Instead, arrogantly relying on the old Russian tradition of the knout and on the forces of the German occupation, they harassed the peasantry with bloody punitive expeditions and pillaging. It was only in the routine of state power that the counterrevolutionaries were superior to the revolutionaries. They lacked the level of culture that makes a conservative stratum useful to the nation as a whole. In general, the ruling strata of the old Russian Empire that had now returned to power in Ukraine were too decadent and dissolute to play a more valuable role in government than the revolutionary democratic strata. Here, too, the Hetman government suffered from an internal contradiction: it entrusted the task of founding a new state to a social stratum with little capacity for rule.

The consequence was an outbreak of fierce peasant uprisings, especially in the Dnipro region, which had a combative population still mindful of its former Cossack liberties. If the uprising did not immediately turn into a general revolt but was ultimately put down, it was only because the German and Austro-Hungarian army of occupation held the country in check. Thus it was not only the occupation and the Hetman government but the very idea of Ukrainian independence that came to be hated among the masses. If the strength of every monarchy consists in its identification with the common people, then the Hetman government, which represented the monarchic idea, found itself in contradiction with the very principle that it was supposed to represent.

Aware of all those deficiencies, the Ukrainian national elements of the Hetman government, which included part of the rather thin ranks of the moderate democrats, attempted to win the support of the radical democrats, who represented the main Eastern Ukrainian political camp and were then standing resentfully aside, for the existing order. The goal of the nationally conscious elements was to bring forth from the revolutionary camp a new pro-Ukrainian bureaucracy devoted to the state and, what was most important, to link the idea of the Hetman government with that of Ukrainian national propaganda and popular education, thereby creating a counterweight to the Russian orientation of the Hetman government. The attempt was correct in principle. Although the all-Russian orientation of the Eastern Ukrainian counterrevolution from which the Hetman government drew its support was hostile to Ukrainian national statehood, the way to overcome this was by no means the destruction of the Hetman regime itself. This all-Russian orientation was dangerous to Ukraine because the Ukrainian movement was inferior to it in every requisite of a well-ordered state—culturally, politically and economically. If the Ukrainian movement was to rid itself of this enemy, the best means of so doing would be to strengthen the existing Ukrainian state order sufficiently to destroy any hope that Ukrainian independence might suffer internal collapse. Within the framework of this state order it could then overcome any opponent by bringing all the forces of the national movement to bear in an open cultural, political and economic competition in which the sheer growing weight of the Ukrainian national element would purge the Russian influence and gradually assert undisputed control over the Hetman government itself. This would settle once and for all the question of the all-Russian orientation in Eastern Ukraine, for the very power center of that orientation would have been overcome. Defeated in the domain where it had held the upper hand, the all-Russian movement in Eastern Ukraine would scarcely have had the strength to resist swift cultural, political and economic assimilation by the now equally powerful Ukrainian movement.

But in order to carry this out, the Ukrainian radical democrats would have required a political outlook that was wholly foreign to them. They would have had to regard the national state not as an abstract program but as an actual exercise of power within their own country, in whatever form it might happen to be. And at that time the actual form was the Hetman government. But the ability actually to see the Hetman government as the embodiment of Ukrainian national statehood required a level of political culture—of education, insight, experience, a sense of political form and tradition—that those radical democrats did not possess. They should have recognized the failures of the Central Rada as Ukrainian democracy's lost opportunity and, in the interest of the Ukrainian state, freely accepted the counterrevolution as the underlying principle of a new attempt to create a Ukrainian state order without, of course, giving up their right of constructive criticism and opposition. Had Ukrainian democracy been capable of such a transformation, the overthrow of the Hetman government would have been completely superfluous, for Ukrainian democracy would have demonstrated its capacity to carry out its political tasks no less successfully than the great democratic-republican nations of the West. Here, then, was another important inner contradiction of the Hetman government: it had overthrown Ukrainian democracy because of the latter's incompetence in the task of building an independent state, but without the support of this same democracy it was itself unable to survive.

However, the Eastern Ukrainian democratic movement had a profound hatred—as profound as that of the all-Russian orientation for Ukraine—of all forms of "reaction," understanding by this almost everything handed down from the old order, all that stood in the way of the revolutionary dynamic, and it could not imagine an independent Ukraine that was not "free" and socialist-revolutionary, or at least radically democratic. A monarchic system, such as that of the Hetman government, was for them an absolute horror. Moreover, enthusiasm for the revolutionary slogans of 1917 was still very much alive in Ukraine. The revolution had not yet run its course or, more precisely, the reality of the revolution had not yet exposed and compromised such slogans. The Hetman government was not produced by any collapse of the revolution. The demand for a rational counterrevolution had not yet emerged. Indeed, the premature imposition of the Hetman government by a foreign power put a sudden stop to the process of disillusionment with the revolution and gave new impetus to its idealization because of general fear of the return of a reactionary system as narrow-minded as it was vindictive. The broad mass of the population had not yet reached the point of seeing clearly that this democratic ideology, developed in the very different world of Western Europe, would lead to something quite different when transplanted to the former Russian Empire, with its uneducated masses, its undeveloped middle classes still incapable of self-government, and its corrupt elite. It could only lead to disintegration, chaos, and Muscovite Bolshevism. More decisive, perhaps, was the fact that the Eastern Ukrainian democratic movement, for all its numerical strength, was incapable of taking the place of the Hetman government. Nor was its cultural standing such as to allow it to compete successfully with the vastly more educated and refined all-Russian movement. A rapid and forceful elimination of this embarrassingly superior minority seemed easier than the arduous effort to achieve cultural, political and social equality with the Russian opponent. A sense of their own inferiority and fear of a new Russification of Ukraine led them to believe that, instead of a difficult struggle perhaps lasting decades, a brief one-time explosion could destroy the all-Russian forces in Ukraine at a blow. Thus the revolutionary orientation of Eastern Ukrainian nationalism at the time was by no means an expression of strength that impels one toward the revolutionary seizure of power. On the contrary, it was an expression of inner and outer weakness that saw a revolutionary coup as the only salvation from the threat of demise.

Whereas the knout was the preferred instrument of rule of the all-Russian reactionary elements in Ukraine, for the Eastern Ukrainian revolutionary democrats it was the incitement of the masses. This gave a false impression of the strength of the stratum led by the Eastern Ukrainian national movement. One bold revolutionary could control a whole area simply by arousing the popular masses. This gave the Eastern Ukrainian democrats a decisive superiority over the all-Russian forces as long as the revolutionary turmoil lasted and the revolution had not run its course. The Hetman government and the all-Russian stratum ruled externally and mechanically by means of the presence of foreign occupation troops and through their control of the restored state apparatus. The Eastern Ukrainian democrats, however, ruled the hearts and minds of almost the whole mass of the population, and this made it a most dangerous opponent. Now they made use of this powerful weapon. They did everything in their power to arouse the masses, especially the landless peasantry, against the Hetman government, the return of privately owned large estates, and the whole new system in general. In this they were greatly assisted by the reactionary regime's practice of mounting punitive expeditions against the peasantry.

In spite of all these difficulties, a hetman who was an exceptional leader could have united the warring elements into a great nation, established the Hetman State as a great power within the borders defined by the Treaty of Brest-Litovsk, and perhaps even made Ukraine the leading East European center of struggle against Bolshevism. Neither nations nor general sociopolitical conditions can withstand the magic of a great leader. In Skoropadsky, however, the command of the German army of occupation had made a most unfortunate choice. Quite narrow in outlook, with little understanding of the broader context of events, seeing only the most immediate task, more a general than a sovereign ruler, this hetman was far from being the father of a nation who could inspire the imagination and love of his people. His overwhelming interest was not the creation of a great nation from almost nothing, not battle and victory, and certainly not great diplomatic or military deeds, but his personal standing. At best he could have been a vassal prince. A more appropriate path for him, from which he had been driven by the revolution, was that of a general making a career that exceeded his capacities, thanks to his connections at court. It was his misfortune to be the descendant of a house that had produced a Ukrainian hetman [Ivan Skoropadsky—Ed.] at the beginning of the eighteenth century—the successor to Ivan Mazepa, an antagonist of Peter the Great and an ally of Charles XII [of Sweden—Ed.]. Had it not been for this family tradition, which linked him with Ukraine, Skoropadsky—a divisional general in the Russian army during the war—would have been just one more of the countless and now forgotten generals of the Russian counterrevolution, which would have spared him many disappointments. But this family tradition gave him the timid wish to attain the dignity of hetman. To that end, in 1917, he participated in the "Ukrainization" of the Ukrainian sections of the Russian army and headed a Ukrainized army corps. In that position, however, Skoropadsky was not summoned to a task like that of General Lavr Kornilov, who founded and led the strike force of the Russian counterrevolution. Unlike the valiant Kornilov, Skoropadsky lacked military drive and the inventiveness of an inspired statesman who shapes situations to suit his own ends. The fire of a born leader was not in him, and thus he lacked the one characteristic that could have enabled him to hold his troops together at a time when the army was disintegrating. The great chance of his life came in 1917, before the Bolshevik coup, when at a blow he might have united the whole of Ukraine around the renewal of the Hetmanate, leading an army inspired by that idea. But the opportunity was lost. His army corps shared the fate of the whole army of the revolution, falling apart ingloriously as a result of revolutionary agitation. Thus Skoropadsky, half-heartedly toying with the Ukrainian Hetmanate, set himself a goal that far exceeded his capacity: it was the source of the misfortune that never lost its hold on him and prepared an unbecoming end to all his enterprises. He was a thoroughly unimaginative man with a very limited mental horizon. In every situation he would grasp for the immediate advantage, lacking the capacity to foresee its generally disastrous long-term consequences. Coldly self-seeking, he resorted to pursuing fortune by means of trickery and deceit, attempting to gain his ends through external circumstances alone. Raised from insignificance to the office of hetman by the German military command amid the internal conflicts of the period, he sought merely to hold on to his post through a policy of deceiving one and all. To Eastern Ukrainian nationally minded circles he presented himself as a champion of the cause of Ukrainian independence. To the all-Russian reaction, however, he hinted that he was not unaware of his duties as a Russian general. To be sure, there was something very enticing about being hetman of an independent state, especially a state the size of Eastern Ukraine, but Skoropadsky lacked the passion that makes the royal purple seem the finest burial shroud. He could equally well have played the role of vassal hetman to a Muscovite tsar. He adapted to every situation, bet on all his cards at once, and thought himself too clever for anyone to see through. His proper domain was that of political intrigue, not on a large scale but on one in which it is hard to tell whether the overriding motivation is one of ambition or of miserliness and greed. Consequently, no one took him at his word or respected him as a great leader. He was not the kind of hetman that Ukraine needed. What Ukraine needed was either a great hetman or none at all. And so Skoropadsky was just an interim hetman, one who stood and fell with the German occupation of Ukraine, doomed to downfall, for he had no integrity.

Thus none of the elements that made up the Hetman government served to stabilize the Ukrainian state. The Hetmanate was not an established form of Ukrainian statehood but merely a theater of conflict between two opposing forces—the all-Russian reaction and Eastern Ukrainian revolutionary democracy. In the middle were the rather weak forces of the nationally minded Ukrainian conservatives and the moderate democrats, who honestly supported the Hetman government and were prepared to make sacrifices for it, but they counted for little. The real power in the country was the German military command. At first the reactionaries were stronger. Only a fraction of them supported the idea of Ukrainian independence. In their overwhelming majority they wanted to see the former unity of the Russian Empire restored after the defeat of the Bolsheviks. They hoped to make use of Hetman Ukraine as a means to that end and strove constantly to gain control of it. In this they were successful, for the all-Russian element pervaded the Hetman government, and the Hetman State became increasingly Russified. The all-Russian element felt so confident that ultimately it refused to tolerate the national and cultural demands of the Ukrainian movement, aspiring to eradicate it immediately and openly reintroduce the old system of Russification. Against this all-Russian force the hetman himself and his government were powerless: their rule was limited to Kyiv. In the provinces they had little or no power. Even in Kyiv, the central offices were divided between Ukrainians and Russians, with the most important posts under Russian influence. The Ukrainians soon found themselves in a state that should have been and wanted to be Ukrainian but was controlled in every respect by the forces of Russian nationalism. To the social and political dissatisfaction of the Eastern Ukrainian parties with the Hetman government was now added a national dimension. In external appearance as well as in essence, the Hetman State, thoroughly sabotaged by the Ukrainians, was becoming more and more Russian, giving rise to a vicious circle: the Ukrainians undermined the state because it was becoming Russian, and the state became ever more Russian because it was being undermined by the Ukrainians. In the end, the Ukrainians suspected the hetman himself of excluding nationally minded Ukrainian circles from important offices of state in order to facilitate the reincorporation of Ukraine into the Russian state after the defeat of Bolshevism.[84]

The fate of Ukraine at the time, like that of the rest of the world, was being decided by the massive world-wide conflict between the Central Powers and the Entente. Moscow and St. Petersburg were in the hands of the Bolsheviks. At the time of the German occupation of Ukraine, the armed resistance of the Russian counterrevolution was just beginning. Russia had ceased to exist. The most important province of the old Russian Empire, Ukraine, was in the hands of the Germans, who seemed intent on keeping under their control the whole zone between the Baltic and the Black Sea, of which Ukraine was the most significant part. As long as the outcome of the world war remained uncertain, and as long as the state of affairs established by the Central Powers in Eastern Europe appeared to be permanent, it was almost hopeless for the all-Russian element in Ukraine, who were the most favorable to the Entente, openly to oppose the existing order in general and Ukrainian independence in particular. Initially, therefore, they adopted a realistic attitude and recognized the Hetman government, however unwillingly. They were glad to have been saved from the Bolshevik flood, even if the price for this was the disintegration of the old Russian Empire. Had the Central Powers been victorious, an independent Ukrainian state would have been established under the hetman. In time, and probably not such a long time, the all-Russian movement would have come to terms with Ukrainian statehood. The next generation would probably have been Ukrainized, giving permanence to the situation created at Brest-Litovsk. This Hetman Ukraine would have been a rather dubious state, not having arisen from the struggle of its own population, although a later struggle against the Bolsheviks might have changed this. Nonetheless, it would certainly have become a viable state. However, as it became clear in the summer of 1918 that the war was turning against the Central Powers and that the arrangements in Eastern Europe were not to be permanent, for the Entente was intent on the restoration of Russia and the elimination of German influence in the buffer states, the all-Russian forces in Ukraine gained courage and went over to an ever more open offensive against Hetman Ukraine. As soon as Turkey and Bulgaria collapsed and the victory of the Entente was no longer in doubt, the all-Russian counterrevolution began to arm itself and, in October 1918, became a threat not only to the Hetman government but also to Ukrainian independence. In November

1918, just before the final collapse of the Central Powers, an all-Russian armed uprising against hospitable Ukraine was imminent.

Was the fate of the Hetman government now sealed? Under a different hetman, such an outcome would by no means have been inevitable. For, in spite of everything, the Hetman government had rendered outstanding services to the Ukrainian national cause, especially in the field of national culture. Among a certain, by no means small, section of the national movement, the Hetman government therefore enjoyed support. Of course, the Hetman's army was small. It was really just the core of a future army, as the Germans did not allow the growth of large Ukrainian armed forces. But the troops that supported the Hetman government were still stronger than the all-Russian forces, which were made up partly of elements of the Ukrainian army itself and partly of all-Russian volunteer formations, which came to be organized quite openly. The Sich Riflemen, who would later deliver the coup de grace to the Hetman government, were then fully prepared to defend it against an all-Russian coup. A decisive appeal to the whole Ukrainian nation to defend its state against the Russians—Bolsheviks as well as the internal all-Russian foe—would have divided the opposition in the Ukrainian national camp at one blow and made the Hetman government, which disposed of armed forces, at least equal in strength to the dissatisfied extreme social revolutionaries among the Eastern Ukrainians. But this would have confronted the hetman with a real struggle, perhaps a horrendous one, for he would have had to fight not only the external Muscovite Bolshevik enemy but also two internal foes, the all-Russian reaction and the internationally oriented social revolutionaries of the Ukrainian national camp. And he would have had to do this without giving up his own conservative, socially counterrevolutionary base. But commensurate with these dangers was the promise of a very great reward: either to create a Ukrainian nation-state with blood and iron against all obstacles, and even in defiance of all sociological laws, or to go down with all flags flying, leaving for posterity an indelible act of national heroism that could have served as a model of the struggle for statehood.

But such abilities—indeed, such considerations—were foreign to Hetman Pavlo Skoropadsky. The Central Powers, to whom he had been a tributary up to this point, were now collapsing, as the days of the German occupation were numbered by November 1918. Unable to stand on his own two feet and intimidated by the tumult of the all-Russian elements, Skoropadsky thought he could save himself by adapting to the new situation and simply replacing his orientation on the Central Powers with a policy friendly toward the Entente. He therefore yielded to the demands of the Entente and of the all-Russian forces in

Ukraine, established an all-Russian ministry and, on 14 November 1918, proclaimed the return of Ukraine to a future Russian federation.

Was the Ukrainian cause now lost? If the Eastern Ukrainians had been a well-established political nation, such a proclamation would have had no importance. To all appearances, Russia did not yet exist. For the moment, the main task was to defeat the Bolsheviks in order to prevent the influx of Bolshevism into Ukraine itself. It would therefore have been extremely advantageous to settle the quarrels within the general Ukrainian and Russian counterrevolutionary bloc so as to make its striking force all the greater. If the proclamation of a future Russo-Ukrainian federation was useful for this purpose, it did not necessarily imply that such a federation would actually come into existence. The struggle against Bolshevik Moscow might have left the Bolsheviks in power in Russia but forced them to leave Ukraine, just as they were later obliged to leave Poland. The federative proclamation would then have lost its validity. Thus the Ukrainian movement would not have been party to the restoration of Russia but, on the contrary, the Russian counterrevolution would have been engaged, against its will, in supporting the establishment and consolidation of an independent Ukraine. In any case, a nation possessing internal unity, governing its own territory independently, with a national army at its disposal, and capable of standing up to the armed forces of any other great nation has nothing to fear from union or federation with another state.

Such considerations, which would have been appropriate in other circumstances, were wholly irrelevant in Eastern Ukraine in 1918. At that time Ukraine as a nation was in fact no match for Russia. Russia was not an external partner for Ukraine; it was much more of an internal enemy. Neither was Russia an element of the "future" for Ukraine nor, strictly speaking, is it quite true, as was said earlier, that Russia did not yet exist because the Bolsheviks were temporarily in charge of St. Petersburg and Moscow. Russia was, indeed, very much of the present; present in Ukraine itself. By federating with Russia because he feared that otherwise it would remove him by force, the hetman simply deserted the field of battle without a struggle and turned Ukraine into a base from which to launch the restoration of the Russian Empire. All that he saved, assuming the Russians proved sufficiently loyal not to get rid of him at a later date, was purely and simply his own personal position. But his status as hetman was now no more than that of a Russian governor general with extended powers. Under the circumstances that existed in Ukraine in mid-November 1918, the Russians were already in control of the Hetmanate's whole state apparatus. With complete freedom to develop its own military forces, the Russian movement would quickly have become so well established in Ukraine that it would easily have dominated the sparse nationally minded Ukrainian leading stratum. The leaderless Eastern Ukrainian masses would then have been overcome by the reintroduction of an even more relentless Russification drive similar to the one used against the Kuban Cossacks, who were ethnically Ukrainian and inclined toward separation from Russia. In 1919, their territory was turned into a fortress of the all-Russian counterrevolution under General Anton Denikin. The Ukrainian movement was left with no choice: confronted with the decisive superiority of the all-Russian forces, it had to resort to arms to defend not only the principle of statehood but its very existence.

The result was a decisive turnabout in Ukraine. By proclaiming the federation, the Hetman government let slip the opportunity to place the socially counterrevolutionary element in Ukraine at the head of the movement for a Ukrainian national state. The leadership of that movement now inevitably fell once again into the hands of the Ukrainian social revolutionaries. This meant that the later uprising against the Hetman government suffered from an inner contradiction. For as a result of its social-revolutionary orientation, this uprising, whose task it was to rescue the idea and the existence of the Eastern Ukrainian state, became merely the overture to the Bolshevik inundation of Eastern Ukraine. The Hetman government, under its weak and incompetent leadership, was overthrown by the combined determination of the all-Russian reactionaries and the Eastern Ukrainian revolutionaries, but at the cost of the destruction of both parties, since this overthrow merely paved the way for a third force—Bolshevism. But the Ukrainian national movement really had no other choice. The failure of the Hetmanate doomed the cause of Eastern Ukrainian statehood in any event. Still, the uprising against the Hetman government, which could not have led to the creation of an independent Eastern Ukrainian state under any circumstances, at least accomplished what the hetman, had he been the right individual, should have done instead of proclaiming the federation; namely, it raised a resolute armed struggle in the defense of Ukrainian freedom and made a final heroic defense of the unsuccessful attempt at Ukrainian independence. It was precisely in this, and only in this, that the revolution in Eastern Ukraine, otherwise so disastrous, was of greater importance from the Ukrainian national viewpoint than all the policies of Hetman Pavlo Skoropadsky.

This, then, was the general course of events that preceded the uprising of November 1918 in Eastern Ukraine. The radical Ukrainian parties had been considering an uprising for a long time. Some months before this, individual members of the Ukrainian National Union (Ukraïns'kyi Natsional'nyi Soiuz), a bloc of all the democratic and socialist Eastern Ukrainian parties—most notably the president of the Union, Volodymyr Vynnychenko—had had secret meetings with the Moscow Bolsheviks and received assurances from them that they would remain neutral in the event of an uprising against Skoropadsky.[85] Had the hetman survived, such preparations would of course have been wasted. After the proclamation of 14 November, however, even the moderate democrats who had remained loyal to the hetman were won over to the idea of revolution. The uprising itself unexpectedly gained added impetus from the collapse of the Central Powers. The Austro-Hungarian army of occupation was making a rapid and completely disorganized retreat from southern Ukraine. The German troops, who would have been a threat the week before, could now be expected to play a neutral role, especially after the outbreak of revolution in the German Reich itself. The uprising took place the day after the hetman's proclamation, on 15 November 1918. At first the military prospects seemed rather hopeless. The peasantry had been put down long before, the whole of Ukraine had been pacified, and it was still unclear what the German troops would do. The country was firmly in the hands of the hetman's police and the Russian counterrevolutionary officers. The Directory, the revolutionary government elected by the parties under the leadership of Vynnychenko and Symon Petliura, had at its disposal nothing more than a number of conspirators spread broadly across the land and an appeal that it distributed in the small town of Bila Tserkva, about 150 km from Kyiv, where the Directory had established itself. It also had a detachment of Sich Riflemen stationed in the town: four companies of infantry, a field battery, twelve heavy machine guns, and half a squadron of cavalry. The Sich Riflemen intended to make their way to Kyiv and go down to defeat in street fighting, proclaiming by their action that Ukraine would no longer freely submit to union with Russia.

The fate of the uprising was decided by a single battle. Although the numbers involved were very small, this battle was one of the most decisive for the subsequent history of Eastern Europe. On 19 November the two sides clashed at Motovylivka, between Fastiv (Khvastiv) and Kyiv, with all the forces at their disposal. There was a battalion of Sich Riflemen and three battalions of Hetman troops, the core of which was a truly courageous battalion of Russian officers. Both sides were fully aware of the importance of the battle and fought with extreme bravery. For hours the Sich Riflemen held off the strong attacks of the enemy forces, which outnumbered them twelve to one. The actual founder of this formation, Captain Fed Chernyk, was killed in the battle. Angered by the death of their leader, the Riflemen mounted an all-out assault against the enemy forces, which still outnumbered them three to one, and this assault was decisive. Very few of the hetman's troops survived this battle, and not one of the Russian officers.[86]

The consequences of this victory were enormous. The counterrevolution in Ukraine, especially in Kyiv, was disabled at a blow. The flower of the Russian officer corps, assembled in Kyiv, fell in that battle. As news of the Ukrainian victory spread throughout the country, it had a magical effect on the whole Eastern Ukrainian population. Hundreds of thousands of peasants stormed into the cities and towns. Kyiv, defending itself with great endurance and skill from the installations established during the world war, was besieged. The German troops, drawn into the chaos of the fighting in spite of their neutrality, were largely disarmed. The whole of Eastern Ukraine became a sea of turmoil. Finally, on 14 December 1918, enjoying the apparent support of hundreds of thousands of armed peasants, the Directory of the Ukrainian People's Republic entered Kyiv in triumph. The principle of Ukrainian national statehood was seemingly victorious.*

The battle at Motovylivka had incalculable consequences. The Hetman State had made the whole of Ukraine the base of the counterrevolution. In Russia the Bolsheviks were very weak, hemmed in on all sides by the counterrevolutionary armies since the end of 1918. If the Russian counterrevolution in Ukraine been given a little more time to organize itself, which it had been prevented from doing previously by the German occupying power, there is no doubt that victory in Eastern Europe would have been theirs. But now those counterrevolutionary forces were wiped out. Defeated and decimated, they withdrew to the Don region, to the Crimea, and toward Odesa. The counterrevolutionaries had lost their Ukrainian base: almost a year would pass before they managed to regroup in the Don region and recover that base. But by then it was too late, for the Bolsheviks had consolidated their power in the meantime. This one battle decided not only that Bolshevik Russia, not the counterrevolution, should hold power in Eastern Europe. It also had the effect of extending

* The Directory of the Ukrainian People's Republic was conspiratorially elected in Kyiv by the parties on 13 November 1918. Its members were as follows: Volodymyr Vynnychenko (Social Democrat), chairman; Symon Petliura (Social Democrat), commander in chief (*holovnyi otaman*); Fedir Shvets (Peasant Union, an organization subject to social-revolutionary influence); Opanas Andriievsky (Ukrainian Party of Socialist Independentists); and Andrii Makarenko (independent, representative of the Railway Workers' Union) (Khrystiuk, *Zamitky i materiialy*, 3: 130–31).

for a full year the existence of what appeared to be Eastern Ukrainian statehood and made possible an armed struggle under national slogans that imparted an inextinguishable national consciousness to the entire Ukrainian population, down to the last village in Ukraine. The foundation was thus laid not only for the later Soviet Ukraine but also for the future national development of Ukraine, whatever that may be. Herein also lies the weakness and vulnerability of Bolshevism. Nor is it without significance that almost all of the Sich Riflemen officers had formerly served as officers of the Eastern Galician Ukrainian Sich Riflemen and that three-quarters of the troops were Western Ukrainians. They owed their victory to the spell exercised by their heroic young captain, Fed Chernyk, and to the very hard discipline and training that they took over from the German storm troopers and supplemented with their own experience. In this regard, they were greatly superior to the Eastern Ukrainian troops, trained in the traditions of the Russian military, for whom such a system of discipline would have been unbearable. That system suited the Western Ukrainians, who were inspired by Western culture. And so, through its warriors, Western Ukraine again intervened decisively in the destiny of Eastern Ukraine, as it had done in January 1918, when the Sich Riflemen put down the Bolshevik uprising in Kyiv.

The Western Ukrainians saw the massive scale of the unrest in Eastern Ukraine as proof that national consciousness and the desire for national statehood were as strong among the masses here as they were in Western Ukraine, and there was great enthusiasm for the unification of the two republics. The Western Ukrainians also felt confident of assistance from Eastern Ukraine in the war against Poland, as the Directory seemed to have at its disposal a massive military force of some hundreds of thousands. Under these circumstances the State Secretariat of the Western Ukrainian People's Republic now decided to put into effect the decision of the National Rada of 10 November 1918. On 1 December, in Fastiv near Kyiv, representatives of the State Secretariat signed a preliminary unification accord with the Eastern Ukrainian Directory. In this accord both governments declared their intention of uniting both republics in the near future into a single state in which the Western Ukrainian People's Republic would relinquish its sovereignty in favor of the Ukrainian People's Republic but would retain territorial autonomy in view of its particular history, culture, and social and legal system. The exact form of this autonomy, which was a fundamental precondition of the merger, was to be determined later.[87]

In the course of December 1918 the Directory reached the peak of its apparent power. Kyiv was under its control, and the last remnants of the Russian counterrevolutionary volunteer units were leaving Ukraine. The Muscovite Bolshevik troops, for the time being, did not cross the demarcation line that had previously been established between them and the German and Ukrainian forces in the north. It seemed that the Directory was about to succeed in harnessing the apparent national enthusiasm of the Eastern Ukrainian peasant masses to the task of peacefully constructing an independent Ukrainian state on the ruins of the Hetman regime. They dreamt of recognition of the Eastern Ukrainian state by the Entente.[88] All this convinced the Western Ukrainians that they should promptly relinquish their separate statehood and find military and diplomatic support in Eastern Ukraine against the Poles.

Without delay, on 3 January 1919, the Ukrainian National Rada, meeting in Stanyslaviv, ratified the preliminary agreement reached at Fastiv and announced triumphantly, as an accomplished fact, the amalgamation of Western and Eastern Ukraine into a united and sovereign people's republic. A delegation of sixty-five members was elected to convey this decision to the Directory in Kyiv. This was at once the high point of Western Ukrainian hopes with regard to Eastern Ukraine and of the idea of Ukrainian national unity.[89]

The decline, however, was as rapid as the rise. It was not the principle of Ukrainian independence that drove the Eastern Ukrainian peasantry to revolt but rather their social discontent. The revolutionary parties in Eastern Ukraine made full use of this discontent, portraying the future Ukrainian state as one that would bring contentment and liberty to the peasants and promising the elimination of the large landlords and capitalists. As long as the mass struggle was directed against the Russian counterrevolution, the authority of the Directory was more or less universally recognized. But the Directory stood at the head of a social revolution, not of a national and political one. As soon as the true and legitimate master of the social revolution in Eastern Europe—Bolshevism—arrived on the scene, the Directory's authority abruptly collapsed.

Various circumstances within the Eastern Ukrainian movement itself promoted this process. In keeping with the Russian tradition that students were the avant-garde of the revolution, the younger an Eastern Ukrainian, the more socially radical he was. In the most radical parties, especially in the Eastern Ukrainian Socialist Revolutionary Party, it was the youngest members who wielded highly disproportionate influence. What emerged out of this was a real youth politics, for which we need to invent a new name, "pediocracy," so as to leave no doubt about who actually made up the extremely active "popular forces" that were at work in these tremendously important parties in Ukraine during the revolution. Soon this most radical pediocracy broke with the Directory because it was too "bourgeois." The radicals went among the agitated masses, established soviets, and stirred up "revolutionary energies" in the belief that, if these were released, and if the parties "listened to" the "voice of the revolution," then the "revolutionary masses," in their mystical urge to promote "human happiness," would of themselves lead Ukraine to some blissful utopia of "people's power." All that was asked of the Bolsheviks was that they not interfere with the "development of the revolution," as it was called, in Ukraine. But in this assiduous popular agitation the youngest and most radical of the Eastern Ukrainians hardly differed from the Bolsheviks. The only real difference lay in the fact that the Bolsheviks agitated among the masses but did not "listen to" them. Rather they led them toward their own chosen goal, the dictatorship of the Communist Party, while the Eastern Ukrainian pediocracy set its hopes on a distorted form of parliamentarism, something approaching the automatic establishment of radical democracy by means of the "voice of the revolution" once the bourgeoisie had been eliminated. But for the masses, who constituted that mysterious "voice of the revolution," such distinctions were too subtle. The masses wanted to be led, not listened to. The result was that, having done the work of stirring up the masses, the radical pediocracy did its wretched best to lose popularity to the Bolsheviks.

With the destruction of the Hetman regime, the small landowning peasants, who had some interest in the maintenance of order, promptly dispersed. The already undisciplined troops of the Directory were now made up almost exclusively of rural proletarians and other haphazard elements—a true "avant-garde of the world revolution" of the kind with which the Bolsheviks fought their battles. Moreover, the whole state apparatus of the Hetman regime had disintegrated. A country the size of the German Reich, with a population of thirty million, suddenly found itself without any form of state machinery. Given the low level of self-management ability in the population at large—a legacy of the tsarist regime—the commissars whom the Directory appointed in each region were unable to improvise any kind of order in this vast land. Educated Ukrainians were too few in number to take over the leading positions in the state and military: had it been otherwise, the Russification of the state under the hetman would not have proceeded so successfully. It is no wonder, then, that under such circumstances the whole country dissolved into anarchy. The property-owning majority of the country, those who had something to lose from all the chaos, took cover in hopes of somehow surviving the adversity, as they were incapable of organizing and helping themselves. It was the minority of the population—the active, propertyless, nomadic element—that became the "voice of the revolution." Among the armed masses as well as throughout the country in general there now emerged local leaders, calling themselves otamans, and the ranks of the "people's army of the Directory" turned largely into armed bands. Whom those masses followed was a matter of chance. Sometimes it was the Directory, sometimes the Bolsheviks, and sometimes the social-revolutionary pediocrats, who opposed everything. It all depended on the whim of some local leader or otaman. In some places the social-revolutionary regions rebelled against the Directory. Elsewhere common mobs, under Ukrainian nationalist, Bolshevik or, most often, anarchist banners, carried out bloody anti-Jewish pogroms in the cities and towns. During the final days of December 1918, just as the Western Ukrainians in Stanyslaviv were deciding on union with Eastern Ukraine, the whole huge country plunged into complete chaos. The Directory was incapable of bringing this chaos under control. Even its garrison in Kyiv, numbering some tens of thousands, completely disintegrated. What happened now among the armed Eastern Ukrainian masses, although at a much faster rate, was what had happened in Russia in 1917, when the military disintegrated into armed bands and the quasi-revolutionary Provisional Government under Kerensky was forced to give way to the Bolsheviks.

Now, their time come at last, the Moscow Bolsheviks pushed into Ukraine from the north. But the Bolshevik forces were small in number and not exclusively Russian. Altogether, hardly more than two thousand Eastern Ukrainian peasants marched on Kyiv. They came from the region of Tarashcha on the Dnipro, where they had held out against the Germans for a long time before retreating into Soviet Russia. Otherwise, the number of Russian Bolshevik forces that invaded Ukraine was very small. But the Directory was unable to offer any resistance. The most radical pediocrats joined forces with the Bolsheviks and began to organize peasant uprisings against the Directory in the foolish belief that the Bolsheviks would give them a role in government. The Directory had no more reliable and battle-ready troops. Even the regular Sich Riflemen in Kyiv, who had recruited tens of thousands of insurgents at the time of the overthrow of the hetman, were unable to discipline this huge mass in such a short time, with the result that they lost all control over the Kyiv garrison, now known as the Sich Riflemen Army Corps. Just barely, but successfully, they managed to prevent Kyiv from becoming the scene of anti-Jewish pogroms, as was happening throughout the rest of Ukraine. The rash of pogroms now reached its peak. It seemed to many of the otamans that the Jews alone were responsible for the Bolshevik invasion. The Directory had no idea what to do. It vacillated between the "development of the revolution" in agreement with the Bolsheviks in Moscow on the one hand and, on the other, promotion of the counterrevolution and the interventionist policy of the Hetman regime concurrently with the Entente. It was unable to take firm control of the turbulent masses and the local leaders. Among the masses in its own country who had taken up arms against the Directory, the government was no match for the propaganda and organization of the Bolsheviks. Against the approaching Bolshevik mob, it was as good as defenseless. The Directory was living out its final days of glory in Kyiv when, on 16 January 1919, the official delegation from Western Ukraine entered the city for a triumphant proclamation of the unification of Ukraine.[90]

With great ceremony, the act of union approved by the Ukrainian National Rada on 3 January 1919 was promulgated in Kyiv on 22 January. In this act Western Ukraine gave up its sovereignty in favor of the Ukrainian People's Republic. The Directory responded with its own solemn "universal" (proclamation). This solemnity would have been meaningful if it had symbolized the triumph of a maximum exertion of national strength or the willingness of the whole people to make some sacrifice for their own state. But in the midst of the general chaos in Eastern Ukraine, it was merely a propaganda spectacle for the troops in Kyiv and for the Congress of Toilers (Trudovyi Konhres), a kind of preparliament that was convened in Kyiv at the time. The festivities were therefore false, and this falseness was apparent in every phrase, in almost every word, of the Directory's universal.

It was part of the political style of the Directory to attempt to deceive both itself and everyone else. It tried to hoodwink the masses with social-revolutionary slogans in order to enlist their support for an independent Ukrainian state, even if it were to be a bourgeois state. It pretended to the Bolsheviks that it saw itself as part of the world revolution. It promised the Entente that Ukraine would take up the fight against the Bolsheviks as soon as it received the Entente's recognition and support. It was therefore only natural that the Directory would try to use the presence of the Western Ukrainian delegation and the act of union itself to suit its own purposes. The Directory was suspicious of its Congress of Toilers. It believed that under the influence of the revolutionary pediocrats the congress wanted to proclaim a proletarian dictatorship in Ukraine, relinquish Ukrainian sovereignty, and proceed not only de facto but formally to commit Ukraine to Moscow's plans for world revolution. In an attempt to strengthen the moderate element in the congress, the Directory unceremoniously gave the Western Ukrainian delegation the right to participate in the proceedings. But this move was superfluous, as the majority at the congress, frightened by the massive unrest in the country, did not want to be the "voice of the revolution." Although in favor of democracy and the greatest possible degree of local self-government in principle, what they really longed for was the kind of strong leadership that could put down the "people's freedom" by force of arms. Nevertheless, this participation by the Western Ukrainian delegation in the Congress of Toilers was the first occasion on which Western Ukraine participated officially in the leadership of the Eastern Ukrainian state. It also sealed the conquest of Western Ukraine by the Eastern Ukrainian chaos.[91]

This was promptly followed by other Eastern Ukrainian legislative acts. At its first session on 23 January 1919, the congress unanimously ratified both acts of union—the resolution of the Ukrainian National Rada of 3 January and the Directory's universal of 22 January. A few days later, on 28 January, the congress resolved to augment the Directory with a representative of Western Ukraine. In view of the uncertain situation in Ukraine, both internal and external, the congress decided to adjourn and give the Directory unlimited legislative and executive—in other words, dictatorial—powers.

On the basis of this congress decision, the Executive Committee of the Ukrainian National Rada appointed its president, Yevhen Petrushevych, a member of the Directory. The process of unification was now complete. The leader of the Western Ukrainian state became part of the Directory, making it the state authority not only of Eastern but now also of Western Ukraine. The Ukrainian National Rada accepted the logical consequence of this and changed the official name of the country that it governed: the "Western Ukrainian People's Republic" became the "Western Province of the Ukrainian People's Republic" (Zakhidnia Oblast' Ukraïns'koï Narodnoï Respubliky, ZOUNR).[92]

Incomparably more important than these acts of union, however, was the actual structure of the relationship between Western and Eastern Ukraine. This was, and remained, a relation between two completely independent countries, although a close one. Of the two, Western Ukraine was by far the stronger partner.

While the act of union was being celebrated in Kyiv, the Directory lost the whole of the Left Bank of the Dnipro to the Bolsheviks, and by 4 February 1919 Kyiv, too, was already lost. The remnants of the Directory's troops retreated, in complete disarray, to Podilia and Volhynia (Map 2). The Directory established itself at first in Vinnytsia, but very soon, with its constantly declining forces, had to begin its peregrinations in western Podilia and central Volhynia. However, as a consequence of inner conflicts and the demands of the Entente, the Directory itself soon collapsed, leaving the military commander, Symon Petliura, as the actual dictator of Eastern Ukraine.[93]

Now, during February and March 1919, the situation in Eastern Ukraine became clear. The Ukrainian People's Republic under Petliura was no more a state than any of the other counterrevolutionary enterprises in Eastern Europe in 1919, such as those of Aleksandr Kolchak or Anton Denikin. It was merely a military organization. Just as in the case of the reactionary armies in Russia, the masses of the people did not take part in this organization. In some areas they approved of it; in others, they rebelled against it. But that was the full extent of their relation to this organization.

Everything depended on the person of Petliura. From modest origins he had become, even before 1917, a social-democratic publicist of repute. In 1917 and during the uprising against the hetman he was a hugely popular idol of the masses. He was a brilliant orator with a winning personality, witty, modest and gentle. Petliura was indeed the most important personality among those who led Ukraine between 1917 and 1920. No one had greater love for the fatherland than he. He never sought his own personal advantage but gave his whole heart and soul to Ukraine. His name became practically synonymous with the whole enterprise of the Ukrainian People's Republic, so that both the Bolsheviks and the Russian counterrevolutionaries invariably referred to it simply as Petliurism (Petliurovshchina). In time, this name became a symbol for the whole Ukrainian peasantry, and it was the rallying cry of the Eastern Ukrainian peasants when they later rose up in anger against the Bolsheviks—"Petliura" was the name of Eastern Ukrainian nationalism. Recognizing clearly that Eastern Ukrainian nationalism would stand or fall with this man, the Bolsheviks succeeded in identifying the rash of pogroms in Ukraine with this Petliurism as well. This would later cost Petliura his life. He was murdered in Paris in 1926 by a Jewish agent as the putative organizer of the pogroms. His name, freely abused by the world press, accompanied him to the grave. But the name of Petliura was and remains unbesmirched, for he was one of the leaders in Ukraine who did everything in his power at that time of dissolution to protect the Jews. Many hated him deeply. But just as many loved him profoundly and would have died for him. He considered that Ukraine needed him. That he stood, and wanted to stand, at the head of the country, he saw as a service to the fatherland. It was seen by his enemies, unjustly, as unlimited personal ambition. Petliura was a product of the radical democratic, revolutionary socialist and internationalist development of the Eastern Ukrainian movement since the turn of the century. In 1917 he still opposed national independence for Ukraine and argued for the revolutionary community of interest between the Ukrainian and Russian movements. Only after the first Bolshevik invasion of Ukraine at the end of 1917 was he converted, along with the rest of the Ukrainian movement, to the idea of independence. This became for him a fanatical religion for which he would live and die. But this was only a fanatical emotion, without insight, without understanding. At the level of the state he had no political experience. His experience until then had been that of the proletarian and Ukrainian national revolution against the state—the Russian state. Thus he had no understanding of what constituted the underlying strength of a state or of what moral and intellectual preparation was necessary for a position in the service of that state. He was a tribune of the people, not a statesman. He considered national sentiment an adequate basis on which to found a state. He sought without scruple to arouse national enthusiasm among the people and was prepared to use any means to that end, whether socialist demagogy to whip up the masses or an appeal to defend civil order in Ukraine against the threat of Bolshevism. He was accused of deceit in his dealings with the leaders of the Eastern Ukrainian parties, but this was merely the ruthlessness with which he used some and cast aside others in the interests of the idea of statehood that he himself served. He was also no military commander. He thought of an army only as a mechanical concentration of forces. He had no understanding of a modern army as a living organism galvanized by strength; he even failed to recognize that an army is better fitted to the task of building a modern nation-state if it is strongly disciplined in its military behavior and in its dealings with the civilian population and has a strong sense of honor. He therefore distrusted the senior officers of the former Russian army, looking instead for the kind of carelessness that, in his mind, went with a proper warlike spirit. The ebb and flow of enthusiasm with which the Eastern Ukrainian commanders today would fearlessly attack the enemy, only to hold back in a dispirited mood tomorrow, was more comprehensible to him than the iron steadfastness of a regular army. On the other hand, he was very impressed by the discipline and elan represented at times by the Sich Riflemen, and he dreamed of turning the whole Ukrainian force into such an army. Nonetheless, he did not give leadership to the army, nor did he impose discipline or order, and if the latter gradually emerged, it was not his achievement but that of his junior officers. Equally limited was his understanding of foreign policy. He never understood the actual situation in which Ukraine found itself, and he believed—in fact, never doubted for a moment—that Eastern Ukraine as it then stood was capable of establishing a state if only the military campaign continued to be waged. His whole foreign policy was oriented toward this single goal of continuing the armed struggle. Foreign policy meant for him one thing only: the securing of adequate supplies for the troops. And there was only one struggle, as he saw it—the struggle against Russia—and for its sake he was prepared to sacrifice everything, even to allow the Ukrainian People's Republic to assume a shadow existence and become a mere instrument in the hands of foreign powers, with no reward for itself.

There were indeed many unblemished patriots in the Petliura camp who, though repelled by the deplorable state of affairs within the movement, did all they could to promote the formation of an Eastern Ukrainian state. But it was not their spirit that prevailed, and that was their tragedy. The abuses were stronger, as they are in all counterrevolutionary actions. The civil administration and the courts that the Eastern Ukrainian governments set up behind their lines were makeshift, corrupt and arbitrary in the extreme, as they also were behind the lines of the Russian counterrevolutionary forces. Also, because of the constant movement of the front, they lacked the time to establish themselves and become effective. Indeed, the whole of the Ukrainian People's Republic at this time was like a wagon train constantly on the move. The extent of order in the country depended entirely on the personal characteristics of individual functionaries, whose relation to the central government was largely illusory. The whole apparatus was characterized by a lack of discipline and sanction, making it impossible for anyone to compromise himself by his actions or make a fool of himself. There was also a total absence of any unifying will. Lenin's maxim prevailed: "A state is a large enterprise that can even make use of rags. " Just as in the armies of the Russian counterrevolution, the greatest nuisance was the stream of cowardly soldiers making their way from the front to the rear. At the front one found all the elements that were at least warlike and possessed that one virtue, but the state of affairs behind the lines was deplorable. Wherever Petliura and his government were stationed, order and security prevailed, and that was about the extent of it. In other areas it all depended on whether the military commander was an honest soldier. There was a degree of primitive public order in the vicinity of some, not all, of the frontline troops. This was certainly true in the case of the Sich Riflemen. After a few lamentable attempts at political action—trying to set up a military dictatorship in Kyiv or to change Eastern Ukrainian policy following the retreat—they gave up politics once Kyiv was lost. The riflemen then turned their attention to a more appropriate task—that of establishing some military order among the fifteen thousand or more troops that they had taken with them from Kyiv. Reinforced by a few thousand new recruits from Western Ukraine, they set about this task with energy and firmness. They did not hesitate to use the death penalty in imposing order on the rebellious Eastern Ukrainian troops and appointed Western Ukrainian officers and subalterns to command them. The rest were brought up to standard in March 1919 at the Battle of Berdychiv. They lost that battle, suffering huge casualties of 1,200 men and 250 officers, but what remained after the defeat was a competent fighting force. The riflemen, a good half of whom were Western Ukrainians, did not tolerate any pogroms or plundering in the areas that they controlled, even during the periods of greatest anarchy. Any such attempts were promptly and mercilessly suppressed, often at great risk to the riflemen's lives in this turbulent land. This was perhaps a more useful achievement than the utmost defiance of death in battle that characterized many of the Eastern Ukrainian forces. The Western Ukrainians understood instinctively that the Bolsheviks could not be defeated by means of counterrevolutionary or nationalist agitation, but only by overcoming arbitrariness and lawlessness in the counterrevolution's own camp. Only in this way could the moderate, settled part of the population, so important to the state, be won over. Neither the Russian counterrevolution nor the Ukrainian People's Republic understood this—a failure that led to their ruin. The Eastern Ukrainian forces thus gradually lost many of those who had participated in the uprising against the hetman. Those who remained, such as the Zaporozhian Corps led by Colonel Petro Bolbochan, were extraordinarily courageous. In any case, there was an unmistakable improvement in relations between the troops and the Eastern Ukrainian population.[94]

The Eastern Ukrainian army* now had to fight two opponents: the Poles, who were pushing into western Volhynia in hopes of surrounding the Western Ukrainian army from the north, and the Bolsheviks, who now had as many fighters in the field as the Eastern Ukrainians and

* Its best-known officers were Generals Vasyl Tiutiunnyk, Volodymyr Sinkler, Mykola Kapustiansky, Mykola Yunakiv, and Oleksander Osetsky, as well as Volodymyr Salsky and Marko Bezruchko, chief of staff of the Sich Riflemen.

could also rely on inexhaustible reserves. They attacked from the north by way of the Mazyr–Korosten and Luninets–Rivne railway lines, from the east by way of the Kyiv–Berdychiv and Kyiv–Zhmerynka lines, and from the southeast by way of Kremenchuk and Katerynoslav (Dnipropetrovsk) (Map 2). A military defense on those two fronts was possible only because the Ukrainians disposed of the meager remains of Russian military equipment left over in Ukraine from the world war.[95]

What problems and tasks now burdened Western Ukraine because Eastern Ukraine had no proper state organization and the Eastern Ukrainian People's Republic was in fact nothing but an army?

It was not just a feeling of national unity that prompted the Western Ukrainians to unite with Eastern Ukraine but first and foremost the prospect of Eastern Ukrainian assistance in the war against the Poles and the belief that Eastern Ukraine could deliver this assistance in spite of the Bolshevik threat. For this reason, Western Ukraine's willingness to subordinate itself to the Ukrainian People's Republic was both universal and profound. Had the same conditions existed in Eastern as in Western Ukraine, a victorious war on both fronts, against the Bolsheviks and the Poles, would have been possible, and an all-Ukrainian state would have arisen in Eastern Europe whether the neighboring and other European powers wanted it or not. But the same conditions did not exist, and both Western and Eastern Ukraine were faced with the prospect of being defeated by the Poles on one side and the Bolsheviks on the other, with the consequence that neither Eastern nor Western Ukraine would achieve national independence. In order to establish a Ukrainian state in Eastern Europe, it was essential to end the war on one of those fronts. Peace with the Bolsheviks was impossible. Unlike the Poles, the Bolsheviks were not interested in the acquisition of some part of Ukrainian territory. They wanted complete control of Ukraine at all costs in order to ensure that it would not become a base for the counterrevolution. Until they secured Ukraine, the existence of the Bolsheviks in Russia hung by a thread. Only after securing Ukraine could they push westward into Central Europe and pursue their plans for world revolution. But now that Western Ukraine was involved in a war with Poland, it had to pay the price and sue for peace on highly unfavorable terms—if peace with Poland could be concluded at all—not only because of Poland's growing strength but also in order to be able to come to the assistance of Eastern Ukraine. This was one of the problems posed for Western Ukraine by the weakness of Eastern Ukraine.

There was a second problem. If Ukraine wanted to pursue only one war, that against the Bolsheviks, then the existence of two independent governments was senseless, for it could only further weaken the already inadequate forces at the disposal of the whole country. It was essential that the country be firmly united behind a single leadership, otherwise catastrophe was inevitable. It was therefore thoughtless of the Western Ukrainians to subordinate themselves precipitously to Eastern Ukraine. Western Ukraine was, after all, a state, which Eastern Ukraine, as noted, certainly was not. After the overthrow of the Hetman government the political center of Ukraine was no longer on the Dnipro, in spite of its larger territory and population, but in tiny Western Ukraine, which constituted barely a tenth of the population and territory of Ukraine as a whole. The subordination of the superior to the inferior, of the stronger to the weaker, of Western to Eastern Ukraine, was thus the wrong way to go about creating a unified state.

But the Western Ukrainians did not fully realize this. They saw the collapse of Eastern Ukraine simply as a result of inadequate national consciousness among the Eastern Ukrainian masses. They therefore thought it quite appropriate for the Directory to have attempted to arouse that national consciousness by means of social demagogy. They also thought that Petliura's basic idea was reasonable, namely, that in order to arouse the national enthusiasm of the population and win it to the banner of the Ukrainian People's Republic, and to establish a national state in Eastern Ukraine in spite of the hostility of foreign powers, all that was required was to persist in the armed struggle against the Bolsheviks while carrying out large-scale national propaganda among the population. It did not occur to anyone that there were many perfectly conscious Ukrainian nationalists among the Bolsheviks, as well as among the forces of the Russian counterrevolution. They also ignored the fact that national consciousness among the Eastern Ukrainian masses had been very high in 1917, but the Central Rada's attempt to establish a national state had failed lamentably and was rescued only by the German occupation. These experiences were evidence enough that national sentiment is clearly an inadequate basis on which to found a nation-state. They failed to realize that it was not just national consciousness that had helped the Western Ukrainians. Among them there had also been very strong resistance to social revolution, a spirit of moderation on the part of the leadership and, among much of the population, especially in the educated strata who now made up the officer corps and the state bureaucracy, a deeply rooted sense of duty, a sense of order and discipline, law and justice—in a word, a spirit of rural conservatism. The Western Ukrainians were successful only where those characteristics prevailed. But wherever mere nationalist sentiment predominated, wild and half-baked as it was in Ukraine, dissolution and chaos were the order of the day even in Western Ukraine. The Hetman State required such a spirit as was found in Western Ukraine, but even among the ruling strata of the Hetman government that spirit was too weak, and the consequence was the collapse of the state. The overthrow of the Hetman government also completely destroyed the small and insufficient cadre of moderate elements who were capable of ruling in Eastern Ukraine. Another factor that influenced the destiny of the country from now on was that the Eastern Ukrainians who rallied around Petliura were, in the final analysis, only freedom-loving rebels. They were capable of incredible feats of arms but not of establishing order either among themselves or in the country around them.

Thus the chasm that opened up in 1919 between Western and Eastern Ukraine was far deeper than the differences resulting from their immediate past—in the one case, the link with Russia; in the other, with Austria. It was the chasm that separated the peasant, settled since time immemorial, from the wild, romantic and nomadic Cossacks of the steppe. After the collapse of the Hetman government, it was the Cossacks—an eastern, Eurasian element from the borderlands of Eastern Ukraine—who profoundly influenced the Eastern Ukrainian national movement. In many respects the free Cossack was far superior to the peasant: he was active, daring and ambitious. The peasant was ponderous, deliberate, narrow-minded, almost crude, but this peasant doggedness could establish and maintain a state. The Cossack could only destroy.

The Western Ukrainians did not understand that, after the fall of the Hetman government, the strength of the revolutionary movement in Eastern Ukraine was inadequate to the task of founding a national state. Eastern Ukraine could now only provide space for the territorial expansion of the more highly developed powers. "Petliurism" and other outbreaks of Eastern Ukrainian nationalism were mere death throes. The only question now was how long this would take and how much more blood it would cost the Eastern Ukrainians, and, above all, which of the foreign powers would become lord and master of Eastern Ukraine.

If Eastern Ukraine lacked the inner strength to protect itself from the sad fate of becoming mere booty for other nations, and if at least some part of Eastern Ukraine were to be saved from such a fate, then there was only one possible course of action. The Western Ukrainians should have intervened in Eastern Ukraine, not in order to subordinate themselves to the Ukrainian People's Republic but to place themselves at the head of it, to establish order, to bring their own political culture to the east and create a united Ukrainian state on their own. The situation in Western Ukraine made such an action necessary. They could not avoid losing some of their western territory to Poland, at least Lviv and probably the oil region of Boryslav–Drohobych as well. The rest of Eastern Galicia would have been too small for a viable state. In order to maintain the existence of their own state, the Western Ukrainians would have had to annex territory to the east. The only alternative would have been to continue the war with Poland until the inevitable defeat. Had they intervened forcibly in Eastern Ukraine, they could have established their state on Eastern Ukrainian territory and then resumed the armed conflict with Poland. Only in this way could the Western Ukrainians have overcome the loss of territory to Poland.

This amalgamation of the Western and Eastern Ukrainian causes was the second burden that Western Ukraine had to bear, and it was much greater than that of the whole war with Poland. Although the Western Ukrainians did not fully realize it at the time, they now faced a dangerous task. As a result of the many upheavals that had taken place, by 1919 the Eastern Ukrainian populace was extremely distrustful and prepared at any moment to mount a guerrilla war against any authority it did not like. The Eastern Ukrainian troops were haunted by the spirit of unruly local leaders; even Petliura was not entirely secure from them.[96] In the Eastern Ukrainian parties, personal ambitions played an immense role. The petty intriguers making up the pediocratic groups and factions were always ready to pop up from among "the people" (whom they took themselves to be) whenever they felt that they were not receiving enough attention. The popularity of Symon Petliura was a great potential danger that could explode at any time if he were to stir up the people. Since he considered himself the only possible dictator for Eastern Ukraine, there was little prospect that he would submit without resistance. Thus it would have been a most dangerous game for the Western Ukrainians to put their hands into the wasp's nest of Eastern Ukraine. Even if they had the good fortune to master the Eastern Ukrainian chaos, further prospects were not exactly bright. The chances were that they could only have established a Ukrainian rump state consisting of the central and eastern parts of Eastern Galicia and Volhynia, along with Podilia, a territory extending not even to the Dnipro or the Black Sea. Given the prevailing balance of power in Eastern Europe, this was probably the limit of what the combined forces of Western and Eastern Ukraine could have achieved. But despite all that, the Western Ukrainians had no other choice than to take their chances in this risky game. The Western Ukrainian cause could not survive on its own. Indeed, the Western Ukrainian political and military leadership proved incapable of carrying out the limited tasks assigned to it in Lviv a short time earlier. How much less capable were these leaders, then, of carrying out this much larger project, although it was suggested to the Western Ukrainians by the moderates of the Eastern Ukrainian movement. And so, in spite of all the acts of union, everything remained as it had been. Ukraine continued to exist as two states with two independent sovereign governments. To be sure, there was no opportunity to change this for a long time. A purely military project, such as that of the Ukrainian People's Republic, needed the support of some actual state organization. Accordingly, Petliura negotiated with the French mission in Romania to get French support for Eastern Ukraine in the war against the Bolsheviks. The first actual state to offer support, however, was Western Ukraine, and that is why it stood high in the estimation of Eastern Ukrainian patriots. Large numbers of Western Ukrainians were called upon to take leading positions in Eastern Ukraine, and they proved themselves worthy of the task. Time and time again the Western Ukrainians sent one unit of recruits after another to help the Eastern Ukrainians fight the Bolsheviks. Petliura wanted nothing quite so much as that Western Ukraine's war with Poland should come to a swift conclusion in one way or another so that its three army corps, organized in January-February 1919, could be used against the Bolsheviks. This also explains why the Eastern Ukrainian government was so accommodating, for the time being, to the Western Ukrainian government.

The Western Ukrainians, however, were prompted less by feelings of national unity than by recognition that the Eastern Ukrainians were doing them a good turn by protecting them from the Bolsheviks. At the military level, as well as at the level of finance, economy and foreign policy, quite a few measures were taken by both governments acting in unison. One of the most important such measures was the decision, made at a conference of both governments on 30 March 1919, to send a joint diplomatic mission to the Paris Peace Conference and notify foreign governments of the unification of Ukraine. Thereafter, both governments would retain separate diplomatic representations only when the special interests of either part of Ukraine made it necessary, as in Western Ukraine's relations with the successor states of the old Austro-Hungarian Empire. But even in the latter cases it was agreed that both parties should maintain the closest possible contact. In this way Western Ukraine renounced any form of active foreign policy in Eastern Europe and encapsulated itself in a kind of regionalism, which, under the circumstances, was the weakest position it could have taken.[97]

But there was also some discord. Western Ukraine isolated itself from the east, extremely wary lest propaganda for social revolution penetrate its own territory. But the Eastern Ukrainian influence did seep through. A number of radical socialist factions, encouraged by their amazing success in undermining Eastern Ukraine, now tried to extend their influence westwards. But the Western Ukrainians expelled them, and they then expressed great indignation at Western Ukraine's inability to adopt any progressive measures. Moreover, the east did not receive enough troops from the west, and dissatisfaction began to be expressed over Western Ukrainian egoism. At the same time, Western Ukrainians began to adopt a disdainful and even hostile attitude toward Eastern Ukraine, which was unjust, certainly from a military point of view, since really courageous troops were to be found more often in the Eastern than in the Western Ukrainian army. In this manner a breach developed, becoming almost an unbridgeable chasm, between both tendencies in Ukraine, an ever-widening breach that divided the already hard-pressed Ukrainian people into two hostile camps, almost into two independent nations.[98]

The causes of this breach were there from the beginning in the existence of two completely independent governments, two states built on entirely different principles, and consequently two very different foreign policies and spheres of interest. Petliura was interested only in the war against Russia. His foreign policy was concerned only with the supply of military equipment for his troops. To that end he tried to establish links with France. In order to facilitate dealings with the French, he refused to regard Eastern Ukraine as being at war with Poland, in spite of the actual fighting in western Volhynia and the Western Ukrainians' demand, given their union with Eastern Ukraine, for an open declaration of war. As long as Western Ukraine held out in the fighting with Poland and was able to give occasional assistance to Eastern Ukraine, and as long as there was still hope that the whole Western Ukrainian army could be fielded against the Bolsheviks, Eastern Ukraine's policy toward Poland remained unclear: a Western Ukrainian bird in the hand was worth two Polish ones in the bush. But a Western Ukrainian military defeat would inevitably drive Petliura, sooner or later, into the arms of Poland—which is what happened later, in 1920. The Western Ukrainians, on the other hand, were interested only in the war with Poland, and since they had to fight that war alone, as Eastern Ukraine was in no position to help them, they inevitably turned their attention toward Russia, with one eye on the Bolsheviks and the other on the counterrevolutionaries. For the time being, in early 1919, this was only thought of as a last resort, but it was always one of the options available to the Western Ukrainians in the event of an Eastern Ukrainian collapse. Toward the end of 1919, that option was being openly considered.

Because of the split over foreign policy and over the question of the war, there was never a joint command over the Eastern and Western Ukrainian front against Poland.[99] The Western Ukrainians, with their view that the war with Poland was all that mattered for the whole of Ukraine, were just as reckless as the Eastern Ukrainians. They were politically interested in Eastern Ukraine only insofar as it offered them protection from the Bolsheviks. But they were, in the end, so bitterly disillusioned with Eastern Ukraine that they wanted to have nothing more to do with it and behaved almost as a separate nation. After the eventual row with Eastern Ukraine it became official Western Ukrainian policy, from 1920, to establish a neutral state on the territory of Eastern Galicia under the protection of the League of Nations. The only purpose of the joint diplomatic agreement with Eastern Ukraine was to convince the Entente to force Poland to leave Western Ukraine in peace on the grounds that Ukraine was a major factor in the struggle against Bolshevism. In this, as in everything else, the Western Ukrainians were short-sighted. Had they intervened in Eastern Ukraine and established order there, this argument would have had some weight. But the state of affairs after the Eastern Ukrainian explosions was such as to make hardly anyone believe that Ukraine was in any condition to defeat Bolshevism.

The relationship between Western and Eastern Ukraine was therefore an unhealthy one, dangerous and debilitating for both parties. The situation had forced the Western Ukrainians to attempt to play an active role in East European politics far beyond the capacity of the tiny Eastern Galician territory. But Western Ukraine lacked ambitious and enlightened statesmen. Its leaders were propelled by circumstances into which they had very little insight and over which they had no clear vision.

4. Western Ukraine and Bolshevism

We have already seen how, at the end of 1918 and the beginning of 1919, Western Ukraine, in its state and military organization, was superior to its neighbors, especially the Poles and, militarily at least, the Czechs. Socially and politically it was less divided than those other countries. Its external situation, however—namely, the dual burden of the war with its stronger neighbor, Poland, and the need to create some kind of order in the turmoil of Eastern Ukraine—required a much higher degree of statecraft of the Western Ukrainians, if they were to maintain independent statehood, than was demanded of the Poles and the Czechs. Historically, Western Ukraine was at a disadvantage. Not having inherited an established state apparatus from Austria, it had to begin by creating one. Western Ukraine was a "non-historic nation." The

Poles and the Czechs, like so many other peoples in Europe, had a living memory of their previous existence as historical states. Their task was, ultimately, only one of reconstruction. But the historical statehood of Western Ukraine was lost without trace behind six centuries of history. What they were creating was therefore something completely new for Europe. And in this attempt they failed.

Western Ukraine had now improved the favorable conjuncture of the Entente victory for Poland and Czechoslovakia, providing a protective barrier for them with its successful defense against Bolshevism. It acted as a dike against the tempest from the east, behind which both nations, no longer threatened by any external danger, now gained time to strengthen themselves in makeshift fashion and then put themselves forward as the supposed protectors of Europe from the anarchic East, extending their rule over the territories that they still occupy today. This as yet completely unrecognized effect of the brief existence of Western Ukraine as a state is significant for world history.

The Paris Peace Conference began its work in January-February 1919 at a highly critical moment for Europe. Victors and vanquished were exhausted; traditional state machinery had either collapsed completely, as in Russia and the Central Powers, or was on the verge of collapse, as among the South Slavs, in Italy, and even in France.[100] The real "Bolshevik threat" was not what was happening in Russia but the internal disintegration of Europe itself. In Europe, both victors and vanquished were equally confronted by imminent social revolution. Everything hung by a hair; the smallest action could tip the scales. Fear of the kind of wild disorder and misery that Russia was undergoing acted as a restraining influence. But working against this was the turmoil of the dissatisfied masses, the spirit of rebellion in the "victorious" armies, the helplessness and powerlessness of the traditional ruling strata, and the despair among the vanquished patriots, who, like those in Hungary, were forced into catastrophic actions, including even service to the communists, as long as they seemed to offer the prospect of avoiding servitude to the Entente. Bolshevik Russia threatened to upset the delicate balance in Europe. If Russia's armed hordes reached the gates of Germany, penetrating Poland, Hungary, Bohemia, and Austria, who could reckon the consequences? Perhaps in the revolutionary turmoil the Central European masses would have established soviets everywhere and spread the armed revolution further westwards. The revolutionary upheavals in March and April 1919 in Bavaria and Hungary, as well as the social-revolutionary turmoil during this period in Czechoslovakia, Austria and Germany, show what could have happened all over Europe if the armed Russian Bolshevik hordes had been able to link up with the revolutionary masses of Central Europe.

As far as the maintenance of the capitalist order in Europe was concerned, military action against the Moscow Bolsheviks was the last thin thread holding everything together. If it broke, then everything might well be lost. If that was the case, then the fate of Europe depended on two borderlands, the Baltic provinces and anti-Bolshevik Ukraine, both East and West.

The armies of Estonia, Latvia and Lithuania, as well as those of the German Reich and of the Russian counterrevolution, which were posted in the Baltic provinces, protected Congress Poland. As long as this territory remained secure, there was only one line of access open to the Bolshevik troops, the route to Warsaw by way of Minsk and Brest-Litovsk. But until well into February 1919 this route was blocked by the German army of occupation in Belarus, and even afterwards, it was just a dead end into which the Bolshevik hordes, threatened by the forces from the Baltic provinces, would not have ventured. With the few thousand soldiers that Poland had deployed for this purpose,* it was a simple matter, after the withdrawal of the German army, to block and push back the equally small number of Bolshevik troops from this sector.

But the greater part of Poland and Romania was protected by Ukraine. At that time, in February and March 1919, Ukraine had more than a hundred thousand men in the field, fighting against the Poles, the Kyiv Soviet government or, in the ranks of the latter, against Petliura. If these troops had joined forces with the tens of thousands of Bolsheviks fighting under the Soviet banner, nothing would have stood in the way of a victorious Soviet march on Warsaw, Cracow, Budapest, and Prague. But that did not happen. Like a besieged fortress, Western and Eastern Ukraine fought alone, with no outside support or reliance on any foreign power. They were, in a sense, outside the life-and-death conflict of world capitalism and world revolution, and yet they were at the very center of that conflict. They fought against the Poles and, in that sense, against Entente capitalism, but at the same time they protected the Poles from direct contact with Bolshevism. The Polish-Ukrainian conflict therefore played itself out within the capitalist sphere, and this struggle between two similar sociopolitical formations actually strengthened Poland,

* The Polish struggle for the Belarusian and Lithuanian regions did not actually get under way until March 1919. Until then the Poles could organize the troops designated for that purpose virtually unmolested. That organization proceeded very slowly. Not until the end of April 1919 did the Poles have twenty-six and a half infantry battalions (some twelve thousand men) assigned to their "Lithuanian" and "Belarusian" fronts (Hupert, *Zajęcie Małopolski Wschodniej,* pp. 11, 13, 14).

preventing it from falling prey to the Bolshevik ferment. At the same time, the Western Ukrainians were fighting on the side of Entente capitalism against the Bolsheviks, blocking their path to Central Europe, the only path that led to world revolution.

This world-historical effect and significance of the Ukrainian liberation struggle remains a fact even if the Ukrainians, given their perceptions at the time, could not have acted differently. After having shown itself incapable, during the existence of the Hetman State, of placing itself at the head of the East European counterrevolution, Ukraine was confronted with the necessity of choosing between Entente capitalism and world revolution. Its choice, whether for good or ill, could have been a major world-historical turning point only in the event of its opting for the Bolsheviks. But to place Kyiv alongside Moscow in the leadership of the world revolution; to bring the whole nation, united and independent, into union with but not subservience to Moscow; to make such a decisive attempt at tipping the scales of history—for this, a very high level of political leadership ability was required. Only the appearance of a Ukrainian Genghis Khan or a second—Ukrainian—Lenin could have given the necessary impetus to the Ukrainian national and social revolutionary movement. But the Ukrainian movement did not produce any such "scourge of humanity." It is doubtful whether the highly unstable foundation of the Ukrainian movement could have provided a base for a forceful leader of that caliber. The misfortune of the Ukrainians, especially the Eastern Ukrainians, was their individualistic and anarchistic conception of freedom, which made them unsuitable for any major task requiring unity and stability. They were always thrown back and forth between extremes. Rebels such as the young pediocrats who overthrew the Directory in January 1919 and joined forces with the Bolsheviks would soon tire of any order, even a Leninist one. They were not a reliable base of support. The Kyiv Soviet government, just like the Hetman government before it, had to find its support in the Russian sector of the population, the difference being that this time it was among the Russian proletarians in Ukraine. This led, once again, to national discontent among the Eastern Ukrainian pediocrats, who now took up arms against the soviets just as they had previously done against the Hetman government and the Directory. If even the Eastern Ukrainian social revolutionaries were unable to join forces with Bolsheviks, then how could one expect this of the Eastern Ukrainian nationalist supporters of Petliura, or of the peasant reactionaries of Western Ukraine, who could almost be said to have more in common with absolutist monarchy than with the problems of the modern world, class struggle, soviets, and the dictatorship of the proletariat?

The internal situation and political culture of the country meant that the Western Ukrainians could only create what the Bolsheviks called a "petty-bourgeois" peasant state. Bolshevism threatened the existence of that state; hence it had to be fought. In such a rural political environment Leninist propaganda, with its abstract and clichéd way of thinking, could naturally make little headway.

Nevertheless, certain factors were making for a possible sovietization of Western Ukraine: the influence of the intellectual decline of "revolutionary democracy" in Russia, doubts about the country's ability to hold out against Poland, and, finally, the emergence of Soviet Hungary.

Under the leadership of previously unknown people, there emerged in Western Ukraine, ca. January 1919, a Peasant-Worker League (Selians'ko-robitnychyi soiuz), which became the oppositional avant-garde against the "petty-bourgeois" parties then in power, the National Democrats and the Radicals. Some of the Western Ukrainian Social Democrats gave timid support to this organization.[101] These social democrats did not really know what direction the small Western Ukrainian state should take. They admitted that in a "backward" country like Western Ukraine ("backward" being the relevant Marxist technical term), only a "petty-bourgeois" and not a "socialist" domestic policy was possible.[102] But their socialist conscience persuaded them that they had a duty to put up some kind of opposition.

In the Peasant-Worker League, which even published its own newspaper, the program and slogans of the Social Democrats, the Russian Socialist Revolutionaries, and the Bolsheviks were all mixed together in an amazing mishmash. The Leninist political doctrine was not properly understood; the dictatorship of the proletariat was something incomprehensible; they remained democrats but, just like the Eastern Ukrainian social-revolutionary pediocrats, they wanted to exclude from the parliamentary order all those who did not truly represent the workers and peasants. It was claimed that the Ukrainian National Rada was carrying out the policy of the Ukrainian "bourgeoisie" against the workers and peasants. There was in fact no bourgeoisie: what they meant by this was the other Western Ukrainian parties. The workers and peasants could defeat Poland, they claimed, but the "bourgeoisie" did not want to turn over the government to them. The Western Ukrainian bourgeoisie was alleged to have made a pact with the Polish and Entente bourgeoisie and to be cleaving to the large Polish landowners, and that was why the Ukrainian National Rada would not give way to a properly elected popular assembly and refused to introduce agrarian reform and the eight-hour day. They demanded that Western Ukraine not orient itself on the Entente but rather on the "revolutionary world proletariat," the avant-garde of which was Soviet Russia, for the Entente could not defend Western Ukraine against Poland, whereas an alliance with the Bolsheviks would give Western Ukraine victory over Poland. At the same time, however, "petty-bourgeois" nationalism was thrown into the mixture, and the Peasant-Worker League supported the Directory. Protesting the Moscow Bolshevik invasion of Eastern Ukraine, they nevertheless considered the Bolshevik government in Kyiv a legitimate Ukrainian authority and called for an agreement with it.[103]

This whole mishmash would be quite unimportant were it not for the light that it throws on the essence of Russian and Eastern Ukrainian "revolutionary democracy," the precursor of Bolshevism. That "democracy," though perhaps at a higher intellectual level, jumbled together all possible tendencies and slogans, creating such total chaos in political thought that it only prepared the way, first among the leading intellectuals and then among the popular masses, for Leninist Bolshevism. In the more limited and therefore more clearly apparent circumstances of Western Ukraine were mirrored all the chaotic events of the whole of Eastern Europe and, indeed, of the whole world of that day. The mirror distorts, to be sure, but precisely in this distortion, as in a good caricature, we see the most characteristic, most essential features all the more clearly. This was a time for great, unequivocal decisions, a time in which it made sense to be unreservedly for or unreservedly against Bolshevism. But the East European "revolutionary democracy," with all its noise, writings, discussions, speeches, divided into innumerable factions, tried to stake out a middle ground between the two great fighters, Bolshevism and the counterrevolution. It refused to link up with one or the other outright and, within this framework, to try to overcome difficulties and problems through positive activity and thus strengthen one or other tendency. With all its demagogic activity, it only clouded the real issues of the struggle and its true meaning. It was merely disruptive, held in contempt by both camps, considered by both to be worthless and meaningless, mere anarchic turmoil, a true product of the printer's ink that had made the literati unbearably popular since the nineteenth century. It was, ultimately, not Bolshevism but this "revolutionary democracy" that unleashed unspeakable chaos in Eastern Europe in 1917 and 1918, and thus it was a greater threat than Leninism itself. The Leninists agitated but, at the same time, they organized a new dictatorial leading stratum and established the foundations of a new and stable, if savage, order in their "revolutionary committees," "communist cells" and "soviets." The democrats, however, with their demands for indeterminate freedoms, disorganized everything, tore apart every social bond, and made of society an amorphous mass without being able, at the same time, to establish something new in place of the old.

The mishmash of the Peasant-Worker League only created anarchic discontent among the population of Western Ukraine and in the armed forces. It undermined trust in the leadership and weakened the resistance of the troops at the front. And it did so without preparing any replacement for the "petty-bourgeois" regime. In this way the Peasant-Worker League grew in popularity, especially as the war with Poland began to go badly for Western Ukraine. This popularity prevailed among anarchist malcontents, but it was good enough for Eastern Ukrainian Social Democratic and Socialist Revolutionary refugees, as well as for the Western Ukrainian Social Democrats, and soon these circles were ever more openly supporting the Peasant-Worker League.[104] This was their way of "deepening the revolution," as the saying went, while remaining blind to the experience of Eastern Ukraine. Things went so far that at its conference in Stanyslaviv on 30 March 1919 the Peasant-Worker League demanded that sixty-one of its representatives be given seats in the National Rada. Anonymous leaflets were distributed throughout the country calling on the people to march to Stanyslaviv and overthrow the Ukrainian National Rada, precipitating a civil war. It is not hard to discover which power was pulling the strings behind the scenes in this political puppet show. On 25 March 1919 Moscow Radio, triumphantly proclaiming Béla Kun's communist victory in Hungary, announced at the same time that the Peasant-Worker League had overthrown the Ukrainian National Rada, arrested the State Secretariat and proclaimed the Western Ukrainian Soviet Republic. In other words, Moscow already knew on 25 March 1919 what was supposed to happen in Stanyslaviv on 30 March.[105] It also appears that the well-developed Polish secret service, with its extensive network, was busily creating disorder in Western Ukraine. In February 1919 anonymous leaflets called on the peasants to divide up the large estates and initiate pogroms against the Jews, who were the true cause of their misery.[106]

The Ukrainian National Rada was of course quite incapable of doing anything to counter this movement, especially as it seemed inappropriate to place restrictions on speech and the press in that period of freedom. The National Rada was also held back by the consideration that it would be unwise to start an armed conflict inside the country while trying to carry on the war against Poland. The military force of the League was of course negligible. When the National Rada rejected its ultimatum, the

League threatened "consequences," but it was an empty threat. They had no intention of starting an actual uprising.[107] Only a few drops fell from the threatening dark clouds of the "world revolution." Nor was there any "white terror," and the only effect of all this was to weaken the military capacity of the Western Ukrainian army. The attempt to sovietize Western Ukraine thus collapsed because of the chaos among the social revolutionaries.

Much more serious was the despair among patriots, such as was also seen in Hungary, which led such people to consider supporting Bolshevism. An example of this despair appears in the following quotation from the nationalistically inclined Western Ukrainian publicist Vasyl Pachovsky:

> We are now confronting a question of the most serious consequence. Should we join forces with the Poles, who are engaged in a bloody campaign against Ukraine, and direct the whole might of our forces against the northern enemy?... But let us consider: although Muscovite Bolshevism threatens Dnipro Ukraine with national and economic ruin, the invasion of Polish rule is by far the greater danger for Western Ukraine.... We know from historical experience that the advance of Polish imperialism will not stop at the Galician-Volhynian line of the Buh River but will continue to Kharkiv, and that the mob of Polish henchmen and robber barons, who have stolen our land and liberty from us, will collude with the Russians to make us slaves in our own country. We must therefore insist on the following condition: Poland is to evacuate Lviv, Peremyshl and Kholm, and the population in the region of Rzeszów and Nowy Sącz should decide whether to join Poland or Ukraine. If Poland does not accept this condition, then nothing remains for us but to fight to the finish. The spread of Bolshevism cannot harm Western Ukraine: the naked man does not fear the thief. Let the Poles and the Entente tremble before it—we are convinced that, in the long run, we will not be able to hold out against this powerful current, this new religion of the masses, this tremendous upheaval. Ultimately, we will have no choice but to enter into this movement and attempt to guide it so as to ease the suffering for ourselves and ensure that it spills the least possible amount of our blood. It is true that the advance of Muscovite Bolshevism threatens the fall of the Ukrainian state on the Dnipro to the autocracy of the Muscovite barbarians, but this current also carries within it the seeds of a future democratic order. When that comes about, our people

> will inevitably become rulers of their own land. The peasants received land and liberty from the Directory; now they must defend those gifts. If the peasants do not understand this, they will fall under the rule of the Moscow Soviets—but that will serve them right; it is a lesson they need to learn. It will be a bloody lesson, but that is a historical necessity for a nation that does not know how to value a state of its own.[108]

This article is remarkable in many respects. In 1920, hardly a year after conquering Eastern Galicia, Poland did indeed seek to extend its rule to the Dnipro. It was also the case, as will be shown later, that the Polish invasion of Ukraine in 1919 took place on the basis of the assumption that Poland would come to some agreement with Russia on the division of Ukraine and that, together with the Russians, the Poles would throttle Ukraine.

What is really noteworthy here is the clear formulation of the dilemma: either to hold fast to the doctrine of national statehood and relinquish to Poland Ukrainian territory in Eastern Galicia up to the Buh River, make peace with Poland if the latter should be willing to accept it, and join, with all the forces at the Ukrainians' disposal, in the struggle against Bolshevism, or, just as definitely, to give up the doctrine of national statehood, accept orthodox Leninist Bolshevism unconditionally so as to crush Poland once and for all, and later, once Bolshevism had run its course, create an independent Ukrainian state in Eastern Europe encompassing all Ukrainian national territory between the Carpathians and the Don. It was impossible to fight the Bolsheviks and, at the same time, to strive for the ethnic border in the west. It was equally impossible to ignore the true essence of Bolshevism and merely "orient oneself toward it" in the belief that the Bolshevik world revolution would stop at the borders of the "petty-bourgeois" Eastern Galician state, defend it against Poland, and not seek to sovietize it.

There were few who recognized this dilemma clearly, and the Western Ukrainians lacked the qualities of intellect and character required to confront it head-on. It was necessary to decide which of those alternatives, both equally achievable with the Ukrainians' own forces at the time, was best for their native land: either a Ukrainian national rump state or the crushing of Poland and the unification of all Ukrainian territories under the rule of Muscovite Bolshevism. In the meantime, however, everyone became involved in pure speculation about what would be the better course: should one adopt an orientation on the Entente or on the Bolsheviks in order to receive the gift of a Ukrainian national state from one "constellation" or the other, just as the Poles and the other "self-determining" peoples had been given their national statehood by the "constellation" of Entente victory? One side—represented, for instance, by the official policy of the Ukrainian National Rada—insisted that the Entente would recognize the "right of self-determination of peoples" with regard to Western Ukraine, force Poland to accept a peace favorable to it, and support Western Ukraine in order to create a base for the struggle against Bolshevism. This was known as the "Entente orientation." The other side believed that Western Ukraine would gain nothing from an Entente intervention and wanted to join forces with the Bolsheviks, persuade them to leave Ukraine, win their support in the war against Poland, and obtain their recognition of a Western Ukrainian national, even "petty-bourgeois," state. This was known as the "Bolshevik orientation." The Entente orientation was by far the more popular, but that meant little, for both orientations sought salvation from an outside power. Both lacked the capacity to alter the basic situation, and both were prepared, at any moment, to change their attitude if that seemed likely to promote the "right of self-determination."[109]

Thus not even national desperation sufficed to drive the Western Ukrainians into the arms of the Bolsheviks. Meanwhile, these Western Ukrainian waverings were being watched uneasily by another people, namely, the Hungarians. On 21 March 1919 the Allied Supreme Council in Paris communicated the unbearably harsh terms of armistice with Romania to the democratic Hungarian government of Count Mihály Károlyi, who resigned and handed over the government to the extreme left. Under the leadership of Béla Kun the communists took up the struggle against the Entente in order to save Hungary. This soviet-style government, which later collapsed because of Kun's complete inadequacy, immediately placed itself at the service of the Hungarian patriotic movement: it ventured to do what the Western Ukrainians had also considered, as has just been shown. Hungary was in an extremely difficult situation. The country was surrounded by hostile foreign troops: French, Italians, South Slavs, Romanians, Czechs, and Slovaks.[110] There appeared to be no possible deliverance from this situation, unless the East European Bolsheviks could break through Western Ukraine and attack the Romanian and Czechoslovak troops from the north by way of the Carpathians. But the Eastern Ukrainians under Petliura blocked the way as best they could, and this barrier was strong enough to prevent a breakthrough by the Moscow Bolsheviks. And beyond Eastern Ukraine was "petty-bourgeois" Western Ukraine. Hungary was completely inaccessible to relief forces from the north.

The Hungarian communists then turned to Volodymyr Vynnychenko, who had just resigned as president of the Eastern Ukrainian Directory, proposing that he mediate between the left socialist parties in Ukraine and the Moscow Bolsheviks so as to establish in Ukraine a soviet government predominantly or entirely Ukrainian in national composition. The Hungarians hoped that this new government could do away with the Directory as well as the Western Ukrainian government and unite all the Ukrainian military forces. A united soviet front made up of Hungary, Eastern and Western Ukraine, and Russia would then strike a decisive blow against the satellites of the Entente in Central Europe. Soviet Hungary, with which Western Ukraine had good relations, just as it had had previously with the Károlyi government, loyally offered to mediate between the Western Ukrainian State Secretariat and Soviet Russia.[111]

To be sure, the Bolsheviks were Russian chauvinists who controlled the "Soviet Ukrainian government" and rejected any accommodation of Leninism to Ukrainian national sentiment. But, quite apart from this, the Moscow Bolsheviks were well aware that the Ukrainian "revolutionary democrats," who, as the Hungarians wished, were to be given the government in Kyiv so as to mobilize their national sentiment in support of the world revolution, were in a state of internal turmoil. To hand over the ship of state to such an unstable element would mean, in practice, to relinquish the dictatorship of the proletariat in Ukraine and reintroduce a distorted form of parliamentarism such as the Central Rada had been—a mixture of social-revolutionary phraseology and "petty-bourgeois," nationalist and separatist practice. Only one thing could be expected with certainty from such an arrangement, namely, that the Ukrainian revolutionary-democratic pediocracy would soon rebel against and destroy the united front of the world revolution, and that the Ukrainians, though unable to provide any leadership themselves, would soon reject the leadership of Moscow and begin a "liberation struggle" against the communist dictatorship. Being good judges of both the situation and the measures required, the Moscow Bolsheviks were obliged to reject the mediation of Béla Kun in the interests of the world revolution. They gave him to understand, with some degree of irony, that they saw no need to replace the already existing Ukrainian Soviet government. They demanded instead that the Ukrainians either become Bolsheviks and submit without protest to the leadership of Moscow or, in the interests of their petty-bourgeois separatist conception of national freedom, fight just as resolutely against the Bolshevik world revolution. The Hungarian attempt at mediation thus came to nothing, and this marked the passing of the last opportunity for the sovietization of Western Ukraine.[112]

As far as its relations with the Bolsheviks were concerned, all that now remained for Western Ukraine was to maintain good relations with Soviet Hungary.* In April 1919 the two countries signed a trade agreement.[113] This did not, of course, interfere with the continuation of the war against the Moscow Bolsheviks. War on two fronts, against the Bolsheviks and the Poles, thus continued to define the Ukrainian situation.

The question that now arises is what part Western Ukraine played in the grand strategy of the Entente powers, whose representatives were just then conferring in Paris about the structure of postwar Europe. The answer to this question must begin with Poland's plans in relation to Ukraine, for which it sought the support of the Entente.

* The assumption, almost universal in Polish historiography concerning developments in Eastern Galicia in 1918–19, that the Western Ukrainians were supplied with military equipment by Soviet Hungary, is a complete fabrication. Soviet Hungary lacked such equipment even for itself. Its initial military successes were due exclusively to the almost inexplicable panic fear that its opponents had of it. In military terms the Western Ukrainians were incomparably stronger than the Soviet Hungarians, who in any case were very lamentably led by Béla Kun.

Chapter 3

The Paris Peace Conference and the Polish-Ukrainian War for Eastern Galicia

1. Polish Diplomacy and the "Question of Eastern Galicia"

The Entente victory naturally brought to the head of Polish foreign affairs the camp that had championed a pro-Entente orientation, namely, the National Democrats under the leadership of Roman Dmowski. To obtain a clear picture of Poland's diplomatic superiority over Western Ukraine in 1918–19, it is essential to summarize the origin and growth of the influence of the Polish National Democrats among the Entente powers during the war.

As is well known,* at the beginning of the war the National Democrats continued the foreign policy that had been theirs for a decade, looking to the defeat of the Central Powers and the reunification of all Polish territories by Russia. Such an outcome would strengthen Poland not only in relation to Russia but also to the rest of Europe and make the formation of an independent Polish state, within a union with Russia or outside it, inevitable. But by 1915 it was already clear that this Russia-oriented policy was leading nowhere, and not only because Russia was in no position to defeat the Central Powers. Roman Dmowski himself, the originator of this orientation on Russia and the Entente, was forced to admit at the time[114] that Russia had no intention—not even at the beginning of the war, in the event of its military victory—of keeping the promise made on 15 August 1914 by Grand Duke Nicholas in order to strengthen Russophilism among the Poles. Thus Russia would not annex any predominantly Polish territories of the Central Powers, especially Germany, for fear of strengthening the Polish movement within its own borders. And Russia allowed no interference by the other Entente powers in its Polish policy.[115] As the price for giving France a free hand on the Rhine, Russia demanded from France a free hand for itself in the question of its western borders and, at the beginning of March 1917, received a guarantee** that under no circumstances would it be forced

---

* For an extensive discussion of Polish policy in the course of the world war, see Recke, *Die polnische Frage*, pp. 174–284; this work also gives detailed references.

** Following the collapse of Russia, which ensued shortly thereafter, the other Entente powers did not recognize this Franco-Russian agreement, as Arthur Balfour announced in the English Parliament on 19 December 1917 (Temperley, *Peace Conference*, 1: 184n). Cf. Seyda, *Polska na przełomie dziejów*, pp. 458–61 (Dr. Recke, to whom Temperley's work was unavailable, does not cite this detail).

to keep its promise to unite the Polish lands. Russia, then, was the main obstacle to the solution of the Polish problem in Europe. Only a defeat or at least a weakening of Russia could alter this situation, which was so desperate for the Polish National Democrats.

The Central Powers' military victories over Russia in 1915; their attempts to gain the sympathy of Congress Poland, which was conveniently distinct from the Russian system of government;[116] and, finally, such demonstrative gestures as the speech by Theobald von Bethmann-Hollweg in the German Reichstag on 5 April 1916, announcing a solution of the Polish question by the Central Powers, shook Russia's position. In this new situation the National Democrats made a very clever diplomatic intervention. These moves by the Central Powers awakened in the Entente, especially in France, the fear that Poland as a whole would declare itself for the Central Powers and raise a volunteer army of some hundreds of thousands to be placed at the latter's disposal.[117] The National Democrats took advantage of these fears in order to convince France thoroughly of the importance of the Polish question and win full French support for their own political goals. National Democratic propaganda succeeded in eliciting the first cautious proposals from France intended to persuade Russia to compete with the Central Powers on the Polish question. Although such interventions brought no results as long as Russian tsardom remained in place, they were the first indications that the Polish question was gradually becoming an international problem as a result of the undertakings given by the Central Powers.[118]

The proclamation of the Kingdom of Poland by the Central Powers on 5 November 1916 took the Polish question out of Russia's hands and established it finally as an issue of international significance, strengthening the diplomatic activity of the National Democrats. They were no longer satisfied with the reunification of Poland under Russian rule: they now demanded of the Entente complete independence for a united Poland.[119] Although the Western Entente powers, fearing a separate Russian peace, continued to leave the solution of the Polish question to Russia and were extremely cautious in dealing with the question so as not to antagonize the Russians,* the need to outbid the Central Powers compelled Russia

* Cf. Recke, *Die polnische Frage*, p. 259. This caution is also apparent in the Entente's note of 10 January 1917 to Wilson containing its peace conditions: "The intentions of His Majesty the Emperor of Russia in regard to Poland have been clearly indicated by the manifesto he has just addressed to his armies" (Temperley, *Peace Conference*, 1: 172n. Recke does not cite this note). The reference was to the tsar's order of 25 December 1916 to his army, issued as a response to the German peace offer, which promised, inter alia, the creation of a "free Poland." This promise had so little significance that the commission convoked by the tsar to advise on measures to be taken to carry out the order to the army could refuse even to consider the question of a

gradually to accept the establishment of a Polish state as one of its war aims and lend a more favorable ear to the emissaries of the National Democrats.*

The final stage of this development was initiated by two tremendous catastrophes that lay beyond the scope of all political reckoning—the Russian Revolution of 1917 and the complete collapse of the Central Powers in 1918. The proclamation of Polish independence by revolutionary Russia allowed the Entente openly to proclaim as one of its war aims** the establishment of an independent Polish state, an aim previously considered only on the theoretical level. The collapse of the Central Powers made it possible for them to achieve this by means of a simple dictate, although an independent Poland with access to the Baltic seemed pure fantasy to the Americans and the British, and even to the French, as late as November 1918.[120]

Such was the course of events, unleashed by the Central Powers, that created and extended the scope of activity of Polish National Democratic diplomacy. The situation forced the Poles to pursue a dual strategy, so that both camps in Poland, one supporting the Entente and the other the Central Powers, worked for an independent Poland. Decisive in this respect, however, was the activity of those Poles who supported the Central Powers. The Polish question gradually became important

---

"free Poland" (cf. Recke, *Die polnische Frage*, pp. 259–69; Seyda, *Polska na przełomie dziejów*, pp. 455–60).

* The initiative came from Wilson's message of 22 January 1917 to the U.S. Senate, even before the United States entered the war. It says, among other things: "I take it for granted, for instance, if I may venture upon a single example, that statesmen everywhere are agreed that there should be a united, independent, and autonomous Poland, and that henceforth inviolable security of life, of worship, and of industrial and social development should be guaranteed to all peoples who have lived hitherto under the power of governments devoted to a faith and purpose hostile to their own" (cf. Recke, *Die polnische Frage*, pp. 285–86; Seyda, *Polska na przełomie dziejów*, pp. 461–63).

** Poland's right to independence was proclaimed by the Petrograd Soviet of Workers' and Soldiers' Deputies on 28 March 1917, and its sovereignty was proclaimed by the Provisional Government on 30 March 1917. (The texts of both documents appear in Roth, *Die Entstehung des polnischen Staates*, pp. 127–28.) But it was not until 28 October 1917 that the Russian foreign minister, Mikhail (Mykhailo) Tereshchenko, could announce that France and England had committed themselves to the restoration of an "independent and undivided Poland" as one of the bases of the coming order in Europe. Italy adhered to this commitment a few days later (Temperley, *Peace Conference*, 1: 183–84; Kumaniecki, *Odbudowa Państwowości Polskiej*, p. 109; Seyda, *Polska na przełomie dziejów*, pp. 464–69; Recke does not mention this announcement). The announcement was then made for France by its foreign minister, Stéphen Pichon, on 27 December 1917 (Dmowski, *Polityka polska*, p. 318), for England by David Lloyd George on 5 January 1918 (Temperley, *Peace Conference*, 1: 191), and for the United States in point 13 of Woodrow Wilson's peace conditions of 8 January 1918 (Temperley, *Peace Conference*, 1: 413). This series of declarations by individual powers was crowned by the joint resolution of France, England and Italy at the inter-Allied conference in Versailles on 3 June 1918 (Kumaniecki, *Odbudowa Państwowości Polskiej*, p. 118).

to the Entente not because there was a camp in Poland that expected all possible benefits from the Entente powers but because the other camp had persuaded the Central Powers to take up the Polish question. Thus, when the National Democrats campaigned energetically against the opposing Polish camp and called on all Poles to adopt an uncompromising hostility toward the Central Powers, they were sawing off the branch on which they themselves were sitting. The beginnings of the organization of a Polish state were made by the camp that supported the Central Powers, not by the National Democrats. It was also this camp that created the Polish Legions, from which the Polish army developed in 1918–19. One can hardly exaggerate the advantage that Poland would have enjoyed upon the collapse of the Central Powers if, two years previously, the National Democratic sabotage of those powers had not prevailed and Poland had created its own strong army, even if it had initially been under German command.* It was also the camp supporting the Central Powers that created the Regency Council. Although despised by the Poles, the council was nevertheless the institution from which the Polish state developed at the end of 1918, at a time of most dangerous crisis for Poland. Finally, it was also the work of this camp that ensured that the legal and educational systems of Congress Poland were in Polish hands and that the autonomous institutions of Galicia were able to function as the beginnings of Polish state administration in that region.

In other words, the National Democrats created nothing during the world war but very astutely reaped what the conjunctures of world politics made possible at any particular moment. They were active only on the level of political virtuosity, in other words, diplomacy, and not on the level of statesmanlike insight and understanding that brings about a new reality and creates new situations—the level of politics. They were complete masters of diplomacy. Closely following the course of events,

---

* With regard to the Treaty of Brest-Litovsk and the entrance of troops of the Central Powers into Ukraine, Michał Bobrzyński observes (*Wskrzeszenie Państwa Polskiego*, 1: 212–13):

> Many a Pole who was averse to the Legions and the Polish army [that the Germans wanted to organize in 1916–17] now thought to himself how different the occupation of those territories would have looked if it had been carried out by a Polish army, even if it had been under the command of a [Hans von—Ed.] Beseler. If he went further in his thinking, he also asked himself whether the Treaty of Brest-Litovsk would have looked as it did and whether it would have come to such an elimination of the Polish presence in the Ruthenian regions if the Legions, supported by the whole nation and built up into a powerful army, had been posted to the Russian front.

This recognition does not, however, prevent Bobrzyński, a few pages later (2: 10), from presenting Poland as a victim of the Germans from the military viewpoint. He writes: "After the Germans crushed the Legions and thwarted the formation of a Polish army, Poland could not [in November-December 1918] claim the intended boundaries that extended past its own ethnic territory."

it was they who were the first to convince the Entente how useful the Polish question would be as a way of "cutting the sinews of Prussia," as Bismarck had expressed it in 1848. The great achievement of Dmowski and his colleagues on behalf of the Polish cause at this time was not their orientation on the Entente per se, considered as a political factor among the Polish masses, but the determination and boldness with which the National Democratic diplomats carried out their propaganda campaign in the Entente countries themselves to promote the destruction of Germany and the creation of an expanded Polish state at a time when such an idea seemed impossible to the Entente governments.

The organization of this diplomacy was very extensive. It was started by Dmowski in November 1915 when, despairing of Russia, he left the empire in order to win support for the Polish cause in the West. For a long time the only financial support came from the National Democratic organization in the Poznań region and from Count Maurycy Zamoyski.* In September a Central Polish Agency (Centralna Agencja Polska) was created in Lausanne, headed by the Poznań journalist Marian Seyda. Its task was to influence the Western press in favor of Poland.[121] Soon afterwards, the initially loose association of Dmowski and his friends from the National Democratic Party and the Realists, who were close to them, gave rise to an unofficial Polish diplomatic corps in all the Entente capitals.[122] Dmowski established himself in London, where he undertook with great perseverance to instruct British journalists and politicians on the situation in Poland. In 1917 it became clear that some kind of official organization of pro-Entente Poland was necessary, and on 15 August the Polish National Committee (Komitet Narodowy Polski) was established in Lausanne. It soon moved its headquarters to Paris and functioned more or less as a future government of Poland.[123] The National Committee was headed by Dmowski, and its members were Erazm Piltz and Count Maurycy Zamoyski in Paris; Count Władysław Sobański in London; Marian Seyda and Jan Rozwadowski, who remained in Switzerland as representatives of the Polish territories in Prussia and Austria; Konstanty Skirmunt in Rome; and Ignacy Paderewski in the United States.[124]

Dmowski's plans for the reunification of Poland naturally won favor first of all among the French.** The French, whose main goal

---

* Dmowski, *Polityka polska*, pp. 168–69, 293–94. Financial assistance from the National Committee (Wydział Narodowy) in Chicago came later, and finally, in 1918, there was a bond issue guaranteed personally by the members of the National Committee, to be repaid by the Polish state, in the amount of 175,000 francs monthly from France and 75,000 francs monthly from England. The Polish state did indeed subsequently take over this debt (Roth, *Die Entstehung des polnischen Staates*, p. 240).

** Recke (*Die polnische Frage*, pp. 183–88), considers that even Dmowski's adoption of a Russophile policy in 1907 can be traced back to some secret agreement of this Polish politician with France.

was the destruction of Germany, were the first to attempt to convince Russia, however cautiously, of the importance of the Polish plans.[125] French support for the Poles became even stronger after the outbreak of the Russian Revolution in 1917 because the end of the old Russian Empire meant that France had to seek a new and more reliable ally against Germany in Eastern Europe. Even before the formation of the Polish National Committee, a decree of the French president dated 4 July 1917 created a volunteer Polish army, soon to be headed by General Józef Haller.[126] With French support, the National Committee set itself the following tasks: 1) to obtain from the Entente governments an unambiguous declaration on how they intended to deal with the Polish question after the victory over Germany; 2) to organize a Polish army to fight against Germany; 3) to look after the interests of Poles living in the Entente countries; 4) to develop a political propaganda campaign on behalf of the Polish national cause.[127] The National Committee soon managed to obtain recognition from all the Entente governments as the official representative of the Polish nation. This recognition was given in France on 20 September 1917, in England on 15 October 1917, in Italy on 30 October 1917, and in the United States on 1 December 1917.[128] As the official representative of an allied nation of the Entente, the National Committee signed an agreement with France on 20 March 1918 in which the French premier confirmed the autonomy of the Polish army in France. This statute of autonomy was replaced on 28 September 1918 by a military convention between the committee and the French government according to which the Haller army in France was recognized as an allied fighting force under the leadership of the Polish National Committee (*armée autonome et belligérante sous un commandement polonais unique*), subject to certain restrictions.[129]

In its relations with the Entente powers, the Polish National Committee was recognized at the end of the war as the national government of Poland. On 4 July 1918, as the Americans celebrated Independence Day, the Polish flag flew alongside the other flags of the Entente for the first time, a symbol of Poland's equal standing among those powers whose dogged and bloody struggle had made that independence a reality.[130]

Support for Poland came from numerous organizations and individuals with important social and political connections in Europe and America. Some of these were supporters of the National Committee and followers of Dmowski's ideas; others acted on their own initiative. After France, Polish influence was strongest in the United States. A powerful organization of American Poles, which also provided considerable funds for the National Committee, built up popular support for the Polish cause in the United States by means of rallies, lobbying of leading statesmen, and publications and articles in the press.[131] In 1918 a major newspaper, the *New York Times*, gave its full support to Dmowski's basic idea that without the establishment of an extensive Polish state, including the Vistula (Wisła) estuary and Danzig (Gdańsk), the outcome of the war would represent a defeat for America and the Entente.[132] The influence of individual Polish political figures reached to the highest levels of the American administration.[133]

The ground was thus superbly prepared for Ignacy Paderewski, the most important National Democratic leader after Dmowski and a personal friend of President Wilson. In spite of everything, Wilson was long hesitant to consider the newly reconstituted Poland a state that, along with indisputably Polish territories, should also include ethnically non-Polish lands, especially on the Baltic coast. It was Dmowski who came to America in August 1918 and finally persuaded Wilson to accept the Polish point of view by frankly threatening him with the loss of "four million Polish votes" in the coming Congressional elections due to be held in November 1918.[134] There was also direct Polish influence in the American commissions that were preparing material for the forthcoming peace treaty. The special group established in the summer of 1918 to deal with the Polish question was led by Dr. Robert Howard Lord, professor of history at Harvard University, who was very well disposed toward Poland.[135] There were two Polish-American professors among his colleagues in the group.[136] Consequently, not only were the Polish diplomats in a position to know Wilson's intentions with regard to Poland, but that rather weak statesman was unable to withstand all this Polish influence. With the greatest naïveté, Wilson supported Polish claims at the Paris Peace Conference almost without exception—claims that the French diplomats had supported all along. Thus Wilson's whole program of national self-determination and world disarmament was stood on its head.[137]

The least successful of the National Democratic groups was that in England. The powerful Liberal camp in England was not happy with plans for the permanent crippling of Germany by the French and the creation of a Polish superpower in Eastern Europe. Not only the prime minister, David Lloyd George, who explicitly rejected such plans, but even the foreign minister, Arthur Balfour, who showed a certain interest, held back on the issue. There was the additional fact that since 1917 London had become the foreign center for the Polish Liberals and Social Democrats—the camp of Aleksander Lednicki, which had taken part in the Russian Revolution in 1917. These Poles in London, led by August

Zaleski, had friendly relations with the circle around Lloyd George.[138] Their program called for peace without delay and the unification of Congress Poland with Galicia. They left open the question of Polish territories in Germany, thereby thwarting the National Democratic propaganda that called for the continuation of the war until the complete defeat of the Central Powers.[139] The Dmowski policy, however, had quite a few highly placed supporters in England, and the National Committee was backed by influential anti-Liberal circles, most notably the Catholic Conservatives, whose spokesman was the writer Gilbert Keith Chesterton. The *Morning Post*, for example, was completely open to National Democratic propaganda.[140] Paderewski also had close personal contact with Lloyd George,[141] so that even in England, where the Polish movement was weakest, it was not entirely without influence.

Then the Central Powers collapsed, and as the whole of exhausted Europe disintegrated into chaos and Eastern Europe became the scene of internal conflicts, the representatives of the victorious nations made haste to Paris to dictate a new world order to the vanquished. Since a de facto state already existed on core Polish territory and was being ruled from Warsaw by an independent government under Piłsudski's leadership, the National Committee in Paris, having engaged in unsuccessful intrigues to overthrow Piłsudski by force,[142] was obliged to relinquish its plans to become the first Polish government.* Under pressure from the French, who impressed upon the National Committee the need for moderation, it had to come to some arrangement with the hated Piłsudski government in Warsaw.[143] On 16 January 1919 Paderewski became prime minister of the Warsaw government,[144] and the Paris National Committee, led by Dmowski and later augmented by delegates from Warsaw, was designated the diplomatic representative of the Warsaw government at the Paris Peace Conference.[145] This new Polish state, now an actual fact and no longer merely a propaganda project, was officially accepted as a member of the Entente. By means of a letter from the French government to the National Committee on 15 January 1919, the inter-Allied conference invited the Polish state to send two plenipotentiaries to the Peace Conference, which opened in Paris on 18 January 1919.[146]

* Initially this ambition was supported by France: it sought England's agreement for the recognition of the National Committee as the de facto government of Poland, but Balfour declined in his note of 30 November 1918 (cf. Roth, *Die Entstehung des polnischen Staates*, p. 51). On 29 December 1918 Pichon still referred to the committee in the French Parliament as "a regular (*regulier*) government" but was already insisting that it reach an understanding with Piłsudski (Bobrzyński, *Wskrzeszenie Państwa Polskiego*, 2: 38). Thus the National Democrats were more annoyed than the French themselves by the fact that their Warsaw compatriots had once been Austrophile or friendly to Germany.

Thus Poland became one of the "allied and associated powers," one of the "victorious states" that would now dictate the peace. The ranking of the Entente states was now also determined. America, England, France, Italy, and Japan would have five plenipotentiaries each. Serbia, Belgium and Brazil were each to send three, while China, Greece, Hejaz, Poland, Portugal, Romania, Siam, and Czechoslovakia had two each. The South American republics were given one plenipotentiary each.* Russia, where the Bolsheviks now held power in Moscow and St. Petersburg, and on whose remaining territories civil war was raging, was not allowed to attend the Peace Conference. Neither were any of the new states that had emerged on the territory of the old Russian Empire. Poland alone represented the whole of Eastern Europe.**

"It seems to me," wrote Roman Dmowski, "that I have every right to say that it was we Poles who first formulated and substantiated as a whole the program for the reconstruction of Europe implemented by the Treaties of Versailles and Saint-Germain."[147] It was indeed a massive program that this Polish diplomat gave the British foreign minister, Balfour, in April 1917.[148] The treatise was issued for English political circles in July 1917 under the title *Problems of Central and Eastern Europe*.*** This was done at a time when the power of Germany and its allies seemed unstoppable and Germany appeared to be on the verge of victory. Dmowski's program for Europe may briefly be summarized as follows:

> Germany, which has become the greatest power on the Continent, threatens to bring all of eastern and southeastern Europe under its direct and indirect rule. Austria-Hungary, Bulgaria and Turkey have become mere dependencies of the German Reich in the course of the war and are a base from which Germany can advance into the Middle East. A peace on the basis of the slightly altered status quo of 1914 would soon lead to a new war in Europe in which Germany would certainly emerge as the complete victor. Nothing could then

* Temperley, 1: 247–48. India and the British dominions also had their own representatives.

** Moreover, the Warsaw government was soon also recognized de jure in 1919: on 30 January by the United States, on 24 February by France, on 25 February by England, on 27 February by Italy, on 6 March by Belgium, on 8 March by Finland, on 12 March by Switzerland, on 13 March by Greece, on 22 March by Japan, on 30 March by the papal curia, on 15 April by Brazil, on 21 May by Norway, on 22 May by Spain, on 28 May by Czechoslovakia, on 31 May by Denmark, on 3 June by Sweden, on 21 June by Romania and Portugal, on 7 July by Argentina, on 28 August by Chile, on 29 August by Persia, and on 9 October by Paraguay (Kutrzeba, *Polska odrodzona*, p. 187).

*** The complete text of the treatise appears in Polish translation in Dmowski, *Polityka polska*, pp. 450–505. The sections of the English original concerning the boundaries of the future Poland also appear in *Akty i dokumenty dotyczące sprawy granic Polski*, 1: 21–31.

> save Europe from German domination. The present world war, therefore, must not end until the German danger has been completely eliminated. Any peace with Germany must deny it all possibility of maintaining its stronghold in southeastern Europe. This means the end of Germany's dependency, Austria-Hungary. To promote the general European tendency toward the creation of nation-states, the Austro-Hungarian territory must be divided among Italy, Serbia, Romania, and Poland. A new state, Czechoslovakia, must be created, and Hungary, which, because of its location, is strongly pro-German, must be restricted to purely Magyar ethnic territories. The rest of German Austria should then become part of Germany. This last, as Dmowski says elsewhere, should be done by strengthening the less dangerous south German elements in order to weaken the predominance of Prussia, the bastion of German militarism. This new anti-German Central Europe will only be stable if it has the support of a powerful Poland. Russia has no interest in opposing Germany. Now, after the outbreak of the Revolution of 1917, it has entered a period of internal turmoil, the to-and-fro of revolution and counterrevolution that may last for generations. This excludes Russia as a factor in the European state system and, in fact, leaves it completely open to German influence. Only a large and powerful Polish state can put a stop to the possibility of German expansion into the disintegrating Russian Empire. Only the incorporation into Poland of Silesia, the Poznań region, West Prussia and Danzig, as well as the creation of a small East Prussian state more or less closely associated with Poland, can deliver the death blow to Prussian militarism, which draws its strength from all these lands. Alsace-Lorraine should go to France and Schleswig to Denmark. Hemmed in this way, with a strong Poland as the central axis of the new order in Central Europe and in the rest of the continent, the German people will gradually be forced to accept their new situation, give up their ambition to dominate Europe, and play their proper role to the benefit of a peaceful Europe with no injustice to the other nations on this continent.[149]

In this overall context, analyzing the general situation and its particular problems, Dmowski also deals occasionally with the newly arisen Ukrainian question in Eastern Europe. He says several times that

> this problem is part of the profound and probably unstoppable process of the disintegration of Russia resulting from

> the penetration of the empire by the ideas of European nationalism. In Eastern Galicia this takes the form of a national political movement directed against Russia as well as against Poland. Although this is undoubtedly the most important of the new national movements on the territory of the former Russian Empire, since it will probably grow rapidly and strive for complete Ukrainian independence,* its future is not yet definite enough to permit any judgment about it because the bearer of this movement is an immature people without a history. This is all the more true as Germany already wishes to be its protector, and it is receiving support against Poland from both Vienna and Berlin. Germany's goal is to establish a Ukrainian state alongside a small Polish state limited to the territory of Congress Poland. These would then be part of a system of border states between the Black Sea and the Baltic, a system of German dependencies that would establish and secure German domination in Eastern Europe. A strong Polish state must be able not only to prevent German interference in the internal affairs of Great Russia but also to head off the possibility of German intrigue in Ukraine. The eastern border of Poland should therefore extend to include the territories of the former Russian gubernias of Kovno (Kaunas), Minsk and Grodno (Hrodna), as well as the greater part of the gubernias of Minsk and Volhynia. For the same reason, Eastern Galicia must belong to Poland. Once the intrigue from Berlin and Vienna has been eliminated, there will certainly be a just Polish-Ukrainian compromise in Eastern Galicia.

Although the Polish uprising in Lviv on 1 November 1918 was more the result of Polish national temperament than of political calculation, the political grounds for the uprising, as well as its significance in the context of world politics as he perceived it, had already been established by Dmowski almost two years earlier. Whether right or wrong, his way of treating the Polish and Ukrainian questions was infinitely superior to the Western Ukrainians' notion of "ethnic rights." Among the Western Ukrainians no one, since the good old generation of Drahomanov in the second half of the nineteenth century, had really concerned himself with the big questions of world politics. No one had really attempted to understand the different and opposing interest groups that existed in Europe or to which of those interest groups Ukraine and its possible

* This was written, nota bene, in the first half of 1917, when Eastern Ukrainian public opinion was still demanding a federal restructuring of Russia and the idea of Ukrainian independence was almost frowned upon.

statehood belonged. What was not stated explicitly in Dmowski's text, although it was absolutely clear from its whole argumentation, is that he had made calculations about the future development of Eastern Europe with regard to the Ukrainian question. These calculations could be summarized more or less as follows:

> After the radical changes of 1917, Russian domination of Eastern Europe from Moscow and St. Petersburg and the possibility of Russia's linking up with the Germans against Poland is out of the question for an indeterminate period. The emergence of nationalism among the non-Russian masses of the former Russian Empire has strengthened the centrifugal forces at work to such an extent that Great Russia will be completely preoccupied, for an indeterminate period, with the task of maintaining its own unity and dealing with outbreaks of nationalist separatism. It will be in no position to threaten Poland from the east by linking up with Germany. The danger to Poland from Moscow and St. Petersburg is therefore excluded for some considerable time. If there is any threat to Poland from the east, it comes not from Great Russia but from Ukraine. If the Ukrainians succeed in establishing their own state, it will be on much friendlier terms with Germany than Russia ever was, and then Poland will have on its eastern border an enemy that could pose a real threat in alliance with Germany. It therefore lies in the interest of the Polish state to cripple the Ukrainian movement, and this can best be done by Poland's annexation of Eastern Galicia, for it is precisely here that the Ukrainian movement has reached its highest level of development. This would mean that the rest of Ukraine, which previously belonged to Russia, would be unable to win the battle against Russia and establish its own state, as it has not yet matured to that degree. But the level of national consciousness there is such that the Ukrainians would continue the struggle, thereby weakening Russia as a whole and preventing it from playing any significant part in foreign affairs for a long time. If Poland can win for itself this extended period of external security, then, by the time the situation in Eastern Europe has once again turned to our disadvantage, we will already have succeeded in Polonizing the Ukrainians in Eastern Galicia and Volhynia and thereby eliminated the Ukrainian danger from within. The most essential thing is, however, that once we manage to prevent the establishment of a Ukrainian state, there will inevitably emerge an ongoing community of interest between Poland and Great Russia of the type that existed

> between Prussia and Russia after the partition of Poland—a shared interest in the suppression and defeat of the Ukrainians that will guarantee a lasting peace between Poland and the rest of Russian-dominated Eastern Europe.

In addition to the national and historical sentiments that influenced the Polish attitude toward Eastern Galicia, the National Democratic diplomats were demanding the annexation of Eastern Galicia and other Ukrainian territories of the former Russian Empire to Poland, as well as the complete annihilation of any attempt to establish a Ukrainian state not only in Western but also in Eastern Ukraine, so as to exclude Ukraine completely from the developing European state system and thus establish Poland's security against Germany. Just as in the case of the oppression of Hungary, this was meant to lay the foundations of a new European order based on the untrammeled domination of the continent by France and Poland.

As propaganda for the establishment of Poland as a great power, Dmowski's program was brilliant. As a description of the true state of affairs, however, it was misleading. The Central Powers did not have any preconceived plans as far as Ukraine was concerned, and they began to pay attention to Ukraine only at the end of 1917, having failed to win the support of the Poles and at a time when Russia was already in a state of collapse. Thus it was not any recognition of the real situation that prompted Dmowski's attitude toward Ukraine but rather his preconceived ideas. He always suspected a hidden German hand in anything that he saw as a threat to Poland, and since the Western Ukrainians were threatening the Eastern Galician Poles, he could see in this only the workings of German intrigue.*

But Dmowski believed his own propaganda, and when his prediction of 1917 that the Ukrainians would soon be demanding independent

---

* In general, Dmowski was prone to resentment on many scores. Thus, for example, he believed in the existence of some worldwide German-Jewish-Masonic-socialist conspiracy, endowed with an almost clairvoyant capacity for intrigue, that took advantage of the smallest opportunity anywhere on the globe to harm Poland. With regard to "German support for the Ukrainians," he was convinced (*Polityka polska*, p. 311) that Germany had intended to establish a Ukrainian state as one of its protectorates ever since the end of the nineteenth century. Elsewhere (ibid., p. 74) he writes that "The draft of the Treaty of Brest-Litovsk as one of the possible ways of resolving the Polish question in the event of a war with Russia must already have been worked out, at least in general outline, and must have been ready in Berlin by the year 1907." "Naturally, there were also other drafts," he adds sagely. He even went so far—and here his thinking borders on the pathological—as to maintain (ibid., pp. 336–37) that the Ukrainian student Myroslav Sichynsky, who shot the Galician governor, Count Andrzej Potocki, in 1908, was "the executor of Berlin's large-scale plans" and consequently was not hanged but spared in order to make possible his subsequent escape from prison in Stanyslaviv to the United States.

statehood came true at the beginning of 1918, he and the rest of the National Democrats immediately began a most persistent campaign against the emergence of an independent Ukrainian state—a campaign based on Dmowski's memoranda of 1917 as just outlined. The peace of Brest-Litovsk gave apparent confirmation to his view that Germany had always wanted to create a Ukrainian state in order to encircle Poland, so now Dmowski counterposed to this encirclement the idea of partitioning Ukraine between Poland and Russia. This idea, first suggested by Dmowski in April 1917, was now given explicit formulation by the National Committee in Paris in its decision of 28 February 1918 to oppose Ukrainian statehood at all costs, so that Poland could not be threatened from the east in its struggle with Germany. According to this resolution, "the security of the Lithuanian and Ruthenian lands to the east of Poland against the threat, direct or indirect, of German domination can only be guaranteed if Poland and Russia have a common border and if, in view of the impossibility of establishing a truly independent Ukrainian or Lithuanian state, these lands are brought under Polish and Russian instead of German influence."[150]

From then on the Polish National Democrats followed this line without regard to the changes that were taking place in Eastern Europe. In October 1918 the Hetman government was still in place in Ukraine; because of the defeat of the Central Powers and its coalition with the Russian counterrevolution, this regime was seeking increasingly to ally itself with the Entente. The Hetman government was also preparing for a decisive struggle with the Bolsheviks, in which it could almost certainly rely on the support of the Entente. But the Polish National Democrats, in their dealings with the Entente, ignored the fact that this existing state was no longer pro-German and sought instead to frustrate any attempt to construct a power center in Ukraine, regardless of where the Ukrainians stood in relation to Russia, with the result that the collapse of the Hetman government objectively paved the way for the victory of Bolshevism in Ukraine and corresponded completely to the Polish desire to annihilate Ukraine.

The Dmowski memorandum given to President Wilson on 8 October 1918 initiated a campaign intended to discredit Ukraine in the eyes of the Entente and win the latter to the idea of partitioning Ukraine between Poland and Russia.[151] The memorandum, which dealt with the territorial extension of the future Polish state, contained all the arguments against Ukraine that were used from then on in every Polish note to the Entente and in every piece of Polish propaganda. The tenacity with which the Poles carried out this campaign was devastating to the Ukrainian cause, especially in Western Ukraine. "The Ruthenian-speaking population," says the memorandum in relation to the Polish claim to all of Galicia, "lives in Eastern Galicia, where Poles make up only 25 percent of the population. A Ruthenian national movement, sometimes also known as Ukrainian, developed in Eastern Galicia in the second half of the last century. It was supported from the beginning by the Austrian government, which saw in it a means of weakening Poland. For the same reason, Berlin has readily supported this movement for the past fifteen years." This image of "Austria and Germany playing off the Ruthenians against the Poles," in which the Poles appeared as the injured party, was given the greatest emphasis. It was later claimed that the Western Ukrainian army had been created by the Austrians and supported by the Germans. It is easy to imagine how the feelings of the Entente were aroused against Ukraine when we remember the kind of propaganda that was so widespread during the war and made the Germans so hated in almost the entire world. "The Ruthenian leaders," continues the memorandum, "demand the separation of Eastern Galicia from Poland on the grounds that most of the population is Ruthenian. We must realize, however, that this Ruthenian national movement, the existence of which we do not dispute, has not penetrated the great mass of the Ruthenian population, which is largely uneducated and indifferent to nationalism, nor has it created a strong and independent educated stratum. Official statistics show that in all the trades and professions in Eastern Galicia, with the exception of small landowners, the Ruthenians make up less than 5 percent. Under such circumstances it is difficult to see how the Ruthenians could govern the country. If under Austrian rule the government of Eastern Galicia is in the hands of the Poles, it is not because Austria wants it that way but because there is no other element in the country capable of taking on this role."

This argument about the political incapacity of the Western Ukrainians was later accompanied by horror stories directed against them by the Poles during the Polish-Ukrainian war, as well as by the claim that the Western Ukrainians had allied themselves with the Moscow Bolsheviks. There were only very limited possibilities of testing these Polish claims, as Western Ukraine was practically cut off from the rest of the world. No one in Western Europe had any great knowledge of those far-off East European lands; hence even the claim that Austria only reluctantly used the Poles to govern Eastern Galicia appeared credible. The suggestive power of this Polish propaganda must have been immense, considering how persistently, doggedly and systematically it was promoted by a network of Polish organizations that extended almost around the world.

The final link in this chain of arguments was the Polish claim that the Western Ukrainians had no reason to fear any injustice at the hands of the Poles or any attempt at Polonization. According to various speakers at the session of the National Committee held on 2 March 1919,* "the territories we want to acquire in the east are essential for Polish expansion, but, of course, we cannot say this to the Peace Conference.... The eastern territories are our colonies. That has always been their status to some extent, and so it should remain.... When, among ourselves, we talk of our eastern borders, we know that the territories not settled by Poles today will in fact be settled by us in a short period of time.... If we succeed in implementing the committee's plans and acquire a large territory in the east that we can merge with Poland through a process of Polonization, then we will have brought about a situation in which we can push even farther eastwards and, in a few decades, reach our historical borders." But Dmowski's presentation to Wilson was somewhat different: "At least for the near future, the Polish administration [in Eastern Galicia] is the only possible one that can guarantee the normal development and progress of this country. The national aspirations of the Ruthenians must be satisfied, and this will be done by granting them complete freedom in their national culture, by recognizing the official status of the Ruthenian language, by having Ruthenian classes in the schools, and so on. But as long as the Ruthenian nationality is at an embryonic stage, and as long as the level of Ruthenian intellectual life is too low to permit the creation of a progressive modern Ruthenian government, Eastern Galicia must remain an inseparable part of the Polish state." These promises were later strengthened by undertakings to grant Eastern Galicia territorial autonomy, and this argument was so convincing that Wilson was won over and later, at the Paris Peace Conference, strongly supported the incorporation of Eastern Galicia into Poland.[152]

Polish territorial claims in Eastern Ukraine were argued with equal ingenuity. "In the last fifty years," maintained Dmowski in his presentation to Wilson, "there has been a certain degree of literary activity among the Ukrainians, combined with a rather feeble movement for political separation [from Great Russia]. This movement, however, was limited almost exclusively to university students, mostly sons of the clergy and peasants. It remains too underdeveloped to have produced a strong intellectual stratum among the Ukrainians. If Germany recognized the Ukrainian nation in the Treaty of Brest-Litovsk, this was not out of any consideration for international justice but simply out of a desire to defeat

* These are the statements of Antoni Sujkowski, Menard Downarowicz, Count Jan Żółtowski, and Joachim Bartoszewicz (*Akty i dokumenty*, 1: 82, 94, 100).

Russia and diminish Poland. Germany did this with full awareness that the Ukrainian state could not be truly independent and would inevitably come under a German protectorate.... Poland is too weak at the moment to rule successfully over all the [historically Polish] eastern provinces. Given that there is no other sufficiently strong cultural element in those provinces, the question of their political future is an almost insoluble problem. The formation of an independent Lithuanian or Ukrainian state would mean either anarchy or foreign—in this case, German—rule. The return of those provinces to Russia would mean no less anarchy and the stagnation of intellectual and economic life. The reestablishment of Polish rule in those territories [to the borders of 1771] would be too great a task for the Polish state and would deprive it of unity. Such unity is essential to any state, but especially to Poland, which has Germany as its immediate neighbor. There is no adequate solution to this problem, and we must choose the solution that appears to have the least disadvantage. Such a solution would be the division of the territory of the eastern Polish provinces into two parts. The western part, where the Polish population is more numerous and Polish influence predominates, should belong to the Polish state. The eastern part should remain a possession of Russia. This would give Poland a border somewhat farther east of that established by the second partition (of 1793)."

This way of presenting the argument was incredibly astute. The National Democrats realized that the Polish borders of 1771 took in too much Ukrainian territory and that there was no real chance of their being able to control them. It was also clear that the Entente, especially England and America, would not be won over with a mere historical argument. A clear and simple formulation of the Polish claim would make the whole problem appear rather too plain, and an equally clear case could then be made for another solution, namely, that the Ukrainians, especially in Eastern Galicia, should have their right to national self-determination and be given a free hand to establish a state on their own territory. But if the Ukrainians' ability to establish their own state could be put into serious doubt and, at the same time, the disadvantages of giving the territory between ethnic Poland and the Dnipro either entirely to the Poles or entirely to the Russians could be demonstrated, then the whole problem would become so clouded as to appear insoluble and, in practice, Poland would have a free hand to divide this territory with Russia, however well it might come off. Such an argument also had the appearance of complete objectivity. "The territorial program described herein," continued Dmowski for Wilson's benefit, "is not the expression of a desire for national expansion, nor is it dictated by any hostile attitude toward Poland's neighbors. There is no nation in Europe more interested in the establishment of a firm and lasting peace after the present war than Poland. Poland suffered not only throughout this world war but also from the war waged throughout the whole previous century by those who oppressed the Polish movement. Poland is now faced with a massive creative task, that of healing the wounds of war, reestablishing economic prosperity, raising the standard of its people's education, organizing its political life according to modern principles, and becoming a healthy, creative democracy capable of surviving, prospering, and contributing to the well-being of all mankind."

Polish claims in Eastern Galicia did not therefore amount to a mere border dispute, as in the case of Poland's conflict with Czechoslovakia over Cieszyn (Těšín). What was at issue here was the complete destruction of Ukrainian aspirations toward statehood; the complete frustration of any attempt to establish, out of the rubble of the world war, any kind of Ukrainian state alongside Poland. Polish diplomats at the Paris Peace Conference therefore demanded not only Eastern Galicia but also the greater part of Volhynia and western Podilia, with Proskuriv (Khmelnytskyi) and Kamianets-Podilskyi. Dmowski presented those demands verbally to the Supreme Council on 29 January 1919.[153] They were also contained in the Polish delegation's note of 28 February (or 3 March) 1919 to the Commission on Polish Affairs, which was established by the Peace Conference.[154]

As clever as these activities of Dmowski were, they were completely lacking in foundation by 1919. In other words, it was not the case that Ukraine, under all circumstances, would be hostile to Poland and therefore had to be partitioned between Poland and Russia. If the Hetman State, within the borders it had at the time of the German occupation, had been able to survive in alliance with the Central Powers, and if Ukraine had won its independence from Russia on the field of battle, and if it had then formed a close diplomatic, military and economic alliance with Russia, as the Hetman State indeed wanted, then such a major power might well have been a threat to Poland, allying itself with Germany in order to force Poland back to its own ethnic territories. But with the collapse of the Hetman government, it was clear that the Ukrainians would not be able to keep their whole territory; at best, they might establish a rump state in the western Ukrainian lands extending, at most, to the Dnipro. What role such a rump state would play in Eastern Europe was made dramatically manifest in the first months of 1919: it gave Poland effective protection against the rest of Eastern Europe and, thanks to this protection alone, Poland was able to proceed undisturbed in the task of establishing its own state organization. This was no accidental episode. A Ukrainian rump state between Poland and the Dnipro would exercise an ongoing pull on Eastern Ukraine on the Left Bank, whether the latter was under Bolshevik, democratic or reactionary Russian rule. Such a state would find itself bogged down in a long-term conflict with Russia, with no end in sight. Under those circumstances, whether the Ukrainians loved or hated the Poles, such a rump state would be forced sooner or later to seek support from Romania or Poland, as Petliura attempted later, in 1920. Such a Ukrainian state could only become a dependency of Poland and not of Germany, as Dmowski believed, no matter how friendly the Ukrainians were toward the Germans. By absorbing the pressure from the rest of Russian-dominated Eastern Europe and providing a protective shield for Poland, a Ukrainian rump state would strengthen Poland in its relations with Germany and, within the European continent as a whole, promote Franco-Polish rather than German domination.

There was a brief moment in February 1919, as we will show in greater detail later, when the French general staff recognized the true situation in Ukraine. To this real situation, however, Dmowski remained blind. The experience of the first three months of 1919 demonstrated the inadequacy of Dmowski's plans for the partition of Ukraine. The course of events themselves made it possible for Poland to achieve a much more effective destruction of Ukraine: a division not into two but into three parts. Such a tripartite division would be as follows: western Volhynia and the western part of Eastern Galicia, including Lviv, would go to Poland; the rest of Eastern Galicia and Volhynia, along with Podilia, would be part of a Ukrainian rump state; and the rest of Eastern Ukraine would go to Russia. This arrangement would not only give Poland long-term protection from the East but also eliminate any Ukrainian danger for an indeterminate period, since no part of Ukraine would then be strong enough to emerge as a threat to Poland. The western part annexed by Poland would not be strong enough to withstand Polonization, while the rump state would not be able to take the rest of Ukraine from Russia, and Eastern Ukraine on the Left Bank of the Dnipro would succumb completely to Russia. But Dmowski did not recognize any of this.

Thus the Dmowski program contained neither real insight into the play of forces in Eastern Europe nor the moderation required for statesmanlike thinking. It was the product of a basically unpolitical and rigorously dogmatic frame of mind, inadequate not only in its presuppositions but also in its dogmatic expectations. For it failed to take into account that whether the Ukrainian movement gained strength under Russian rule or fell prey to Russification, the part of Ukraine remaining with Russia would necessarily constitute an ongoing and exceptionally serious threat to Poland. It would always be open to a strongly developing Ukrainian movement to ally itself with Russia against Poland, just as Dmowski himself and his National Democrats had made common cause with Russia against the Germans. For the Ukrainians could always turn the tables on the Poles and, in place of a Polish-Russian deal to keep down Ukraine, create a Russo-Ukrainian alliance for the destruction of Poland. That is how the partition of historical Poland began in the seventeenth century. The idea for it came from the great Ukrainian Cossack hetman Bohdan Khmelnytsky, and the partition of Poland in the eighteenth century was the expression not of a Muscovite but of a Ukrainian historical conception. If the Eastern Ukrainian movement were to succumb to Russification, then this new "all-Russian" nation, a Great Russian-Ukrainian political and cultural entity, would be a real threat to Poland, just as it was to Austria in 1914. Moreover, Dmowski greatly underestimated the political goals of Moscow. Under the Bolsheviks, a permanent Polish-Muscovite alliance was ruled out entirely, and Polish-Muscovite relations in general were reduced to short-term agreements from one case to another. What did Poland have to gain from forcing thirty million Ukrainians into the camp of such an unpredictable power as was, at this time, the Bolshevik Golden Horde?

Meanwhile, whether Dmowski understood the situation in Ukraine rightly or wrongly, whether the success of this diplomacy would really be to Poland's advantage or not, it was Dmowski's diplomatic activity within the Entente that was the real enemy of Ukraine, and it was now the Entente that would decide the outcome of the Polish-Ukrainian war in Eastern Galicia. Dmowski's diplomatic activity was guided by two goals, the destruction of Germany and the destruction of Ukraine. He pursued them by attempting to draw the future Poland's borders in the east and in the west in such a way as to do the greatest damage to both Germany and Ukraine. Every other aspect of Polish diplomacy in Eastern Europe was determined by its effect on the Ukrainian question, and the whole inner and outer structure of the contemporary Polish state is determined by its attitude to Ukraine as much as by its attitude to Germany. After the understanding between the National Committee and the Warsaw government, there were two different conceptions in the committee. The National Democrats wanted a unified Polish state with the Polonization of the annexed territories, while Piłsudski, some of the Polish socialists, and the Cracow conservatives wanted a Polish-Lithuanian federation. A meeting of the National Committee on 2 March

1919 was to decide this question and determine which territories should be annexed by Poland. "If we apply the federative idea to Lithuania," said one speaker, "then we will have to apply it to Ruthenia as well, and that will lose us Eastern Galicia."[155] Dmowski's program for a unified state was better adapted to Poland's interests, said another speaker, "because it solves the Ruthenian question favorably, as the federative policy does not. There are not many Poles who would want a Ruthenian state as a partner in any federation." The desire to stop the emergence of a Ukrainian state was overwhelming, and the idea of a unified state won the day, even though it meant the loss of the Lithuanian region of Kowno (Kaunas).

The only thing that now remained for the committee to decide was the precise shape of Poland's eastern border. The Warsaw federalists coopted onto the committee wanted to cut more cloth than the master tailor, Dmowski himself. It was the latter who established the general task: "Between the very strong German nation on the one side and highly anarchic Russia on the other, we must strive to become a greater nation than we are" through the Polonization of the Ukrainians and Belarusians.[156] This diplomacy did not set itself tasks that the Polish nation was already in a position to carry out, but, concerned to eliminate Ukraine, it sought to increase the Polish population in order to fill out the territory that would be "tailored" for Poland. Dmowski advised caution: "Of course, it would be good to have everything, but that is not possible. Let us not make the mistake that brought about the downfall of the Russian state. It was a characteristic of this state that its appetite was too big for its stomach. It had a craving for more than it could digest. I know that we, too, have an appetite, but we are a Western people and know how to control our cravings. These cravings must be controlled, or else we will create for coming generations a fatherland that they will not be able to keep, just as the Russians could not keep theirs, for they had too great an appetite."[157] This "moderation of cravings," since a smaller number of Ukrainians would be easier to Polonize, led Dmowski to demand significantly more for the Polish state than it possesses today: almost all of Volhynia and western Podilia, with Kamianets-Podilskyi and Proskuriv. The controversy about "cravings" led to general agreement on a Polish great power whose size corresponded to Dmowski's "appetite."

It was the Paris Peace Conference that was now to make the final decisions about Polish "cravings" and the fate of Eastern Galicia, and thus on the existence or nonexistence of the Ukrainian state of 1919. This decision was entirely in the hands of the Supreme Council, the joint organ of the United States, England, France, Italy, and Japan. It was chaired by

Georges Clemenceau, and its members were President Wilson, Prime Minister Lloyd George, Prime Minister Vittorio Orlando, two Japanese delegates, and the foreign ministers of the other four powers: Robert Lansing, Arthur Balfour, Stéphen Pichon, and Sidney Sonnino. In March 1919, this "Committee of Ten" turned into the "Committee of Four," the "big four": Wilson, Clemenceau, Orlando, and Lloyd George.[158]

On 22 January 1919 the Supreme Council decided to send an inter-Allied mission to Poland to carry out an on-the-spot investigation,[159] and this mission, chaired by the French ambassador Joseph Noulens, left for Poland on 29 January 1919, following Dmowski's submission to the Supreme Council.[*] In Paris itself, a Commission on Polish Affairs was established to look into Polish claims; it, too, was chaired by a Frenchman, Jules Cambon.[**] On 1 March 1919 this commission established a subcommission chaired by yet another Frenchman, General Henri Le Rond, to work out the details concerning Poland's borders.[***] In spite of differences of opinion in the Supreme Council, both commissions took a favorable view of Polish claims.[160]

The situation of the Poles at the Peace Conference was as follows: Poland was an allied nation of the Entente, an officially recognized Entente state whose restitution had become one of the principal war aims of the whole Entente; Polish diplomacy and propaganda had an extremely active organization covering the whole of Western Europe and the United States, with important connections and influence in the public bodies of the Entente and extensive financial resources; Polish claims were supported unconditionally by France and, in almost all cases, by the United States; in the other Entente states, with England at the bottom of the ladder, Polish attempts at winning influence were very successful; the working commissions that prepared the decisions of the Supreme Council were entirely favorable to Poland. There was one other much weaker party in this diplomatic game, that of the Western Ukrainians.

---

* The other members of the mission were General Henri Niessel (France), Major General F. J. Kernan and Professor Robert H. Lord (United States), Sir Esme Howard and Brigadier General A. Carton de Wiart (England), and G. C. Montagna and General Romei Donghena (Italy) (Kozicki, *Sprawa granic Polski*, p. 62).

** The other members of the commission were Dr. Isaiah Bowman (United States), Sir William Tyrrell (England), Marquis Pietro della Torretta (Italy), and Kentaro Otchiai (Japan). The secretariat of the commission consisted of Lieutenant G. de Percin (France), Stewart Montgomery (United States), Colonel F. H. Kisch (England), and G. Brambilla (Italy) (Kozicki, *Sprawa granic Polski*, p. 62).

*** The other members of the subcommission were Dr. Bowman (United States) and Colonel Kisch (England) (Kozicki, *Sprawa granic Polski*, p. 63).

2. *Ukrainian Diplomacy and the Entente Powers*

The passivity of Western Ukraine's foreign policy in relation to both Poland and Eastern Ukraine can be explained by its trust in the Entente's solemnly proclaimed policy of the "right of national self-determination." The Western Ukrainians feared, in fact, that they might weaken their case if they pursued too aggressive a foreign policy, especially by negotiating directly with Poland. They assumed that the Entente would decide on the question of their borders by a process of arbitration and would then keep the Poles out; in other words, that the Entente would create a Western Ukrainian state, just as it had in the cases of the Poles and Czechs. For this to happen, however, two preconditions were required. First, it was essential that the Entente recognize the Ukrainians, at least the Western Ukrainians, as a politically developed nation. Second, one of the Entente powers would have to consider the establishment of an independent Western Ukrainian state sufficiently advantageous to itself to be willing to take up the Western Ukrainian cause and defend it with all its might against the "appetites" of the Poles, as France had done for the Czechs in the case of Těšín and England for the Germans over the question of Danzig. Both these preconditions, however, were lacking.

An English historian formulated the general attitude of the Entente toward Poland as follows: "On the central point all the Powers were agreed—that it was necessary to establish a Polish state and to establish it with a real chance of existence, that is to say with the greatest possible stability and strength. Opinions differed only as to the manner in which Poland could be made most strong and most stable."[161] On the other pan of the scales, however, which was to contain something in favor of the Western Ukrainians to balance the concretely perceived Polish reality, there lay something nebulous, an item of special knowledge possessed by Entente experts on Eastern Europe—the "Ukrainian question." This was something new to the Entente and aroused its suspicions: before 1917 or even the Brest-Litovsk treaty of 1918, who had ever heard of any "Ukraine"? To be sure, the Entente's hopes of making the Hetman State a base from which to fight the Bolsheviks had given some concrete reality to their idea of Ukraine, but in December 1918 those hopes proved false, and Ukraine became once again the "Ukrainian question," as it had been in 1917.

Even Dmowski, a ferocious enemy of Ukraine, did greater justice to the "Ukrainian question" than the nonpartisan experts of the Entente. In his memorandum of 1917 to Balfour he played down the political ability of the Ukrainians but recognized, at least, that they were a different people from the Russians, that the Ukrainian national movement was an unstoppable development, and that at some time in the future the Ukrainians might be capable of establishing their own national state. But as late as 1923 the English historian cited above, who was rather well disposed to the Western Ukrainians, still believed that a particular Ukrainian national consciousness was a myth and that such a thing could only come about if it were created by the Poles. "The feeling of nationality may be specially dangerous in this case because in spite of artificial attempts to regard it as distinct from and opposed to the Russian, as well as the Polish, nationality, it may at any moment in the case of the White and Little Russians become merged in a general Pan-Russian movement. The Russians themselves regard these people as simply branches of the one Russian people, and, apart from the Poles and the Ruthenian leaders in Galicia, it is difficult to find any large body of people who take a different view. The Poles might possibly have been able to develop a non-Polish, non-Russian national feeling in these areas, but the chances were heavily against their being successful, and there is little doubt that at the present time such a feeling is relatively insignificant."[162]

If it was possible to express such views in a work on the Paris Peace Conference published in 1923 with the support of the Foreign Office, then how much murkier this "Ukrainian question" must have been at the time of the Peace Conference itself in 1919! For the Entente powers, the meaning of the "Ukrainian question" was, first and foremost, whether there existed any Ukrainian ethnicity that could be distinguished from the Russian. In Entente diplomacy, Eastern Ukrainian interests were hindered not so much by the Polish National Democrats as by Russian reactionary forces—this despite the fact that in the uprising against the hetman this Russian reaction was defeated and smashed into a thousand pieces not by the Bolsheviks but by socially radical Ukrainian nationalists.

The situation with regard to the Western Ukrainians was of course somewhat different. It was all too obvious that the "Ruthenians" did not want to belong to Poland, so that there was no possibility of considering them part of the Polish nation in the way that the "Little Russians" were thought to be part of the Russian nation. It was also known that linguistically the Ruthenians and the Little Russians belonged together. But because the Ruthenians were considered more highly developed than the Little Russians, they were dealt with separately from the latter, as if they were a small newly emerging national entity. As the national particularity of the Western Ukrainians was now no longer denied, this attitude tallied with that of Dmowski. Just as the attitude of the Entente toward Eastern Ukraine was decisively influenced by the Russian reactionaries, so it was the Polish National Democrats who became the sole source of information for the Entente concerning the "Ruthenians."

Another factor that worked against the Ukrainians, especially the Western Ukrainians, was the unfortunate attitude of the Entente "specialists." They did not take into account that the nationality question in the East required an altogether different set of criteria from what they were used to applying in Western Europe, and that in times of revolutionary upheaval hidden nationalities can come into view anywhere. But the scholarly advisers on Eastern Europe, drawn into the "peace work," operated within a framework of assumptions established in the nineteenth century, according to which there were only two powers in Eastern Europe: Russia and Poland. To now recognize three, albeit unequal, nations in Eastern Europe—Russia, Poland and Ukraine—would have meant coming to terms with those erroneous assumptions. It seemed predetermined, therefore, that the views of the Russian reactionaries and the Polish National Democrats would be confirmed and strengthened by the authority of the scholarly experts. It was therefore no accident that if anyone among the Entente personalities regarded Ukraine and the Ukrainian national movement as real, it was not the experts but the soldiers.

Professor Robert Howard Lord, one of Wilson's most trusted advisers and perhaps the most pernicious of the Peace Conference specialists in Central European and German affairs, may have believed that his own erudition, exalted far above any doubt, was the sole source of expertise available to Wilsonian justice, but in practice he was nothing more than a mouthpiece for the views expressed in Dmowski's memoranda, notes and conversations. Although Dmowski, as an interested party, might not have been entirely trusted in this matter, who could doubt the word of an expert? It was one of the greatest misfortunes for the Ukrainians at the Paris Peace Conference that the Entente experts were capable only of confirming and reinforcing the tendentious views of the Poles and Russians.

If we compare the opinions cited above, those of Harold W. Temperley in his book on the Peace Conference with the views of Robert Lord in 1920, then it would be reasonable to claim that those views represented the common viewpoint of the Entente experts on the "Ruthenian" question. Lord went even further than Dmowski:

> During the five or six centuries in which the two races have lived side by side, their relations have on the whole been relatively satisfactory and amicable. To a large extent they are

> so still, whenever the politicians do not intervene, as is shown, for instance, by the high percentage of mixed marriages. In the nineteenth century, however, a nationalist movement grew up among the Ruthenians, which assumed a marked anti-Polish tendency and which has led to the rather bitter racial feud that has raged in Eastern Galicia in the past thirty years. It is likely that this contest would never have assumed so fierce a character had it not been for the insidious activities of the Austrian government, which lost no opportunity to stir up the two races against each other, aiding now one and then the other in accordance with the traditional Austrian maxim, "divide and rule." In the last twenty years the German government has also taken an active hand in the affair, secretly exciting and aiding the Ruthenians against the Poles; for the latter were always *the* enemy for Berlin, and decades before Brest-Litovsk German statesmen appreciated the possibilities of the "Ukrainian idea," which might be used with equal effect against both Russia and Poland.[163]

But perhaps even more disastrous for Western Ukraine was the insidious activity of its own Russophiles, the miserable remnant of the once strong Russophile camp that had developed out of the Old Ruthenian movement in Eastern Galicia. In 1918 in Western Ukraine the situation with regard to Russophilism was such that even those who had remained most faithful to the old idea of all-Russian national unity, both those who had stayed in the country and those who had returned from Russia, admitted that they had gone wrong with that ideology. In practice, then, Russophilism was all but eradicated. Given that the Ukrainian national idea had triumphed so completely in the country itself, the few remaining Russophile leaders, still turning up now and then among the Russian reactionaries or settled in Paris, would seem not to have had much choice, in view of the hard-fought Western Ukrainian war with Poland, but fully to support the Ukrainian diplomatic effort in Paris or at least not to hinder it. For the main thing at that moment was that Western Ukraine stand up to Poland, and even if they did not want to give up any of their Russophile convictions, they could always postpone action on this issue until later, when Western Ukraine was victorious. They could then have taken up their campaign among the Western Ukrainians themselves and tried to convince them to give up their independent statehood and unite with Russia and the "all-Russian" nation. But this clique, defeated in their own country, now made Paris a showplace for their own intrigues, which they carried out with the support of the Russian reactionaries. Having failed to convince their own people, they now set about trying to convince the English, the French and the Americans. How insidious this attack was, and how treacherous not only against Western Ukraine, their own homeland, but even against the "all-Russian" movement itself, can be seen from the judgment of an English historian:

> The position of the Ruthenians was, however, enormously weakened in Paris by their own internal discord, which, as is seen in the past history of the Poles themselves, appears to be the special temptation of a defeated people. So far as can be judged the majority of the Ruthenian people pride themselves on their separate nationality and express a hostility to Great Russia second only to their hostility to the Poles. There is, however, a considerable minority lying chiefly along the slopes of the Carpathians and in certain other regions who are definitely pro-Russian and regard themselves as simply a branch of the one Russian race. Hence the representatives of Eastern Galicia came to Paris speaking with two voices, and this made it easier for their opponents to maintain that they were a people politically undeveloped and nationally ill-defined. Such uncertainty served in some quarters to confirm the Polish claim.
>
> Each party also laid itself open unnecessarily to a special argument—thus weakening its own case and distracting attention from the real situation. The Russophile party wished to bring Russia to the very summits of the Carpathians. Who, it was asked, could support the responsibility of causing such a menace to the stability of Europe, especially at a time when Russia was in the hands of the Bolsheviks? The Ruthenian or Ukrainian party, on the other hand, proclaimed their intention of acting as the "Piedmont" of Ukrainia, and of becoming a centre of propaganda in Russia on behalf of an independent Ukraine. Who would venture to set up such a storm-centre in the heart of Europe, a source of sedition and disruption for the Russian Empire? In this way by focussing attention not only on their own disunion, but also upon academic questions of no possible practical importance at the moment, the two parties allowed the fundamental contention upon which they were really united to become obscure, that it was contrary to every principle of self-determination to hand over three million people to the Polish State without securing for them the right to make some free and public expression of their will.[164]

The Western Ukrainian trust in the Entente was a serious error, but this action by the Russophiles was madness. After all, the Western Ukrainians did possess an army and a state organization and would have been able to manage quite well once Poland withdrew from their country. But the Russophiles insisted that the Entente should militarily occupy Western Ukraine and rule it until such time as Russia recovered and could take over responsibility.[165] The consequences of these fantastic views were all the more serious in that the Russophiles actually had access to the ears of the Entente diplomats via the well-known politicians and diplomats of the old Russian Empire. The Western Ukrainians, lacking the right social connections, found closed doors everywhere.

Given this situation, an expert like Lord had no lack of arguments to prove that his judgment of the "Ruthenian" question was perfectly correct. He argues further: "For a nation so backward in its development, so divided against itself, and so accustomed to look to Berlin and Vienna for aid and direction, the World War arrived at the wrong moment."[166] "If one might judge from the relative strength of the two Ruthenian parties as they existed before the war, the party which wanted an independent Ukrainian state might be a majority among the Ruthenians, but was only a minority in the total population."[167] In this manner the conclusion was reached, quite expertly, that even from the viewpoint of democracy there was no injustice in the later Polish annexation of Eastern Galicia. There was no Ukrainian nation in this country, only a "Ukrainian party" that was, after all, a mere minority of the Eastern Galician population. But that is not all. Lord even ventured to conclude that the Polish conquest of Eastern Galicia was in fact a liberation of that country. "The majority of the population—Poles, Jews, and Ruthenians alike—were relieved when this government collapsed and the Polish troops came in."[168]

If such was the dominant attitude toward the Ukrainian question, then any kind of direct observation was unlikely, in the nature of things, to change it. At the beginning of 1919 the internal situation in Poland, the effectiveness of its government, was much worse than in Western Ukraine. But the Poles were a universally known historical nation and, however bad the conditions in their country, no one was really concerned. It was considered an insignificant, transitory crisis, not a sign of Poland's incapacity for independent statehood. But from the very beginning, the Entente missions and agents that came to Western Ukraine were only interested in defects. Only if they could find none would they allow themselves, against their inclinations, to be convinced by the Western Ukrainians. But in their "on the spot" studies in Western Ukraine they generally listened only to the local Poles, which made their trips quite superfluous. There were, in addition, the imponderables of the personal well-being of those Entente tourists. With relief, even joy, they left this rather gray Western Ukraine to return to the delights of Warsaw. Polish hospitality and noblesse were on a par with those of the great Western nations. The Western Ukrainians, on the other hand, weighed down by so many troubles, were gloomy, hard, perhaps even socially tactless at times. The Poles were masters of the dashing parade. Among the Western Ukrainians, however, one saw only hulking great barbarians. Such subsequent confirmation of a preèstablished opinion is admitted by Lord. "It was rather doubtful, moreover, whether the Ruthenians were capable of taking over the government of the country. They had had no independent state for nearly six hundred years, and their national development had been so retarded and unsatisfactory that it was not easy to believe that they were fitted for independent statehood today. Where were the elements on which a viable state could be constructed? Such elements were not to be found in the ignorant and inarticulate masses of the peasants nor in the small class of intellectuals. These intellectuals had already given the measure of their ability: for six months they had tried to run a government, and the result—nearly all the many Allied officers who were sent in to study the situation were unanimous in the opinion that this Ukrainian government had been, to put it mildly, a sorry failure."[169]

An additional factor in all this was the not incorrect perception that one had in Europe of Eastern Ukraine after the fall of the Hetman government. This perception was expressed clearly by Lloyd George in his discussion with the Allies in December 1918 about the guidelines of Entente policy in Eastern Europe. The Hetman government had appeared to the Entente to be an alliance-worthy state, but after its collapse the Entente statesmen regarded Eastern Ukraine as a place of anarchy infested with robber bands, a space perhaps for the eventual colonial expansion of the Western powers. At best, in the event that some kind of Ukrainian rump state did come into being, it would be a semi-colonial dependency open to foreign dictate and interference in its internal affairs. "The allies had counted," said Lloyd George to Clemenceau, "on the establishment of a firm government in Ukraine, but then we saw how this adventurer, Petliura, at the head of a few thousand men, managed to overthrow that government with the greatest of ease. This uprising was Bolshevik in character, and its success showed clearly that Ukraine was not the solid front against Bolshevism that we had assumed it to be. What had happened in Great Russia was now beginning to be copied in Ukraine."[170]

Since the Western Ukrainians lacked the strength to intervene in Eastern Ukraine during the period of Petliura's government so as to establish a firm state order there, their own position vis-à-vis the Entente deteriorated even more. The failure of the Eastern Ukrainians was seen as proof of the political inability of the Ukrainian movement as a whole and, as such, was used against the Western Ukrainians.

In view of all these circumstances, it is amazing that not all but only the great majority of the Entente envoys shared Lord's opinion of the Western Ukrainians' state-building capacities. One of those who did not was an American officer, General F. J. Kernan, who took the trouble to travel independently in March 1919 throughout much of Poland and part of Western Ukraine. He was surprised to discover that the Western Ukrainians were by no means as bad as the description of the Entente envoys, isolated in Warsaw, had led him to believe. What those descriptions had been like can be visualized when we read his report to President Wilson, written on 11 April 1919: "The distinct impression I brought away from Eastern Galicia was that the Ukrainians were exceedingly anxious for a truce and that their leaders were intelligent men by no means Bolshevik.... Besides my own observations I talked with quite a number of disinterested observers who had been travelling through the Ukraine quite recently and as a result I am convinced that the present Ukrainian Government and the Ukrainians in the mass are by no means Bolshevik.... The Ukrainians are wholly isolated from Europe and they have, I believe, been misrepresented in a large degree to the world, it being the policy of their enemies to denounce them as bandits and Bolsheviks. Reiterated statements of this kind have their effect, however groundless they may be."[171] However strongly General Kernan might want to correct the conceptions that were dominant at the time, those conceptions were and remained even more unfavorable to the Western Ukrainians than the judgments of such experts as Lord, both among the average politically interested and active citizens of the Entente countries and among the Entente missions operating in Eastern Europe. They were similar to the perceptions people had had fifty years earlier about Albania. The Western Ukrainians had the respect and sympathy of individual English front officers who had had some experience of the Western Ukrainian frontline troops, but that had no effect.[172]

Thus the first precondition for their receiving justice at the hands of Wilson was not fulfilled, namely, that the Entente should regard them as a politically and nationally developed people. For the Entente, the Ukrainian people and their national movement were a *quantité négligeable*. Of course, it was highly damaging to the Western Ukrainian cause that in the war they had been on the side of the Central Powers,[173] but this had been so insignificant to the Entente that it even hesitated to hold that circumstance against them. As Lord said, "as to the Galician Ukrainians, Paris could never quite make up its mind whether to count them as friends, enemies, or neutrals."[174]

Meanwhile, the specialists and reporters did not decide what was to become of Ukraine but only what weight to give the Ukrainian question in the political deliberations of the Entente. That decision lay with the Entente politicians. Conditions at the front or rear for General Kolchak or even General Denikin might have been much worse than they were for Petliura—indeed, that was the case in Siberia—and the Entente may even have reckoned with the defeat of those Russian leaders. But they were seen as representatives of Russia, and no one doubted the ability of Russia itself ultimately to overcome even the most severe internal crisis and become once again a powerful empire. In the event of a victory for Kolchak or Denikin, Russia would have some value as an ally. In the reports on Ukraine, the Entente politicians were not interested in academic judgments as to whether the Ukrainians were a nationality distinct from the Russians. Their only concern was the practical political question of whether the Ukrainians, those "adventurers wanting to be a nation," would ever assert themselves sufficiently to organize a state, with or without help from the outside, and whether such a state could be allowed to develop into a power strong enough to merit consideration as an ally. Since the judgment of the experts was so unfavorable to Ukraine, the attitude of the Entente politicians to the Ukrainians was completely different from the one they adopted toward Kolchak or Denikin. The Ukrainians were not considered reliable allies but only instruments or spoils. If the "Ukrainian adventurers" failed to be of any use in the momentary pursuit of some goal by the individual Entente powers, then they could be denied any assistance and confidently abandoned as loot for neighboring countries. If it turned out that the Ukrainians could be of some use in achieving a particular goal, then they could be "supported" for a while with weapons, regardless of what might happen to them later—whether they asserted themselves as a state or perished in spite of the "support" offered them.

In such a situation it made little difference what kind of diplomatic activity the Ukrainians pursued in Paris to ensure that Ukraine would become at least an instrument and not an object of booty. Do as they might, it was not their astuteness that would decide the question but rather the general attitude of the Entente powers toward Eastern Europe. It is this general attitude that we shall now discuss.

It is of course premature, before the Entente archives are made accessible, to make absolutely reliable judgments about the details*—some of them extremely important—of the policies of the individual Entente powers at the Paris Peace Conference. At this stage we are dependent on the revelations of individual Entente politicians and on our knowledge of the facts themselves, the background to which is not always entirely clear. It does seem possible, however, even now, to produce a fairly accurate picture of what happened in Paris.

The Ukrainian question was part of two major international political problems: the future of Germany and that of Russia. Both these issues dominated the tension that existed between England and France despite all the sentiments arising from their alliance in the war. If French goals were consistent and clear, English policy toward the European continent had never perhaps been more vacillating and unreliable than it was at the Paris Peace Conference.[175] Although the English were totally united in their goal of English naval dominance and the greatest possible expansion of their colonial power,[176] they were deeply divided on their policy toward Germany and Russia. Leading English politics at the time were the Liberals with Lloyd George at their head. But the Liberals were not much stronger than the Conservatives, represented by Lord George Curzon and Winston Spencer Churchill. In order to stay in power, Lloyd George had to outbid now Liberals, now Conservatives with policies and slogans intended to win the greatest possible support both among the English public and in Parliament.[177] The Conservative camp saw the Germans, now as before, as the main danger to the British Empire. Expressed in simplest form, the policy of this camp was as follows: destroy Germany once and for all, as Rome once destroyed Carthage; complete economic independence for the British Empire, even if this meant the permanent impoverishment of Europe, by creating alternative markets and alternative sources for the supply of raw materials; complete self-sufficiency for England, even if this meant the long-term domination of the European continent by France.[178] In relation to Russia, the Conservative camp stood for the complete destruction of Bolshevism by the military forces of the Entente, as it was nurturing social dissatisfaction in England and throughout the world and was, at the same time, a potential ally for Germany.[179]

* Thus, for example, Margolin (*Ukraina i politika Antanty*, p. 120) considers that he has grounds for the assumption that by 1917 England and France had already concluded a secret agreement to partition Russia into their spheres of interest. According to the agreement, the Baltic region, northern Russia, the Caucasus, the Kuban region, and the eastern Don region were to be assigned to the English sphere of interest and Poland, Ukraine, the Crimea, and the western Don region to that of France. Not until the beginning of 1920, thinks Margolin, did certain indications appear that the agreement had been allowed to lapse, but he offers no evidence.

There was no place for Ukraine in this English Conservative scheme of things. This was not only because the English knew little about Ukraine apart from what they were told by Russian reactionaries.[180] It also seemed to the English Conservatives that the best prospect of defeating the Bolsheviks lay in the counterrevolutionary armed forces being put together by General Denikin in the Crimea and in the region of the Don and the Kuban. They did not want to interfere in the nationality problems of the Russian Empire. For them the most acute problem of the moment was Bolshevism, and everything else in Eastern Europe had to be subordinated to that question. Since Denikin's project appeared to be the most powerful anti-Bolshevik force, it seemed reasonable to the English to insist that the various nationalities or groups that were fighting the Bolsheviks, such as the Eastern Ukrainians, should unite under Denikin.[181] In spite of all the experts, the English realized, of course, that movements such as the one in Eastern Ukraine constituted a real force, but the solution they offered was typically English: such movements should unite under Denikin on the basis of a federal transformation of Russia.[182]

The Western Ukrainians fared little better under this approach. In order to keep down Germany, Poland was to be as large and powerful as possible, encompassing Germany's erstwhile eastern territory. But as the restitution of Russia was also eagerly awaited, the question of Poland's eastern border was put off to some time in the future, when the reestablished Russian Empire could be involved in the decision. As the Entente had been committed since the war to recognizing Russia's claim to Eastern Galicia, Western Ukraine was one of the disputed territories. No matter how much opinions may have differed, there was no question of energetically defending Western Ukraine against Polish claims. Western Ukraine itself was considered merely a provisional entity. For the time being, therefore, in spite of all theoretical considerations, the decision about Western Ukraine was simply left to the outcome of the Polish-Ukrainian war.[183] Neither Western nor Eastern Ukraine could expect any help from the English Conservatives.

With the Liberals it was quite a different matter. This camp, so firmly wedded to the capitalist prosperity of England, wanted, in addition to colonial acquisitions, to strengthen the English economy as rapidly as possible by means of the peace treaty. The views of this camp were so strongly colored by capitalist economic considerations that "In their eyes one of the greatest achievements of the war was the establishment of Great Britain's control over the oil-fields of Mesopotamia."[184] With reference to the English Liberals, an American historian has written that

"Great Britain was desperately anxious to get back on a sound economic basis."[185] "She wanted all the world economic power she could seize upon: she was keenly conscious of the dependence of the rest of Europe upon her; but, on the other hand, Germany and the other enemy countries—and Russia!—must at least be left alive economically, for British economic power was also tied up with European economic prosperity: how could Britain sell if no one had anything to buy with?"[186] For the English Liberals, therefore, the emergence of voracious nationalisms, either among the smaller groups now developing their own nation-states or among the expanding nations that exhibited militarism, attacked their weaker neighbors or attempted to create a general confusion out of which they could emerge as major powers, was a most unwelcome development. For "as long as they would not settle down, there could be no return to peace, and no revival of normal trade and commerce in which the British (and to a lesser degree the Americans) were vitally interested."[187]

For these reasons Liberal England attempted to placate Germany commercially as much as possible and make it economically dependent on England, especially against the Poles. If Polish "cravings" could be tempered and satisfied, and if Poland also could be made dependent on English capital, then Western Ukraine would have a certain value for the English. All the more so as Western Ukraine had petroleum resources that, although by no means major, were not without significance. It would be easier for the English to take control of them from a small and weak Western Ukraine than from a much stronger Poland supported by the French.[188] These capitalist economic considerations made their public appearance in the form of idealistic catchphrases such as "national self-determination," "peace and disarmament," and "freedom and the democratically expressed will of the people." To anticipate later developments, English considerations of this kind were the only point of support that the Western Ukrainians had in their diplomatic efforts to win over the Entente at the Paris Peace Conference. But however energetically Lloyd George supported the Western Ukrainians on occasion, this point of support was actually quite fragile. The French supported Poland exclusively for power-political reasons. For the sake of that power or, as the French themselves perceived it, for the sake of the very existence of France, the existence of a strong Poland was absolutely essential, even if the price were economic loss.[189] For the English, however, Western Ukraine was only a minor matter. Even Liberal England never intended to contest the whole of ethnically Ukrainian Eastern Galicia with Poland. It always took for granted that the western border of Eastern Galicia would be some line to the east of the Sian River. Thus, even when the English spoke of the "right of self-determination" of the Western Ukrainians, they still expected that significant border regions (including Przemyśl) in which Ukrainians constituted the majority would remain in Poland.[190] Since the British were interested only in capitalist economic considerations, they were always ready to drop the issue of Western Ukraine in return for some economic compensation or as soon as insistence on national self-determination appeared to offer fewer advantages than an alternative solution, even if this meant the Polish occupation of Eastern Galicia. This was clear from the fact that England did not strive for the establishment of an independent Western Ukrainian state but was only intent on keeping Eastern Galicia out of the hands of the Poles.[191] England was prepared to reserve this territory for Russia or turn it into some form of English-controlled mandate. The Western Ukrainians hung desperately onto Lloyd George, not realizing that his support was completely unreliable and not seeing that for England Western Ukraine was nothing more than an object of barter, not even a political entity. While the English did nothing to help them in their military struggle against the Poles, the Western Ukrainians, by maintaining their national defense, were doing everything possible to increase, as it were, their exchange value for England. The dispute between England and France over the question of Western Ukraine concerned nothing more than the question of whether France could obtain Eastern Galicia for the Poles without compensating England elsewhere or whether, as a price for Eastern Galicia, France would have to hand over to the English some tens or hundreds of thousands of Syrians, Arabs or Mesopotamians. The eventual publication of the Entente archives is almost certain to demonstrate the connection between the Eastern Galician question and the dispute between France and England over the colonies.

English liberalism offered even less to Eastern than to Western Ukraine. As in the case of Germany and Central Europe, so also with regard to Russia and Eastern Europe the English Liberals were only interested in the quickest possible resumption of trade and economic relations with the lands of the former Russian Empire. The English Liberals were as hostile to the Bolsheviks as were the Conservatives, not only because the Bolsheviks were instigators of social unrest who threatened the whole capitalist world but also because the turmoil that they were stirring up in Eastern Europe was cutting Russia off from the world market. If the Liberals had believed, as did the Conservatives, that the united forces of the Entente and the Russian counterrevolution were adequate to defeat the Bolsheviks, then they would have pursued that policy arm in arm with the Conservatives. But the Liberals did not clearly recognize the extent of the threat to the world capitalist order and were thus unwilling to commit themselves to the kind of armed struggle against the Bolsheviks that they had carried on against the Germans during the world war. In this, as in everything else, they believed that prosperity was the highest goal of human existence, and they considered that the best guarantee against the spread of the "Bolshevik disease" in Europe was the economic revival of Germany and the other countries of Central Europe.[192] The Liberals misunderstood the nature of Bolshevism and therefore failed to grasp that, although internal stabilization was essential, it was not enough to ward off Bolshevism: military action was also required. The Liberals therefore were not inclined to give material support to the war against Bolshevism, without which the Russian counterrevolution was unlikely to be victorious. In fact, the Liberals did not agree at all with the need for a military struggle against Bolshevism. They thought that the political policies followed in Western Europe, policies of "self-determination," "freedom," "democracy," "economic revival" and so on, would also suffice to defeat the Bolsheviks in Eastern Europe without recourse to arms in a kind of free and peaceful competition with Bolshevik ideas.

The superiority of the power-political approach to politics, as practiced by the Bolsheviks, over the capitalist-economic approach was nowhere demonstrated more crudely or with more terrifying clarity than in the unofficial contacts between Anglo-American world capitalism, as represented by Lloyd George and Wilson, and the Bolshevik world revolution, as represented by the envoys of Lenin. These capitalist powers, which had just trounced the German and Austro-Hungarian Empires and were now dividing up half the world, were completely bewildered when confronted with a political methodology totally different from their own, which was to make political decisions on the basis of the calculation of the economic interests of individual capitalist concerns. As a result, they considered Bolshevism to be some sort of madness brought on by famine and seriously considered whether the best way to deal with it might be some form of "humanitarian action," such as flooding Russia with foodstuffs from America.[193] This capitalist ignorance of Bolshevism was so great and the arrogance with which they considered capitalist prosperity the best possible condition for mankind was so extreme that they believed Bolshevism would be unable to withstand the Russian people's desire for capitalism once they had seen these fruits of "self-determination" and "democratic freedom." They seriously thought themselves in a position to grant the peace that the peoples of Russia themselves were unable to find. As Lloyd George aptly expressed it,

"When the Allied representatives leave the Peace Conference in Paris, they will not be able to congratulate themselves on having contributed to a better world if half of Europe and half of Asia are still in flames."[194]

Given their impressive understanding of capitalist psychology, the Bolsheviks operated with such superiority and refinement that there were times, at the turn of the year 1918–19, when the administrators of world capital appeared to be serving as unconscious instruments of the Bolshevik world revolution. The Bolsheviks wanted to limit Entente support for the Russian counterrevolution. They needed a breathing space in which to consolidate their position and bring about an internal collapse in the areas under the control of the counterrevolution before unleashing a storm against Central Europe. They also wanted social unrest in the Entente countries to develop to the point where they would be ripe for communism. By means of certain false economic enticements, such as vague promises to repay the debts of tsarist Russia, which were transmitted to the world capitalists by their own intermediaries, the Bolsheviks succeeded in getting the Peace Conference to formulate the program of Lloyd George and Wilson, of the English Liberals and the American Democrats, with regard to Eastern Europe in line with their suggestions. On 16 January 1919 Lloyd George presented this program to the inter-Allied conference in Paris. His proposal for ending the chaos in Eastern Europe was that all de facto governments on former Russian territory be recognized officially, a truce arranged between them and the Bolsheviks, and then all parties be invited to iron out their differences at a conference.[195] This last and most authoritative word of capitalist economic policy proved meaningless: both France and the Russian counterrevolutionaries rejected the idea with the greatest indignation. Although the English Liberals remained embroiled in Bolshevik diplomacy for quite some time, right up to April 1919, they were eventually forced to give it up entirely in view of extremely dangerous opposition from the Conservatives, and Lloyd George was obliged to declare in Parliament on 16 April 1919 that he had no knowledge of any dealings with the Bolsheviks.[196] From then on the English Liberals had no real policy of their own with regard to the territories of the former Russian Empire; and the leadership of England's East European policy was left uncontested to the Conservatives.* Eastern Ukraine had nothing more to expect from Liberal England.

In Europe at this time the Bolsheviks were unsurpassed for their insight into the overall context of European politics. Ranking second were

* On 6 February 1919 Denikin received his first delivery, by ship, of English military supplies (cf. Hurwicz, *Geschichte des russischen Bürgerkrieges*, p. 137).

the French, not the English: in the midst of all the turmoil and confusion, they had a clear perception of their goals and how they were to be achieved. Motivated by an irreconcilable hatred of Germany, the French were absolutely decisive about one thing: the solution to all the problems of Europe would have to be considered from one point of view only—the extent to which they injured and weakened Germany. The French saw clearly that there was nothing more likely to unite Germany's neighbors in an anti-German alliance under French leadership than the fear of German revenge for the loss of German territory. Therefore France energetically supported Belgium, Denmark and Poland in their desire to take as much German territory as possible. It even took an interest in minor territorial issues, such as the question of whether Czechoslovakia should have a tiny part of Silesia, in order to surround Germany with an iron ring of enemies. Breaking up the Austro-Hungarian Empire into separate national states and trouncing Germany's allies, the Hungarians and the Bulgarians, was another way of isolating Germany. The common fear of all the non-German nations of Central Europe that they might become the prey of a resurgent Germany would unite them all under French leadership to form a second line of opposition to Germany. The third aspect of this policy related to Eastern Europe. In view of the collapse of Russia, the French adopted Dmowski's plan for the creation of a strong Poland encompassing as much German territory as possible, thus leading to an irreconcilable opposition between those two countries. The foundation of this whole system was to be the firmest possible footing for France on the Rhine and the impoverishment of Germany by means of the most oppressive system of reparation payments. This more or less sums up French policy at the Paris Peace Conference. Just as all of France was united in this single sentiment, so the whole of France's destructive hostility toward Germany was embodied in a single man, the French prime minister, Georges Clemenceau.[197]

Bolshevism now threatened to overthrow this whole system. If Bolshevism were to penetrate Central Europe, uniting the different nationalities in the struggle against world capitalism—in other words, against the Entente—then the metropolis of all those nations would not be Paris but Moscow and, at best, France would stand alone against Germany. But if Germany itself were swept up in the world revolution, then the metropolis might not be Moscow but Berlin. The need to destroy Russian Bolshevism was therefore generally accepted in France. Differences existed over the appropriate means, but those differences tended to complement rather than contradict one another—an ensemble of rare ingenuity.[198] Clemenceau himself, as well as the dominant elements in French public life and at the Paris Peace Conference, defended the view that the forces of the Entente were insufficient to restore order on the vast territory of the former Russian Empire. What France wanted was the consolidation of a zone of nation-states under French dominance: first of all, Poland and Romania; then Czechoslovakia, where English influence would have to be overcome. This would create a *cordon sanitaire* to fend off the "Bolshevik disease" from Europe and, at the same time, establish an impregnable barrier between Germany and Bolshevik Russia.[199] The fate of Russia would have to be decided by its own warring factions. This self-flagellation of Russia might go on for some considerable time, in which case there would still be an opportunity, by means of a strengthened Poland and Romania, to divide up Eastern Europe in a manner suitable to France. If, on the other hand, there should be any indications that a solution to the East European confusion was forthcoming from within Russia itself, then there would still be time to adapt to the new situation and make the appropriate decisions. As far as Poland was concerned, what mattered was that it have firm borders against Germany, while in the east it should extend itself as much as possible in order to act as a solid dam vis-à-vis the rest of Eastern Europe. If the Poles could draw the Western Ukrainians into this *cordon sanitaire* without having to conquer the whole of Eastern Galicia, that would be even better, since France, unlike Dmowski, had nothing against an "independent" Ukrainian rump state dependent on Poland.* If Poland were to be unsuccessful in this, and if unruly Western Ukraine were to disrupt this Polish-Romanian operation, then Eastern Galicia would absolutely have to be incorporated into Poland so as to give the latter a common border with Romania. In any case, this Polish-Western Ukrainian war was disruptive and unwanted. The simplest thing would be for Poland to defeat Western Ukraine.

Eastern Ukraine, however, belonged to those countries that were beyond the *cordon sanitaire*. Initially, there was not a great deal of interest in those countries, unless, of course, Eastern Ukraine were willing, under the leadership of Poland and Romania, and with their "support," to become an advance outpost of this *cordon sanitaire*. Its eventual fate,

---

* Later, on 19 May 1919, when the Poles were already conquering Eastern Galicia, the French foreign office also referred in its letter to the Ukrainian delegation in Paris to the need for a direct Polish-Ukrainian compromise as the prerequisite of French support for Ukraine. According to the letter, "It is necessary that the Ukrainians and the Poles unite for battle against their common enemy, Bolshevism, forget their stubborn (*personnelles*) mutual claims, and abandon their hostility to each other, which has gone on too long." Even now, the Ukrainians failed to understand that the path to France's favor lay through Warsaw (Margolin, *Ukraina i politika Antanty*, pp. 372–73 and 144–46, cites the full text of this highly characteristic letter).

whether it be "national independence," annexation by Russia or, as Dmowski wished, partition by Russia and Poland, could be decided once the situation in Eastern Europe had become clear. This complete lack of prejudice with which the French recognized that the Ukrainians, no matter how pro-German they might have been during the war, were not inevitably so, and could easily become an instrument of French and Polish policy, demonstrated, in spite of the apparent similarity of Dmowski's and Clemenceau's policies, the difference between the creative ability of a genuine statesman, Clemenceau, and the mere ability to manipulate a given situation cleverly that is the hallmark of a doctrinaire politician such as Dmowski.[200]

If France did not harbor the same kind of prejudice against Ukraine as did Dmowski, and if it considered the possibility of incorporating Ukraine into its plans for Eastern Europe, then one might think that this opened up the possibility of a successful diplomatic approach in which Ukraine could offer itself as an ally and not just as a tool of France. But this lack of prejudice on France's part only demonstrates what the possibilities for Ukraine might have been if its political maturity at the turn of the year 1918–19 had been greater than it actually was. Had the Hetman State, with its whole sociopolitical order, been able to withstand Russification and maintain itself as an independent Ukrainian state, then this Hetman Ukraine, within its established Brest-Litovsk borders and with a stable internal sociopolitical order, could have become a power of the first rank in Eastern Europe capable of equal partnership with France. Under certain circumstances such a Ukraine could even hope for French help against Russia, just as France fully supported the Poles against Germany. That would have laid a firm foundation for the Ukrainian state. If, after the fall of the hetman, Petliura's Eastern Ukraine had established an orderly democratic state at least on the Right Bank, as Western Ukraine had succeeded in doing, then such a state could also have become a valuable ally for France. Indeed, even if Poland had come to some agreement with Western Ukraine, allowing the latter to intervene in Eastern Ukraine, establish order there, and push back the Bolsheviks from the Right Bank, then such a state, although small in size, would have been firmly established internally. If such a Ukrainian state were to normalize relations with its neighbors, such as Poland, by means of an active independent foreign policy, then it could count on French support. Being drawn into the *cordon sanitaire* as an ally of France, Ukraine would have been able to maintain a greater degree of independence and even rely on France to intervene directly in the Paris Peace Conference on its behalf.

But at the turn of the year 1918–19 Ukraine was actually in no position to take advantage of this French openness. Western Ukraine was enmeshed in a disastrous war with Poland. In other words, it was in direct conflict with France, since France, as we have seen, regarded the well-being of Poland as a life-and-death question for itself. Western Ukraine undertook no steps to end this war, for it had not resolved to settle it by negotiating directly with the Poles, even if that should entail great losses to itself. By submitting to the arbitration of the Paris Peace Conference, the Western Ukrainians did not improve their relations with France. They simply became a bargaining chip for Liberal England in an incontestably French sphere of interest in Eastern Europe, which gave the French one more reason, in addition to the well-being of Poland, for wanting Western Ukraine completely eliminated. We can assume with a great degree of certainty that the French had a higher estimation of Western Ukraine's viability as a state than did the English and that they were fully aware that, by eliminating Western Ukraine, they were destroying any possibility of the emergence of a Ukrainian rump state in Eastern Europe.

With Western Ukraine excluded from French considerations, what remained, namely Petliura's Eastern Ukraine, was so obviously unviable as a state that even an Eastern Ukrainian Talleyrand, had the Eastern Ukrainians possessed one, would not have been able to convince France that his country was a serious partner worthy of being drawn into the *cordon sanitaire*. As a result, this French lack of prejudice, which could have become a base of support for Ukraine in European diplomacy had Ukraine been a stable state clear about its own goals and methods, was now turned against it—not only against Western but also against Eastern Ukraine. The opportunity was offered by Eastern Ukraine itself. Unable to assert itself on the basis of its own powers and incapable of establishing order on its own territory, the Directory, as early as December 1918, saw its only hope for survival in the military support of the Entente, just as the Central Rada before it had looked to the German army of occupation. The Directory believed that it could establish a state with foreign tanks in the absence of its own ability to govern.[201] Its cry for help to the Entente became even more desperate as the Bolsheviks grew in strength. But the only possible effect of such actions by the Eastern Ukrainians could be to convince the French to make use of them as temporary border guards for Poland and Romania, should they wish to do so, with no need to commit France in any serious way to the creation of a Ukrainian rump state.

The general attitude of France in the Ukrainian question was like a pendulum that swung sometimes in favor of the creation of a French dependency in Ukraine and at other times in favor of the complete destruction of Ukrainian national aspirations. It was not Clemenceau but rather the French military, led by Marshal Ferdinand Foch, who were willing at times to become involved in the business of Western and even Eastern Ukraine.

Clemenceau's *cordon sanitaire* was the main battle line of French policy in Eastern Europe. The lighter tactical troops might make tactical diversions forward of that line, but their only purpose was to strengthen it. Driven back, they could take refuge behind the line, which remained firmly in place. On the one hand, then, the French foreign ministry had friendly contacts with the Russian counterrevolution and sympathized with the restoration not of a federative Russia, as did the English, but of a united centralized Russia. This kept open for France the possibility of an understanding with Russia in the event of a victory for the counterrevolution, an understanding behind the backs of or even at the expense of the Poles.[202] As late as 17 June 1919 the French foreign minister, Pichon, declared in the French parliament his support for the restoration of a united Russia.[203] On the other hand, however, as another tactical diversion, Marshal Foch directed the French military policy of armed Entente intervention in Russia. But in this case the goal was not the restoration of a united Russia; rather, first and foremost, it was the destruction of the Russian Bolsheviks by the united forces of the Entente itself, the Russian counterrevolution, and the nationalities. Only when this had been achieved would the French decide which option to take—either a united Russia or some other arrangement in Eastern Europe.[204]

This plan already existed at the end of the war. The truce conditions stipulated that the German army of occupation in Eastern Europe should only be withdrawn at the behest of the Entente. The intention was to replace the Germans later with the anti-Bolshevik forces that existed on the spot, as well as with Entente troops. As is clear from Lloyd George's above-cited letter of December 1918 to Clemenceau, the basis of this large-scale action against Moscow was to be Hetman Ukraine, but the uprising against the hetman disrupted this plan. Before the Entente could replace the German troops, it was confronted with a completely new situation in Eastern Europe. Hetman Ukraine was now under the control of the revolutionary Eastern Ukrainian movement, while the base of the counterrevolution was restricted to the narrow strip of territory under the control of General Denikin—the Crimea, the southernmost part of steppe Ukraine, and the Kuban region, as well as the part of the Don region subject to General Petr Krasnov. The whole counterrevolution was so disorganized as a result of the uprising against the hetman that it became clear that the Foch plan would require a much greater number of troops than had been previously assumed—much greater, in fact, than the Entente had at its disposal in Eastern Europe. More money would also be required than previously thought. Foch's undertaking now depended not only on the military readiness of France but above all on English and American capital. With the most checkered army they could muster together, mainly from the Salonika front—French, Poles, Greeks, Russian volunteers—Odesa was occupied under French command on 18 December 1918 after a battle with the troops of the Directory. The French authorities immediately made contact with the Russian counterrevolution and even established a "southern Russian government."[205] At the same time, steps were taken in Paris to win England and America for the French action. On 12 January 1919 Marshal Foch recommended to the Supreme War Council* that an inter-Allied army, mainly American in composition and under American command, should be created. This army should be sent to Poland, and from that base it should begin an immediate and unremitting campaign to destroy the Bolsheviks. But the Supreme War Council declined this proposal, especially as Foch was insisting at the same time on long-term French occupation of the Rhineland. Having failed to get Entente troops, the French military now entered into various intrigues whereby not only Poland and Romania but also Ukraine should become a base for a later Entente intervention against the Bolsheviks. They also attempted to put pressure on England and America to accept the Foch plan and make more troops and money available to the marshal.

This action in relation to Eastern Ukraine was directed by the head of the French military mission in Romania, General Henri Berthelot.[206] On 15 January 1919 General Philippe d'Anselme, with his chief of staff, Colonel Henri Freydenberg, was named commander in chief of the hastily assembled South Russian Army. Their territory was initially limited to Odesa and its environs.[207] The initial plan was to establish a base in occupied Ukraine using Russian counterrevolutionary troops.[208] But it soon became clear that the troops of the South Russian Army commanded by the French in Odesa were too weak and unreliable to venture into the turmoil of Ukraine under the Directory. It was also clear from the many envoys[209] who pleaded urgently for Entente assistance that the Directory was by no means "half Bolshevik," so there was no reason why the Directory's troops could not also be incorporated into

* The Supreme War Council consisted of Marshal Foch and General Maxime Weygand (France), Sir Henry Wilson (England), and General Tasker Bliss (United States) (Baker, *Woodrow Wilson*, 1: 137 [U.S. ed., 1: 164]).

the South Russian Army. So the French decided, finally, to make use of the Eastern Ukrainians, along with auxiliaries of many other nations, in the Foch plan. The conditions laid down, however, were hard for the Eastern Ukrainians. For France, on the other hand, this was an excellent opportunity to use Eastern Ukraine against the Russians. Later, it could be handed back to Russia in return for certain compensation or kept on as an "independent" Ukrainian dependency of France.

At a meeting of representatives of the Directory[210] with Colonel Freydenberg in Birzula on 6 February 1919, the French military laid down the following conditions as an ultimatum: 1) The socially radical members of the Directory had to step down. These included the president of the Directory, Volodymyr Vynnychenko, as well as the "adventurer" Petliura and Opanas Andriievsky, who was considered an irredentist by the Russian reactionaries. The socialist cabinet of Volodymyr Chekhivsky had to be disbanded. The Directory and its government would have to be reorganized according to the instructions of the French commander in chief of the South Russian Army; 2) The railways were to be placed under French control; 3) Control of finance was to be in French hands; 4) The Directory's troops were to be subordinated to the French commander in chief of the South Russian Army; 5) In case of a lack of Ukrainian officers, Russian officers from the army of General Denikin were to be used; 6) The Ukrainians were to write a letter to the French government expressing regret for their errors—the alliance with the Germans during the war and the attempts at socialization after the overthrow of the hetman—and promising to continue the war against the Bolsheviks. They were to request French support, first of all, in raising a Ukrainian army and then in the organization of the whole of the "economic, financial, military and political life of Ukraine." The letter was to emphasize particularly that this Ukrainian request for French assistance sprang from their trust in the French; from their knowledge of France's historical glory and generosity.[211] The French also insisted that the agrarian reform could only proceed on the basis of compensation for the estate owners and that the Directory's whole policy "should not harm the economic or social interests of any particular social stratum."[212] In return for carrying out this ultimatum, the French military authorities promised to supply military equipment to the Eastern Ukrainians,* to assist in sending a Ukrainian mission to the Paris Peace Conference, and to give secret recognition to the Directory. However, to avoid impairing relations with

* The Don Cossack General Petr Krasnov was favored with a similar offer of a French protectorate over the Don region, which had been an independent state since 29 April 1919, but declined assistance on such terms (Hurwicz, *Geschichte des russischen Bürgerkrieges*, p. 141).

the Russian counterrevolution, the French military officials insisted on referring to Ukraine officially as "Southern Russia" and describing the Directory as the "government of the Ukrainian zone."[213]

The Germans in 1918, at the height of their power, leading an army of some hundreds of thousands that had Ukraine firmly in its grip, who actually protected the country from internal anarchy and external aggression, had never demanded as much as the French commanders were now demanding. The French, unlike the Germans, barely occupied a single port in Ukraine and led an army of hastily assembled cowards that even the Directory could disperse and, as one young Eastern Ukrainian captain put it, "throw into the sea" at any time.[214] Very soon afterwards, at the end of March and the beginning of April 1919, these troops of the "Odesa Entente" were in fact forced to make a very rapid exit from Odesa by an Eastern Ukrainian captain, Nykyfor Hryhoriiv, who had rebelled against the Directory and allied himself with the Bolsheviks. Petliura and the moderate Eastern Ukrainian elements accepted the French ultimatum for a number of reasons: a sense of their own weakness; a hatred of Russia that led them to prefer French colonial status to Russian rule; their desire for Entente support and their willingness to go any lengths to obtain it; and their conception of national statehood not as a real exercise of power in their own country but merely as something in the nature of a "principled program," a conception that prepared them, in the worst case, to rest content with semi-colonial status if only their "free" Ukraine could formally be accepted as an "independent state," as the French vaguely promised. On 9 February 1919 the president of the Directory, Vynnychenko, and the socialist cabinet of Chekhivsky resigned. On 13 February a new cabinet, led by Serhii Ostapenko, was formed from parties that had given occasional support to the hetman.[215] On 17 February 1919 the text of the letter demanded by the French was secretly drafted and sent to General d'Anselme.[216] But all this was not enough for the French. On 1 March 1919 they demanded the resignation of Petliura and Andriievsky, holding out, in return, the prospect of immediate assistance.[217] They even sent the draft of a truce between the Directory and the South Russian Army to indicate the nearness of the ultimate solution that France had to offer.[218]

In one sense, the French ultimatum was a benefit for Ukraine inasmuch as it eliminated the baleful man of letters Vynnychenko from Ukrainian public life. Up to that point Vynnychenko had played a major role in Ukrainian literary and political affairs. Politically, the influence of his "revolutionary democratic" politics had done a good deal of damage to Eastern Ukraine in 1917–18, just as in the decade before 1917 his clever pen had poisoned the intellectual atmosphere. Owing to the ultimatum, he disappeared from Ukrainian public life once and for all, despite his later attempt to come to an arrangement with the Bolsheviks. But the acceptance of the ultimatum by Petliura negated the whole purpose of the uprising against the hetman and of the revolt against the rule of the Russian counterrevolution in Ukraine. For at least the beneficiaries of that rule had been the native, territorially Ukrainian, if somewhat Russified elements in the country. The Ukrainian national movement was at all times free to enter into positive competition in culture and other fields with this all-Russian element, with all its political experience and material power, and win it over to the Ukrainian national cause. Now, for the sake of a phantom, for the sake of this completely meaningless "independence" for Ukraine, the country was thrown into a situation from which retreat was very difficult, a situation in which Ukraine would become an object of exploitation for foreign and anonymous cliques and concerns. Their rule in Ukraine could only corrupt the whole of Ukrainian national life. The entire meaning of the Ukrainian-Russian struggle was thereby lost, for that struggle made sense only as a means of settling relations between Ukrainians and Russians arising out of the immediate and direct confrontation of both parties on Ukrainian territory. Even a pact with Denikin would have been more statesmanlike, assuming that the latter were willing, than this pact with the French. Petliura's Eastern Ukrainians acted like rebels, not statesmen, in accepting this French ultimatum. For now it was the French who would dictate what happened in the "Ukrainian zone," and they would do so in the interests of France, without regard for the balance of Ukrainian-Russian forces or for the wishes of the Ukrainians. This French interest could dictate that Ukraine be annexed by a united Russian state or be turned into an exploited "Ukrainian" rump state. The latter solution might be a worse fate than reunification with Russia. This was the role of Eastern Ukraine as envisaged by the French generals, Berthelot and d'Anselme—the role of a tool in the hands of France.

The course of events then took an unexpectedly favorable turn for Ukraine, not as a result of Eastern Ukrainian influence, which we have shown to be very small indeed, but as a result of the much greater weight of Western Ukraine. In keeping with the intrigues of Berthelot and d'Anselme in Eastern Ukraine, Foch, in Paris, argued in February 1919 for a completely different plan of intervention from what he had envisaged in January. If America refused to supply more of its own troops, then some other source of military assistance would have to be found. There was also the unpleasant experience of Archangel, where British,

American and Italian troops had been landed to fight the Bolsheviks,[219] and the ruthless defenders had properly trounced the victorious but extremely war-weary Entente troops. Thus, what Foch wanted from the United States and England was not troops but money. On 25 February 1919 he outlined his specific proposals concerning troops to the Council of Ten. He proposed that an army made up of Greeks, Serbs, Romanians, Poles, Czechs, Slovaks, Estonians, etc. be raised and sent into Eastern Europe under French command.[220] The South Russian Army was not forgotten either: on 19 February 1919, a representative of the French war ministry, General Henri Alby, delivered a note to the Committee for Romanian Affairs at the Peace Conference in which the French foreign ministry strongly emphasized that the Romanian army under General Berthelot "must be kept ready for disposal and possible employment in South Russia."[221] According to a communication from Foch dated 25 February 1919, he planned to strengthen the South Russian Army immediately by sending three Greek divisions to Odesa.[222] Greek troops did indeed arrive in Odesa, only to be "thrown into the sea" a month later, along with the rest of the "Odesa Entente" troops. Foch's situation in Paris was somewhat improved in mid-February because Lloyd George and Wilson were no longer there, and Lloyd George's representative, the Conservative leader Winston Churchill, immediately placed a demand before the Peace Conference in the name of England for immediate and energetic action against the Bolsheviks.[223] Taking advantage of this situation, on 26 February 1919 Foch approved the truce conditions laid down by the Council of Ten for ending the Romanian-Hungarian conflict. These conditions were so devastating for Hungary that the government of Mihály Károlyi was not immediately informed of them. Foch had thus gained an excellent means of eventually forcing Lloyd George and Wilson to accede to his plan. If they approved the planned crusade against the Bolsheviks, then the Foch army, on its way to Russia, would impose the truce conditions on Hungary. If they rejected the plan, then one could expect that the communication of these conditions would provoke some desperate act on the part of the Hungarians, most probably the sovietization of the country. The Anglo-Saxons would then be forced to support Foch's crusade against Bolshevism, which was already making its presence felt in Central Europe.*

* This is Baker's explanation (*Woodrow Wilson*, 2: 24 [U.S. ed., 2: 30]) of why the truce conditions were suddenly communicated to Hungary on 19 March 1919, only after the rejection of Foch's proposals on 17 March, even though they had already been adopted by the Council of Ten on 26 February. "Every evidence in these secret documents [of the Peace Conference] goes to prove clearly that the French military and diplomatic authorities not only welcomed but stimulated this outcome [the sovietization of Hungary] with the idea of forcing military action and military

We have already indicated that Foch wanted to raise an army of "Greeks, Serbs, Romanians, Poles, Czechs, Slovaks, Estonians, etc." This "etc." now included the Western Ukrainians. The whole operation against the Moscow Bolsheviks had developed most unfavorably in the course of February 1919. In the second half of March, there were appeals for help from the South Russian Army in Odesa.[224] A few days later, the British-American troops in northern Russia were threatened with extermination.[225] At that time, every soldier that could be mustered by the counterrevolution was very valuable. The Western Ukrainians had a fighting force of almost fifty thousand soldiers on the Polish front and almost as many again behind the lines. Even with their unusually bad leadership, they pressed the Poles so hard that it is difficult to understand why they did not succeed in driving them out of Lviv and throwing them back beyond the Sian. There were desperate calls for help from Lviv, but the Poles were in no position to do anything about them.[226] Under a proper leadership, advised by French officers, this army, which was all but impervious to Bolshevik sloganizing, had the ability to deliver a strong blow to the Bolsheviks. Since Poland was unable to defeat even the Western Ukrainians, to say nothing of marching on Kyiv or Moscow, the reckoning was clear: the Polish-Western Ukrainian war tied down more than twenty thousand Poles and almost fifty thousand Western Ukrainians. At one blow, the liberation of seventy thousand soldiers to fight the Bolsheviks would have changed the whole balance of forces in Eastern Europe decisively in favor of the counterrevolution. Never before or after, perhaps, did the fate of the Bolsheviks hang by such a slender thread: it depended on whether or not the Polish-Western Ukrainian war in Eastern Galicia could be brought to an end.* In January 1919 a French mission led by General Joseph Berthélemy was sent to Poland to familiarize itself with the war and arbitrate an end to it.[227] The results of these dealings promised to be much more favorable for the Western Ukrainians than the negotiations with Berthelot and d'Anselme had been for the Eastern Ukrainians. Doubtless with Foch's agreement, Berthélemy clearly and openly offered the Western Ukrainians what Berthelot and d'Anselme had persistently refused the Eastern Ukrainians, namely, the recognition of Ukrainian state sovereignty. In accordance with Foch's new

---

settlements," writes Baker.

* For the sake of comparison, let us cite the numerical strength of Denikin's combat forces: by the beginning of 1919 (before joining forces with the Don Cossack Army), Denikin's Volunteer Army (including the Kuban Cossacks) numbered approximately forty thousand men and disposed of more than 193 field guns, 621 machine guns, eight armored cars, seven armored trains, and twenty-nine airplanes (Hurwicz, *Geschichte des russischen Bürgerkrieges*, p. 144).

plan, the Berthélemy mission, which arrived in Lviv on 28 February 1919, proposed a Polish-Western Ukrainian truce and called on the Western Ukrainians to turn all their might against the Bolsheviks. Although the truce conditions were extremely unfavorable to the Western Ukrainians, this truce proposal offered the only opportunity that they had for the duration of the Paris Peace Conference to establish an independent Ukrainian state with the support of the Entente, that is, France. The truce conditions stipulated that the Western Ukrainians would have to give up not only Lviv, which they were strongly attacking at that point, but also the oil region, which they firmly controlled. This would mean a loss of nearly half their territory to Poland. But in return Berthélemy promised Entente recognition of the Ukrainian state and somewhat compromised Berthelot's action with the Directory by declaring that he had greater authority than the powers in Odesa and could bring about a favorable outcome for the Directory in its negotiations with Berthelot and d'Anselme.[228]

This Berthélemy intervention appears to have been a decision of the first importance, and it is worth examining from a number of angles. The Foch plan in its purest form of February 1919, namely, to exclude the nationalities of the former Russian Empire and attack the Bolsheviks with forces of "Greeks, Serbs, Romanians, Poles, Czechs, Slovaks, Estonians, etc.," seems to have been a catastrophic policy whose implementation could have led to the collapse of capitalist Europe. For all those countries, with whose troops Foch was preparing to march into Russia, were themselves in such internal disarray that their own forces were barely adequate to hold down social revolt. The Foch plan proposed sending these armies, which, as the Odesa experience demonstrated, were undisciplined and seething with revolutionary ferment, into the heart of Russia. The enemy against whom they were being sent would be hard pressed and would therefore fight back with an energy born of desperation. Finding themselves in the barren wastes of Russia, those "Greeks, Serbs, Romanians, Poles, Czechs, Slovaks, and Estonians" would most probably conclude that the fight in which they were being asked to spill their blood was a senseless one; that they were not fighting for the good of their homelands but were being used as cannon fodder for American, French and English capitalism. Their courage eaten away by doubt, and fearful of the desperate Bolshevik enemy, these disorganized and rebellious troops would probably return to their homelands as bearers of social revolution.[229]

If, however, the idea of a united centralized Russia were given up and Clemenceau's *cordon sanitaire* policy were extended in the direction of a progressive containment of Moscow Bolshevism through support for the building of independent states by the nationalities on the periphery of the former Russian Empire, things would look different. This would then resemble the policy pursued by the Germans when they occupied Ukraine and by the Hetman State, namely, the creation of independent states closely allied against Moscow, including the Ukrainians and the Don and Kuban Cossacks. No matter how disorganized the Ukrainian movement may have been at the turn of the year 1918–19, the center of gravity of any such containment policy against the Moscow Bolsheviks would have to lie in Ukraine. Once the lever of the fringe nationalities was set in motion, and the nationalities with an immediate interest in the destruction of the Bolsheviks were made the advance guard of the counterrevolution, the Ukrainians first and foremost among them, and these latter were in the front line of battle with the Bolsheviks, then there would be no problem in having the "Greeks, Serbs, Romanians, Poles, Czechs, Slovaks, and Estonians" in the rear. Spared the risk of frontline fighting, there would be little danger of their becoming Bolshevized. This appears to have been the only way that "Western civilization" could penetrate and dominate Eastern Europe, if such a thing were at all possible. It was in this way, some centuries earlier, that the Western crusaders had conquered the Byzantine Empire while protecting it from Islam. If the Western Ukrainians had accepted the oppressive terms of the Berthélemy peace with Poland, if they had then marched on Kyiv, and if in their rear a veritable flood of "armies of Western civilization" had engulfed Eastern Europe, as Foch wanted, then not only the poor Western and Eastern Ukrainians but all the nations of Eastern Europe would have had to prepare themselves for the worst. For, as one can judge from the ultimatum of the "Odesa Entente," those Western crusaders, having wiped out the Moscow Bolsheviks, would have been unlikely to remove themselves from Eastern Europe. Rather, in return for having dealt with the Bolsheviks, they would have divided up this very rich area into colonial or semicolonial spheres of interest. Although Russia, because of its greater distance and larger population, might have been able to avoid this fate, it would have been difficult for Ukraine, the latter being very accessible and weak. The spirit of Generals Berthelot and d'Anselme would have triumphed in Ukraine. But if, as actually happened, the Anglo-Saxon powers opposed this whole plan of Foch, and the marshal failed to get the flood of Western armies that he wanted, then it is highly probable that the Western Ukrainians, at peace with Poland and supported by the French, would have managed, with their own forces and those of Eastern Ukraine, to establish a Ukrainian rump state that could then have become part of the *cordon sanitaire* alongside Poland and Romania and kept the Bolsheviks at bay. Because of the greater strength of Western Ukraine, such a state would have had a less oppressive dependence on France than that which the Directory was willing to accept. This would certainly have been the case if the Western Ukrainians had got rid of the Directory altogether and created a unified Ukrainian government in league with the moderate Eastern Ukrainians.

This, in outline, was the only possibility that existed in 1919 for the Ukrainians to create an independent state as a client of the Entente, that is, of France. But it was not Liberal England, with its slogan of "self-determination," that offered this possibility, as the Western Ukrainians believed. It was, rather, the French military, as Petliura and the Eastern Ukrainians correctly realized.

This possibility, however, did not last very long, and it receded as quickly as it had emerged. The Western Ukrainians did not accept the Berthélemy proposal but, rather, enmeshed themselves even more in the war with Poland in the belief that Liberal England would force Poland to accept a just peace. The Directory hesitated over the resignation of Petliura and Andriievsky, but before the French in Odesa could make up their minds what to do about this, the Directory itself was finally shipwrecked in March 1919. The French conditions were so outrageous that the Directory troops, including the Sich Riflemen, were about to appeal for help from the Soviet government. On 9 April 1919 another socialist cabinet came to power under the leadership of Borys Martos. The Bolshevik armies were victorious everywhere. An attempt by the right-wing parties, on 29 April 1919, to overthrow Petliura finally sealed the fate of this government, and the Ukrainian People's Republic was able to maintain itself with great difficulty only in certain parts of central Volhynia (Map 3).[230] In Paris the Foch plan was once again rejected; hence the reinforcement of the South Russian Army in Odesa became impossible. Odesa itself became indefensible, and on 3 April 1919 the French withdrew, giving up the city to the Bolsheviks.[231]

As a result of all this, the Ukrainians lost all value for the French military at a blow, and Foch returned to Clemenceau's position of a defensive *cordon sanitaire* against the Bolsheviks. But now Foch developed a third plan. Whereas previously the recognition of Ukrainian aspirations to national statehood had been seen more or less clearly as the central axis of Foch's February plan, now, in March, Foch turned all his attention to the task of completely eliminating the Western Ukrainians. They were a major obstacle to Foch, as their war against Poland greatly complicated the whole situation in Eastern Europe, and they confused matters by preventing a clear division of Eastern Europe into two camps, revolutionary and counterrevolutionary. In France the decision was made at this time to organize several strong Polish divisions in General Haller's army, which was to be well equipped and advised by French officers. Foch now centered his plans on this army. He persistently demanded of the Supreme Council of the Peace Conference that it immediately send the Haller army to take up the defense of Lviv. On 17 March 1919 he advised the Supreme Council to send the troops by way of Vienna. But the Supreme Council did not authorize him to do so and adopted instead the English proposal, which called for a truce between the Poles and the Ukrainians.[232] The English wanted to delay the transport of the Haller army because they knew that, once in possession of such a force, Polish "appetites" would become uncontrollable, and they feared above all that the Haller army could be turned against Danzig.

Foch now attempted to force the Supreme Council to approve the conquest of Western Ukraine by the Haller army. On 19 March 1919 he ordered that the above-mentioned Hungarian-Romanian truce conditions be presented to the government in Budapest. The Károlyi government immediately resigned, and Béla Kun took over the leadership of Soviet Hungary.[233] Hardly had the Supreme Council given its final rejection, on 21 March, of Foch's plan to send the Haller army to Lviv than on 27 March Foch was again demanding Allied intervention.[234] Indicating the emergence of Bolshevism in Hungary, Foch demanded that the Supreme Council organize an army of French, British, American, Greek, Serbian, and Romanian forces to surround Hungary from Odesa, occupy Vienna, and wipe out the Bolshevik forces in Hungary. From Budapest this army should then "close the `Lemberg Gap,'" in other words, finally get rid of the Western Ukrainian problem.[235] The Supreme Council again rejected Foch's plan.[236] He continued to insist, however, that the Western Ukrainians should be attacked and defeated. Foch did, in fact, carry out his ideas later, when the Haller army was transported through Germany to Poland in May 1919. What finally remained of Foch's world-shattering plan was the concentration of those crusading forces that were to have brought "Western civilization" as far as the Volga on tiny Western Ukraine, a country not much more than two hundred km wide and two hundred km long. Just as a hungry lion will not hesitate to fall upon a mouse, so now the mighty marshal turned his towering rage on unfortunate Western Ukraine, this tiny country caught in the struggle of the world's great powers.

Even before the Western Ukrainian delegation arrived in Paris to plead their modest cause before the benefactors of mankind who wished to bestow eternal peace upon it, their fate was already sealed without their knowing it. Among the French, Clemenceau as well as Foch, Dmowski had already won his case. France now supported Poland's plans to conquer all of Western Ukraine, and, given the persistence with which France supported the Polish cause, there remained very little for Liberal England to do but protest against this fait accompli. This protest, however, would do nothing to save the Western Ukrainians from the maw of the Franco-Polish lion, although it might increase England's trade with the East by a couple of boatloads.

In the Ukrainian question at the Paris Peace Conference, as in all others, the most pathetic figure of all was Wilson, the prophet of "national self-determination" in whom the Western Ukrainians had placed all their hopes of obtaining justice. If Wilson had not existed, then the Western Ukrainians might have pursued a more active and aggressive foreign policy. They might even have fought all the more desperately against Poland to escape their fate and avoid losing all their territory. As it was, they only hurt themselves by placing so much trust in Wilson, who was no more than a puppet in the hands of anti-Ukrainian specialists like Lord, who in turn was nothing more than a puppet in the hands of Dmowski. Although on the issue of German territories he supported Lloyd George against Poland, if rather weakly and, in the last phase of the Peace Conference, most unreliably,[237] when it came to the question of Western Ukraine, the "Eastern Galician question," he unhesitatingly supported Poland and France against the Western Ukrainians. At most he was willing to grant them some form of autonomy within the Polish state.[238] The American attitude to the Eastern Ukrainians was even worse. "Our conversation with Lansing left us absolutely astounded," reported one of the Eastern Ukrainian representatives in Paris, Arnold Margolin, commenting on his visit to the American secretary of state on 30 June 1919.[239] "Lansing was utterly ignorant of the situation in Eastern Europe, and he had a totally blind faith in Kolchak and Denikin. He insisted categorically that the Ukrainian government recognize Kolchak as its head of state and as commander in chief of all the anti-Bolshevik armies. When we discussed Wilson's principles, which were already being applied to the nationalities of the former Austro-Hungarian Empire, he declared that he knew of only one united Russian people and that a restored Russia could only exist as a federation on the American model." It is true that Russia could only have been reconstituted as a federation—but it would be a Bolshevik Russia! In any case, what did it matter to the Americans whether Russia was restored or not? America's only interest in this affair was the fact that the United States and Japan were financing Kolchak, and they feared losses to their Siberian concessions should the Kolchak operation come to nothing. Similarly, the English financed Denikin and extolled him to the Eastern Ukrainians, hoping that in this great Russian "clearance sale," under his protection, they would at least manage to take control of the oil region around Baku. France supported Poland and lured the Ukrainians in that direction so as to isolate Germany. All this was at the expense of the peoples of the former Russian Empire, whose bloody slaughter in 1914–15 had made the glorious victory of the Western powers possible in the first place.

"The Italians," wrote an English historian, "had no special interest or strong views in regard to the frontiers with Germany. They supported the Poles in Teschen [Cieszyn / Těšín—Ed.] against the Czechs and in Eastern Galicia against the Ruthenians. As regards territory formerly Russian they felt strongly the obligations incurred by the alliance with Russia, and held that while it was desirable to give to Poland the ethnographic frontier which had been recognized by Kerensky's government, it was undesirable to go farther in deciding the fate of regions in which the Russians were concerned. The decision on these matters had in the end to be postponed."[240]

"The Japanese," continues this English historian, "were not directly interested in the Polish question so far as it was settled by the Conference. The boundary with Russia, with which they were more immediately concerned, never came up for final decision."

Of all the other Entente nations, only the Czechs thought it advisable to support the Western Ukrainian claim to self-determination. They took advantage of the fact that practically all of Poland's military forces were involved in fighting the Western Ukrainians and laid claim to the Těšín industrial region of Austrian Silesia, which Poland had taken over in November 1918. On 23 January 1919 the Czechs attacked the Poles in this region and occupied it. But the fact that, thanks to the Western Ukrainians, the Czechs were able to take over and hold this territory was not their only reason for supporting the Western Ukrainians. Polish and Czech industry were engaged in fierce competition, and Polish control of Eastern Galicia would cut off Czechoslovakia from the East European market. It was therefore very important for the Czechs either to have a Western Ukrainian state on their border that could provide a transit route for its products into Eastern Europe by way of Slovakia and Carpatho-Ruthenia or for Western Ukraine to be incorporated into Eastern Ukraine or, as the Czechs preferred, into Russia.[241]

From February 1919 the Ukrainian delegates made their way one by one to the witches' caldron of the Paris Peace Conference. The numerous battlefronts had practically cut off their country from the rest of the world. There was, first of all, their own battlefront with Poland, and then the Romanian-Hungarian and Czech-Hungarian fronts in Central Europe. Almost the only means of contact between the Peace Conference and the Ukrainians had been the telegraph. The other countries, especially France, created numerous passport difficulties for the Ukrainian representatives, so it took weeks, and in some cases months, before they all arrived in Paris. Like the representatives of many other nationalities of the former Russian Empire, they were recognized only as a political committee with no diplomatic privileges. Their participation in the Peace Conference was limited to handing notes to the conference secretariat, which acknowledged them from time to time. Any official contact between them and the Peace Conference was the rarest of exceptions and concerned only the "Eastern Galician question."[242] Their access to the powers that be was made extremely difficult. They depended on the favor of the junior diplomatic staff of secretaries and specialists. As a result, their diplomatic activity was largely a cry in the wilderness.

The first to succeed in reaching Paris was the head of the Ukrainian People's Republic's delegation to the Peace Conference, an Eastern Ukrainian, Hryhorii Sydorenko, whose memorandum of 10 February 1919 demanding recognition of Ukraine and its admission to the conference was the first official step taken by the Ukrainians in Paris.[243] A month later, in the final days of February, the vice president of the delegation, the foreign secretary of Western Ukraine, Vasyl Paneiko, was admitted to Paris. The second most important representative of Western Ukraine, Stepan Tomashivsky, was not given an entry visa until two months later, at the end of April 1919, and only after the Americans and English intervened on his behalf with the Supreme Council. The French did not hesitate to use the pettiest of means, such as the refusal of entry visas to the Western Ukrainian delegation, to do damage to this small country, whose fate already lay in France's hands. But even before all the members of the Ukrainian mission reached Paris during April and May,* the decision on Ukraine's existence as an independent state had already been taken by the European diplomats: Foch had given up his game involving Ukraine, and England's position on the restoration of

* Aside from those just named, the delegation consisted of the following: Arnold Margolin, who came in April 1919 as a representative of Eastern Ukraine, Oleksander Shulhyn, Serhii Shelukhyn, Makar Kushnir, and Dr. Borys Matiushenko. On 7 May, the Western Ukrainians Dr. Mykhailo Lozynsky and Colonel Dmytro Vitovsky arrived in the matter of a Polish-Ukrainian truce. In June the Western Ukrainian Dr. Teofil Okunevsky also joined the delegation. In addition, the delegation had a small number of interpreters and office workers (Margolin, *Ukraina i politika Antanty*, pp. 105–6, 134 ff.; Lozyns'kyi, *Halychyna*, pp. 114–17).

Russia had remained unchanged. Not only the Ukrainian question in general but even the specific cause of Western Ukraine was already lost in European politics. England had not found it worthwhile to intervene energetically on Western Ukraine's behalf by refusing, for instance, to deal with the question of Poland's western borders until Poland had made peace with Western Ukraine, as England wanted. Poland and France were not intimidated by England's protests and decided to proceed with a policy of fait accompli as far as Western Ukraine was concerned. Under such circumstances, there was little that Ukrainian diplomacy could do but try to delay the formal international recognition of those faits accomplis. There was never any question of their being able to win a favorable decision for Western Ukraine in material terms. That was the extent of the success of the Western Ukrainian diplomatic representatives in Paris, Paneiko and Tomashivsky, perhaps the most politically cultivated and competent diplomats in Western Ukraine at the time. Under the circumstances, they could not have achieved more.

The difficulties caused for the Ukrainian diplomats by the desperately difficult external circumstances in which they had to operate were compounded by their lack of unity in Paris, which completely paralyzed them. The blame for this disunity lay not with the Ukrainian diplomats but with the state they represented, which had no clear and decisive foreign policy for them to implement. The establishment of the basic principles of Ukrainian foreign policy was left to the diplomats themselves, and as there was not one but several possible guidelines, it is obvious that the individual diplomats would have starkly divergent views. There were in reality two Ukrainian states, not one. As long as Ukraine was contending with the Poles and Bolsheviks and opposing the Russian counterrevolution as well, it could not align itself with any of the political systems wrestling for control of Eastern Europe. One or the other of its war aims would have to be dropped. Ukraine was too weak to fight against all sides, relying entirely on its own strength. It would have to seek support from some political system outside itself.

The fundamental line of policy that was objectively most correct from the viewpoint of establishing a Ukrainian state in Eastern Europe was that of the Hetman government's foreign policy, and that line was followed in Paris by the Eastern Ukrainian representatives, Arnold Margolin and Oleksander Shulhyn. This policy was worked out by Margolin after negotiations in Odesa with representatives of the Don and Kuban Cossacks, General Cherechukin and Luka Bych, as well as with the Belarusians—General Aliaksandr Bakhanovich and Consul Stsiapan Nekrashevich. It was outlined in a joint memorandum submitted to General d'Anselme on 5 February 1919—a document remarkable not for its general argumentation, which was weak indeed, but for its overall approach.[244] All those more or less legitimate representatives of Ukraine, the Don and Kuban regions, and Belarus pointed out that, in view of the strong emergence and growth of the non-Russian national movements after 1917, the continued insistence of the Entente and the Russian counterrevolution on the reconstruction of a united Russia, even on the basis of a federal system, would not lead to the defeat of the Bolsheviks. Only support for the establishment of independent national states on the territory of the former Russian Empire, they said, would liberate forces in Eastern Europe that could then link up with the Russian counterrevolution, thereby creating a movement strong enough to defeat Bolshevism. In order to facilitate such a shift in policy by the Russian counterrevolution and the Entente, the memorandum suggested that the only way to restore a unified Russia would be to leave it to the constituent assemblies of the established national states, after the victory over the Bolsheviks, to decide whether the unity achieved in the course of their struggle should be given permanence in a federation.[245]

In hindsight it can hardly be doubted that, as far as the restoration of a united Russia was concerned, it was the Bolsheviks and not the Russian counterrevolutionaries who had the capacity to bring this about. But if the goal was the destruction of Bolshevism, as indeed it was for the Entente, then it was not the Russian counterrevolution alone that could achieve this but a united effort of the Russian counterrevolution with the non-Russian national movements for the purpose of restructuring Russia as a regional union of national states. The Russian counterrevolutionaries, however, were dissatisfied with Margolin's and Shulhyn's proposals for a Ukrainian-Russian settlement, insisting that a future all-Russian Constituent Assembly would decide the fate of the nationalities. To that end, they demanded that Eastern Ukraine submit to Admiral Kolchak or General Denikin. Thus Margolin's negotiations with representatives of the various Russian parties in Paris in April and May 1919 came to nothing.* Since England accepted this Russian position, which the Ukrainians could not approve, and France was perhaps the only power that might have been won over to Margolin's program, it would have been necessary to make some deal with the French at the expense of Western Ukraine. But the consequences for

* Discussions were held with Vasilii Maklakov, the Socialist Revolutionaries, and other representatives of Russian democracy: Konstantin Sokolov, Mark Slonim, Vasilii Sukhomlin, Aleksandr Kerensky, Mark Vishniak, Nikolai Avksentiev, Prince Georgii Lvov, and Nikolai Chaikovsky (Margolin, *Ukraina i politika Antanty*, pp. 138–43; Lozyns'kyi, *Halychyna*, p. 117).

the particular goals of Western Ukraine were unacceptable, and this Margolin line was consequently paralyzed.

Since England insisted on the restoration of Russia and, at the same time, on the self-determination of Western Ukraine, there was little that the Western Ukrainians could do in Paris but distance themselves from Eastern Ukraine as a particular and independent state—a state disinterested with regard to Western Ukraine, so to speak. And that is exactly what Paneiko and Tomashivsky did. They strongly emphasized that Western Ukraine was completely independent of Eastern Ukraine, while concealing this from the rest of the Ukrainian delegation in Paris. However, if they had wanted to strengthen their position in England and interest the English not just economically but also politically in Western Ukraine, then the only way to do this would have been to arrange an Eastern Ukrainian federation with Denikin and then make Western Ukraine, in alliance with Denikin, into an Anglo-Russian bulwark against the extension of French influence in Eastern Europe. In fact, Paneiko sought contact with the Russian counterrevolution[246] on this basis, but such contact could lead to nothing because irredentist and separatist Eastern Ukraine stood in the way. So this line of approach also meant diplomatic paralysis for the Ukrainians.

Diplomatic acumen was weakest among those representatives who stood for the maintenance of Ukrainian unity and continued to press Ukrainian claims not only against Poland but also against Russia. The defenders of this policy were Dr. Mykhailo Lozynsky and Colonel Dmytro Vitovsky. They protested Margolin's and Shulhyn's acceptance of a possible federation with Russia, as this contradicted the principle of national statehood. They made accusations against Paneiko and Tomashivsky because their separate action had contradicted the principle of Ukrainian unity. They demanded that emphasis be placed on the Ukrainian desire for national statehood and not on Ukraine as a factor in the struggle against Bolshevism.[247] It was indeed inexplicable why they bothered to come to Paris at all to seek justice and support from the Entente if, from the very beginning, they had made up their minds to accept none of the conditions laid down by the Entente. The many memoranda with which the head of this faction, Hryhorii Sydorenko, bombarded the Peace Conference were among the most unedifying emanations of Ukrainian political culture. Those dilettantes, who had no idea of the state of world politics at the time, believed that the best way to "interest the Entente in Ukraine" was with fantasies about Ukraine as "a bulwark for the defense of the Dardanelles, the Suez Canal, the Persian Gulf, and India."

So the final and weakest factor in the process of decision-making about Ukraine, namely, Ukrainian diplomacy, was exhausted. In relation to all the other factors it was, in fact, quite insignificant.

The double dilemma that confronted the Peace Conference was now clear. As far as Eastern Ukraine was concerned, the question was how best to defeat the Bolsheviks—by supporting the restoration of counterrevolutionary Russia or its dismemberment into national states? After some hesitation, the Entente came down firmly on the side of the first solution, and from then on there was nothing to obscure the clarity of the dilemma. As far as Western Ukraine was concerned, the issue was equally clear: should Eastern Galicia be annexed by Poland or should Western Ukraine be recognized as an independent state? Since England and France had different ideas on this, the dilemma, though very clear in reality, became a test of the specialists' astuteness and of the ability of great-power diplomacy to hide its actual goals behind a smokescreen. It also became a test of the Poles' ingenuity in muddying the waters so that they could go ahead and do what they wanted anyway. In other words, this question became an insoluble puzzle, and the more carefully and profoundly it was discussed the more insoluble it appeared to become, since a compromise was being sought that was in fact completely impossible. "Of all the questions affecting Poland," complained the English historian, "that of Eastern Galicia was perhaps the most complicated and the most difficult of solution."[248]

The English argument went as follows:

> ...if Poland was to be strong both internally and externally it was necessary that self-determination should be the guiding principle of the settlement. Internally Poland must in any case possess very large minorities of Jews on the one hand and Germans on the other—neither of them likely to make the wheels of political life run more smoothly. If besides this inevitable alien minority Poland were to receive in the west more than the necessary minimum of Germans and in the east quantities of unwilling Lithuanians, White Russians, and Ruthenians her political effectiveness would decrease with the increase of her size, and she would become like the former Austrian Empire, a conglomerate of nationalities incapable of securing even-handed justice and of working a democratic form of government. Externally she would be surrounded by a ring of enemies, smarting under a sense of injustice, preaching a gospel of irredentism, fostering faction within her borders, and waiting an opportunity—which would not be difficult to

> find—for military aggression. And these enemies would be two of the greatest Powers of Europe—Russia and Germany. Germany, indeed, would always have causes for dispute with Poland. It was, however, possible and desirable to reduce these causes to the minimum demanded by justice. In such circumstances the Poles would be wise to avoid all possible cause of quarrel with Russia, even if it meant in some cases recognizing Russian claims whose justice they disputed. Above all, it was dangerous to take advantage of Russia's temporary weakness and annex border peoples without securing a free expression of their wishes. Such action, as it separated Russia and Germany in space, would bring them together in spirit and might easily result in a new and this time perhaps a final Partition of Poland from which no human power could save her.[249]

The French, on the other hand, insisted that "the duty of the Conference was to create a large Poland as a barrier against the Bolsheviks and as an ally of France in any future war against Germany."[250]

But there were other considerations as well:

> The Poles could with every reason occupy portions of the border countries in order to free them from anarchy and to defend Poland itself against attack. Yet while these countries were being fought over, it was impossible to secure self-determination, and hazardous, if not foolish, to legislate for a quite uncertain future. There were, indeed, hopes that first Kolchak and then Denikin could succeed in establishing a Russian Government with which it would be possible for the Poles and the Allied Powers to treat in regard to the ultimate fate of the disputed territories. It was partly such hopes which prevented the Conference from dealing with these regions, but these hopes were gradually destroyed. The difficulties caused by this situation were enormous. Threatened by Bolshevik armies and assailed by Bolshevik propaganda, weakened by war and famine and disease, the border peoples were, to say the least, not in the best condition to establish a stable form of government. The Poles, on the other hand, even apart from national ambitions, could hardly be expected to hand over willingly to a Bolshevik régime large areas where members of their race constituted the bourgeois element and possessed the bulk of the land.[251]

"Among those border peoples," went the argument, "the Ruthenians have staked their claim for self-determination. But it is extremely doubtful that they are capable of governing themselves.[252] They will not be able to stand up to the Bolsheviks or block their passage to Hungary.[253] The Poles are strong enough to occupy this eastern territory. If the conference prevents them from doing so, there will be such an outcry in Poland that the Polish government will be swept away and nothing but anarchy will be left in its place."[254]

"There are tasks," cried an appalled Englishman or American when confronted by the Eastern Galician question, "there are some tasks which are almost too great for mortal men."[255]

The English historian writes:

> To declare the whole county independent would have satisfied the Ruthenians, but the Poles would certainly not have submitted, and even if they had there was no guarantee that the Ruthenians could have set up a stable government or that the Polish minority would be adequately protected. To hand the whole country over to the Poles could be done only by force of arms and would be manifestly unjust. It was necessary to seek some sort of solution which would at least attempt to do justice between the contending parties.... There was no possible solution which did not receive serious consideration by the Polish Commission in Paris. Even the most improbable contingencies were envisaged, including such remote possibilities as a temporary occupation of the whole territory by Czecho-Slovakia or Rumania. All the Delegations in Paris, except the British, were, however, strongly in favour of assigning the whole territory as a natural unit to Poland in some form or other and with such safeguards and limitations as might be thought necessary. There were, indeed, proposals to split up the country by a frontier running east of Lemberg and Drohobycz. Such a frontier would have assigned to Poland a large area in which the majority was definitely Ruthenian; it would not have satisfied the Poles; it would have meant bitter hostility on the part of the Ruthenians; and it would have left the portion of Eastern Galicia excluded from Poland a mere mutilated fragment resting on nothing and incapable of existing by itself. These proposals were, however, put forward as desirable only in case the British view should be accepted, that sooner or later the Ruthenians should be given a real opportunity for self-determination. If the future fate of the country was to be left in any reasonable doubt, then such

doubt, it was maintained, should not be allowed to affect Lemberg and Drohobycz, both of which should be secured for Poland. The possibility of self-determination—if this should be thought desirable—ought to be given only to the east of the Lemberg-Drohobycz line.

There were two serious possibilities before the Conference; one was to attempt to secure a free expression of the people's will under proper international safeguards, the other was to give Poland some sort of authority and control at least for a time.

Of these the first was very difficult—its opponents said impossible. An immediate plebiscite could not be held unless the country was occupied by a neutral force, it would have taken place at a time when men were inflamed by passion and little inclined to vote from a reasonable consideration of the true interests of the country. Further, what alternatives could be put before them at a time when Russia was in chaos, and independence would lead to internal troubles and perhaps, it was urged, to co-operation of some sort with the Bolsheviks? Clearly it was desirable that the plebiscite should be postponed till passions were cooler and Europe had taken definite shape again after passing through the furnace of war and revolution. But to secure this it would be necessary to have some sort of supervision by the League of Nations. If a representative of the League of Nations arrived without forces in a country seething with civil war what chance was there that his wishes would be obeyed? On the other hand, it was impossible to send a large international force to this remote inland area with hostile forces all around and the Bolsheviks hammering at the gates. Similarly, what Great Power would accept from the League of Nations a temporary mandate over this country at a time when troops were urgently needed elsewhere, when demobilization was being demanded, and when all the nations were on the point of exhaustion? Even if a Great Power did accept such a mandate the result would be economic dislocation and political instability, and the country would continue to be a hotbed of agitation and strife until some permanent settlement was secured. Poland, it was urged, was the only Power in the vicinity, Poland alone could bring about a permanent and immediate settlement, and Poland was both willing and anxious to undertake the responsibility.

In spite of strong protests from the British Delegation these considerations appeared to be conclusive to the majority of the Powers at the Peace Conference. The matter was, however, to

> some extent taken out of their hands. As related elsewhere, in May 1919 the Poles attacked successfully and the Polish advance stopped after protests from Paris only when the greater part of Eastern Galicia had been occupied by Polish troops.[256]

So everything was against the Western Ukrainians. Not even the people's war against Poland sufficed as an expression of their desire for an independent state. Even the Ukrainians' struggle against the Bolsheviks was used against them: "How," it was said, "can a nation that is weakened by war, hunger and sickness and threatened by Bolshevik armies found a state?" Since everyone assumed that Ukraine would collapse, it was thought better that it be occupied by the Poles than by the Bolsheviks.

Thus the Western Ukrainians went to Paris in vain. Whether they made that pilgrimage or not, what really decided the fate of their country was the war with Poland. The Peace Conference in Paris was merely a stockbroking operation in which the decisions of the Supreme Council reflected the state of the action on the Polish-Ukrainian battlefront.

3. The Course of the Polish-Ukrainian War and the Decisions of the Allied Supreme Council

I.

To get a proper understanding of the scope of the military problems confronting Western Ukraine immediately upon its emergence as an independent state, we have to look at the military position of Poland at the turn of the year 1918–19.

At the end of November 1918, the state power established in Warsaw extended over Congress Poland and Western Galicia. To the west and north of this state territory were the old borders of the German Reich, but Germany was in no way a threat to Poland. In the southwest, in Austrian Silesia, a preliminary Czech-Polish agreement went into effect on 5 November 1918, leaving Poland in control of the Cieszyn region. In the southeast, in Eastern Galicia, the Poles were fighting the Western Ukrainians in the Przemyśl–Khyriv region and in Lviv, as well as south of Zamość in the direction of Rava-Ruska, but this was an offensive war on the part of Poland. In the east, the Poles were holding or had crossed the Buh, the border between the Chełm region and Volhynia. The Eastern Ukrainians were stationed on the eastern side of the Buh, not with the intention of invading the Chełm region but in order to stop the Poles from marching into Volhynia. A foreign invasion of Congress Poland was theoretically possible from only one direction, the northeast, the direction of Moscow. But in Brest-Litovsk and in the Belarusian regions to the north and east of it, the German occupation army was still stationed as a sentry against the Bolshevik troops, so to speak, until February 1919. Poland was thus militarily secure and protected on all sides. Although the Poles complained incessantly to the Entente about the danger of their situation, this danger had nothing to do with any threat to the Polish state. Their only fear was that they might not be able to take all the territories to which they laid claim. The Poles looked upon this as a form of foreign interference in their own country and spoke of a "Ukrainian invasion" of Eastern Galicia. In order to defend itself against such invasions, the whole Polish nation was mobilized into aggressive military actions on all its borders. The first war to break out was that with the Western Ukrainians in Eastern Galicia. Following on this was the war against the Eastern Ukrainians in western Volhynia. On 27 December 1918 the Poles in Poznań staged an insurrection against the Germans in order to push the Polish border as far westward as possible. Finally, with the evacuation of German troops from Pinsk, Baranavichy, Volkovysk, Hrodna, and Vilnius, the Poles began to push into Belarus. The only truly defensive war that Poland had to fight was the one that broke out with Czechoslovakia on 23 January 1919, but it was brought to an end by the Entente on 25 February 1919. This was a small territorial dispute over the possession of Těšín/Cieszyn that, like the other conflicts, involved no threat of an invasion of Western Galicia.[257]

In all these military actions Poland was in an unusually advantageous situation. The countries attacked had no intention, in the event of a Polish defeat, of invading the central territory of Congress Poland and Western Galicia. The Poles therefore risked nothing in such border disputes. These military actions were generally carried out by small improvised armies made up mostly of volunteers from the border areas where the fighting took place. The central Polish government only had to give them as much support as they needed not to be defeated. In the meantime, Poland kept building up its reserve army, and only when this organizational work had been carried through did it intervene decisively in those border disputes. The organizational work proceeded very slowly. It really did not get under way until February 1919, as increasing amounts of military supplies began to arrive from France. Until then the troops on the front, just like those of the Western Ukrainians, were often overhastily and unsystematically built up. For instance, they were reinforced with untrained recruits. In spite of all this, the Polish military was sufficiently well developed to undertake a decisive offensive against Vilnius in April 1919. With the arrival of some Franco-Polish divisions of the Haller army in May 1919, at the time of the decisive military push against the Western Ukrainians, Poland was undoubtedly the strongest military power in Eastern Europe, with three hundred thousand men in training and one hundred fifty thousand soldiers ready for action. In short, from November 1918 Poland had almost half a year of peace to prepare its military before intervening with all its might in its border conflicts. Although, compared with Western Ukraine, Poland had an incomparably more numerous and better-trained officer corps, its military and organizational achievements at the turn of the year 1918–19 were certainly much smaller than those of Western Ukraine.[258]

For the situation in Western Ukraine differed greatly from that in Poland. From the very first day of its existence as a state, it was involved in a war on its own territory. According to one Polish military historian, the Western Ukrainians had to improvise an army for frontline fighting under circumstances in which "they had such a lack of officers that even the Polish military, itself not very well supplied with officers, would have difficulty in imagining the situation."[259] The Poles in the border regions had raised such an army spontaneously, without placing any burden on central Poland. In the midst of this war, Western Ukraine had to carry out a military organization of its three million people. Central Poland, however, was able to carry out such military organization more or less systematically in conditions of peace, disposing of a large territory and a population of almost fifteen million. This situation demanded a high level of achievement from the Western Ukrainians. Extreme effort, which alone could have brought victory, was not forthcoming. The actual effort was nonetheless very great, much greater than anything required of the other national states that were being established in postwar Europe.

As described earlier, the first units of the Western Ukrainian army came into existence spontaneously on 1 November 1918. In response to the appeal of the Ukrainian National Rada, militias were formed throughout the country to take control of the territory up to the Sian River. This spontaneous military organization was initially very small, as most able-bodied men had not yet returned from the world war. The few soldiers then in the country were war-weary and did not enlist. A certain section of this militia was made up of Ukrainian formations from the Austrian period, but the majority was made up of rapidly improvised and partly untrained volunteer units. As a result of the poor preparation for the insurrection of 1 November 1918, those companies and battalions throughout the country were not under a unified command. They acted on their own initiative wherever Polish opposition broke out. In Lviv and Przemyśl, where this Polish opposition was greatest, the Ukrainians were not strong enough to assert their authority.[260]

Having first lost Przemyśl and then Lviv, the Western Ukrainians found themselves in the following military situation at the end of November 1918: east and south of Przemyśl, Polish troops were keeping open a line of communication between central Poland and Lviv. Most of the Polish forces were in Lviv, which resembled a besieged fortress. Small numbers of Polish militia with armored trains guarded the railway line between Przemyśl and Lviv. The whole country south and north of this railway line was completely under Ukrainian control: its border ran northward from Przemyśl, past Jarosław to the former Austro-Russian boundary, more or less following the river Sian. At both ends of the Przemyśl–Lviv line, small numbers of Polish troops created diversions: in the south they operated along the Carpathians from Sanok (Sianik) to Khyriv, and in the north around Jarosław on the Sian. The supreme commander of this whole Polish front was General Tadeusz Rozwadowski. Much farther north, and completely separated from the Polish forces in Galicia, a small independent unit of Polish troops operated out of Zamość toward Rava-Ruska in the south (Map 1).[261]

The strategic position of the Lviv Poles was highly unfavorable. They were confined to this city and therefore doomed to passivity. Their goal was to hold out at all costs until reinforcements from Poland could unite Polish positions in Przemyśl, Lviv, Jarosław and Rava-Ruska into a solid front capable of securing the line of communication between Lviv and central Poland. They were also waiting for Polish forces from the north, in the area of Rava-Ruska, to attack in the direction of Lviv north of the Przemyśl–Lviv railway line and clear that area of Western Ukrainians; finally, they were waiting for Poland to be ready to launch a major offensive that would defeat the Western Ukrainians and take all of Eastern Galicia.

This situation forced the Western Ukrainians to adopt the following strategic plan: in view of their experience of the relief for Lviv from Cracow and Przemyśl in November 1918, it was essential to retake Przemyśl with their strongest and best-led troops in order to break the link between Lviv and central Poland and then to hold that crossing on the Sian River at all costs. With their next best troops they had to conduct an active defense by retaking Rava-Ruska, capturing Jarosław, and penetrating into the Chełm region around Zamość. Around Lviv, on the other hand, it was only necessary to leave behind a strong observation corps ready to strike at any time so as to keep the city in a constant state of unease and tie down the Polish troops there, preventing them from taking large-scale action elsewhere. Protected by such an aggressive military policy on the front, they would have to raise a regular reserve army in the rear so as to take Lviv sometime around January 1919, unless it capitulated earlier. Polish troops in the city would be destroyed and the whole Western Ukrainian army would march to the Sian and into the Chełm region. If along this front they could prevent the Polish attackers from retaking Lviv, then they could hope for a peace with the Poles that would give them the whole country, including Lviv. If they failed in this endeavor, they would have no choice but to make the best possible deal with the Poles before Warsaw invaded Western Ukraine with all its forces.

But there is no such thing as pure strategy. The way in which a war is waged corresponds in very large measure to the political leaders' conceptions of how peace with the enemy is to be achieved. The Western Ukrainian political leaders, however, were actively striving not for peace with Poland but for Entente recognition of their right to national statehood. Their goal therefore was the occupation of as much Eastern Galician territory as possible by the Western Ukrainian army as proof for the Entente that the population really aspired to national self-determination. Such a policy demanded the concentration of all their military forces, from the very beginning, around a strategically peripheral point—Lviv—in the hope that its capture would impress the Entente favorably with regard to the Western Ukrainian cause. This strategy, however, led nowhere: in fact, it delayed the capture of Lviv. If they had carried out successful military operations on the flanks, against Przemyśl and on the Rava-Ruska–Jarosław line, it would have been easier to bring about the fall of the capital than through this concentration of forces around the strong Polish defenses of Lviv. In the mind of the Western Ukrainian military leaders, however, the goal was not the defeat of Poland but the capture of Lviv. This limitation, this narrowing of their strategic vision robbed them of all freedom of movement. They tied themselves down to the enemy's strongpoint in Lviv, condemning themselves to a wholly defensive strategy against military operations from the periphery, from their right and left flanks, where the war was actually decided in its first stage. From the very beginning, therefore, the Western Ukrainians relinquished the possibility of a daring war of movement, leaving the enemy all the advantages of a well-planned and extensive campaign. Their numerically superior forces were bogged down by the enemy for months. This was the most fateful error made by the Western Ukrainians in the course of the whole war.

II.

Although in November 1918 the Western Ukrainians were weary of war, the loss of Lviv brought about a complete revitalization. The Western Ukrainian government ordered an immediate mobilization of all able-bodied men between eighteen and thirty-five. The people now clearly saw the danger of a Polish victory in Eastern Galicia, and the mobilization, carried out in December 1918, when most of the Western Ukrainians serving in the Austrian army had returned, proceeded with no serious difficulties. In fact, in many areas volunteers were mobilized up to the age of forty.[262] Polish military historians are therefore wrong when they speak of a failure of mobilization in Western Ukraine. They simply extend to Western Ukraine the problems that the Poles themselves had in attempting to mobilize their population in Western Galicia.[263] This can easily be demonstrated by looking at the numbers. After the first mobilization in November and December 1918 there was no new recruitment drive in Western Ukraine, although in many cases the recruits of November and December were not enlisted immediately. As of 17 April 1919[264] the Western Ukrainian front army alone, regardless of its great losses through illness and the desertions that set in after March 1919 (the reasons for which will be explained below), still counted 1,412 officers and 53,224 men.* This figure does not include the numerous guard troops and militias of every sort that were organized throughout the country after the November mobilization. Nor does it include the units, made up mostly of recruits, that were continuously being sent to Eastern Ukraine after December 1918. These units must have numbered at least 60,000 men under arms.** Together with the front army, that makes 115–125,000 men. To this we must add the Western Ukrainian losses after December 1918 owing to illness, death, and the numbers of wounded and prisoners of war, which may have amounted to some 10,000 men by April 1919. The toll of the world war in dead, wounded, refugees, and prisoners of war who had not returned from Russia and especially from Italy must have numbered at least 100,000 men in this period.[265] Thus in April 1919 the military strength of Western Ukraine must have been at least 225,000

---

* At least until about the end of January 1919 the number of Ukrainian troops at the front was much greater than that given in official statements. A bad habit had set in among the troops (also evident among the Poles from time to time) of reporting much lower numbers in order to obtain reinforcements as quickly as possible (cf. Shukhevych, *Spomyny*, 1: 105).

** The Western Ukrainian commander in chief, General Mykhailo Omelianovych-Pavlenko, cites much higher figures in his memoirs (*Ukraïns'ko-pol's'ka viina 1918–1919*, p. 61): twenty thousand Western Ukrainians fighting in Eastern Ukraine and fifty thousand behind the lines—seventy thousand altogether.

men, probably 235–240,000. It follows that in the same month, at the time of Western Ukraine's military defeat, with a mobilization of everyone up to the age of thirty-five out of a population of three million, the loss resulting from desertion or nonenlistment was probably no higher than twenty percent. In other words, in November and December 1918 the Western Ukrainian population must have fulfilled its military duty to the full. Could any other nation exhausted by the world war have done any better?

This massive army of more than 100,000 men was created practically from scratch in the course of December 1918 by the Western Ukrainian war minister, Dmytro Vitovsky. Materially this was aided by the military stores left behind by the fourteen Austrian reserve battalions that had been stationed in the country during the world war. From the outset, however, this army was beset by very serious problems. The mobilization was undertaken very hastily, before a proper organizational framework could be established, and an army assembled so inorganically was hard to discipline. There was, in addition, a catastrophic lack of junior officers. At first there were no professionally trained military leaders. It was thanks only to the tremendous effort of the very sparse officer corps that this massive and improvised army was held together at all.[266]

These independent battalions, regiments and companies, so inadequately organized and even less adequately staffed with officers, were now dispatched little by little, in December 1918 and January 1919, first of all against Lviv and then against Przemyśl and Rava-Ruska in the north. It was hoped that they would win a quick victory over the Poles. But this was done in such haste that even untrained recruits were being sent into the field. The result was that frontline troops had to organize the recruits into groups in order to give them the most basic military training at the front itself. The number of officers was inadequate to deal with the huge mass of recruits. In December 1918 and later, many thousands of these recruits were sent into Eastern Ukraine to reinforce the Sich Riflemen.[267]

At the end of December 1918 the Western Ukrainians had almost twice as many frontline troops in their improvised army as the Poles, who may have disposed of 15–18,000 men on the Eastern Galician front. Nevertheless, the Western Ukrainians were not up to winning a victory, for they were far less of an organic whole than their opponents.

The individual Western Ukrainian soldier had a different character from his Polish counterpart, although the great majority of both could fight well if led by good officers. The Polish soldier, a volunteer selected from a large population, was much more intelligent than the Western

Ukrainian soldier. He was also more imaginative and dashing, with greater initiative, but had less endurance and was subject to sudden changes of mood. Although he accepted military discipline with enthusiasm, he was inconsiderate and violent in his treatment of the civilian population, especially enemy civilians. The Western Ukrainian soldier had been called up in a mass mobilization and was therefore somewhat inferior to the average Polish volunteer. He was undemanding and tenacious, not very imaginative or daring, but under good leadership he was very solid in the attack, level-headed and composed in defense. When operating under military discipline he was courteous and helpful to the civilian population. When not under such discipline, he was barbaric. Both opponents had a burning hatred for each other. The Pole had no respect for the Western Ukrainian and was sometimes inhuman in his treatment of him. The Western Ukrainian, however, respected his enemy and treated him well in victory, as the fighting in Lviv in November 1918 demonstrated. But once he had experienced Polish mistreatment at first hand, he exhibited typical peasant vindictiveness and cruelty. The character of the conflict was determined by the fact that the Polish soldiers did not respect the Western Ukrainian soldiers as equals but treated them as rebels. It was similar in this respect to the fight to the finish between the Bolsheviks and the Russian counterrevolution, with the Poles acting systematically and the Ukrainians retaliating.

The Poles had an incomparably more numerous and much better trained officer corps than the Western Ukrainians. The typical Polish front officer was sympathetic and easygoing, proud and with a developed sense of honor, conscientious in service and daring in battle. During breaks from fighting they tended not to bother too much about their units, preferring to leave the soldiers to their own resources. They were well trained, with many officers on active duty and serving on the general staff, and were much faster than their Western Ukrainian counterparts in instilling in their improvised troops a capacity for collective action, not only in the smaller units of companies and battalions but also in the larger formations. The small Polish volunteer army was therefore very mobile, much more so than the Western Ukrainian army. The Polish military leadership mastered the situation only because it was always strongly inclined to a war of movement. Polish strategy, just like the Western Ukrainian, was also determined by political goals. Their goal, however, was the opposite of the one pursued by their opponents: not just to take Lviv but the whole of Eastern Galicia. Numerically inferior to the Western Ukrainians along the whole front, in the decisive battles the Poles always had adequate forces, generally more than the Western

Ukrainians and sometimes even twice as many. This was largely the result of their excellent intelligence service. They were also helped by the fact that, behind their lines, they controlled the railway between Przemyśl and Lviv. Within hours they could send their troops through Lviv from one section of the front to another, even the most distant. The Western Ukrainians had to march around Lviv to achieve the same objective, this operation often taking days. Thus the leadership of the Polish troops was generally well-informed, intelligent, quick, and daring. The Polish soldiers were also much better clothed, equipped, and provisioned.

Things were quite different among the Western Ukrainians. Most of their junior frontline officers were characterized by a spirit of simplicity and modesty seldom found among military leaders. Whereas the Polish officer won the obedience of his troops by means of his success in battle, the Western Ukrainian officer won the same by suffering greater deprivation than the least of his soldiers. In difficult battles he was the first to attack and the last to retreat. From the very beginning of the war, in order to set a good example to the men, the Western Ukrainian officers were forbidden alcohol, and there was almost no case of this prohibition being ignored. The corps of Western Ukrainian front officers was permeated by a deep seriousness. If they sometimes made hard demands of their soldiers, they were even harder on themselves. The whole discipline of the Western Ukrainian army rested on these qualities of the junior officers.

The military training of the front officers, however, did not measure up to those qualities of character. The average company commander was good. Good battalion commanders were harder to find, and there were very few good commanders of larger units. Within battalions the cooperation of troops in battle was relatively good, but cooperation among battalions hardly existed, to say nothing of cooperation among even larger units. On the whole, the army's operations were cumbersome.

The military value of the various fighting units was therefore quite uneven. Alongside troops of the highest caliber one found units of only average ability and in many cases units of no military value whatsoever. The human material was, of course, similar throughout. Because of the way in which the whole war was conceived, as a mere struggle for territory and not as a fight for final victory, the army was satisfied with keeping the enemy at bay and was not motivated by any great desire to seek the enemy out, find him, break through his ranks, and destroy him. It lacked the drive that sees hand-to-hand combat as the ultimate goal of every battle. The troops very soon developed an overwhelming fear of an enemy breakthrough, of being surrounded—a fear that was so characteristic of the Austrian army in the world war. The Western Ukrainian troops were therefore less intent on threatening the enemy than on securing their own position. To a large extent, this was also true of the Poles, but in their case it was somewhat justified by their defensive position. The norms by which a good soldier was evaluated were also very low. Aware of their own weaknesses and constantly threatened by the possible disintegration of this loosely organized and improvised army that was exhausted by four years of fighting in the world war, the Western Ukrainian officers tended to praise the mere fulfillment of ordinary duty as something approaching heroism. The ambition to set and achieve great goals was weakened. Only where improvisation was not possible in any case, as in the infantry, and where the soldiers and officers had to be carefully trained, as in the artillery, did it become apparent how great was the unused military potential of the Western Ukrainian soldier. The Western Ukrainian artillery was one of the best in technical accuracy, as well as in tactical ability and bravery in battle. Far superior to their Polish counterparts, they were the best troops the Western Ukrainians had. In general, with the exception of the period of general dissolution in April and May 1919, the Western Ukrainian army fought well. Judging by their losses in May and June 1919, the Poles may have lost more than 10,000 dead and wounded in this war, while the Western Ukrainians lost considerably more—in excess of 15,000, or about 15 per cent of their armed forces. For an army waging war so sluggishly, this was quite a significant loss.[268]

An army assembled like that of the Western Ukrainians could be trained and molded with time into a competent regular army by one means only—through great victories in the course of an offensive and mobile military action, organized according to a great strategic plan and led by a brilliant general staff. This was how the Eastern Ukrainians turned their originally mediocre troops into a highly competent regular fighting force. The Western Ukrainians lacked such a vision. At the beginning they had no superior military leaders capable of inspiring an irregular mass of soldiers and transforming them into a regular military organism, and few such leaders appeared later.

Very soon, the Western Ukrainians began to look around for superior officers. As early as December 1918 they took on a number of former Austro-Hungarian officers, accepting any nationality except, of course, Poles. But what they got at the beginning was usually an embodiment of the typical Austro-Hungarian military ineptitude that was a favorite subject of caricature at the time. Not until the end of February 1919 did they acquire a few competent German and Austrian general staff officers, but by then it was too late to make any difference. To the basic weaknesses of the army was now added another: the foreign officers lacked the spirit and fire indispensable for carrying out daring and warlike actions, arousing enthusiasm in the troops, and fusing the various units into a united and organic body of fighting troops. The military leadership became highly bureaucratized.[269] As a result, the Western Ukrainian people's army remained a mere mechanism, a machine without life, and soon the fatal process began that infected every soldier who had fought in the world war—the process of dissolution.

The inability of the troop commanders to lead the army to victory was compounded by the failures of the supreme command. The Western Ukrainians had asked the Eastern Ukrainians very early on for a commander of their own nationality. On 10 December 1918 an Eastern Ukrainian became the supreme commander of the Western Ukrainian army. He was General Mykhailo Omelianovych-Pavlenko, a senior officer in the former Russian army. As his chief of staff, he brought another Eastern Ukrainian and onetime officer of the Russian general staff, Colonel Yevhen Myshkivsky. As a human type, General Omelianovych-Pavlenko did not suit the Western Ukrainians. A descendant of a highly regarded line of Zaporozhian Cossacks who had entered Russian service in the 1820s and were later used against the nationalities of the Caucasus, the general was also descended on his mother's side from Georgian nobles who had been in the Russian service for generations. He thus had grown up in a family tradition of military service to the Russian Empire. Soldiers of this type, who had a great love of weaponry, considered war to be the life form of nations and the barracks to be the life form of man. These, along with personal bravery, were the main virtues of General Omelianovych-Pavlenko. The lifetime goal of this military aristocrat was a well-ordered career in the army and decorations in return for professional zeal—that was how the Russian Empire managed to bring him up and how it wanted him to behave. A serviceman through and through, the general was very modest in ideas and general cultural interests. He was unable to grasp a broader totality, be it political or strategic, consider it from different viewpoints, and chart a way forward. Personally extremely courageous, a Ukrainian patriot committed body and soul to the cause he served, General Omelianovych-Pavlenko was unfortunately no military leader. He would have made a conscientious regimental or divisional commander, capable of following orders from a higher authority on some limited section of the front and of carrying out definite limited tasks within a routine army. He had a vague patriarchal geniality and was a father figure to the troops, especially to the common soldiers, as was indeed the tradition in the Russian army and especially among the Cossack fighters. He was a sentimental Ukrainian nationalist, a feature of the Ukrainian upper strata that had survived the worst periods of Russification in the nineteenth century. He had a naïve attachment to folk songs and customs and to Ukrainian Cossack traditions. These were the qualities of General Omelianovych-Pavlenko's faintly glimmering existence that made him appear to be a modest figure. In the Western Ukrainian army that he led, whatever happened appeared to do so of its own accord, not as a result of his purposeful will. Beneath this modest attitude was an invincible stubbornness that the general regarded as willpower. He courted popularity and took for granted respect and honor shown to him. He took very unkindly to criticism, and whenever his own precedence was not spontaneously recognized he preferred to stay in the background and not fight for his own position. What the Western Ukrainians needed was a strategist who could take an overall view of the war against Poland and breathe into it the spirit of some guiding idea. The general's special ability, however, lay in training troops, not in leading them in warfare. His military vision extended only to particular sections of the front. Indeed, this general did not regard the Polish-Western Ukrainian battle line as the main front, which it actually was, but saw it as one of the peripheral theaters of the principal war that the Eastern Ukrainians had to fight with the Bolsheviks. The Western Ukrainians needed a harsh, decisive, purposeful and firm military leader who could train his subordinate officers, turn the whole Western Ukrainian military organization into an effective instrument, and demand the highest possible achievements from the troops in a rapidly moving war. The general's fatherly attitude to the troops was accompanied by a casualness that did nothing to win him the love of soldiers who were, in any case, quite alien to his type of character. Soldiers can only love a leader who impresses them. So General Omelianovych-Pavlenko was not a military leader for the Western Ukrainians, nor was he a man who could build an army for them. Only a bold military leadership could have won the war for the Western Ukrainians, but the general had no conception of this war as a historically decisive event. He therefore conformed completely to the existing Western Ukrainian policy, which saw the war merely as a struggle for territory. He led the operations of the army entrusted to him in a careful, timid and rather small-minded manner. This exaggerated caution and absence of any kind of broader and more daring vision was to be the ruin of this army.

The chief of staff, Colonel Yevhen Myshkivsky, inhibited by the stubbornness of his supreme commander, was later made the scapegoat of Western Ukraine's military failures. But Myshkivsky was not the tactician that the Western Ukrainians so desperately needed. He was praised for his ability to design military organizations, and those designs actually became the basis, later, of the Western Ukrainian military structure. But while Myshkivsky may have been a brilliant theoretician of military organization, he certainly was no practical organizer capable of managing those placed in his charge. Myshkivsky failed to create a competent general staff capable of leading the troops. Not a single section of the general staff functioned properly. In fact, both military leaders only succeeded in contributing another vice to those already existing in the Western Ukrainian army: an eastern, Russian, patriarchal carelessness in the supreme military command.[270]

So far we have considered the manner in which the Western Ukrainian army emerged. We have looked at the ordinary soldier and the frontline officers, the troop commanders and the character of the larger military units, and, finally, the supreme command. We have described the remarkable effort of the people and the inadequacy of the leadership. Now we must look at the other side of the front—the troops behind the lines. There were certainly men throughout the country who recognized the seriousness of the situation, and it was their conscientiousness that really held the country together and kept the newly emergent state from falling apart. But the number of soldiers in the rear was far too great, compared with the number at the front. In general, the soldiers in the rear were much too undisciplined, making them more of a burden to the country than an asset. Also, unlike the officers at the front, those behind the lines were too numerous and exceptionally bad, with very little sense of duty. Again in contrast to the front, a patronage system existed, and widespread corruption seriously undermined the defensive capacity of the troops. Worst of all, the army in the rear cared very little about the war. It made no effort, for instance, to capture deserters. Conditions were probably no worse than behind the lines of the Polish army at the same time. Compared with the anarchy in Eastern Ukraine and with the situation in the rear of the Russian counterrevolutionary troops, however, the Western Ukrainian situation was a shining example. But for a country as threatened as Western Ukraine, the situation was unbearable.[271]

There has never been a war or an army without difficulties behind the lines. From the point of view of whether Western Ukraine won or lost, this was not of such great significance. Much more decisive for the fate of the country was the lack of proper leadership. This was not a problem just for the Western Ukrainians but a basic flaw among all the nationalities that were now attempting to "determine their own future." A whole stratum of democratic epigones, who had nothing in common with the heroic beginnings of democracy apart from the ideology, had grown up in Austria in the decades before the world war. The internal disintegration of the Danube Monarchy and the victory of the Entente had now brought this stratum to a leading position in the state. The general situation created by the war and by the revolutions of 1918 had made it possible everywhere for philistines to rise to the leadership of "self-determination" movements. Foolhardy in success but without substance in defeat, they rose on a wave of popularity, and their weak rule was kept alive by this popularity alone. As the purely parliamentary activity of the Ukrainian National Rada demonstrated, such a leadership was eminently suitable for the task of building a national state organization according to the accepted international constitutional schema within the family of small Entente nations, as happened, for instance, in the case of the Czechs. The members of this stratum in Western Ukraine would also have been quite capable, as representatives of a small nation protected by the Entente, of making foreign-political gains at the expense of other nations defeated in the world war. They needed only to use the easily mastered methods that proved quite decisive in the new European order established by the Entente, namely, writing memoranda and slandering one's enemies. But, as in all those middle-class circles whose way of thinking, feeling and acting was half revolutionary and half petty-bourgeois, the circle that took over the leadership of Western Ukraine lacked that greatness of mind without which really creative actions are impossible. It was such actions that the Western Ukrainians needed—a genuine and bitter struggle against a hostile world, relying only on one's own strength to establish an independent national state. In all cases, in spite of differences in level of civilization, those epigones who ruled in the midst of general collapse all failed, whether it was in the moment of extreme danger, or at some moment when a major decision required great responsibility, or when it was essential that some decisive action be carried through to the end, come what may. In all such cases, those leaders were found wanting. The republican democracy in Germany, which had emerged not out of a genuine democratic revolution but out of the collapse of the old regime, failed when it confronted the dangerous choice of accepting or rejecting the Treaty of Versailles. The Czech national-revolutionary democrats also showed themselves inadequate when what was at stake was not some parliamentary debate in Prague or a bout of haggling in Paris but the fairly simple task of conducting a war against Soviet Hungary, which they managed very badly. The Polish National Democrats in Poznań, who tried so hard to damage Germany with their foreign propaganda and diplomacy, showed themselves thoroughly foolish and cowardly when, at the time of the Bolshevik invasion in 1920, they found themselves in a situation similar to the one that had faced Western Ukraine in 1919. Territorial programs, appeals, meetings, and rabble-rousing articles in the press were no longer enough to show that they had the actual ability to establish a state through struggle and victory and to maintain it. What was needed then was statesmanship and military know-how. In Western Ukraine, during the decades before the war, there had been no sociopolitical upper stratum capable of producing superior military leaders. On the contrary, what existed was a stratum of small-minded pacifist philistines who understood nothing of war, and it was those philistines who led the Ukrainian national movement. It was for this reason alone that Western Ukraine was so unprepared for the war with Poland, so very poorly equipped for this struggle for its own survival. The ossification and bureaucratization of Austria, with its secure and regulated routinism, continued to have its effect on those middle strata long after the fall of the Danube Monarchy. No brilliant statesman or effective military leader could possibly emerge in such a milieu, for the petty-minded stratum that was in charge stifled every nature that was gifted, courageous, energetic and capable of leadership or else pushed them to one side and rendered them powerless. The poor quality of this whole leading stratum, which exercised decisive influence not only on the contribution of the home front to the war effort but also on the whole policy of the state, was an obstacle to any kind of great achievement by the Western Ukrainian people. No form of dictatorship or organizational reform could have made any difference here, for when it came to technical and organizational matters, the Western Ukrainians were fairly accomplished. It was at the intellectual and cultural level that their fate was sealed. Not external circumstances behind the lines alone but the combination of those circumstances with the intellectual poverty of the government was what brought about the ruin of Western Ukraine.

III.

In the final days of November 1918, just as general mobilization was getting under way in Western Ukraine, Poland began its war against that country with three offensive operations. The Polish forces in Lviv, taking advantage of the disarray among the enemy troops after the loss of their capital, began to move east and south. In northeastern Galicia, Polish troops from the Chełm region took Rava-Ruska with the intention of breaking through to Lviv. South of Przemyśl, more Polish troops marched from Khyriv toward Sambir. The purpose of both Polish flanking operations was to gain control of those sections of the railway line, apart from the Przemyśl–Lviv railway, that were important for this stage of the war, namely the northern line that went from Jarosław in the west through Rava-Ruska to Sokal in the east and the southern line that ran from Khyriv through Sambir to Stryi in the Carpathian foothills. They also wanted to control the line running from Rava-Ruska in the north through Lviv to Sambir in the south (Map 1). In general, these offensives were a failure, at least partly so in the north. The rapidly increasing number of Western Ukrainian reinforcements forced the Polish troops back into the city of Lviv. But the Western Ukrainians did not succeed in permanently breaking the railway link between Przemyśl and Lviv. They captured the small town of Horodok near Lviv, which was on that railway line, but a Polish counterattack drove them out after a few days. The Western Ukrainians were also unsuccessful in the fighting around Przemyśl. In early December they not only repulsed the Polish troops that had attacked from Khyriv but even captured Khyriv itself and forced the Poles to retreat north toward Przemyśl and south toward Lesko (Lisko). On 9 December they penetrated the outer defenses of Przemyśl. But the Polish high command rapidly sent relief troops to Przemyśl that soon outnumbered the Western Ukrainians three to one, and by 17 December the Western Ukrainian troops had been forced back to their starting point east of Khyriv. The fighting in the region of Rava-Ruska was especially hard. The Western Ukrainians repulsed the Polish attack, thus preventing them from reaching Lviv, but the very fierce Western Ukrainian attacks on Rava-Ruska, which was strongly defended by the Poles, led to large losses, and the Western Ukrainians were forced to retreat. The outcome was favorable to the Poles, for now the Western Ukrainians were driven south of the railway line between Jarosław and Rava-Ruska. The Western Ukrainian attacks on that line between Cieszanów (Chesaniv) and Lubaczów (Liubachiv) only succeeded in temporarily disturbing the Polish use of it.

The Western Ukrainian weaknesses therefore became very obvious in the first stage of the war. The military leaders were not in complete control of operations. As in the case of the fighting around Przemyśl, they failed to concentrate their troops in decisive locations at the right time or to provide reinforcements when the energetic actions of subordinates produced temporary advances. The enemy, meanwhile, adapted rather quickly to new situations. The war, on the Ukrainian side, became something of an automatized operation. The improvised Western Ukrainian units poured in unplanned fashion from the hinterland to the front. They were highly uneven in fighting ability, and their officers had been appointed only a few days previously. They were slow-moving, often poorly led in attack, and sometimes completely undisciplined. It was as if the war were just a regional affair and not a question for the national military leadership. Thrown into frontline fighting in this manner, their first act was generally to break through enemy lines. Although the individual soldiers behaved well in such situations, the failure of leadership meant that there was very little cooperation between the different military units, with the result that the more mobile enemy generally repelled them by concentrated attack. The result of the Western Ukrainian mobilization was that a front line came into existence almost automatically. This was an excessively long front, more than two hundred fifty km in December 1918, along the line Khyriv–Przemyśl–Lviv–Yavoriv–Lubaczów–Rava-Ruska–Sokal (Map 1). This front was made up of independent battalions organized by sector commanders into larger frontline units or "groups." Exposed to the enemy, these troops either were not withdrawn to reserve units for relief or, if such an attempt was made, it proved difficult to carry out because of the frontline commanders' limited ability to conduct an active, mobile defense and their inclination toward a war of position. Thus the supreme military command lost control, to some extent, of the forces that it was meant to be leading. It always lacked a ready supply of troops for any large operation. From mid-December 1918 the whole Western Ukrainian front was numerically very strong, but, given such conduct of the war, this advantage was irrelevant, for the army was spread out in the manner of a cordon.[272]

Even so, the situation of the Lviv Poles had again become precarious by the end of December 1918. The offensives undertaken by the Polish army had failed. The Western Ukrainian troops, which were increasing in number every day as a result of the gradual mobilization, were wearing down the enemy in Lviv with continuous small-scale attacks. The Ukrainian artillery bombarded the city day and night. The Polish troops in the city had everything they needed, but the civilian population suffered greatly from privation and cold. Famine was threatening. Central Poland had shown that it was incapable, for the moment, of defeating the Western Ukrainians, and the realization that the fate of Lviv depended on the abilities of the Western Ukrainian high command was almost unbearable for the Lviv Poles. Their mood was worsened by the appearance of Eastern Ukrainian troops outside the city. These were peasant troops that had been involved in the uprising against the hetman, and the Directory had sent them to Western Ukraine in the hope that the Western Ukrainians would find some way of instilling discipline and order into this unruly gang.

The Western Ukrainian high command then decided to launch a general attack on Lviv. This attack was scheduled for 27 December 1918 and was to be accompanied by diversionary attacks along the whole front, especially in the environs of Przemyśl, where the railway line to Lviv was to be broken. The Poles, however, evidently well informed of Ukrainian intentions, redeployed their forces then advancing from Khyriv for an attack on Sambir, moving them to Horodok for the defense of Lviv. These included 2,400 men, 150 cavalry, and 10 field guns. Persistent Ukrainian attacks failed to break through the defenses of Lviv. The sudden appearance of the troops from Sambir and their attack on the Western Ukrainians' left flank brought the latter's offensive to a standstill. At that point, the Eastern Ukrainian peasant troops that were engaged in the fighting mutinied.[273]

This brought the first period of the Polish-Western Ukrainian war to an end. The Western Ukrainians had set out to win this war in a short period of time, but their effort—characteristic of this first period of the war—to overrun the numerically weak but militarily more competent Polish troops with a rapidly improvised Western Ukrainian people's army had failed. The war now entered its second period, in which the weight of central Poland came to be felt more and more. The mobilization in Western Ukraine was now over, and without some new organizational measures, which were undertaken neither then nor later, it was impossible to increase the strength of the Western Ukrainian army. Not only did the continuous stream of volunteers from all over Poland grow dramatically, leading to a rapid growth in the strength of the Polish frontline troops, but more and more new troop units were sent from Poland to mount major offensives. Especially in the region of Przemyśl and Lviv, the Polish army established a firm footing for itself through the construction of a chain of strongly fortified positions. By such means they largely restricted the freedom of movement of the Western Ukrainian troops and made Lviv the strategic central point of the war. Throughout January and February 1919, as the Western Ukrainians carried out a regular troop organization in their people's army, both forces directed their military efforts toward isolated battles, more or less carefully prepared and concentrated. Poland regained the initiative.

The Poles first attempted to capture the railway line between Rava-Ruska and Lviv and the Ukrainian-occupied territory to the west of it. To carry out this action, in early January 1919 Congress Poland raised an army of five thousand men under the leadership of General Jan Romer and sent it into the region of Rava-Ruska. In fierce fighting between 6 and 11 January, and again in the middle of the month, the Polish army in the Rava-Ruska–Sokal–Zhovkva region was beaten by the Western Ukrainians and wiped out in some areas. An especially prominent role was played in the fighting by the later chief of staff of the Western Ukrainian army, then commander in chief of the First Western Ukrainian Army Corps and a former colonel of the Austrian general staff, Viktor Kurmanovych. Only a small part of the Polish army under General Romer succeeded in breaking through to Lviv between 8 and 11 January, at the cost of very heavy losses. The plans of the Polish military leaders came to nothing, and the situation on the front returned to what it had been before this Polish initiative.

Now the Polish high command concentrated between fourteen and sixteen thousand battle-ready men and some sixty field guns in the Lviv–Horodok sector in order to throw back the Second Western Ukrainian Army Corps, which was besieging Lviv, to the south. Unaware of this Polish intention, the Western Ukrainian high command ordered its numerically much smaller army corps to undertake a second general assault on Lviv. Thus, between 11 and 13 January 1919, the two offensives clashed, with the Western Ukrainians moving first. In the hard struggle of attack and counterattack, the Polish initiative was completely defeated, and the situation remained as it had been before the battle.

The third Polish offensive against Sambir, undertaken in the Khyriv region in early February 1919, was equally unsuccessful. The Polish troops were driven back by the Third Western Ukrainian Army Corps with considerable losses. Only the inability of the Western Ukrainians to adopt more mobile tactics prevented this from becoming a decisive defeat for Poland.

But one thing, at least, was achieved by the Poles. Apart from the three great offensives just described, they succeeded in turning the conflict gradually into a war of position. This suited, to some extent, the First Western Ukrainian Army Corps in the north, but was even more suitable to the Second Army Corps around Lviv, which had been in this position since the end of December and remained there until the second half of February, except for the short Polish offensive in mid-January. And it particularly suited the Third Army Corps, which remained passive for almost the whole winter. This drawn-out winter campaign placed demands on the morale of the Western Ukrainian troops with which they were unable to cope and that eventually brought about their downfall.[274]

IV.

The winter of 1918–19 was a hard one, and the Western Ukrainian troops were not at all prepared for the cold weather. In many cases, the soldiers did not even have winter coats. At first, in the expectation of imminent large-scale offensive action, the soldiers put up with the privations bravely. They trusted the leadership. Desertions from the front up to the end of February 1919 were insignificant in number, even though everyone knew that deserters were not being tracked down and punished. Many frontline units took the initiative to help themselves, and workshops of various sorts were established. Peasants near the front lines set up support committees and, in a country already so thoroughly plundered during the world war, gave up the last of their clothing and linen for the frontline soldiers. Other problems, such as poor food supplies, were borne willingly and patiently.

Nevertheless, the Western Ukrainians would not have been able to manage this winter campaign had they not received help from Kyiv. Soon after the Directory took Kyiv on 14 December 1918, the Sich Riflemen did all they could to provide assistance to their homeland. Military supplies of every kind, whatever they could rescue from the anarchy of Eastern Ukraine, were sent to Western Ukraine. Later an excellent artillery regiment of riflemen arrived in Lviv. They brought with them the only heavy artillery that the Western Ukrainians possessed in this war, and it proved a highly effective weapon in their hands. But toward the end of December the attempt to use at Lviv the Eastern Ukrainian peasant troops that had been involved in the uprising against the hetman turned out a complete failure. The same spirit of disintegration that had so gripped the Russian army at the end of 1917 again reared its head, as if summoned up by the Eastern Galician soil itself. Orders from above were discussed by the soldiers in assemblies. Positions were given up without resistance, and there was looting. Eventually they had to be disarmed, even decimated in part, and sent back across the Zbruch as quickly as possible.

But the help from Kyiv did not bring any rapid change on the front. In a popular army of this sort, in which the soldiers want to take the offensive and be on the move but are prevented from doing so by the lack of officers and the weakness of the general staff, ongoing privation soon gives rise to a process of disintegration. Tricked by the truce negotiations during the Lviv street fighting in November 1918, the soldiers were now distrustful of the military leaders, whom they still suspected of wanting to organize some truce with the Poles. They even suspected treason. Disorder and the relative surplus of officers behind the lines also aroused indignation. The soldiers began to complain about the officer corps in general and, from about March 1919, trusted only those among their immediate superiors whom they knew. The troops gradually became apathetic.

This discouragement spread throughout the country. The people were convinced that the number of troops at the front was sufficient to defeat the Poles and could not understand why the latter continued to hold the upper hand. After January and February 1919 fewer and fewer recruits went willingly into the army. In Stanyslaviv the parties began to criticize the army. The oppositional left, especially the Peasant-Worker League, took advantage of the situation and fanned the flames of dissatisfaction with the army, especially with the officers, in order to increase its own popularity. In many places, especially after March 1919, there was local unrest. The skillful Polish intelligence network also made use of this mass dissatisfaction to spread its defeatist propaganda throughout the country according to plan.

The first effect of this general disintegration was to strengthen the hatred felt against the Poles. The increasingly disoriented masses grasped at irrelevant and inessential factors as the causes of this failure. There were demands for the removal of the entire Polish population from the war zone. Some insisted ever more stridently on the immediate internment of the Poles behind the lines. And there was much resentment about the Western Ukrainian government's continuing refusal to institute repressive measures against the Polish population and the military leadership's refusal to evacuate the Poles from the areas of fighting. Ukrainians still living in the city of Lviv continued to send out messages insisting that the troops bombard the city more effectively, even though many Ukrainians might be killed as a result. There was widespread popular indignation when the Ukrainian metropolitan in Lviv, Andrei Sheptytsky, requested the troops not to bombard the city unless they were about to storm it.[275] This was also a result of the hate campaign and the atrocity propaganda that the Poles conducted against the Western Ukrainians, both in central Poland and abroad—a propaganda largely based on free invention or, at the very least, wildly exaggerated.

Even worse for Western Ukraine, as a result of this progressive disintegration during the winter of 1918–19 influence on the masses began to slip out of the hands of the established leaders, who were never, in any case, particularly courageous or responsible. The Western Ukrainians had never had a decisive political leadership, even in Austrian times. But the educated stratum of Western Ukrainians generally enjoyed considerable trust among the popular masses because they had done a great deal for the cultural and economic development of the peasantry before the world war. Now this long-established trust was disappearing, and the Western Ukrainian government, already weak and concerned about its own popularity, was helpless. More and more, the newly emergent state began to drift without direction.[276]

V.

In February 1919, in the midst of this upheaval, the war entered its third stage, which was decisive for the Western Ukrainians. The general process of disintegration that has just been described was still only in its beginnings in January and February 1919. The country's ability to resist had not yet been seriously undermined. On the contrary, at that moment the army at the front was in much better shape than it ever had been previously. In spite of all the difficulties, the army had been thoroughly reorganized by Colonel Myshkivsky in January. It now had a solid structure and could be much more easily directed. The whole army at the front was divided into twelve brigades. Each brigade consisted of four strong and independent battalions, each made up of four companies—altogether about three thousand battle-ready infantrymen. Depending on need, each brigade also had its own artillery (in the whole army there were about fifty batteries), cavalry, and technical troops. The brigades in the Lviv sector were given most of the artillery: each brigade there had two artillery regiments. These brigades, not too big but equipped with all the essential military units, were highly suitable for independent rapid action in a war of movement. The Western Ukrainian army was later to retain this internal structure. Myshkivsky had intended to create ten more battalions behind the lines, but this was never carried out—a serious mistake on the part of the Western Ukrainians, as it was one of the factors that later contributed to their defeat. The whole front army was made up of three army corps, each with four brigades. The Second Army Corps was situated near Lviv and, given the balance of forces at the time, this should have been enough to capture the city. The First Army Corps fought in the north of the country, in the region between Sokal and Lviv. The Third Army Corps fought in the south, in the area of Khyriv, Przemyśl, and Horodok.[277]

Now was the time for the Western Ukrainian state leadership to come to terms with what the army had achieved up to that point and what it could achieve in the future. On the basis of such considerations, and quite independently of opinions among the masses or in the army, this leadership now had to determine its future course of action.

The rapid military organization carried out by the Western Ukrainians in January, long before Poland had achieved anything similar, won great regard in Poland for the Western Ukrainian high command.[278] It was assumed that the Western Ukrainian military leaders would also be most competent in battle. It was only later that they obtained irrefutable evidence to the contrary, namely, that the military leadership was politically incompetent and, in spite of its well-organized army and courageous soldiers, was incapable of instigating or carrying through any great achievement on the battlefield. Thus, despite all the theoretical wishes of Dmowski and the Polish National Democrats, there was real doubt in Poland as to whether they could actually succeed in taking over all of Western Ukraine. The Poles began to reconcile themselves to the thought that they would have to be satisfied with Lviv and the oil region, or perhaps even Lviv alone, leaving the rest of Eastern Galicia to the Western Ukrainians. Even those claims seemed overambitious, for at the beginning of February 1919 the situation in Lviv looked rather grim and soon became catastrophic. The troops in Lviv were utterly exhausted, but at that moment central Poland was simply unable to send any more soldiers to the city. In fact, the situation around Poland's own borders began to be cause for concern. In Poznań there was fighting with the Germans. In Austrian Silesia, war had broken out with the Czechs. In the north of Eastern Galicia, in the region of Lubaczów, Rava-Ruska, and Belz, the Western Ukrainians had gone on the offensive, and the operations of the First Western Ukrainian Army Corps against General Romer were developing favorably for them. In southwestern Volhynia, the Eastern Ukrainians had pushed forward almost to the Buh River. In Belarus the Germans had begun to withdraw their forces, and Poland had to improvise troops very rapidly in order to move into this territory before it was taken over by the Bolsheviks.[279]

If one were to ask at the beginning of February 1919 what the Western Ukrainians had achieved up to then, the answer would be that they had forced the Poles to have second thoughts about the conquest of Eastern Galicia as a whole and reduce their territorial claims to Lviv and the oil region. From the viewpoint of the doctrine of the "right of self-determination" and the "claim to statehood within ethnic borders" this was, of course, not a victory but a defeat for the Western Ukrainians. If one considers, however, that this nation, which had lived under the Polish yoke for almost six centuries and which, not so long before, had given up all hope of achieving independent statehood, had now singlehandedly forced its main historical enemy to reconcile itself to the loss of the greater part of Western Ukraine, then this was indeed an objectively victorious outcome to the struggle of the Western Ukrainians.

But there remained the further question: what more could this army achieve? If one held to the doctrine of "ethnic borders," then the army would have to be able to take Lviv and reach the Sian River. Even more, it was clear that Poland would never give up Lviv unless its whole army were decisively defeated at the Sian River in a counteroffensive—so decisively that Poland would have to give up, once and for all, any hope of reconquering Lviv. But by February 1919 it was highly doubtful whether the Western Ukrainians would be able to drive the Poles beyond the Sian. In fact, those with a little more insight and some intelligence in these matters would have had to doubt whether the Western Ukrainians would even be able to take Lviv, especially given the military and political leadership that they had. At the beginning of February 1919, the Western Ukrainians had some thirty-five thousand infantry in their twelve brigades at the front. But the Polish army of General Rozwadowski already had twenty-one thousand soldiers on the Khyriv–Przemyśl–Lviv front, and General Romer had fifty-six hundred soldiers in the region of Rava-Ruska. This was altogether more than twenty-six thousand soldiers, and the numerical superiority of the Western Ukrainians was no longer so great as it had been a month previously.[280] As far as is humanly possible to judge, the Western Ukrainians were probably in a position to take Lviv, but no more. Certainly they would not have been able to take Przemyśl as well except, of course, in the unlikely event that the whole Polish army in Lviv could be surrounded and destroyed. Were the Western Ukrainians in a position to stop a Polish counteroffensive for Lviv at Przemyśl? If they had been a nation with a higher degree of statecraft and a better ability to wage war than the Poles, then perhaps. But they were not such a nation. In intelligence as well as ability, they were inferior to the Poles. Even the inadequate military efforts that the ruling political circles in Western Ukraine had made up to that point were too much for them, but Western Ukraine was unable to produce a better ruling stratum, certainly not at that point or in the foreseeable future. The Western Ukrainian military leaders had also demonstrated the limits of their ability: they were no match for the Poles. The Western Ukrainian reserve was in disarray, and the number of officers was inadequate. With a big push, perhaps they could have created a reserve army of fifty thousand men, but it is not with numbers of men that battles are won, to say nothing of wars. In any case, the lack of officers and other problems made it extremely unlikely that such a large reserve army could even be held together. Military supplies were also nearly exhausted. How could Western Ukraine fight a major war with Poland if the quality of its national forces was so inadequate and those in leadership positions so weak? It would have been much easier for Poland, on the other hand, to put together a front army of one hundred thousand men within a few months. Confronted with such Polish superiority, what could Western Ukraine do? Conditions in Eastern Ukraine also had to be taken into account. If it fell to the Bolsheviks, then the existence of tiny Western Ukraine as a state, especially if it were to reach as far as the Sian and extend to its ethnic borders, would become an impossibility.

As early as February 1919, at the height of its success and at the peak of its fighting capacity, the Western Ukrainian army, relying on its own forces alone, was in no position to win a complete victory in keeping with the "ethnic principle." If the international environment had been more favorable to Western Ukraine; if any advantage were to be had by gaining time, then the situation would have been different. But that was not the case. The Polish conflicts with the Czechs and Germans were purely local in character. They relieved the pressure on the Western Ukrainians, but, by making a few concessions, the Poles could bring those conflicts to an end at any time in order to throw their whole weight against Western Ukraine.

The time had come for the Western Ukrainians to think of bringing their war with Poland to an end while their situation was more favorable than that of the Poles and they remained militarily strong. To this end they would have to put themselves in the best possible military position to cope with the two choices confronting them: either continue the war, if Poland's situation continued to deteriorate, until all ethnic territory had been conquered or, even at the cost of large territorial losses, make peace with Poland for fear that the Polish situation would soon improve.

Nothing would strengthen the Western Ukrainian position quite so much as the capture of Lviv. Such a success would be important not only from the viewpoint of international relations and negotiations with Poland. It was even more important from the viewpoint of the effect that such a conquest would have on the morale and military competence of the Western Ukrainians.

In February 1919 the Western Ukrainian military leadership finally decided to make the conquest of Lviv its proximate goal. But the Western Ukrainians made no move in the field of foreign policy. Under the spell of the doctrines of "self-determination" and "ethnic borders," they were concerned only with the continuation of the war, while doing nothing to pave the way for an eventual peace treaty. It was of decisive importance that they were totally unconcerned with Entente intervention in the

Polish-Ukrainian conflict and in the "Ukrainian question" in general—this despite the fact that they had the opportunity at least to lessen the damage that such intervention would soon do to their cause.

In view of Western Ukraine's military and organizational achievements, and in view of the fact that the Directory, although it had just lost Kyiv, still held almost all of Volhynia and Podilia (Map 2), it should have been no surprise that just at this moment, in February 1919, Marshal Foch began to think of Ukraine in his plans for intervention against the Bolsheviks. In January 1919 an inter-Allied mission was sent to Warsaw to arrange a peace between the Poles and the Western Ukrainians in the event that the latter turned out not to be Bolsheviks, as Poland had led the Entente public to believe. The members of this mission, led by the French general Berthélemy, were the English general Adrian Carton de Wiart, the American professor Robert Lord, and the Italian commander Giuseppe Stabile.

On 19 January 1919, the English mission headed by General de Wiart, having just arrived in Lviv, asked the Western Ukrainian high command what its attitude would be to a truce with Poland on the basis of a mutually agreed demarcation line. This gave the Western Ukrainians the opportunity at least to attempt diplomatic preparations for a peace treaty with Poland, and perhaps even to persuade the English to work toward reducing Polish "appetites." But the Western Ukrainians saw no need to make peace with Poland as long as it remained weak. Under pressure from public opinion and concerned about its own popularity, the Western Ukrainian government held dogmatically to the "ethnic principle," thinking it better to have a firm policy. Believing that the army was in a position to take Lviv at any moment and paying no heed to the military potential of central Poland, they thought, quite simply, that the conquest of Lviv would mean the end of the war. They replied to the English suggestion that they were prepared to accept a truce with Poland only on the basis of Western Ukrainian control up to the Sian River and without relinquishing their claim to Ukrainian territory west of the Sian. But the Western Ukrainians did not in fact hold that territory, nor was it likely that their forces would be able to take it.[281]

Paying no attention to the many invitations from the Western Ukrainian government to extend its visit to Western Ukraine,[282] the Berthélemy mission now negotiated exclusively with the Poles. These negotiations with the French military representatives clearly concerned what kind of concessions the Poles were willing to make that would enable the French to integrate the Ukrainians into their planned intervention against the Bolsheviks and into their overall plans for French dominance in Europe. What prompted this Warsaw-based mission to intervene decisively in the Polish-Ukrainian war was that by about mid-February 1919 the military situation of the Poles in Eastern Galicia seemed almost hopeless.

VI.

At the beginning of February 1919, Myshkivsky was replaced as chief of staff of the Western Ukrainian army by the Western Ukrainian Viktor Kurmanovych, well known for his role in the fighting around Rava-Ruska and Zhovkva. This change gave new confidence to the army, a confidence that initially seemed justified. Preparations were immediately begun for a major offensive. According to the plan, a section of the Third Army Corps was to break the Lviv–Przemyśl railway line between Horodok and Sudova Vyshnia, while the First Army Corps continued its assault on the line between Rava-Ruska and Sokal. Meanwhile, the Second Army Corps, reinforced by units of the First Army Corps, was to tie down the Polish army in Lviv by means of a major diversion to the north of the city. Following the operation at Horodok and Sudova Vyshnia, the third general assault on Lviv would be carried out. After the capture of the city, which was awaited with confidence, the army would go on to capture Przemyśl.

The Western Ukrainians began their offensive on 14 February 1919, taking Polish positions all along the line between Horodok and Sudova Vyshnia. They reached the railway line and kept it under fire to a depth of about twenty-five km. The Poles held up any further Ukrainian advance, but their desperate counterattacks, intended to drive the Ukrainians back, failed because of the strength of Ukrainian resistance and further Ukrainian assaults. By 20 February there was no longer any railway link between Lviv and Przemyśl. Deprivation in the surrounded city became extreme.

Everyone now expected the capture of Lviv to follow very quickly. The fall of the beleaguered city was taken for granted by all. Reports to Paris from the inter-Allied mission in Warsaw spoke of this as an inevitability.[283]

But now the unforeseen occurred—something that, along with the incompetence of the leadership and the turmoil among the masses, was to be one of the causes of the ultimate ruin of Western Ukraine. In the face of what appeared to be imminent defeat for the Poles, the Entente intervened in the war on the side of Poland.

Without delay, the Berthélemy mission left Warsaw for Lviv on 17 February. Their aim, at the last minute, was to save Lviv for the Poles, not only because it was in France's interest that Poland occupy the western part of Eastern Galicia but also because they knew that if the Western Ukrainians captured Lviv, Polish resistance to the Ukrainian occupation would merely prolong the war and undermine the immediate plans of Marshal Foch.

En route to Lviv on 18 February, the Berthélemy mission sent a telegram to the Western Ukrainian high command demanding an immediate cessation of hostilities. The high command rejected this, stating that negotiations could take place while the war continued. The mission passed through Lviv and, not without difficulty, came through the battle lines, arriving at the headquarters of the Western Ukrainian high command in Khodoriv on 22 February. Here the members of the mission declared that, as plenipotentiaries of the Entente, they regarded the refusal to cease hostilities as tantamount to a breach of diplomatic relations between the Entente and Western Ukraine. They threatened to leave the country immediately. Under such pressure, the Western Ukrainians called off their military offensive, which was proceeding well, early on the morning of 25 February, and their representatives went to Lviv to begin negotiations. This intervention of the Entente saved Eastern Galicia for Poland. For it can hardly be doubted that the capture of Lviv at that particular moment would have given such a boost to the fighting spirit of the Western Ukrainians that any later Polish offensive would have been met by insuperable resistance. Poland would then have been in no position to take all of Eastern Galicia from an undaunted nation but would probably have had to content itself with the occupation of a small section of the western part of the country. The Entente intervention, however, now decided the outcome of the conflict against the Western Ukrainians not only because of the intervention at that moment by the Berthélemy mission but, more importantly, because the Western Ukrainian military effort now became totally confused. It was no longer directed by a clear understanding of the balance of forces between Poland and Western Ukraine but by extremely erroneous assumptions concerning the role of the Entente as an honest broker in the conflict between the two countries.

The negotiations were a travesty of justice. All the representatives of the Allies, including the English, sided with Poland. Even their outward behavior toward the Western Ukrainian representatives was highly insulting, crude and rough. They had already brought the completed truce agreement with them from Warsaw. The Poles were familiar with the contents of the document, and when, under the leadership of Count Aleksander Skarbek, the Poles began to negotiate directly with the Western Ukrainians, they ridiculed their opponents. When the Western Ukrainians demanded that the truce line be on the river Sian, the Poles demanded in return that it be on the Zbruch, which forms the eastern border of Galicia. The Poles' final offer was that the demarcation line be much farther east than the subsequently announced Berthélemy line.[284]

Since the direct negotiations between the Poles and the Western Ukrainians came to nothing, it was up to the Entente to arbitrate between the two. But first the Berthélemy mission paid a visit to Petliura, who had just arrived at the Western Ukrainian military headquarters in Khodoriv. They wanted to have a look at this "adventurer" before making use of Ukraine in their plans for fighting the Bolsheviks. On 28 February General Berthélemy handed over the truce conditions to the Polish and Western Ukrainian delegations separately. His speech to the Western Ukrainian delegation on this occasion ran as follows:

> We, the representatives of the Entente, that is, of England, France, America, and Italy, have conscientiously and thoroughly examined this dispute in which we are called upon to arbitrate. We ask for concessions from both parties, concessions that are only of a preliminary nature and will retain their validity only until a final decision is made at the Peace Conference. It is true that your situation today is a favorable one, but that situation could change. A truce has already been arranged between the Czechs and the Poles, and Poland will now be able to transport munitions across Czech territory. Similarly, a truce will soon be arranged between the Poles and the Germans.* The Bolsheviks have not yet attacked Polish territory, and the Poles are therefore under no compulsion to defend themselves from that quarter. The Poles are aware of all this, which fills them with hope and gives them added strength. If you do not accept our proposal, you will bear the responsibility for your decision before the whole Entente. You will have to wage war with Poland, which will be assisted by Haller's competent and well-organized army. Our observations in France have convinced us of the courage of this army. On the other side, the Bolsheviks are marching against you. They have already occupied Kyiv and the greater part of your territory and are now standing at your own door. But if you accept our proposal, we will

* Such a truce was indeed dictated to the Germans by the Entente as early as 16 February 1919, partly in order to thwart the German counteroffensive in the province of Posen (Poznań) and partly to free Polish forces for action against the Western Ukrainians.

> take steps to recognize your sovereignty. The fact that we are negotiating with you and making such a proposal to you is already something of a recognition of your state, for one cannot negotiate with what does not exist. With our support you will defeat the Bolsheviks and win back the country that you have lost. You will then not appear before the Peace Conference with empty hands. Our decision will influence the outcome of the negotiations now being held between the Directory and the Entente representatives in Odesa because our plenipotentiary powers exceed theirs. We will arrange for your representatives to be present at the Peace Conference. We will send a special mission that will remain here and report to our governments on your needs. We will establish relations between your government and the Entente powers. Think of the proverb: heaven helps those who help themselves. Heaven, in this case, is the Entente. Your decision will represent the beginning of a new life for you and the fulfillment of your aspirations as a nation. Never again will you have the opportunity that you have today. This is a great and solemn moment. The fate of your nation is in your hands.[285]

These admonitions corresponded to the truce conditions. The Western Ukrainians would have to evacuate their forces within fourteen days from almost half of their linguistic territory in Eastern Galicia. The demarcation line was to run from the former Austro-Russian border along the Buh River to Kaminka-Strumylova, then through Bibrka and Mykolaiv to the Dnister, then further southwest between Drohobych and Stryi into the Carpathians to the former Galician-Hungarian border. Lviv and the oil region would remain with Poland (Map 1). The signing of the truce agreement was to take place on 5 March 1919, and at the same time a treaty drafted by the mission was to be signed in order to guarantee oil deliveries to Western Ukraine by Poland. The truce agreement contained the condition that this agreement in no way predetermined the eventual decision by the Peace Conference concerning Eastern Galicia, but it was clear that the demarcation line was to mark the future border between Poland and Ukraine.

The truce conditions were excessive, as was all that the Entente dictated to the defeated nations at the end of the war. The greater part of the Western Ukrainian territory that was to be handed over to the Poles was in Western Ukrainian hands. The Poles held only two cities, Przemyśl and Lviv. As far as Lviv was concerned, its retention by Poland was in some sense justified by the wartime right of military possession.

The Poles had, after all, held on to the city with great courage and perseverance against numerically superior forces. Patriotic Western Ukrainians could possibly have come to terms with the loss of Lviv and the territory lying to the northwest of the city. It was roughly a quarter of their whole country, but that did not exceed the normal conditions of truce agreements. But the loss of the territory south and east of Przemyśl on top of that was almost too much for the Western Ukrainians.

And yet there was not much they could do but accept the Berthélemy peace proposals. For the situation and prospects of the Western Ukrainians were exactly as Berthélemy had described them. Without the support of the Entente, a victory over the Bolsheviks was inconceivable, and Berthélemy offered the Ukrainians the prospect of being accepted into the Entente. That the Western Ukrainians, an unknown nation greatly slandered by its enemies, should, on the basis of its military strength alone, have forced the Entente into the position of making such an offer was indeed a tremendous success. Given the circumstances in Europe at the time, there really was no other option for Western Ukraine except, perhaps, joining the Bolshevik camp. Once Ukrainian statehood had been recognized by the Entente, this was something of a guarantee that Western Ukraine would not be attacked by Poland in the future, unless, of course, the Ukrainians were defeated in the battle against the Bolsheviks. In that case, Poland would certainly occupy all of Galicia.[286] But with Western Ukraine in a much better state of order than the territory under Denikin[287] or Petliura, there was good reason to hope that the Western Ukrainians would be successful in their struggle against the Bolsheviks, as were the Baltic states, and that under those circumstances the eastern borders of the Ukrainian state could even reach as far as the Dnipro and Odesa on the Black Sea. The prospects of such a state, dependent on the good will of France and Poland, were by no means bright, but, given Ukraine's internal and external situation at the time, it was in no position to achieve more. It was a major step forward for a stateless people to be able to set up a rump state if the choice was between this and complete subjection.

In order to accept the kind of peace that Berthélemy was offering, a nation would have to be free of all ethnic conceptions in the realm of politics. International politics would have to be seen as the interplay of real national forces, not as a conflict involving just abstract national rights. Ethnic territory is only the natural spatial context within which politics works. National traditions provide only the raw material that is shaped and molded by politics. But the goal of politics itself is neither to mirror this ethnic territory exactly in national statehood nor to encapsulate the totality of those national traditions in state form. The goal of politics is above all the establishment of a particular order and a particular rule of law on the territory that a nation actually controls. This way of thinking was not entirely alien to the Eastern Ukrainians. They were well aware that they could achieve statehood only on the basis of their own military strength and on such a territory as that strength could defend. Petliura therefore strongly advised the Western Ukrainians to accept the Berthélemy proposals. Such an attitude and such a solution would also have appeared plausible to the Western Ukrainians had not the proclamation of the Wilson principles as the highest norm of international relations brought about total chaos in the political conceptions of European democrats at the time. This proclamation introduced a completely new element into international relations, namely, a conceptual confusion about what constituted justice in relations between nations and states. Up to that time it had been assumed that every nation forges its own destiny and that it was open to every nation, by making a more strenuous effort, to satisfy its own ambitions. It was taken for granted in international relations that a just peace did not correspond merely to some temporary advantage gained by one of the parties but to the vital interests of both parties and to the fundamental balance of forces between them. An unjust peace was one that undermined a nation's vital interests, thereby putting its existence in question, or one that failed to reflect the innermost equilibrium between nations in the international arena. Now, however, as a result of this idea of democratic self-determination, wishes themselves—above all, ethnic and territorial aspirations—became the criterion of international justice. Such a criterion took no account of the actual state-building capacity of any nation, nor of its real cultural and intellectual level, not to mention its military strength. Under the spell of such a mishmash of reality and desire, the Western Ukrainians, taking the wish list as the basic principle of world order, declared that the acceptance of the Berthélemy proposals would be tantamount to a renunciation of their national and political cause. They were, after all, equal to all other freely self-determining nations. No one in the Western Ukrainian camp could regard the Berthélemy conditions in any other light. Nor, for that matter, could the Poles or the Czechs.

A nation so intent on its ethnic borders, in terms of the Wilsonian principles, could only submit its explosive national sentiments to the cold rationality of politics, thereby avoiding catastrophe and saving its state from destruction, if it were ruled by a genuine leading stratum that relied on respect, not just on popularity, and had a strong and effective government at its disposal. But Western Ukraine, just like the other self-determining nations, had neither such a stratum nor such a government. The governments of the newly emergent states kept themselves in power not on the basis of well-established trust and respect but only on the basis of ever-variable popularity. The Western Ukrainian government feared, not without reason, that acceptance of the Berthélemy proposals would provoke disintegration throughout the country, possibly leading to a soviet insurrection. The masses, enthusiastic supporters of the ethnic principle, would have regarded the acceptance of the truce proposals as a final abandonment of the territories that were under Polish control and thus as a betrayal of the national cause on the part of the government.

Since the Berthélemy proposals were put forward in the form of an ultimatum that ruled out any further negotiation, the Western Ukrainian military leaders promptly rejected the truce proposals on the night of 28 February–1 March 1919, ignoring another ultimatum from the Berthélemy mission that demanded a truce. This apparent steadfastness reflected the triumph of the mood of the army and the nation. All too soon, however, the true worth of the popular mood made itself apparent.[288]

VII.

Now the Western Ukrainians would have to show their true heroism on the field of battle. "Let blood and iron decide between us and the Poles" was the proud boast of the military order issued on this occasion. But the big words were not followed by big deeds. The rejection of the Berthélemy proposals would have made sense only if the government were determined to settle this issue by relying exclusively on its national forces. It should then have made an appeal to the whole nation, a call to a life-and-death struggle, and explained clearly to the nation that only the utmost effort could now save it from destruction. But such a mode of behavior was alien to the very being of this ruling stratum. Like the other small nations of Europe, the Western Ukrainians were dazzled by the seemingly almighty power of the Entente. Since the Entente was now the arbiter in a whole series of European conflicts and had proclaimed the Wilsonian principles as its immutable guidelines in settling such conflicts, all the Western Ukrainian politicians needed to do was demonstrate to the Entente by their military operations the need for it to reckon more carefully with Western Ukrainian aspirations and make a decision more favorable to Ukraine. Nothing was done to strengthen the nation's military capacity. On the contrary, its fighting ability was undermined by the government, which, in its attempt to maintain good morale among the population, which it thought of simply as a good mood, led the people to believe that the Entente would eventually realize the injustice of the Berthélemy proposals and grant the Western Ukrainians the right to their own nation-state within their ethnic borders. But this only served to promote the process of decline in the army and in the masses. Why make a great effort if the outcome depended more on the Entente's sense of justice than on what the nation itself could achieve?

The rejection of the Berthélemy proposals could still have been justified, in spite of this attitude of the government, if the military leaders had been fully convinced that they were capable of defeating the enemy with their own forces alone and above all that they would be able to take Lviv within a few days. This would have been a visible demonstration to the Entente that the Berthélemy proposals had indeed underestimated the Western Ukrainians. But the military leaders actually gave up their plan of taking Lviv by storm, to which they had been committed shortly before, and, politically naïve as they were, placed all their hopes in a siege of Lviv in the belief that hunger would force it to capitulate in about a month. From the strategic viewpoint, this plan was seriously misguided. Given the strength of the Polish forces in Lviv and the military capacity of central Poland, it was extremely unlikely that the siege of Lviv would last a whole month without a major relief operation from Poland.

Even tactically, the siege of Lviv was badly organized by the Western Ukrainian military leaders. A siege of Lviv should have been accompanied by a strong offensive against Przemyśl. But all the Western Ukrainians did was renew the operation in the Horodok–Sudova Vyshnia region, which had been interrupted by the Berthélemy mission, against the railway line between Lviv and Przemyśl. Their plan, following the successful completion of this operation, was to wait at Sudova Vyshnia to intercept the Polish relief troops that would be coming from Przemyśl. But the twenty-five km of territory that the Western Ukrainians occupied between Sudova Vyshnia and Polish army positions at Horodok was a very narrow stretch of territory. It would not be difficult for the Polish relief troops from Przemyśl to break through this thin Ukrainian ring around the western end of the city. The Berthélemy mission had given the Poles a welcome break, and the Western Ukrainians were now rapidly approaching catastrophe on the field of battle.

While the Western Ukrainian government protested in a radio broadcast on 4 March 1919 to the Entente and "the whole civilized world" against the Berthélemy conditions—the annexation by Poland of a predominantly Ukrainian territory against the wishes of its population of one and a half million—the Western Ukrainian military offensive was resumed, and on 8 March the army made its assault on the Lviv–Przemyśl railway in the Horodok–Sudova Vyshnia sector. Within a day the Polish lines in this region were completely broken, and this section of the railway line fell into the hands of the Western Ukrainians. Lviv was now completely cut off from the west. Instead of continuing their attack westward toward Przemyśl, the military leaders now directed their forces against the very strongly defended Polish positions at Horodok. This attack was futile. And the Third Western Ukrainian Army Corps, instead of reinforcing its right flank near Sudova Vyshnia to await the imminent arrival of relief troops destined for Lviv, took troops out of that area and employed them in various other regions, where they were of no use. The stage was now set for a massive Polish victory.

Twice during those days fate almost put Lviv in the hands of the Western Ukrainians. They only needed to grasp the opportunity, and Poland would have suffered a major defeat. The first occasion was on 5 March, the day on which the Western Ukrainians were meant to sign the truce agreement of whose injustice they had complained. The heavy artillery of the Sich Riflemen blew up the Polish army's ammunition dump in Lviv. The Poles fled in panic, believing that the Ukrainians had taken the city. The second occasion was two days later, when almost the whole contingent of Polish troops in Lviv was sent to Horodok to prevent a Ukrainian breakthrough. But the indolence of the commander of the Second Army Corps led to both opportunities being missed.

On 12 March Poland sent an army of between eight and ten thousand men to Przemyśl under the leadership of General Wacław Iwaszkiewicz to break through to Lviv. These were troops from all parts of Poland, from the Silesian front as well as from Poznań, for the French had done everything in their power to bring about a truce between the Poles and Czechs in Silesia and the Poles and Germans in Poznań, as Berthélemy had indeed warned the Western Ukrainians, in order to make it possible for Poland to concentrate all its forces against Western Ukraine. The addition of this new army meant that the Polish troops now fighting in Eastern Galicia were numerically superior to the Western Ukrainians. Moreover, the Polish military leaders were superior to their Western Ukrainian counterparts. A Polish counteroffensive therefore began from Przemyśl. First the Poles attacked units of the Third Western Ukrainian Army Corps south of the railway line between Przemyśl and Sudova Vyshnia. Hemmed in by the Polish troops stationed at Przemyśl and Lviv, the Western Ukrainian troops in the Horodok–Sudova Vyshnia region were completely routed. By 18 March, the Western Ukrainians had been driven back to their old positions south of the Lviv–Przemyśl railway line. The ten-day siege of Lviv was over. The link between central Poland and Lviv, this "Polish Verdun," as the Poles liked to call it, was restored and permanently secured. The strength of the Western Ukrainian army was decisively broken.[289]

VIII.

This unfavorable turn in the situation had a deadly effect on the resoluteness of Western Ukraine's timid leadership. The "spirit of irreconcilability," in the name of which the Berthélemy proposals had been rejected, had not yet evaporated. Neither the masses nor the government and military leadership realized that, given the shortcomings of Western Ukraine that made it unable to wage a successful war, the conflict with Poland was already lost, and the only task remaining was to save whatever could still be saved of national independence.

The events in Lviv were not immediately known in Paris. What was known there between 17 and 19 March was that Lviv was surrounded and the Ukrainians were about to march into the city. France therefore took up the Polish cause most energetically, for the loss of Lviv would have done great damage to Poland's prestige and made it much more difficult to argue the issue of Poland's western borders at the Peace Conference. As noted earlier, on 17 March 1919, when the Ukrainian capture of Lviv seemed inevitable, Marshal Foch demanded of the Supreme Council that it send the Haller army to Lviv immediately by way of Vienna. At that stage Western Ukraine's chances with Lloyd George and with the American delegation, in which Isaiah Bowman in particular argued their case, were good. The Western Ukrainian protest of 4 March and the telegram of the Western Ukrainian state secretary, Vasyl Paneiko, on 13 March had some diplomatic effect, and Wilson, in his reply of 17 March, emphasized the Entente's good intentions toward Western Ukraine.[290] Much more important was the fact that the Western Ukrainians appeared to be militarily competent and successful, so that it seemed worthwhile to take them under the wing of the Entente. The Supreme Council therefore rejected Foch's demand and instructed him on 21 March to enter into negotiations with the Germans at Spa concerning the transport of this army through Germany.[291] This was the period of greatest tension at the Paris Peace Conference, and the decisions of the Supreme Council were simply a front for the maneuverings of individual powers. On 17 and 21 March Clemenceau gave in to Lloyd George on the question of the Haller army, but in the meantime, on 19 March, evidently under French pressure, the Eastern Galician question was placed on the agenda of the Supreme Council for the first time. What the French wanted was to use the authority of the Supreme Council to put a halt to the assumed military progress of the Western Ukrainians, just as they had done previously through the intervention of the Berthélemy mission. They intended to drag out the Eastern Galician question in the Supreme Council so as to give the Haller army time to reach Poland, where it could force the Western Ukrainians to retreat or perhaps even defeat them once and for all. Accordingly, on 19 March the Supreme Council passed a resolution calling on both parties in Lviv to cease fighting immediately and remain in their current positions. The railway line to Lviv was to be kept open for the supply of provisions. At the same time, the Supreme Council declared that such a cessation of hostilities was a precondition for hearing both parties, which were invited to send representatives to Paris to begin truce negotiations.[292] This whole resolution was based on the assumption that the Western Ukrainians were about to take Lviv and, just like the Berthélemy mission, its whole point was to stop this from happening.

In Western Ukraine's crippled state, this intervention by the Supreme Council actually made things worse. Without this external intervention, the Western Ukrainians might have pulled themselves together and fought out of desperation or tried to come to some understanding with the Poles. Now, however, their faith in the Entente and their belief that it would recognize their right to self-determination seemed justified. They could now submit to the mercy of the Supreme Council in the hope that its judgment would be more favorable to them than Berthélemy's conditions or any others that might arise out of direct negotiations with the Poles. The dictate of the Supreme Council also absolved the Western Ukrainian government of the need to make an independent decision and of any responsibility for loss of territory. What followed now in Western Ukraine was as inevitable as a forced mate in a game of chess.

The Supreme Council's resolution of 19 March, which was received in Western Ukraine at the same time as the friendly telegram from Wilson, was seen by the Western Ukrainian government and military leadership as a very welcome rescue from a most dangerous situation.[293] The complete irresponsibility of the Western Ukrainian leadership is demonstrated by the fact that, although both the government and the military leadership thought that a truce was their only salvation, they were so worried about their popularity that they did not dare to take this decision themselves. General Omelianovych-Pavlenko left the decision to his already badly shaken army. He gave the order that every battalion was to elect a delegate, a move that began the open disintegration of the army. The elected delegates, assembled at supreme headquarters, were to approve the resumption of negotiations, which they did under pressure of the threat of resignation of the general and his chief of staff. Following this, the supreme command of the Western Ukrainian army sent a favorable reply to the demand of the Supreme Council on 22 March, and the government prepared to send its representatives to Paris to negotiate with the Poles.[294]

According to the resolution of the Supreme Council, the Western Ukrainians immediately proposed a truce to the Polish supreme command. To their great surprise, they discovered that the Poles had no intention of complying with the resolution.[295] The Polish army in Eastern Galicia, now under the command of General Wacław Iwaszkiewicz, was numerically either equal to or stronger than the Western Ukrainian army. Whenever the Polish troops advanced, the Western Ukrainian troops, as a rule, retreated. Instead of a narrow corridor of Polish troops between Lviv and Przemyśl, there was now a well-organized Polish front extending from the Carpathians to Volhynia. Beginning on 23 March, the very day on which the Western Ukrainians proposed a truce, the Polish army began to move north of the Lviv–Przemyśl railway, and by the end of the month they had cleared that whole territory of Western Ukrainian detachments as far as Yaniv–Vyshenka–Nemyriv–Rava-Ruska (Map 3). The troops under Generals Iwaszkiewicz and Romer now established contact with one another, replacing the narrow Polish corridor surrounded by hostile territory with a broad and solid wedge of troops stretching from Przemyśl through Lviv to Rava-Ruska in the north. This would make an excellent starting point for a general offensive aimed at completely wiping out the Western Ukrainians. Given this successful advance of Polish preparations for the takeover of Eastern Galicia and their knowledge of Foch's plans for the Haller army, the Poles decided not to pay too much attention to the resolutions of the Supreme Council.[296]

The Poles' obvious intention to present the Supreme Council with a fait accompli in Eastern Galicia now prompted Lloyd George, with the support of the American delegation, to demand that the Poles implement the resolution of the Supreme Council. Since they had not replied to the council's demand of 19 March, the head of the American delegation to the inter-Allied Polish Commission, General F. J. Kernan, then still in Warsaw, was instructed to see to it that the truce be put into effect in Eastern Galicia.[297] Kernan then arranged a meeting of representatives of both armies in Khyriv near Przemyśl on 27 March. To the amazement of the Western Ukrainians, who assumed that the decision in this matter lay in the hands of the Entente in Paris, the Poles insisted that they would only agree to a truce if the Western Ukrainian government declared its readiness within three days to accept the demarcation line proposed by General Berthélemy. "You are misjudging the situation," said Count Aleksander Skarbek, an outstanding Polish politician of the old school who was much respected by the Western Ukrainians, in a private conversation with one of the Western Ukrainian representatives. "When the Supreme Council passed this resolution, the situation was quite different from what it is now. At that time it seemed that Lviv was about to fall into your hands. Now, as you know, there is no threat to the city. It is now high time for you to accept the Berthélemy line. You must realize that in offering you this deal, we are at odds with public opinion in Poland, which will be very angry with us. Our justification is that it is the will of the Supreme Council. If you do not agree to a truce now, we shall have the Haller army here in a month, and then you will be driven out of Eastern Galicia completely."[298]

The first time it was General Berthélemy who gave the Western Ukrainians, then on the winning side, a lesson in the assessment of their situation. Now on the losing side, they were being given a second lesson in politics, a very frank and honest lesson, again by a representative of the enemy. Count Aleksander Skarbek, a National Democrat, may have been prompted by the knowledge that a resolution of the question of Poland's western borders depended on settling Polish differences with the Anglo-Saxons concerning Eastern Galicia. Trusting in the Entente and unwilling to burden themselves with any personal responsibility, the Western Ukrainians, who were no longer masters of their own public opinion, rejected any considerations such as those suggested by Count Skarbek. They preferred to wait for the dictate of the Supreme Council and consoled themselves with the thought that, if worst came to worst, they would always have another opportunity to make peace with Poland on the basis of the Berthélemy proposals. So the Western Ukrainian representatives rejected the Polish conditions, and the negotiations at Khyriv came to nothing.[299] This was Western Ukrainians' last chance to sign a peace treaty with Poland, and they let it slip through their fingers.

IX.

What the Supreme Council did at this point only added to the disorientation of the Western Ukrainians and led them to believe that their attitude at Khyriv had been appropriate. Clemenceau wanted to pacify his Anglo-Saxon opponents. When the Supreme Council heard of the truce conditions laid down by the Poles, it decided on 2 April to form an inter-Allied commission in Paris under the chairmanship of the Boer general Louis Botha to work out truce conditions for the Poles and the Western Ukrainians. On the next day, 3 April, the Supreme Council sent a telegram to the Polish government informing it that the commission had been established and warning that the conditions of the preliminary truce in Eastern Galicia would not take precedence over what was eventually decided by the commission. At the same time General Kernan, who was already on his way to Paris, was asked to return immediately and try once more to bring about a truce. The general did his duty and again visited the Polish supreme commander in Przemyśl, General Iwaszkiewicz. But Kernan had to return to Paris empty-handed, as the Polish general declared himself unable to alter the instructions of his government concerning the Berthélemy demarcation line.[300]

With the formation of the Botha commission in Paris the Western Ukrainians appeared to have good grounds for hope that now the Supreme Council would really do something on their behalf. But this Anglo-Saxon intervention via the Supreme Council only made things worse for the Western Ukrainians. It was because of this intervention that they refused to accept the Berthélemy line immediately from the Poles. But that did not stop the Poles from preparing and carrying out their offensive with the goal of wiping out the Western Ukrainians. In expectation of some decision from the Supreme Council, the Western Ukrainians completely gave up their war effort, since it appeared senseless to continue when a peace treaty was being drawn up in Paris. This meant, however, the destruction of the last remnant of Western Ukrainian army morale. From the army's point of view, the war had now become entirely meaningless.

While Lloyd George was arguing the Western Ukrainian cause so assiduously in Paris, Ferdinand Foch and Matthias Erzberger signed a treaty in Spa on 4 April concerning the transport of the Haller army through Germany. Two weeks later, on 17 April, the Paris press was able to report the commencement of the transport. On 21 April General Haller himself arrived in Warsaw to undertake preparations for the offensive against the Western Ukrainians. The supreme army command in Warsaw had already decided on 16 March that the offensive should begin in May.[301] Meanwhile, new Polish units were continuously arriving at the Western Ukrainian front. One of them, a strong detachment from Poznań, was deployed in the Przemyśl–Lviv sector, so that by the end of April there were fifty-seven Polish battalions in the Khyriv–Przemyśl–Lviv sector alone, confronting at most forty battalions of Western Ukrainians. Meanwhile in Poland a strong wave of public opinion, encouraged by the National Democrats, was demanding the immediate subjugation of Western Ukraine. On 11 April the Diet in Warsaw passed a resolution to begin an immediate decisive offensive.[302]

The Western Ukrainian leadership was now overcome by panic. On the one side the Poles were gathering all their forces to subjugate Western Ukraine, and on the other side the Supreme Council was promising a just peace. What was to be done? Prepare to fight? But the Supreme Council was insisting that a truce was an absolute precondition of its just decision. Should Western Ukraine prove its good intentions by not responding to the Polish military buildup? But the Poles were actually attacking, and Western Ukraine was threatened with annihilation. The Wilsonian principles were becoming a curse for Western Ukraine because the Ukrainians actually believed in them and thought that the Entente would implement them. The whole political and strategic incompetence of the Western Ukrainian leaders now came home to roost, and their thinking became prey to utter confusion, in which they floundered hopelessly. Their last remnants of willpower perished in doubt and despair. Completely despondent, all the leadership could do was send telegrams to the Supreme Council and to the members of various inter-Allied commissions. In a flood of declarations they declared their readiness to cease hostilities immediately and implored the Entente to force Poland to do likewise.[303]

In vain the Western Ukrainians awaited the Polish negotiating team from one day to the next. Meanwhile, they stood idly by and watched the Polish troops make continuous advances and push back the Ukrainian front from what it had been on 23 March, creating a better starting point for their general offensive against Western Ukraine. But all the Western Ukrainians did was to send a protest note on 7 April from the Ukrainian delegation in Paris to the Supreme Council demanding that the truce be based on the status quo as of 21 March, the day on which the Supreme Council's resolution of 19 March had been announced.[304] This show of activity by the Western Ukrainians finally prompted their Anglo-Saxon patrons to act as well. They got an agreement that the Haller army would not be placed under the command of the Polish supreme command in Warsaw but would be exclusively at the disposition of Marshal Foch, with the strict proviso that it would not be used in Eastern Galicia. General Haller himself was forced to accept this obligation, and the Polish prime minister, Ignacy Paderewski, further agreed that Poland would submit to the decisions of the Supreme Council concerning Eastern Galicia.[305] Their own diplomatic activity on the one hand and Polish commitments on the other finally bewildered the Anglo-Saxons into thinking that the end of the Polish-Ukrainian war in Eastern Galicia was in sight.[306]

Incomparably more important than all these worthless diplomatic achievements of the Western Ukrainians was the effect that the panic among the Western Ukrainian ruling circles had on their army. The detachments defeated in the unsuccessful March offensive returned wrathful, embittered and undisciplined to the brigades from which they had been taken, spreading their dissatisfaction with the self-evidently unsuitable supreme command among the other units. At one blow, hopeless disappointment caused a general outbreak of the war-weariness that had been suppressed for months. Suddenly there was an alarming incidence of desertions among troops who had been sitting inactive in the trenches, waiting apathetically for the enemy to concentrate a few more battalions in their sector and attack them in turn, as he had already attacked the neighboring units. Soon bands of ragged, rebellious marauders began to roam the country, heading for home and sometimes plundering as they went. The embittered troops became reckless in making their requisitions. Mutinies broke out here and there. In many places the Poles, too, felt the helpless rage of their defeated opponents. These people were often interned, and prisoners of war and internees were now subjected to the same treatment that the Poles had meted out for months to imprisoned Western Ukrainians. The supreme command and the government shrank from this disintegration and allowed things to go their own way, so that Western Ukraine gradually became ripe for Polish conquest. Just as in February 1919 almost no Western Ukrainian doubted that the Poles would be defeated, so in April of the same year all the Poles were convinced that their troops would soon reach the Zbruch.[307]

Meanwhile, another blow awaited the already bewildered Western Ukrainian leadership. As a result of a number of circumstances, among them the evacuation of Odesa by the French, the Eastern Ukrainians suffered total defeat in their offensive against Kyiv at the beginning of April 1919. Their troops were pushed back into central Volhynia. The Bolsheviks occupied all of Podilia, and soon afterwards they were stationed all along the Zbruch River on Western Ukraine's eastern border (Map 3).[308] Although the communist revolution in Hungary had taken place only a short time previously, on 21 March, the high point of Bolshevism in Central Europe had already passed, and the threat of a Bolshevik takeover of Western Ukraine no longer had the same decisive importance as in January and February 1919. The Western Ukrainians were still completely unwilling to ally themselves with the Bolsheviks, and their only response to the advance of the Bolshevik troops to the Zbruch was to feel that everything was now collapsing around them. General Omelianovych-Pavlenko entertained the fantastic idea of evacuating part of Eastern Galicia before a prospective Bolshevik invasion, but he did nothing, and everything remained as before. On 19 April a mixed army of Eastern and Western Ukrainian troops, the Eastern Front, was formed along the Zbruch, and from then on it acted as a border defense for Western Ukraine against the Bolsheviks.[309] The Bolsheviks, in the meantime, assuming that the Poles would drive the Western Ukrainians directly toward them, halted at the Zbruch and devoted all their energy to destroying Petliura's troops in central Volhynia. On 7 May the Soviet government in Kyiv informed the Western Ukrainians that it was willing to sign a truce. This government's appeal of 9 May to "the toiling masses of Galicia and the whole world" was a clear and open expression of Bolshevik aims. The appeal called on the "workers and peasants of Galicia" to join a united front with Soviet Hungary and Soviet Ukraine. But as long as the Western Ukrainians themselves did not call on Soviet troops for assistance against the bourgeoisie—in other words, as long as there was no Soviet insurrection in Western Ukraine itself—the troops would not cross the Zbruch except in pursuit of Petliura's Eastern Ukrainian troops. In such a case, the appeal explained, the troops would again withdraw as soon as the action was completed. Petliura's troops had stored their provisions in Ternopil.[310]

With the situation along the Zbruch clarified by the Bolshevik offer of neutrality, the paralyzing immobility of the Western Ukrainians was now total. If they were to confront the approaching Polish offensive, then it was essential for the troops to regroup immediately and make a partial retreat in some areas so as to shorten the front. This would prevent the complete destruction of the Western Ukrainian army, which was split down the middle by the Lviv wedge. But the Western Ukrainian military command did nothing, for in fact it was no longer waging war. Since it had rejected the Berthélemy conditions, a voluntary retreat made no strategic sense. The Western Ukrainians were awaiting a more favorable decision from the Supreme Council in Paris, so any retreat now would only diminish the chances that the demarcation line would be drawn in their favor. In addition, morale among the troops was now so bad that when soldiers left their accustomed trenches, they ceased to have any connection with the military. The whole concept of "ethnic borders" had turned out disastrously for Western Ukraine. Everything—the paralysis of the leadership as well as the tension among the masses—was now working to facilitate Poland's conquest of Eastern Galicia.[311]

Now the first great Polish advances began. While the Western Ukrainian representatives were on their way to Paris to negotiate under the auspices of the Supreme Council, having waited in vain for Polish negotiators and a truce,[312] the Polish army stationed near Lviv, strengthened by considerable reinforcements from Poznań and elsewhere, launched concentrated attacks with greatly superior forces against the Second Western Ukrainian Army Corps and part of the First Army Corps stationed around Lviv and to the north of it, completely routing four brigades between 18 and 29 April. The troops fled, dispersed but not pursued, and later reassembled, taking up positions in the rear, but their military value was completely exhausted, and they were almost incapable of further resistance. The Lviv Poles were thus freed from the proximity of the enemy and his daily artillery bombardments. On 30 April the Polish residents of Lviv welcomed the arrival of General Haller and his staff of French officers with tremendous excitement.[313]

The Western Ukrainians no longer had any opportunity to negotiate with the Poles over the Berthélemy line. Their repeated attempts to arrange a truce directly with the overbearing enemy came to nothing.[314] Meanwhile, the Poles were very cautious in their dealings with the Supreme Council in Paris, for only a section of the Haller army had arrived, and they were afraid that the transport of the remaining troops from France might be held up.[315] They were not attacking the Western Ukrainians, they claimed, but only acting in self-defense and were therefore in no position to lay down their weapons. The Botha commission was finally instructed to begin its work without a truce having been achieved in Eastern Galicia. On 12 May representatives of both warring parties were handed a draft treaty drawn up unanimously by the commission. The proposed treaty, the whole style of which reflected the goals of liberal Anglo-Saxon capitalism in Europe, limited the number of Polish and Western Ukrainian troops in Eastern Galicia to twenty thousand each, even though the Western Ukrainians also had to contend with the Bolsheviks. Lviv and the territory north of it as far as the Buh was given to the Poles. The oil region, however, was given to the Western Ukrainians, which was a considerable improvement on Berthélemy's proposals (Map 1). In a special supplement to the treaty, reflecting Poland's success in persuading the Entente that Western Ukrainian resistance was a product of German intrigue, the Western Ukrainians were obliged to dismiss all German officers in their army (of whom they had none), as well as all Austro-Hungarian officers who had not been born in Galicia. The Western Ukrainians accepted the proposals of the Botha commission on 13 May. The Poles, however, rejected them, ridiculing the Boer general and claiming that a truce would only allow the Bolsheviks to take over the part of Eastern Galicia controlled by the Western Ukrainians.[316]

With the rest of the Haller army already en route to Poland, the National Democrats raised a storm of indignation throughout the country against Paderewski's agreement to submit to the decisions of the Supreme Council. Between 11 and 15 May the Polish Diet rejected this agreement and ordered the complete subjugation of Eastern Galicia. Piłsudski, in his first conversation with Paderewski after the latter's arrival in Warsaw on 11 May, also rejected the commitment not to use the Haller army against the Western Ukrainians. Having carried out a major Polish offensive in Belarus during April and captured Vilnius for the first time on 19 April, Piłsudski saw the conquest of Eastern Galicia as the next major task in order that Poland might obtain not only Lviv and the oil region but also a common border with Romania and access to the Black Sea through Romanian territory. In order to prevent Paderewski's resignation, Piłsudski, as head of state and commander in chief, took complete personal responsibility for this military operation. The Poles then began an extremely active propaganda campaign abroad against the Western Ukrainians. The Poles, who had been able to construct their own state organization in relative peace only as a result of the Ukrainian struggle against Bolshevism, and whose advance patrols first came into contact with weak Bolshevik forces deep in Belarus on 21 February 1919, had declared themselves the protectors of Europe from the Bolshevik menace since the beginning of the Paris Peace Conference. It was on this basis, with French support, that they made their exaggerated territorial claims and their requests for military equipment, which the Entente granted. Now they claimed to be fighting against Bolshevism in Western Ukraine, given that the Western Ukrainians were being supported by the Bolsheviks and Germans alike. Polish historians have completely accepted this falsification, along with the other claim, pulled out of nowhere, that the Western Ukrainians were armed by the Germans in return for Western Ukrainian oil.[317]

X.

The negotiations in Paris and Warsaw were of no essential significance. The decision to subjugate Eastern Galicia had been made much earlier, and military preparations got under way almost a month before the middle of May 1919. The Poles intended not only to occupy Eastern Galicia as far as the Zolota Lypa River but also Volhynia as far as the Styr River, including the town of Lutsk. Their plans originally called for the use of four divisions of the Haller army in addition to the regular Polish forces, but France was reluctant to offend England and America too much by allowing the Haller army to be used against the Western Ukrainians. Eventually the Poles were allowed to use two Haller divisions against the Ukrainians, but not directly in Eastern Galicia. They were used in Volhynia against the Eastern Ukrainians. Nevertheless, the Poles used one Haller division on their northernmost front in Eastern Galicia so that it could operate against the Western Ukrainians on the Eastern Galician side, parallel to the former Austro-Russian border. Thus both Haller divisions, led by French commanders and staff officers, fought arm in arm in Eastern Galicia and southern Volhynia (Map 3). It was a foregone conclusion that the whole offensive in Eastern Galicia and Volhynia would be led by General Haller and his French staff. Up to the last minute, however, this was not officially admitted. Their goal was to confront Anglo-Saxon objections with a fait accompli. The Poles were confident of a rapid victory, since they disposed of twice as many troops, all superbly equipped, as the Western Ukrainians had together with their Eastern Ukrainian comrades in Volhynia. The Poles were also well aware that the military competence of the Western Ukrainians had been completely undermined.

For the military campaign the Poles brought together six already organized infantry divisions, as well as a number of larger and smaller detachments that altogether made up a further three infantry divisions. These were drawn from all parts of Poland, including the Poznań region. Altogether, not counting technical troops, there were 98 to 110 infantry battalions, 31 to 35 cavalry troops, more than 200 light and heavy field guns, more than 900 heavy machine guns, well over 60,000 footsoldiers, and more than 5,000 cavalry. On the Western Ukrainian side, there were only about 60 battalions and some 7 cavalry troops, in addition to the Eastern Ukrainian forces, amounting at most to 8 battalions, about 200 light and heavy field guns, and about 600 heavy machine guns, with barely 30,000 footsoldiers and barely 600 cavalry. Thus the Poles were twice as strong as the Ukrainians in every respect, except for the artillery, where the Poles were not superior in numbers but had guns of higher caliber, and the cavalry, where the Poles outnumbered the Ukrainians almost ten to one.[318]

Even highly competent troops would have had great difficulty in holding out against such superior numbers. A further disadvantage for the Western Ukrainians was the most unfavorable organization of their front. Because of the Poles' Lviv wedge, the whole Western Ukrainian army was now spread out across two loosely connected fronts north and south of the city. Any assault on their northern and southern flanks, together with a cutting-off operation at Lviv, could lead to both fronts being separated from each other and surrounded. The only bright spot in this gloom was that Poland, aware of Anglo-Saxon objections to the use of the Haller army against Western Ukraine, kept the Haller troops in the north of the country around Sokal and did not allow them to penetrate farther south into Eastern Galicia. The frontal assault of the Haller army paralleled the former Austro-Russian border and therefore headed almost due east. As a result of this, the northern half of the Western Ukrainian army was later in a position to withdraw to the south and east, while the southern half, in its eastward retreat, was able to reach the Dnister crossings before the Poles and link up with the northern half (Map 3).

The collapse of the Western Ukrainian fronts began on 14 May, when the Poles broke through in two areas: in the north of Eastern Galicia in the direction of Sokal and north of Lviv in the direction of Kaminka-Strumylova. On 15 May there were two more Polish breakthroughs: on the extreme southern flank near Khyriv in the direction of Sambir and southwest of Lviv along a wide front stretching from Medyka to Mostyska, also in the direction of Sambir (Map 3). With the exception of a small section of the front line east of Lviv that had not been attacked, the whole Western Ukrainian front now collapsed all at once. Only in a very few cases did the Western Ukrainians offer desperate resistance, with disputed positions sometimes changing hands several times a day. The defeat was overwhelming and terrible, bringing to mind the April disaster of the Western Ukrainian brigades near Lviv. The Western Ukrainians had no reserves, and the Poles, in great haste to bring about a fait accompli before the Anglo-Saxons could raise objections, swiftly pursued the Ukrainians because their urgent orders from Warsaw were to occupy the oil region as soon as possible. The Poles reckoned that, with Galician oil under their control, Liberal England would be more inclined to listen to them. They were, of course, absolutely right.

Without fresh reserves behind its lines, a retreating army cannot reestablish itself in a strong defensive position. This is particularly true if that army has been badly beaten, as the Western Ukrainian army was, and is, in addition, very thinly spread out over a long line in which small units of defeated soldiers have little or no contact with one another. Since the Western Ukrainians had no reserves, the Polish pursuit led to ever greater disintegration of the army. The already totally demoralized Western Ukrainian soldiers realized that resistance was useless and, since they were retreating through their own home territory, deserted en masse. The defeated troops came together as they retreated. A whole brigade that had been operating on the extreme southern flank in the Carpathians was cut off from the army and driven across the former

Galician-Hungarian border, where it was forced to capitulate to the Czechs, who had occupied this territory only shortly before. On the night of 18–19 May, the Poles occupied the Eastern Galician oil region in a virtual military walkover, meeting only insignificant resistance from the Western Ukrainian rear guard, and captured Boryslav and Drohobych. On 19 May they took Kaminka-Strumylova in the north and, on the following day, Stryi. The resistance of the Eastern Galicians in central Volhynia is hardly worth mentioning. What could eight battalions do against two Polish infantry divisions when, at the same time, they were fighting for their life against persistent and superior Bolshevik forces attacking them from the east (Map 3)?[319]

Unable to retreat eastward because of Bolshevik positions along the Zbruch, the Western Ukrainian supreme command first planned to withdraw the army to the south beyond the Dnister. Confident of Czech neutrality, they hoped to withstand the Polish assault in the Carpathians. But the Polish troops continued their relentless advance, having received from Warsaw the order to "advance to the Brody–Nyzhniv–Kolomyia line with the greatest speed and energy regardless of fatigue among the soldiers." Behind the lines of the retreating Ukrainians there were local Polish uprisings, so that even the government in Stanyslaviv and the military headquarters in Khodoriv were under threat. The Western Ukrainians were therefore obliged to give up this plan and continued their retreat eastward, where they encountered least resistance.

In this already disastrous situation the Western Ukrainians now suffered another blow—a Romanian invasion. The Romanians wanted to round out their Transylvanian-Hungarian possessions by annexing the mountainous and richly forested southeastern corner of Eastern Galicia with its Chernivtsi–Kolomyia–Deliatyn–Syhit Marmaroskyi (Sighetul Marmaţiei) railway link. On 21 May they made an offer to the Poles to assist in their operation south of the Dnister with an infantry division of ten thousand men stationed in Bukovyna to prevent the Western Ukrainians from establishing themselves in the Carpathians. Before the Poles could reply, the Romanian military authorities informed their Western Ukrainian counterparts in Kolomyia on 23 May that the Romanian troops would enter the southern part of Eastern Galicia on the following morning and occupy the railway line between Kolomyia and Syhit Marmaroskyi in order to secure their front in Transylvania. The Romanian troops had been instructed, however, to avoid a confrontation with the Western Ukrainians, and the latter were asked to withdraw to the Stanyslaviv–Nadvirna line. On 24 May two Romanian cavalry and infantry divisions led by General Iacob Zadik began to march into Eastern Galicia. During the next few days, advancing slowly and cautiously, they occupied the southeastern corner of the country as far as the Dnister, almost reaching the gates of Stanyslaviv (Map 3).[320]

The fate of Western Ukraine was now finally sealed. With the Poles on one side and the Romanians on the other, the Western Ukrainians had to abandon their infantry stores in Kalush and Kolomyia, and the remnants of the army that had previously fought in the south had to cross the Dnister largely unarmed. Supplies for the footsoldiers were quickly running out. The military leaders bore scant responsibility for this. With the Bolsheviks on the Zbruch, it would have been impossible to store supplies in the east of the country beforehand, and in view of the rapid Polish advance, it was impossible to move supplies at the last minute in an orderly manner.[321]

Barely ten days after the initial Polish breakthrough, everything seemed lost. On one side the Ukrainians were being pushed back by the Poles, on the other side by the Romanians, and if they retreated eastward they would collide with the Bolsheviks. They had at most fifteen thousand soldiers left, and these were demoralized and militarily useless. They were covered in their retreat mainly by the artillery, but there was little chance that they would be able to stop and mount a defense. On 24 May the Western Ukrainian government sent four state secretaries to Vienna in order to set up a government in exile, along with the two Western Ukrainian representatives in Paris, in case the government in Western Ukraine should fall into the hands of the Poles. One of those state secretaries, Mykhailo Martynets, was captured by Polish troops en route to Vienna and was murdered together with several companions. The others carried out their task successfully. The government itself left Stanyslaviv on 26 May and headed eastward across the Dnister. The town was immediately taken over by a secretly organized Polish militia. On 27 May Polish and Romanian troops met east of Stanyslaviv. The southern part of Eastern Galicia was now completely lost to the Western Ukrainians.[322]

Although the Western Ukrainian defeat in Eastern Galicia was total, in Paris the Anglo-Saxons continued to pursue a policy apparently on their behalf. Had they been really serious about their support for Western Ukraine, they could have put effective pressure on Poland by making the recognition of its western borders depend on a satisfactory solution to the question of Eastern Galicia. But the Anglo-Saxon delegates were not united among themselves. Alongside the liberal spokesmen there were strong opponents who did not want to increase tensions at the Peace Conference for the sake of some "Ruthenians." Yet Poland had been too brusque and conspicuous in flouting the authority of the Supreme Council, undermining the council's authority among the other newly created states in the European system, for its actions to go unchallenged. It was the Americans, influenced by Isaiah Bowman, who objected most strongly: on 2 May they stopped their deliveries to Poland. The English, however, restricted themselves to a protest against the Polish offensive and, in particular, against the use of the Haller army in the Polish campaign.[323]

But the Western Ukrainians themselves had also provided some incentive for the Anglo-Saxons. In desperation the Ukrainian delegation in Paris, prompted by Paneiko, attempted to intimidate the council by presenting it with a declaration on 21 May that was tantamount to an ultimatum. As the extent of the Western Ukrainian disaster was not yet known in Paris, there were suspicions that the Western Ukrainians might decide to follow the example of the Hungarians and join up with the Bolsheviks in order to take vengeance on Poland and render assistance to Soviet Hungary. It was the Bolsheviks who were feared most of all in Paris, and it therefore seemed advisable to attempt to pacify the Ukrainians. On the afternoon of that same day, the Western Ukrainians were invited to attend the Supreme Council. The meeting was opened by Wilson, the standard-bearer of the Entente: "We have called you here," he said, "so that you might inform us about the situation in Eastern Galicia, which has grown much worse. We are greatly pained by this situation and want to bring it to an end. We hope that you will help us. I would ask, therefore, that one of you give an account of the situation and make the appropriate proposals about what should be done." The Ukrainians insisted on their right to self-determination. Thus the ultimatum and the later notes of the Ukrainian delegation in Paris did have some effect. The Supreme Council reminded Piłsudski of his obligation not to use the Haller army against the Western Ukrainians and demanded an explanation from him concerning the offensive in Eastern Galicia. The Polish press and foreign propaganda promptly responded that the Poles were merely counterattacking to stop a Western Ukrainian offensive. The Supreme Council then became even more energetic under pressure from the Anglo-Saxons and sent a telegram to Piłsudski on 27 May, threatening to stop all deliveries to Poland and cut off support if the Poles continued to ignore its demands. Lloyd George added weight to this threat by informing Dmowski through an intermediary that the satisfactory resolution of Polish claims to German territory depended on a truce in Eastern Galicia. This was the strongest threat England could have made. Dmowski was the representative of a nation that was quite happy at that juncture to take on obligations but unwilling to fulfill a single one. He appealed to England's sense of decency and rejected such pressure as incompatible with England's honor. The threat was never made again.[324]

These diplomatic difficulties had an amazing effect in Poland. The Poles had become so accustomed to the role of martyr among the nations, so used to looking on everything they did or wanted as morally good, that they became extremely indignant about the intervention of the Entente, especially England, which they considered morally reprehensible. They appealed to the honor of the Entente and called on it to bring this unworthy pressure to an end. Although they knew that there was no lack of food supplies in their agrarian country, and that what mattered for them was the supply of arms from America and not the cutting off of food supplies, they appealed to the humanitarian spirit of the world not to let Poland starve by cutting off Entente deliveries. Sympathy for Poland was so great in the Anglo-Saxon countries and the traditional conception of Poland as one of the noblest of nations still so strong that the moralizing propaganda of the Poles made a very strong impression. In England it was generally believed that Poland was being "unfairly" treated and that, as a result of Entente reprisals, it was on the verge of famine. Above all, the Poles insisted, and themselves believed, that Entente intervention was holding back their military campaign in Eastern Galicia. Soon afterwards, when the Western Ukrainians mounted a desperate counteroffensive and dealt Poland a severe defeat, it was regarded almost as a new Polish martyrdom at the hands of the Entente.[325]

Polish historians today still insist that the Entente intervention restricted Polish military operations in Eastern Galicia, although such a claim is clearly false. We have already shown how the Entente intervention restricted the activity of the Haller army only insofar as it prevented that army from attacking south toward the Dnister and shifted it eastward, which was advantageous to the Western Ukrainians. But within less than ten days of the beginning of the Haller offensive the Western Ukrainians were totally defeated, so this restriction by the Entente proved quite ineffective and meaningless. The fact that the remnants of the defeated Western Ukrainian army were able to flee eastward across the Zbruch was actually an advantage for the Poles. The Zbruch region was threatened by the Bolsheviks, and by pushing what was left of the Western Ukrainian army into Galician Podilia the Poles forced the Western Ukrainians, to a certain extent, to act as border guards for them against the Bolsheviks. And these Western Ukrainian troops could not, at any time, pose a threat to the vastly superior Polish army. Poland would have plenty of time to take over the rest of Eastern Galicia once the Ukrainians had been worn out in their struggle against the Bolsheviks. In the meantime, Poland would grow even stronger. It was considerations of this kind, and not the intervention of the Entente, that caused Poland to halt its conquest of Eastern Galicia along a line extending from Brody to the Zolota Lypa River, Nyzhniv on the Dnister, and Kolomyia (Map 3). When Polish troops acting on their own initiative went beyond this line, the military command was extremely dissatisfied with their impetuousness. The fact that they refrained from going on to the Zbruch was then presented as willingness to submit to the wishes of the Entente, but this was sheer pretense.

Although the intervention of the Entente had virtually no effect, another external factor now worked to the advantage of the Western Ukrainians. On 7 May the Germans were handed the first draft of the peace conditions, and there was great suspense not only in Paris but also in Poland about what they would do. The Poles reckoned with the possibility of a new war with Germany. They thought it prudent, therefore, to prepare for this eventuality and keep troops in readiness on their western border. Since the Western Ukrainians seemed totally defeated and incapable of any renewal of military effort, the Poles considered themselves, quite correctly, in a position to withdraw some troops from the Eastern Galician front so as to concentrate them on their western frontier for eventual use against Germany. This pertained above all to the Haller army, for by withdrawing it the Poles would appear to be demonstrating once again their willingness to accommodate the wishes of the Entente. So Piłsudski replied quite straightforwardly to the Supreme Council's telegram of 27 May: the offensive in Eastern Galicia was made necessary by the fact that Germany might reject the peace conditions, and under such circumstances Poland would require a direct link with Romania in order to resist a joint attack by the Bolsheviks and the Germans. Since that goal now seemed to have been achieved as a result of the successful offensive of the Haller army, the division of this army that had been operating against the Western Ukrainians was withdrawn in the direction of Częstochowa on 23 May, and this was followed on 28 May by the withdrawal of some of the Poznań battalions. The rest of the troops were reorganized, as they were no longer needed on the Western Ukrainian front. Eventually, only three infantry divisions remained to deal with the Western Ukrainians. Of course, this still represented a force almost twice as strong as the defeated Western Ukrainian army. On 31 May General Haller and his staff were replaced on the Volhynian-Eastern Galician front by General Iwaszkiewicz. Haller then went to Cracow, where his army was concentrated. As far as the Poles were concerned, the conquest of Eastern Galicia was now essentially complete.[326]

XI.

Now both the Western and the Eastern Ukrainians found themselves in a situation where the destruction of the remnants of their forces seemed almost inevitable. At the same time as the Haller offensive from the west against the Western Ukrainians, the Bolsheviks mounted a concentrated assault against the Eastern Ukrainians in central Volhynia. The Bolsheviks attacked from the north, east and southeast, particularly in the direction of Rivne and Kremianets, making the Poles and Bolsheviks de facto allies in the struggle against the Eastern Ukrainians. Under the weight of this double assault, the Eastern Ukrainian lines collapsed. Retreating from the Poles on one side and from the Bolsheviks on the other, by 1 June the troops found themselves concentrated in a small area north of Ternopil 60 by 90 km in extent (Map 3).[327] The situation of the Western Ukrainians drawing together south of Ternopil was becoming equally hopeless. To the east, on the Zbruch, were the Bolsheviks. In the west were the Polish divisions, which reached Brody, Radzyvyliv, and Zolochiv on 28 May and Berezhany and the Zolota Lypa line on 30 May. They did not stop at the line previously established for them but continued to push forward to the Zbruch on their own initiative. The fighting strength of the Western Ukrainian army was now only about twenty-five thousand men. According to Polish sources, it was only about seven or eight thousand.[328] The people's army created by Colonel Dmytro Vitovsky in December 1918 had all but ceased to exist. What remained was only a guard for convoys of civilian refugees and military trains that rolled eastward and southeastward into the corner between the Zbruch and Dnister Rivers without knowing where they were going or to what purpose (Map 3). No one believed any longer that these troops could put up any resistance to the Poles.[329]

In such a situation, the end seemed near. On 2 June, against the wishes of the military leadership, two Polish divisions attacked Ternopil and occupied it. They found in the city all the military supplies of the Eastern Ukrainians that had allowed them to carry on the war against the Bolsheviks. All this now fell into Polish hands. Polish war reports boasted that these supplies had been taken from the Bolsheviks, although the latter had not occupied Ternopil at that time. Petliura and his staff narrowly avoided capture by the Poles. They escaped between the two lines, that of the Bolsheviks behind the Zbruch and that of the Poles east of Ternopil. Polish and Bolshevik artillery shells met here, a symbolic image of Ukraine's hopeless situation as it fought on two fronts against Russia and Poland (Map 3). The Eastern Ukrainians were thus completely surrounded in the southern part of central Volhynia, trapped in a small area that could be crossed in two or three days' march. The Poles were to the south, and the Bolsheviks were on all other sides. The link between the Eastern and Western Ukrainians was completely broken. The Western Ukrainians were concentrated to the south, about sixty km away from the Eastern Ukrainians, in an area of about eighty sq. km. By 7 June this area was reduced to about thirty-five sq. km, a small triangle surrounded by enemies. The Bolsheviks were to the east, the Romanians to the south beyond the Dnister, and the Poles to the northwest (Map 3). The only thought of the Western Ukrainians now, as they turned their attention to the Romanians across the Dnister, was capitulation. They consoled themselves with the notion that perhaps a Western Ukrainian legion could be created out of this remnant and sent to Eastern Ukraine after a period of rest to help in the fighting against the Bolsheviks. Later, they fantasized, the struggle against the Poles could be taken up again from Eastern Ukraine.[330]

Meanwhile, the Eastern Ukrainians had taken a valiant decision. Although they had very few troops left, those troops had proven their worth in a hundred battles, and many units, led by courageous and competent staff officers, had shown unusual courage and bravery in the war. In the constant advance and retreat of the kind of mobile war that they practiced, this army knew nothing, so to speak, of flanks or dangers from the rear. A retreat for them meant breaking through and operating behind enemy lines in a kind of guerrilla war. Such troops did not capitulate easily. They were not ready to give up now. On 1 June they sent a mission to the Poles, led by General Serhii Delvig, to propose a truce. In the meantime, they decided to move their army east toward Proskuriv so as to break through to the Zbruch. From there they planned to give ground in the north and establish a base in southwestern Podilia, in Kamianets-Podilskyi. With the Dnister and Romania behind them, they planned to create a space for the retreat of the Western Ukrainians across the Zbruch and for joining forces with the Eastern Ukrainians in the struggle against the Bolsheviks (Map 4). On 2–3 June they went onto the offensive—on the Zbruch, for example, where until then their divisions, together with a small number of Western Ukrainian troops, had covered the Western Ukrainian withdrawal from the Bolsheviks. On the same day they took Kamianets-Podilskyi and, on the following day, Proskuriv. They actually created a space for the later retreat of the Western Ukrainians beyond the Zbruch, and not only did they hold this territory for a month, but they actually extended it very considerably eastward and southeastward along the Dnister. Under increasing pressure from the north, however, they began to withdraw more to the south.[331]

This courageous act offered the Western Ukrainians a glimmer of hope. Although the Western Ukrainian government still brooded over the necessity of capitulating to the Romanians, the soldiers, in view of the success of the Eastern Ukrainians, no longer shared this view. They wanted to cross the Zbruch and reorganize themselves to carry on the struggle against the Bolsheviks. A section of the Western Ukrainian military leadership, above all General Omelianovych-Pavlenko, favored the complete liquidation of the war against Poland so as to unite all Ukrainian forces against the Bolsheviks. The government led by Dr. Yevhen Petrushevych was by no means enthusiastic about this but decided to take the possibility seriously. At a conference with representatives of Eastern Ukraine held on 1 June in Buchach, the government agreed with the Eastern Ukrainians that the above-mentioned Delvig mission, which the Eastern Ukrainians had sent to the Poles that same day, should insist on the Berthélemy line as the line of demarcation for any truce. If worst came to worst, however, they would accept the Zolota Lypa River as a demarcation line so that a base could be secured, no matter how insignificant, for an eventual Western Ukrainian war against the Bolsheviks.[332] So the Western Ukrainian government, which had rejected the Berthélemy line only shortly before, now learned from experience that aspirations, even those for ethnic borders, can be freely expressed by any nation, but the extent to which they can be realized depends on that nation's own abilities, as well as on the general situation. The government also learned that a country willing to go to war against its enemy must also be willing to negotiate a peace with that same enemy.

In this situation, in which the Western Ukrainians had in their own minds already given up the war against Poland, what happened now was, against all expectations, a renewal of Western Ukrainian readiness for combat. At the same time, the revival gave evidence of what this peasant nation could have achieved if it had had an intelligent and energetic leadership. On 21 May in Stanyslaviv a Russian general, Aleksandr Grekov, joined the Western Ukrainian military service. The general had previously served in the Eastern Ukrainian army under the Central Rada and the Hetman State and had then gone over to the Directory. He was a courageous and ambitious man, well educated, energetic, and hard when he needed to be. He was one of the few Russians who linked his fate to that of Ukraine and cut his ties with his own camp, that of the Russian counterrevolution. Grekov was a man of stylish appearance who commanded attention. He was an unusually competent man with a sharp sense for the totality of things, whether it be strategy or foreign affairs. His real strength lay in both those areas. General Grekov's world was completely different from that of the Western Ukrainian political and military leaders. In his thinking and in his actions he was a statesman of a great political nation, Russia. He had what the Western Ukrainians lacked—a mature political culture that had developed out of the manifold experience of the Russian Empire. He had the ability to see relations between nations as relations of force. He understood the whole European situation from the viewpoint of the interests of individual countries. In foreign affairs he was flexible and prepared to compromise. He saw both war and peace as instruments of politics and of national advancement. War was a political decision and the conduct of war was, at its highest point, the ability to make political decisions. Unlike General Omelianovych-Pavlenko, he was no serviceman. In his ability to unite strategic and political considerations in military decisions he was of leadership quality. Did he join the Ukrainians after the fall of the Hetman State because his political awareness was far superior to that of the Russian counterrevolution? Did he believe, in other words, that only an alliance of the forces of counterrevolution with those of national liberation could win over the non-Russian nationalities to the fight against Bolshevism? Or was his joining the Ukrainians an act similar to that of the Russian generals who joined the Bolsheviks as specialists? Did he come to the Ukrainians at the time of the Directory with the secret intention of building a military base for himself, an army with himself at its head? Did he see himself as the head of a great country, perhaps even a dictator who could found a new state? Or was he a condottiere type to whom such ambition was alien and whose only enjoyment was the fighting itself? Did he fail because he, a Russian general, had no feeling for revolution or popular movements, or did he fail because Ukraine had nothing to offer such a man, because Ukrainian nationalism was unable to use him to its advantage? Whatever the case, this man, who had been minister of war under the Directory, was unable to assert himself in the atmosphere of mistrust that the Directory built up around the military. It seems that at the time of the negotiations with the French in Odesa the general conspired with the French against Petliura. In any case, Petliura thought he had proof of this, and as a result Grekov had to leave the Eastern Ukrainian military service. He went to Western Ukraine and settled in Stanyslaviv. Two years later, after the final collapse of Ukraine, it seems that General Grekov availed himself of the Ukrainian cause to engage in émigré dealings with the French and the Poles. His dealings came to nothing. He was now a fallen figure, a broken man. In any case, he had no obligations of fidelity to Ukraine. Whatever his other qualities may have been—and, where this mysterious and exceptional man is concerned, they should not be underestimated—General Grekov was at least a competent officer, a courageous soldier, and a bold military leader such as the Western Ukrainians needed at the time.

His time had now come. It was pointless for the Western Ukrainians to try to maintain their burdensome collective government machinery, with its National Rada, the Executive of this Rada, and the State Secretariat. During the retreat they decided to get rid of all this and establish a dictatorship. By decision of the Executive of the National Rada, on 8 June, Petrushevych, the president of the National Rada, was installed as dictator and, at the same time, the State Secretariat was disbanded. The functions of the State Secretariat were entrusted to a small governing group of four.* If this fundamental reform was being carried through in the government, then it seemed obvious that some fundamental changes would also have to occur in the top military leadership, since it had no idea how to avoid the coming military catastrophe and was, in addition, responsible for the failure to capture Lviv. This was made all the more necessary by the fact that General Omelianovych-Pavlenko had lost all sympathy among his troops. In the days leading up to the governmental reform, therefore, General Grekov was offered the top military post.

As an intelligent soldier, General Grekov was well aware that the military disarray had not entirely destroyed the essential virtue of the Western Ukrainian army, namely, its ability to obey orders. In Russia in 1917 it was the system of soviets and the social revolt in the army that had brought about the destruction of that army. This had not occurred in the Western Ukrainian army and, in spite of everything, this army could still be relied on. Some firm action could restore discipline and turn the troops into a useful instrument in the hands of a competent military leader, especially as desertions had only rid the army of its less reliable elements, leaving only the best and most reliable in the temporarily disorganized ranks. The three Polish divisions were pursuing the Western Ukrainians in a frenzy of overconfidence, loosening order in their ranks and links among the various units. This confidence of victory could easily be turned into defeat. The overconfident Poles mistreated the local population and plundered as they went, so that peasants in many areas, especially along the Zolota Lypa, organized behind the enemy lines and began to wage a guerrilla war. There was now a possibility that if the Western Ukrainian troops could make a breakthrough, the population would rally to them for a final desperate struggle against the Poles.[333]

* Dr. Sydir Holubovych, who had been serving as prime minister until then, took over the management of all state affairs; transportation fell to State Secretary Ivan Myron; Dr. Stepan Vytvytsky took over foreign affairs; and Major Karl Dolezhal headed the dictator's military chancellery (Lozyns'kyi, *Halychyna*, pp. 107–8).

The political and strategic situation throughout Ukraine had now changed fundamentally. As we explained in some detail earlier, the establishment of a Ukrainian state in 1918–19 was a possibility only if the Western Ukrainians, from their base in Galicia, were to occupy the western part of Eastern Ukraine. In order for the whole of Ukraine to carry on a successful struggle against the Bolsheviks, the Western Ukrainians would have had to control their own territory at least as far west as the Berthélemy line. This was a small territory, but with a population between two and two and a half million it was large enough to maintain a powerful army of occupation of one hundred to one hundred fifty thousand men, of whom sixty to ninety thousand would be battle-ready. Until the Haller offensive, the existence or establishment of an anti-Bolshevik Ukrainian state depended on whether the Western Ukrainians would give up their useless concept of ethnic borders and conclude a timely peace with Poland along the lines suggested by Berthélemy in order to be able to intervene themselves in Eastern Ukraine.

This whole prospect, namely, the formation of a Ukrainian state on the basis of a Western Ukrainian sacrifice to Poland, had to be postponed because of the Haller offensive. At best, Poland might now permit the Western Ukrainians to establish themselves in the small part of Eastern Galician Podilia east of the line between Brody and the Zolota Lypa River and north of the Dnister. But then Western Ukraine would be so small as to be unable to intervene decisively in Eastern Ukraine. Previously the existence of Ukraine had depended on ending the war with Poland. In this completely new situation, however, the perspective was reversed. It now depended on whether the Eastern Ukrainians, taking advantage of the fact that the Bolsheviks were not about to invade Western Ukraine, would give up to the Bolsheviks some of the forests and swamps they were occupying in Volhynia in order to come quickly to the assistance of the Western Ukrainians, for it was the outcome of the struggle in Western Ukraine that would now determine whether a Ukrainian state existed or not. If the combined forces of Western and Eastern Ukraine could stop the advance of Polish troops in Eastern Galicia and drive them back at least behind the Berthélemy line, making peace with Poland on that line and then devoting all their energy to defeating the Bolsheviks, a final catastrophe for Ukraine as a whole might yet be avoided. If they failed in this, then the Ukrainians, defeated by the superior forces of Russia and Poland, could lay down their arms with a good conscience, for it did not really matter whether the battle against the Bolsheviks continued in Eastern Ukraine for another few months. An independent state would no longer be a possibility.

The Ukrainians, who never had a proper understanding of foreign affairs and were incapable of dealing with really major decisions, completely failed to grasp the significance of the new situation created by the Haller offensive. Not even the Western Ukrainians realized that it was essential, in the interests not only of Western but also of Eastern Ukraine, to combine their forces in the struggle against Poland and not against the Bolsheviks. The Western Ukrainians misjudged the new situation so badly that they were willing to agree to a truce with Poland along the line of the Zolota Lypa in the belief that the final decision about the fate of a Ukrainian state still depended on what happened in Eastern and not in Western Ukraine. Similarly, Petliura and the Eastern Ukrainians never even considered the possibility of postponing their struggle against the Bolsheviks. In the interests of that struggle a truce with Poland was essential, now as before, whatever the cost to Western Ukraine. Inflexible, even naïve, in foreign affairs, and incapable of adapting to a new situation, the Eastern Ukrainian supreme command sent a military mission to the Poles in Lublin to discuss Polish conditions for a truce at the very beginning of the Haller offensive, on 18 May. The mission went so far as directly to betray the Western Ukrainians, whose help Petliura needed in the fight against the Bolsheviks. It was a betrayal, in fact, of the whole Ukrainian cause. The Eastern Ukrainian mission gave the Poles to understand that Polish claims in Eastern Galicia would not stand in the way of an Eastern Ukrainian-Polish agreement. The Poles were of course very pleased with this peculiar attitude of the militarily competent but diplomatically naïve Eastern Ukrainians. What could be better for Poland than to have the Eastern Ukrainian army defending Poland's eastern border for another few months? The Poles were well aware that Eastern Ukraine would never become an independent state capable of threatening Poland or of intervening in Eastern Galicia. Until such time as this Eastern Ukrainian army was finally destroyed, Poland could continue to develop its own strength and eventually manage to defend itself without any help from the Ukrainians. On 24 May the military mission returned with Poland's answer. The Poles were ready to sign an agreement with Eastern Ukraine and would await the arrival of a mission with the appropriate authority. The Eastern Ukrainian military leaders thought they had benefited from this betrayal, for in the final days of May 1919 they were under less pressure from the Polish troops in Volhynia. But in this they were only deceiving themselves. The Polish troops had already been instructed to advance into Volhynia no farther than the river Styr. Even without their betrayal, the Polish threat would have been no worse than it actually was (Maps 3 and 4).[334]

There was only one man among all the Ukrainians who understood the situation, and this was General Grekov, the only one among them with a military mind and the only one who had a sense of the opportune moment when major decisions have to be made in war. He understood that the solution to the whole Ukrainian question depended on what happened in Western Ukraine. He made a careful assessment of both sides fighting on Eastern Galician soil and declared himself ready to undertake the leadership of the Western Ukrainian army, but only on condition that he could lead the troops into an immediate counteroffensive. General Omelianovych-Pavlenko shared this view, although for him the only purpose of such a counteroffensive would be to regain the Zolota Lypa line and try to establish a truce. General Grekov, however, wanted a resumption of the war as such, a decisive onslaught that would take the Western Ukrainian army once more to the gates of Lviv for one final heroic effort, a fight to victory or death. This enthusiasm and strategic and political ingenuity was something that the Western Ukrainians had lacked in their first assault on Lviv. Had they possessed it, they probably would have been able to capture Lviv, Przemyśl, and Zamość and defeat the Poles. General Omelianovych-Pavlenko, lacking in enthusiasm and without a spark of ingenuity, capable only of timid caution and hesitation, accused his rival of madness in undertaking such a venture. The troops, he insisted, had too little ammunition, and such a broadly conceived offensive could only come to grief. "Then we will fight with stones," was General Grekov's reply, for he knew very well that as far as the founding of an independent Ukrainian state was concerned, it was now or never.[335]

On 7 June, his last day as supreme commander of the Western Ukrainian army, General Omelianovych-Pavlenko scheduled the first assault of this campaign, which was to become famous as the "Grekov offensive," for the following day. Although the first breakthrough was made just before his resignation on 8 June, it was inspired by Grekov, who directed the whole war effort from then on.

Early on the morning of 8 June the Western Ukrainians stormed the small town of Chortkiv, which had been occupied by the Poles only three days previously. This assault had an amazing effect. The Polish battalions defending the town fled in a wild panic, leaving behind almost all of their artillery and their whole baggage train, which the Western Ukrainians captured along with about one hundred prisoners. The Polish inhabitants had just gathered in the market square of the town to celebrate the "burial of Ukraine." Suddenly they were overrun by Polish soldiers in full flight, shouting, "Flee! The Ukrainians are here!" and the whole crowd, dressed in their best outfits for this festive occasion, dropped everything and fled.[336]

It was a remarkable event in this war, which had produced very few achievements of note until then. The news of the victory in Chortkiv under the leadership of General Grekov produced an amazing response from the Western Ukrainians. Along the whole thirty-five km of the Western Ukrainian front the soldiers now advanced, eight thousand of them in fighting readiness. Among the people there was a sudden unanimous upsurge of enthusiasm. They realized that now, at last, they were under proper leadership. The soldier who only yesterday had retreated before enemy assaults was now advancing with confident strides. The various units that had been incapable until then of cooperating in combined actions were now operating with an amazing tactical confidence. They made assaults; they broke through enemy lines; they rolled back the enemy flanks; they pursued the enemy and, against the thunder of artillery fire, they marched to the assistance of their comrades. The superior officers, who had known only caution until then, now sought out the enemy, found him, attacked and pursued him, and broke through his ranks. Yesterday's deserters, those barely capable of carrying a gun, young and old, everyone now rushed to join the advancing Ukrainian army. A platoon marched into a village and left it again as a company. The old Western Ukrainian people's army and militia had been practically destroyed by the Poles. Now, within a few days in the midst of battle, the Western Ukrainians created a new army, a regular Western Ukrainian army. They now had a system of military organization, something they had lacked in December 1918. Unlike in December 1918, the soldiers who now returned to the army found a competent and well-organized body of troops held together with an iron discipline. At a blow, this second Western Ukrainian mobilization produced an army as good as any that had gone to war in 1914. From the viewpoint of military organization, this was the secret of the success of the Grekov offensive. It was no wonder that there now developed a real spirit of competition among the various military units. The artillery now advanced bravely in front of the infantry line and overpowered the enemy with its rapid fire; the infantry now threw itself into the breach. The enemy, heedless of orders to resist, dispersed and fled.[337]

Throughout this Western Ukrainian counteroffensive, which lasted almost three weeks, the Western Ukrainians drove back an enemy that was numerically almost twice their size. These were no improvised troops, like those whom the Ukrainians had faced during the battle for Lviv, but orderly, well-knit regiments and divisions with the best of equipment. The offensive of the Western Ukrainians was in fact similar to the Polish offensive of January 1919, when the Poles not only held Lviv but pushed the Ukrainians back to the Zolota Lypa, as they also did subsequently in the Haller offensive.

But from the very first day a shadow hung over this offensive: the Western Ukrainians had a very great shortage of infantry munitions. They had hoped to find Polish munition depots as they advanced, but the Poles were well aware of this Ukrainian problem and, although they left everything else behind when they fled, they did not abandon weapons or ammunition. The Western Ukrainians searched the trains, going through every last wagon; they scoured the trenches of the world war and came up with buried and rusty shells but found nothing of use.[338]

The Ukrainians also demonstrated amazing organizational ability in the territory behind their own lines. The order and security established in the rear of the advancing troops was far superior to that which existed in Polish-controlled territories, even long after they had been occupied. From the first moment of occupation the proper legal authorities and functionaries, who had followed in the wake of the troops, were again playing their appropriate role. The dissolution of the period of retreat was brought to an end in a single day, harshly and often brutally. Those guilty of looting were executed immediately, and even theft was often punishable by death. Only desertions were overlooked, for now the soldier who fled from the rear was on his way to the front.[339]

The spirit of seriousness and decisiveness that permeated this whole operation was the spirit of its supreme commander, General Grekov. Set apart from the rest of the military staff, inaccessible, this man of iron knew neither weariness nor rest. Demanding the greatest physical effort from himself, he kept a firm hand on the operation along the entire front, and in his hand this small army became a precision instrument whose rapid movements clearly exposed the weaknesses of the enemy and took advantage of them. He was hard on himself and demanded similar hardness from his whole staff, but whoever proved himself courageous could count on the commander's greatest favor. The military machinery that functioned to serve the needs of the soldiers and mold them into an instrument for victory worked with a precision never again seen among the Western Ukrainians.[340] As the fighting continued, General Grekov, already the object of general respect and admiration, took the opportunity on 20 June to speak to the commanding officers. "Please forgive me," he said, "for not yet having acquainted myself with all of you, but you know that events have followed one another in rapid succession, and the pressure of work has prevented me from fulfilling this duty. We are now living through a moment that is perhaps the greatest in our history. The fate of Eastern Galicia, whether it is to be Ukrainian or Polish, is now being decided. In Paris negotiations are in progress on the fate of your country. If within a month we manage to establish ourselves on the Sian River, then it is certain that Eastern Galicia will remain Ukrainian, but if we fail in this, then your future is dark and not to be envied. A great achievement now lies ahead of us, and what I call on you to do is work. Help me bring this work that we have begun to a successful conclusion. Do not be upset if I am sometimes rough: this is the army. Do not take offense if my arrangements conflict with your own traditions. I am not familiar with those traditions. But I am grateful to any man who comes to me and says openly: this or that is wrong because it is not in keeping with the way we usually do things. If I see that something is wrong, I will change my command immediately. And now to work!"[341] It was a frank and manly speech, the kind of speech that the Western Ukrainian officers were not used to hearing from their leaders. This was no pep talk, no mere collection of phrases. It was a clear explanation of the dangers ahead, an explanation that called forth the maximum effort.

The Grekov offensive was not only tactically but also strategically bold (Map 4). His first goal was to push forward to Lviv with a powerful show of force, compelling the enemy to concentrate all his forces there. At the same time, Grekov intended to move the Western Ukrainian army along the Dnister until it reached a position southwest of Lviv, where, under cover of that operation, it would rapidly move south across the Dnister to the region of Halych and Mykolaiv. The army's base would thus be transferred out of Podilia south of the Dnister. In possession of the oil region, with their backs to the Carpathians and enjoying the friendly neutrality of the Czechs, they hoped to open up a supply route for arms from the West and continue the war by taking Lviv from the south and southwest and eventually reaching the Sian River.[342] On 9 July and on the following day, as this audacious offensive began, the Western Ukrainians, numbering eight thousand men, defeated two Polish divisions of thirteen thousand men and advanced twenty-five to thirty km north and northwest out of the corner between the Zbruch and the Dnister. As a result of the rapid advance of the Ukrainians and a significant loss of territory on the part of the Poles, the Polish frontline troops overestimated the strength of their enemy, and the Polish military commanders did not know how to proceed. A terrible panic took hold of the Polish population in Podilia, which fled in all directions. Day and night thousands of wagon trains rolled westward. The Poles were deserting Western Ukraine. Almost immediately after the Western

Ukrainian capture of Chortkiv, the refugees spread panic in Lviv and aroused the indignation of all Poland with their stories about the dreadful and bloodthirsty Western Ukrainian troops, supported now by countless Bolshevik forces. These stories immediately found their way into the Polish press and from there into Polish historical writings on these events. Lviv waited in terror for the Grekov offensive and expected a new siege at any time.* The apparently unstoppable Ukrainian advance only served to increase this terror. By 12 June the Ukrainians had advanced farther, taking the small towns of Terebovlia and Skalat in the north and Buchach in the south. On the next day they occupied Pidhaitsi and defeated three Polish divisions, the Poles having sent reinforcements in the meantime. By 15 June they had taken Ternopil in the north and Monastyryska in the south. In the days that followed, the Western Ukrainian army, which now numbered some eighteen thousand men, confronted almost five Polish divisions along its entire front and routed all of them.

At this point in the fighting, Poland's diplomatic game with Eastern Ukraine crossed paths with Western Ukraine—an indication of subsequent developments in 1920. The Eastern Ukrainian military mission of General Delvig, dispatched to the Poles on 1 June along with a Western Ukrainian observer, had meanwhile come to an agreement with the enemy. The negotiations began in Lviv on 3 June and were carried out in such a way that the Eastern Ukrainian negotiators, who had originally insisted on the Berthélemy line, were completely cut off from the outside world and from any information about the military situation. The Poles misled them with a show of sympathy for the Eastern Ukrainians and hostility to the Western Ukrainians, proposing that the Western Ukrainian army be disarmed. Meanwhile the Grekov offensive had begun, of which the Eastern Ukrainian representatives knew nothing. The Poles pretended to make a concession and proposed the front of 3 June as a demarcation line, although the Western Ukrainians had passed it long before. It was indicative of the ruthlessness with which Poland eliminated Ukraine that, while undermining it and destroying it as a nation, the Poles simultaneously demanded of Ukraine that it sacrifice

* The Polish military historian Hupert comments (*Zajęcie Małopolski Wschodniej*, p. 84): "The very fact of the Polish retreat made a tremendous and morally shattering impression." This impression is very accurately reflected in Bobrzyński's concise but horror-struck account (*Wskrzeszenie Państwa Polskiego*, 2: 90), typical of Polish historiography concerning these events: "On the basis of Paderewski's commitment, the Entente forced the Polish government to withdraw the Haller army, and as soon as the Ukrainians noted this, they took advantage of it and went over to the offensive. Their forces, strengthened by large masses of Bolsheviks, attacked Galicia in mid-June, took Brody and Brzeżany [Berezhany—Ed.], and threatened Lwów, murdering and robbing Polish residents everywhere."

itself to the last breath in the struggle against Bolshevism so that Poland would be better able to defend itself. Although the original Polish plans called for the occupation of Eastern Galicia up to the Zolota Lypa, since they placed very little value on the territory east of it, they did not admit this to the Ukrainian negotiators, as they could have done at no real cost to themselves. On 16 June, just as the Western Ukrainians defeated five Polish divisions practically on the Brody-Zolota Lypa line, the Poles declared themselves ready to sign a truce with the Eastern Ukrainians. They hoped that it would compel the Western Ukrainians, who could not be forced by military means, to throw themselves on the mercy of the Poles. The demarcation line, known as the Delvig line (Map 1), was to run from the Dnister along the Zolota Lypa south of Berezhany, then eastward to Ternopil, continuing in a northwesterly direction to the source of the Seret. Ternopil and the railway lines connecting it with Berezhany and Lviv were to remain in Polish hands. This was really a treacherous condition, for it allowed the Poles to concentrate a large number of their troops in Ternopil, making it easy for them to mount a southward assault that could wipe out the Western Ukrainians within a few days. The truce was to take effect early in the morning of 21 June, and the agreement stipulated that peace negotiations would be continued in Warsaw.[343]

To propose such a Western Ukrainian base for the struggle against the Bolsheviks, a territory with a population of about five hundred thousand, was a bloody mockery, and when the Polish negotiators handed over the truce proposals to the Western Ukrainians—this happened in the midst of the fighting around Berezhany, when the situation was desperate for the Poles—General Grekov rejected them out of hand.[344] Ukrainian historians have condemned this decision of Grekov's, since almost all of them start from the false assumption that it was Russia and the Bolsheviks, and not the Poles, who brought about the defeat of anti-Bolshevik Ukraine in 1919. Many Western Ukrainians are also of the opinion that General Grekov should have accepted the Delvig truce.[345] But, as we have already shown, the Ukrainians could only have withstood the Bolsheviks if they had had an adequate territorial base in Eastern Galicia. The Baltic states were successful because they had just such a base. It was not Russia but Poland that destroyed Ukraine, just as Dmowski had planned it. If General Grekov had accepted the Delvig line, this could only have prolonged the death agony of Eastern Ukraine by a few months, certainly no longer than it took the Denikin and Wrangel enterprise to waste away. In no case would it have ensured victory. And had the Poles so wished, they could have perhaps postponed their occupation of the rest of Eastern Galicia up to the Zbruch for another few months. Nothing more could have been achieved with the Delvig line.

So the question would have to be decided on the field of battle. And the battle now raged around the town of Berezhany. As a result of the Western Ukrainian victories to the north and south of it (Map 4), they now had the opportunity of surrounding a whole Polish division, in fact one of the best, the Third Polish Legion Division, in Berezhany. Now at last they had the chance to capture arms and munitions, the lack of which had hitherto prevented them from raising the number of their combat troops to more than twenty thousand men. If they could capture this Polish military center, it would mean a crushing defeat for the Polish army, which would be split in two, with the southern half near the Dnister open to destruction by the Western Ukrainians. The Grekov offensive would then have achieved everything it set out to do. In this dramatic situation, however, a Ukrainian brigade was slow in its attack, giving the Polish division just enough time to escape from Berezhany. This proved a decisive stroke of fate.[346]

The Polish front, consisting of five—almost six—divisions, was breaking up, and on 21 June the Western Ukrainians were in possession of Zboriv and Berezhany, while on the Dnister they had advanced west of Halych. In spite of this successful territorial expansion, however, General Grekov was desperate, not only because he had failed by a hair's breadth to capture a large number of enemy troops, or because of the catastrophic lack of weapons and ammunition in his army, but also because the Poles were still managing to keep their front from collapsing.

Troops were now being sent to Eastern Galicia from central Poland, and on 22 June a Haller division was sent by rail to Kaminka-Strumylova. Reinforcements were also arriving from Poznań, almost two divisions by 27 June. Piłsudski himself hastened to Eastern Galicia to take charge of the counteroffensive in person. He gave the order that the Hnyla Lypa line was to be held, but meanwhile a Western Ukrainian force of about twenty thousand combat soldiers mounted an assault, forcing the whole Polish front of six divisions to retreat in disarray. On 25 June the Western Ukrainians took Brody, Zolochiv and Rohatyn. They advanced almost to Peremyshliany and reached the Dnister west of Zhuravne. In other words, they had already broken through more than half of the Hnyla Lypa line, which was the last Polish defense before Lviv. This Western Ukrainian success was achieved by a force of no more than twenty thousand men whose ammunition supply in the vicinity of Peremyshliany amounted to about ten cartridges per soldier. And it was achieved against an enemy force of almost thirty thousand combat troops who were courageous and well-armed, with a reserve of eleven thousand men in combat readiness immediately behind them. On 7 June the Western Ukrainians had occupied an area of about thirty-five sq. km. Now, on 27 June, they had advanced one hundred twenty km in a direct line along the Dnister and, on their other flank, they had passed Brody, one hundred fifty km away. Their frontline extended one hundred sixty km as the crow flies (Map 4). They were now about a day's march from the Berthélemy line and less than two days from Lviv. The Grekov offensive was thus a remarkable feat of arms, the greatest in this whole war.[347]

Nonetheless, the situation of the Western Ukrainians was desperate, not only because they confronted a courageous enemy that was twice as strong and would not go on retreating forever, but also because they were unable to increase the strength of their own forces. At the very beginning of the offensive, General Grekov began to organize two new Western Ukrainian army corps consisting altogether of eight brigades. The Fourth Army Corps was to cover the Dnister line and eventually cross to the south. The Fifth Corps was to constitute a reserve. But he succeeded in organizing only two brigades. There were plenty of volunteers. Tens of thousands applied to join, but only fifteen thousand were enlisted. The whole of the Western Ukrainian army, including combat and reserve troops, was now more than sixty thousand men. But the organization of this large number of men encountered insuperable difficulties. There were not enough officers but, above all, there were not enough weapons and other military equipment. Weapons were taken from all reserve formations and from the local population in order to arm the two new brigades. This was completed just as the frontline troops were two days' march from Lviv. Up to that point, those new forces had not been able to join the fighting.[348]

XII.

While the Western Ukrainians, now under proper leadership, fought so courageously for their freedom, that other factor, so disastrous for Western Ukraine, continued to operate, namely, the Supreme Council in Paris. We have already shown how France was not at all averse to including Ukraine in its system of dependencies in Eastern Europe, and how Petliura was willing to cooperate. The only hindrance to this was the war between Western Ukraine and Poland. In Paris the delegates from Eastern Ukraine were trying hard, as the saying went, to interest France in Ukraine. They did not realize, of course—the Western Ukrainian representatives prevented them from finding out—that the price of such interest included heavy Western Ukrainian sacrifices to Poland. Now, just as Polish troops marched into the Eastern Galician oil fields in the course of the Haller offensive, and the French assumed that the Ukrainians had become malleable, the French foreign ministry let it be known that the way to Paris led through Warsaw. In response to an Eastern Ukrainian memorandum of 6 May that requested the sending of a French military mission to Ukraine and asked for military assistance from France in the struggle against the Bolsheviks, the French foreign ministry sent a note to the Ukrainian delegation in Paris on 19 May that read:

> The French government is pleased to ascertain that with regard to the Bolsheviks, the true enemies of mankind, the position taken by the Ukrainians corresponds to its own. The French government cannot be indifferent to the appeals that you have made on this question. The government is inclined to send a military mission to Galicia immediately, but its effectiveness will depend on the resolution of certain disputed questions along the lines suggested by the Peace Conference.... At present the French government cannot intervene in any way between the Ukrainians and the Poles on the question of control over Lviv. That is a question for the Peace Conference. But it is essential that the Poles and Ukrainians unite in the struggle against the common enemy, the Bolsheviks. They must put aside their hostilities and claims against each other, which have dragged on for too long. It must be clear that French officers can in no case participate in the action on the Galician front or play any role in the organization of the war on this front. Finally, France can give no assistance to either party for the organization of troops to fight the Russian resistance movement or to fight groups that the French government recognizes, the armies of Kolchak and Denikin, should the latter enter Ukrainian territory in the course of their struggle with the Bolsheviks.[349]

The Eastern Ukrainian reply of 20 May assured the French that under no circumstances would the Ukrainian government use French aid against the Poles or against the Russian counterrevolution. The French were entirely satisfied with this, and negotiations began over the composition of the military mission.[350] But the Ukrainians still did not understand the French diplomatic hint that they should reach a direct understanding with the Poles: instead, they continued waiting for the Peace Conference to settle the question. The Ukrainians had already been made aware on 10 May of the conditions for a direct understanding between Ukraine and Poland. They had been informed of this by Colonel Henri Freydenberg, who was to be the leader of the French military mission to Ukraine, and who was already known to them from his service as chief of staff under General Philippe d'Anselme in Odesa. Freydenberg undoubtedly knew about the planned Haller offensive and its objectives. The conditions included acceptance of the Brody-Zolota Lypa demarcation line, which was as far as the Polish troops planned to advance with the Haller offensive.[351] The Western Ukrainians rejected Freydenberg's suggestion at the time. Their inability to grasp the niceties of diplomatic language on the one hand, and, on the other hand, the amazing success of the Haller offensive, which seemed to indicate that the Ukrainians were militarily much weaker than had been assumed, meant that this French initiative came to nothing.

While the French carried on their maneuverings behind closed doors, although without success, the Supreme Council continued its activity. As the Poles correctly foresaw, their conquest of the Eastern Galician oil fields brought about an immediate change of heart among the Anglo-Saxons. It did not pay to be at odds with whoever possessed the one thing of value in Eastern Galicia, its oil concessions. The reasoning was: "The Poles were strong enough to assert their will in the disputed area itself, and pressure exercised by the Conference might easily have led to such an outburst of passion as would have swept away the Polish Government and left nothing but anarchy in its place." According to the English historian who wrote about those affairs, "The Poles in this way gained both by their strength and by their weakness."[352] The Americans were the first to retreat. Delegates like Isaiah Bowman lost their influence. The victor was Wilson, who voiced the opinion of Lord and wanted Eastern Galicia to be annexed to Poland as an autonomous province. Lloyd George was concerned to establish the best possible conditions for the penetration of English capital into Eastern Galicia and insisted on the greatest possible restrictions on Polish sovereignty in this territory, with some form of international supervision. The possibility was discussed of a neutral Eastern Galicia under League of Nations supervision.[353] The Western Ukrainian nation thus sank to the level of a colored mandate territory.

Meanwhile, the Grekov offensive began, and this far-off nation strove with its last reserves of strength to break out of the iron ring that was closing in on it. But the Western Ukrainians were seen only as troublemakers. For as long as it remained unclear whether Germany would accept the peace conditions—in other words, as long as Europe was still threatened with the outbreak of general warfare—the Eastern Galician question was seen as part of that danger, at least as long as the Western Ukrainians were, or appeared to be, militarily strong. If Germany did not accept the peace conditions, and if hostilities were to break out between France and Germany on the Rhine or between Germany and Poland, then all of

Europe would be thrown into the most terrible confusion of war. From this point of view it was essential to settle all peripheral disputes, such as that between Poland and Western Ukraine, by recognizing whatever claims were justified in order to clarify the overall situation in Europe, especially as there was already another war in progress, the one against the Bolsheviks. But now Germany accepted the peace conditions. The main war danger in Europe had been eliminated, and the smaller conflicts were now seen as petty, tiresome local disputes.[354]

Given the overall situation in Europe at the time, the Grekov offensive came too late. But this was not the only problem. Only the Polish military leaders knew exactly what the situation was in Eastern Galicia. And the French knew, to the extent that the Poles informed them. The Polish military leaders were well aware, as the Polish public was not, that there were only eight thousand Western Ukrainian soldiers at the front when the Grekov offensive began and only twenty thousand when it ended. Thus the Western Ukrainians had been fighting a numerically far superior army the whole time. The Polish military leaders also knew that there were no ties between the Western Ukrainians and the Bolsheviks, for the simple reason that a large territory controlled by Petliura lay between them.[355] But this was a Polish state secret, for Poland had cut off Western Ukraine completely from the rest of the world. The Western Ukrainians did not even have a good radio station through which to inform the world of their situation and their intentions.

The Western Ukrainians were now swamped by a veritable flood of mendacious Polish propaganda. The Poles proclaimed to all the world that they had given in to the pressure of the Peace Conference and withdrawn the Haller army. But the Western Ukrainians had taken advantage of this and, having allied themselves with the Bolsheviks, were now advancing against the heroic Polish defenders of Western civilization, an overwhelming horde of murderers and plunderers that would drown the civilized world in Bolshevik barbarism. The Delvig truce of 16 June between the Poles and the Eastern Ukrainians was held up in Paris as proof of the fact that Poland had already come to an agreement with Ukraine on the need to fight the Bolsheviks, but the Western Ukrainians had joined those same Bolsheviks.[356] The Poles appealed to the Supreme Council for help, calling on it in the name of humanity to allow Poland to stop this "Ukrainian-Bolshevik invasion," as the Grekov offensive was called, by employing the Haller army and occupying all of Eastern Galicia up to the Zbruch.

With Eastern Galician oil threatened by Bolshevik anarchy, there was no question that Poland would be allowed to protect and preserve this holiest of human values.[357] Lloyd George changed his tune immediately and, together with that other Anglo-Saxon prophet of liberty and the right of self-determination, Wilson, set about the destruction of Ukrainian statehood so that the Polish nation could revive the freedom and independence of its state. Ukraine would be partitioned among the Poles, the Bolsheviks and the Romanians—this despite the fact that the Polish nation, which itself had experienced such partitioning, had been calling this kind of action a crime for almost a century and a half. And the Entente itself had morally justified the breakup of the Austro-Hungarian Empire and the German Reich as necessary to expiate the "crime of a partitioned Poland." Just at the moment when the Polish army made its narrow escape from Berezhany, on 25 June, the Supreme Council sent the following hypocritical and insidious message to the Western Ukrainians: "In order to protect the property and the peaceable inhabitants of Eastern Galicia from the threat posed by Bolshevik bands, the Supreme Council of the Allied and associated powers has decided to authorize the armed forces of the Polish Republic to extend their operations to the Zbruch River. This authorization does not prejudice any subsequent decision that the Supreme Council may make to control the situation in Eastern Galicia."

On the same day this part of the Supreme Council decision was telegraphed to Warsaw. In fulfillment of their duty toward the Entente, which had solemnly undertaken to bring peace, liberty and justice to the nations, the Poles were now to be the official executioners of Western Ukraine.

There was, however, a second part of the resolution that the French foreign minister, Pichon, passed on to the Polish prime minister, Paderewski, on 29 June, but not to the Ukrainians. An English proposal that an Entente High Commission should immediately be established in Eastern Galicia "to protect the rights of the Ruthenians" was rejected. But the Supreme Council decided to inform the Polish government that it was also empowered to establish a civilian administration in Eastern Galicia as soon as it had reached an agreement with the Entente concerning the autonomy of the country and the political, confessional and personal freedoms of its inhabitants. This agreement was to give the Poles a limited mandate in Eastern Galicia, lasting from fifteen to twenty-five years, after which period the population of the country would be given the opportunity to decide its own fate.[358]

The Ukrainian delegation in Paris was kept in the dark for a long time concerning the entire contents of the Supreme Council's decision. The decision was made known to them only bit by bit, as if gradually to accustom them to their new role as sacrificial lamb of European diplomacy.

By the time they were given the first part of the Council's resolution that dealt with "Bolshevik bands," on 26 June, the Peace Conference's Commission on Polish Affairs had been given the task of working out with the Poles the details of the treaty with the Entente that would establish Poland's Eastern Galician mandate. Once Pichon informed Paderewski on 29 June, secret negotiations between the commission and the Poles, Paderewski and Dmowski, began on 2 July. It was on this same date that the General Secretariat of the Peace Conference informed the Ukrainian delegation in Paris that it was to present its demands to this commission "in the context of the discussion concerning the possibility of a provisional annexation of Eastern Galicia to Poland." The next bit of information, which came the following day, was that only native Western Ukrainians should attend the negotiations with this "Polish Commission," since "it does not concern the question of Ukraine but only an internal statute for Eastern Galicia." Only much later, on 11 July, was the Ukrainian delegation given the whole text of the resolution. This was the same day on which the Polish supreme command gave the Western Ukrainian government, which knew nothing about any of this, the text of the first part of the resolution dealing with "Bolshevik bands" and the Polish military occupation of the whole of Eastern Galicia. In other words, from the time the decision was made, it was two and a half weeks before the Ukrainian delegation in Paris was fully informed of the extent of the injustice that had been perpetrated against it. For their nation, this was effectively a death sentence. They protested, but their protests were now to no avail.[359]

Meanwhile, the end was also approaching for the Western Ukrainians on the field of battle. On 27 June the Western Ukrainians confronted a Polish army twice their own size: almost nine Polish divisions, with 38,613 footsoldiers, 2,144 cavalry, 797 heavy machine guns, and 207 light and heavy field guns. The Western Ukrainians numbered no more than 20,000, with about 376 heavy machine guns and 144 light field guns.[360] The Western Ukrainian infantry had practically no ammunition. Owing to the breakdown of the Western Ukrainian intelligence service, General Grekov was unaware of the imminence of the Polish counteroffensive.

Early on the morning of 28 June, exactly half an hour before the Western Ukrainians were due to begin a general offensive against the Polish lines that, it was hoped, would take them as far as Lviv, the Poles, under the command of Józef Piłsudski, mounted their assault. There were sections of the front that the Western Ukrainians were unable to defend because entire units possessed no ammunition whatever. The Polish soldiers knew this and did not even bother to cover themselves.

Artillery itself is not enough to drive back an enemy, and the whole Western Ukrainian front retreated.

Covered by the artillery, which often held up the Polish advance with caseshot, the Western Ukrainians retreated in full order. Although they were aware of the enemy's lack of ammunition, the Poles advanced cautiously. Their various units remained in close contact and did not risk advancing beyond the line ordered by their commanders: they knew that they were confronting an enemy of superior courage. The Western Ukrainians were composed but gloomy in retreat, realizing that they were leaving their homeland forever. Between 5 and 14 July, facing frequent but rarely large-scale Ukrainian counterattacks, all the Polish troops reached the line of the Strypa (Map 5). Only now did the Western Ukrainian government discover that the Supreme Council, as early as 25 June, had empowered the Polish army to occupy Eastern Galicia as far as the Zbruch in order to drive out the "Bolshevik bands." On 10 July a Polish negotiator arrived at the front line of the First Western Ukrainian Army Corps with the message that the Polish army had an important document from the Entente. A staff officer of the Western Ukrainian corps command was sent to the Polish side, but the Poles insisted that a plenipotentiary of the supreme command should be sent. This was done. The dictator Petrushevych and Petliura came to the Western Ukrainian military headquarters in Chortkiv to hear the news as soon as possible. They waited through the night, speculating whether the outcome would be good or bad. It occurred only to one lieutenant to suggest that the Poles had been given Eastern Galicia; his view was dismissed. Early on the morning of 12 July the letter from the Polish high command, containing the first part of the Supreme Council's resolution, finally arrived.[361]

The order was given for a retreat across the Zbruch. A massive wagon train carried the army provisions into an uncertain future. Long lines of civilian refugees, in excess of 100,000 souls, left their homeland. With them went the army of more than 60,000 men, with more than 20,000 of them in combat readiness. On 16 July the first lines of the rear guard crossed the Zbruch.[362]

"Those were terrible days," writes an eyewitness of this exodus. "The Poles were advancing on one side and the Bolsheviks on the other. The territory of both Ukrainian states now consisted of a small strip of land on both banks of the Zbruch. From this tiny territory we could hear the thunder of guns from east and west.

Endless lines of Western Ukrainian trains passed by....

The artillery could be heard thundering in the distance. This was the Western Ukrainian artillery, which, with great bravery, was holding up the Polish advance so that the trains would have time to move out with the sick, the wounded, and the provisions. The artillery still had some ammunition, but the infantry had none. The footsoldiers helped the artillery where they could, even resisting the enemy with their empty guns and covering those last few fields of their Western Ukrainian homeland with their corpses."[363]

Chapter 4

The Downfall of Ukrainian Statehood

1. The Ukrainians in the "Rectangle of Death"

We have already described the desperate situation of the Ukrainians after the Haller offensive, now under attack from both the Poles and the Bolsheviks. On 2 June the Eastern Ukrainians were hemmed in by the Poles and the Bolsheviks in south-central Volhynia north of Ternopil. At the same time the Western Ukrainians, cut off from the Eastern Ukrainians, were surrounded by the Poles, Bolsheviks and Romanians south of Ternopil in the triangle between the Zbruch and the Dnister. In spite of all this, there was still a chance of rescuing Ukrainian statehood, as the Grekov offensive demonstrated. This chance lay in the suspension of the war against the Bolsheviks, enabling a united Western and Eastern Ukraine to fight Poland for control of Eastern Galicia. Had they followed this course of action and signed a peace with Poland more or less along the lines proposed by Berthélemy, they could later have used Eastern Galicia as a base from which to continue the struggle against the Bolsheviks and perhaps succeeded in establishing a Ukrainian rump state. Failure to follow this course could only mean the more rapid defeat of the Ukrainians. Their fate was already sealed by the loss of Eastern Galicia.

At this moment, however, when this one last chance was still available, there existed not one but two independent Ukrainian states. At no time did the leadership of Western or Eastern Ukraine extend its authority over the whole of the Ukrainian nation. On the contrary, each leadership rigidly followed policies that profoundly contradicted the other's. The Eastern Ukrainians failed to realize that victory over the Bolsheviks on their own territory depended on the support of an orderly Western Ukrainian hinterland, just as the Western Ukrainians had previously failed to grasp that they should accept the Berthélemy line and make peace with Poland in order to support the Eastern Ukrainians against the Bolsheviks, thereby securing their own existence. Instead of one united attempt to rescue Ukrainian statehood, there were two, and this final opportunity was lost. While the Eastern Ukrainians offered a peace treaty to the Poles and mounted an assault against the Bolsheviks on 2–3 June to establish a new base for themselves in southwestern Podilia close to Romania, the Western Ukrainians began an assault against the Poles on 8 June in order to create their own base south of the Dnister in the Stryi region near Czechoslovakia (Map 4).

Those separate but nonetheless successful offensives marked the end of Ukrainian statehood in 1919. Up to that point the fate of Ukraine depended not only on external circumstances, such as the superior strength of the enemy, but also on the success or failure of the Ukrainians' own internal policies. But from now on their own political activity made no difference to their eventual fate. No amount of political insight, diplomatic dexterity or martial courage could bring about the successful establishment of a Ukrainian state. At most, these activities could postpone eventual defeat by a few months or allow the Ukrainians to confront their downfall with greater or lesser dignity. Just as, in the days of success, the Ukrainian leadership had never really known how to lead the nation forward, so now, in this final hour of national disaster, this leadership failed to understand the true situation. Even now, the Ukrainians failed to unite under a single government, and the country went down to defeat to the accompaniment of petty discord and rivalry between its own two hostile governments.

It was external circumstances, however, that brought about the final collapse. Ukraine was now in conflict with four powerful enemies who were in no way sympathetic to the establishment of an independent Ukrainian state.* These four powers, which constituted a veritable "rectangle of death," were the Poles, the Bolsheviks, the Denikin army, and the Romanians. They either fought the Ukrainians directly or cut them off from the rest of the world.

The two separate Ukrainian offensives went ahead brilliantly for about a month. The Bolsheviks, as well as the Poles, were overrun by much smaller forces. The territorial gain for the Ukrainians was significant. In the final days of June, the Eastern Ukrainians occupied all the territory along the Zbruch. They were retreating from central Volhynia north of Ternopil, but they held on to Proskuriv in the north and to Mohyliv on the Dnister in the southeast. This was a territory of about 100 to 150 km from north to south and more than 160 km in a southeasterly direction along the Dnister from the mouth of the Zbruch.[364] In the west, the Western Ukrainians held on to the whole eastern part of Eastern Galicia north of the Dnister, a rectangular piece of territory measuring 120 by 160 km. The whole territory then occupied by the Ukrainians was therefore about 100 km wide and 350 km long (Map 4).

* Naturally, there was still the possibility of making peace with Poland on the Zbruch or on the boundary that Dmowski demanded for Poland, but an understanding on those terms would have reduced the territory available to Ukraine to such an extent that no small Eastern Ukrainian state north of the Dnister could have remained in existence.

This did not, however, lead to any permanent gains for the Ukrainians. These victories were achieved against numerically superior and, in some cases, very courageous troops. It was inevitable that the enemy's counteroffensive would be crowned with success, since the Western Ukrainians had no more ammunition for their infantry, and the Eastern Ukrainians were exhausted. Just as, in May 1919, the offensives of the Haller army and the Bolsheviks began at almost the same time, leading to the catastrophe at Ternopil, now, too, the Polish and Bolshevik counteroffensives began on almost the same day. The Poles were the first to mount their assault. Led by Józef Piłsudski, they attacked the Western Ukrainians on 28 June, and the latter began their slow but final retreat to the Zbruch. Two days later, on 30 June, the Bolsheviks, with fresh reserves newly arrived at the front, began a determined counteroffensive. Their goal was to break through the Eastern Ukrainian front, which ran from north to south, at Proskuriv, thereby separating the Western from the Eastern Ukrainians, so as to be able to wipe out the Eastern Ukrainian troops at Kamianets-Podilskyi and east and southeast of it along the Dnister before the Western Ukrainians, retreating from the Poles, could cross the Zbruch and join forces with Petliura (Map 5). Their reason for this move was the advance of the Denikin army in May 1919 from the Kuban region against the territory of the Don Cossacks, which had been occupied by the Bolsheviks in the meantime. This advance led to the capture of Kharkiv on 14 June and, on 1 July, the capture of Tsaritsyn (Volgograd) on the Volga, as well as the eastern and southern parts of Eastern Ukraine north of the Sea of Azov (Map 6). The Bolsheviks, who still held the rest of Eastern Ukraine on both sides of the Dnipro, as well as the Black Sea coast with Odesa, wanted to inflict a decisive defeat on Petliura before the crucial battle with Denikin and force the Western Ukrainians, after the final loss of Eastern Galicia, to link up with themselves in creating a pro-Bolshevik force along the Zbruch to ward off the Poles.[365]

The Eastern Ukrainians, exhausted from all the previous fighting and lacking reserves, gradually retreated from the Bolsheviks at Proskuriv. What had happened at the beginning of June 1919 now happened again one month later. The Ukrainians were attacked simultaneously by both the Poles and the Bolsheviks. Although the military situation of the Ukrainians did not seem as catastrophic now as it had at the beginning of June, it was nevertheless the case that the Ukrainians now had no hope of victory over the Poles, as they had had a month previously at the time of the Grekov offensive. While the Western Ukrainians were still deep in Eastern Galicia, on the Strypa and to the west of it, without being able to mount a decisive attack on the Poles, the Bolsheviks, after the capture of Proskuriv on 6 July, had a clear path along the Zbruch to the site of Petliura's government in Kamianets-Podilskyi.[366]

The defeat of the Ukrainian armies, which could be split at any moment by the Bolshevik wedge on the Zbruch all the way to the Dnister, now seemed inevitable (Map 5). The Eastern Ukrainian troops under Petliura were already attempting to make their way through the Bolshevik front in order to wage a guerrilla war behind their lines in Eastern Ukraine, while the Sich Riflemen, made up partly of Western Ukrainians, were trying to join forces with the Western Ukrainian troops on the Zbruch west of Kamianets-Podilskyi and share their as yet unknown fate.[367]

The Western Ukrainians were in a difficult but very clear situation. They had lost Eastern Galicia completely; hence the maintenance of a fictional separate government had become pointless. Objectively, there was no question that the Western Ukrainian government had to be wound up, apart from an official delegation in Paris that would be needed to negotiate autonomy for Eastern Galicia within the Polish state. The Western Ukrainian politicians now had to decide with which of the powers contending for Eastern Europe their army would join forces. The choice was between the Soviet government in Kyiv or the government of Petliura. If they opted for the former, they would have to call for a Soviet government in Western Ukraine and turn their troops against Kamianets-Podilskyi in order to help the Bolsheviks defeat Petliura and force the rest of the Eastern Ukrainian troops to accept either capitulation or Sovietization. In that case, the Western Ukrainians, as a Bolshevik army of Western Ukrainian origin, would be able to get military supplies from the Bolsheviks and continue the war on the Zbruch against the Poles—no longer, of course, under the banner of Ukrainian independence but under that of the world revolution. Later, perhaps, after the Bolshevik victory over the counterrevolution, they could have united Eastern Galicia with the rest of Ukraine under Soviet rule. The other possibility was to join forces with Petliura. But in this case, too, the Western Ukrainians would have to take their troops immediately across the Zbruch, not for the Bolsheviks but against them, in order to recapture Proskuriv and create a space in Eastern Ukraine for the retreat of the whole Western Ukrainian army. The war against Poland would then have to cease. Perhaps the improbable would happen and Petliura, with the help of the Western Ukrainians, would succeed in establishing an Eastern Ukrainian statelet with the support of the Romanians and the Poles.

But the Western Ukrainians did not think like this. On the contrary, they continued to maintain the fiction of a separate Western Ukrainian government in exile. This pointless and senseless behavior—opportunism prompted by constantly changing situations—was characteristic of the Western Ukrainians as they found themselves surrounded in this "rectangle of death."

While the Eastern Ukrainians were still fighting the Bolsheviks at Proskuriv, and the territory beyond the Zbruch seemed secure to the Western Ukrainians, the latter informed the Eastern Ukrainian government on 4 July that they intended to cross the Zbruch to Kamianets-Podilskyi. This information was received as if it were the harbinger of a wondrous rescue. Preparations were made for the Western Ukrainian move. The Western Ukrainian dictator, Petrushevych, was well aware of the rivalry between Petliura and General Grekov and, on 6 July, dismissed the general on short notice. The Western Ukrainians owed Grekov their only truly great action in the war with Poland, the salvation of their military honor. It was due to him that their retreat across the Zbruch was that of a regular and competent army and not of a defeated armed rabble. It was because of the Grekov offensive that this war against Poland could later become an inspiring part of national memory.[368] Like a brilliant meteor, the energetic and gifted general disappeared from the darkening skies of Western Ukraine. His place was taken by someone closer in character to the rest of the Western Ukrainian leadership. This was the commander of the Second Army Corps, General Myron Tarnavsky, whose indolence had lost them Lviv in March 1919.

With the departure of such a clear-minded and superior military leader, the Western Ukrainian leaders once again fell prey to the short-sighted opportunism that was so characteristic of them in difficult situations. It was simply a result of the law of inertia, and not of any clear awareness that, if they were not going to join the Bolsheviks, then they would have to do all in their power to help rescue Petliura, that the Western Ukrainians, on hearing of the capture of Proskuriv by the Bolsheviks, sent a Western Ukrainian brigade from Pidvolochyske on the northern Zbruch in the direction of Proskuriv on 8 July (Map 5). This lucky accident—we can hardly call an unplanned action of this sort anything else—saved the Eastern Ukrainians, as became clear later, and created a space for the Western Ukrainians beyond the Zbruch at the last moment. The Bolsheviks had already advanced a long way south from Proskuriv and were almost at the gates of Kamianets-Podilskyi when this unexpected appearance of significant numbers of Western Ukrainians behind their lines forced them to halt their southward advance. They had to reckon with the possibility that this was not simply an isolated diversionary action by the Western Ukrainians but a large-scale military maneuver that could lead to their own encirclement. For the Eastern Ukrainians, however, this was an illusory relief. Almost immediately, on 12 July, this Western Ukrainian brigade, lacking support from its own army, was defeated by a local Bolshevik uprising halfway between the Zbruch and Proskuriv. The brigade had to retreat to Eastern Galicia. Even without the help of this local uprising, it would not have been difficult for the Bolsheviks to discover that the Western Ukrainian action behind their lines was a weak effort incapable of interfering with their advance on Kamianets-Podilskyi. Nevertheless, this action did hold things up beyond the Zbruch. It won a short reprieve for the Ukrainians, extending the existence of a Ukrainian state in this "rectangle of death" by a few months.[369]

Now, in the midst of such a difficult situation beyond the Zbruch, the Western Ukrainians had a dictatorship. Whereas previously the weaknesses of the Ukrainian leadership had been concealed by the anonymous collective rule of the National Rada, they were now incorporated in this one man, the dictator Dr. Yevhen Petrushevych. A provincial lawyer and one of the pillars of the Western Ukrainian National Democratic Party, as well as a former member of the Vienna parliament, Petrushevych, as a human being, had one notable characteristic, namely, the complete honesty and respectability of a model notary and keeper of the seal, along with its usual accompaniment, the stubborn rigidity generally known as character. This stubborn rigidity alone made him unfit to be a statesman. A man of strong moral principles that added a certain sternness to his appearance, he evoked personal trust, and his assumption of the dictatorship of Western Ukraine was generally greeted with favor. A man strictly devoted to duty who sought no personal advantage, he assumed this honor with full awareness of the heavy responsibility that it entailed. He seemed to carry the burden of his people's fate on his own shoulders, and this burden dug even deeper lines into his sculptured face. The inner discipline that ruled this man also restricted his political intellect, which operated only in the narrow realm of a puritanical simplicity. He saw the Ukrainian national cause not as some particular force outside the framework of moral judgment, collaborating or competing with other similar forces, but rather as an immutable principle of justice of the kind that Wilson proclaimed with regard to nations. Just as the personal life of the dictator was almost completely dominated by the principle "Let justice prevail, though the world perish," his sense of justice in politics condemned him to a stubborn, not fanatical but puritanical inability to compromise. As president of the National Rada, he was certainly the one mainly responsible for the rejection of the Berthélemy peace proposals. The mere principle of justice itself was not enough for this mind bound by rigid formulas. For this civil lawyer, the Ukrainian national cause was also a question of two separate and juridically unequal Ukrainian legacy claims: one legacy from Austria and the other from Russia. He considered himself the only legitimate advocate of the Western Ukrainian claim to Eastern Galicia. It therefore seemed to him that he himself was indispensable and his dictatorship irreplaceable as a separate government of Western Ukraine in exile, otherwise the Western Ukrainian people's right of self-determination, which had taken effect on 1 November 1918, would lose its validity and the Polish occupation of Eastern Galicia would be approved, forfeiting the claim of the Western Ukrainians to their country. Since that claim was confirmed not only by the principle of justice but also by juridical considerations, Petrushevych had no doubt that the future decision of the Entente would return Eastern Galicia to the Western Ukrainians. For this man, formal legal niceties were a more tangible reality than the Polish military occupation of the country. Compared with those legal nuances, the occupation was a bad dream; a fantasy; a rash, senseless act on the part of the Poles. He took pains to avoid associating the Western and Eastern Ukrainian causes. As far as he was concerned, the Western Ukrainian cause was unshakably based on legal principle. This was not the case for Eastern Ukraine because the validity of the Wilson principles extended only to the former Austro-Hungarian Empire, and not to Russia. Hence the jealousy with which the dictator tirelessly defended the dual statehood of Ukraine, although that division had almost brought about the downfall of the whole country. And he defended it even more stubbornly when its fictional character became fully apparent, as both governments resided in the same city of Kamianets-Podilskyi. This insistence on the part of the dictator only hindered the Eastern Ukrainians, as they were well aware, without doing anything to help the Western Ukrainians themselves. The political role of this ossified Western Ukrainian Cato, whose only merit was that he did not allow Western Ukraine to follow a separate military policy, was a crippling one as far as the Ukrainian national cause was concerned. This crippling effect became even worse not only because his strength of character made him impervious to intelligent political arguments for compromise or adroitness, and not only because his fundamental stubbornness entrenched him in his prejudices regardless of any reasonable objections, but mainly because, like every puritan, he was easily outwitted. He was therefore surrounded by a mob of clever intriguers who well knew how to take advantage of his weakness. It was by such people that he was easily led and directed. A man like General Grekov, who was above intrigue, constituted a danger to them, and that is why he was dismissed.[370]

The fate of the Western Ukrainians in the "rectangle of death" cannot be properly understood without taking into account the personal characteristics of the dictator. This is apparent from what happened when the Western Ukrainians became aware of the threat to Petliura in Kamianets-Podilskyi. Early on the morning of 12 July Petrushevych received from the Polish supreme command the resolution of the Supreme Council of 25 June empowering Poland to take possession of the whole of Eastern Galicia. One would think that this news would have made the Western Ukrainians—if they did not want to join the Bolsheviks—rush immediately to the aid of Petliura beyond the Zbruch so that at least the Eastern Ukrainians might win a victory, now that the Western Ukrainian cause was completely lost. But the decision of the Supreme Council came as such a severe blow to the dictator's puritanical world view that he completely lost his head and was incapable of coming to any decision. One of his close colleagues has written about the fantastic political conceptions of the Western Ukrainian dictator in this difficult but clearly understandable situation: "Petrushevych could not grasp how it could be possible that the same Entente that had won the war under the banner of the liberation of the oppressed peoples could now deliver such an age-old Western Ukrainian land as Eastern Galicia to its traditional enemies, the Poles, just as all of Europe was supposed to be rebuilt on the basis of these new principles. He thought it could only be a passing maneuver by the Entente, which had been misled by Poland as far as the Western Ukrainian question was concerned. He had such a deeply rooted sense of justice and fairness that he could not believe what had actually happened. He refused to accept that the great leaders of the Western nations, Wilson, Lloyd George, and the others, could break their word. He held firmly to the belief that the prospects for Western Ukraine would improve very soon and that in a short time the Western Ukrainian government would return to this country as its rightful master. But how? With guns in their hands! At the head of an army made up of Ukrainian prisoners of war still being held in Italy!"[371]

What resolute decision could be expected from such a leadership? Its whole wisdom consisted in the belief that its army and government must be maintained in exile so that the Entente would later have someone to install in power in Eastern Galicia. Eastern Ukraine, the Bolsheviks, the Russian counterrevolution—all these counted as equal as far as the Western Ukrainian leadership was concerned. Anyone was welcome with whom a temporary alliance allowed the maintenance in exile of the Western Ukrainian government. As long as Petliura's precarious situation in Kamianets-Podilskyi was unknown to the Western Ukrainians, it seemed that Eastern Ukraine was the best place to allow the army to rest and recover, the place best suited for a brief visit from the dictator and his troops. But when, in the meantime, the desperate situation of the Eastern Ukrainians became known to them, they began to waver on whether or not to implement their decision of 4 July to march into Eastern Ukraine. Suddenly they began to consider whether it might not be better, in spite of the complete lack of ammunition, to try to hold on to some small part of Eastern Galicia against the Poles. But this was obviously impossible. On the other hand, the brigade that had been sent against Proskuriv on 8 July was sending reports about the unfriendly, even hostile attitude of the local Eastern Ukrainian population. The Western Ukrainians soon received news that this brigade had been beaten by a local Bolshevik uprising on 12 July. Since they had become accustomed, in Eastern Galicia, to the willing support of all the Western Ukrainian population and most of the Jewish population, the blood froze in the veins of the Western Ukrainian leadership at the thought that the Western Ukrainian army, threatened with defeat on all sides, should be delivered up to the unpredictable Eastern Ukrainian lions. And this threat really came from all sides: from the Bolshevik armies, from local Bolshevik uprisings among the people themselves, and from the radical socialist propaganda of the Eastern Ukrainian parties that could undermine their army. For these reasons, as well as the fact that the Eastern Ukrainians seemed too weak to offer secure shelter to the Western Ukrainian dictator and his army, crossing the Zbruch suddenly seemed as undesirable as the capture of some small part of Eastern Galicia was objectively impossible.[372]

Although there should have been no reason for this indecision, the Western Ukrainian leadership lived through a hell of uncertainty and doubt during those days. In vain, the delegations from Eastern Ukraine tried to make clear to the dictator that the Western Ukrainians now had no choice but to join the Eastern Ukrainians in the fight against the Bolsheviks, and the sooner they did so, the better it would be for Western Ukraine.

On 12 July, in this inglorious frame of mind, the Western Ukrainian leaders received an offer from the Bolsheviks that threw them into total confusion and left the Eastern Ukrainians suspended between heaven and earth awaiting their fate. The Soviet government in Kyiv laid down the following conditions: 1) the handing over of Petliura and the withdrawal of Western Ukraine from any participation in the state organization of Eastern Ukraine; 2) the public announcement of this break with Petliura and of the alliance of Western with Soviet Ukraine; 3) a Western Ukrainian alliance against Poland and Romania; 4) the placing of the Western Ukrainian army under the supreme command of Soviet

Ukraine; 5) the attachment of Soviet Ukrainian commissars to Western Ukrainian military units; 6) the nonintervention of Soviet Ukraine in the internal affairs of Western Ukraine. "Your only choice is either to go with us or die a heroic death," added the Soviet government from Kyiv.[373]

The aim of the Bolshevik offer was clear. On the plains of the Don steppe, the decision was now being made whether Russia was to be ruled by Lenin or by another tsar. The Bolsheviks must have considered that perhaps Denikin would be clever enough not just to bring back to power the old reactionary and corrupt figures but also to draw new, young and powerful forces from the still chaotic but nonetheless strong non-Russian national movements. What if he were to make a deal with Petliura so that the latter, with the support of the Entente, could explode the seething cauldron of Ukraine and put an end to Bolshevik control over the southern part of the former Russian Empire, as the Hetman State and the Russian reactionaries had been defeated earlier? The whole of Eastern Ukraine was in turmoil with peasant uprisings against Soviet power. The need of the hour, therefore, was to get rid of Petliura, but this could not be done without the help of the Western Ukrainians. The Bolsheviks also desperately needed an army against Poland to prevent it from joining up with Denikin. Who was better suited for this than the Western Ukrainians? The Bolsheviks were well aware of the political naïveté of the Western Ukrainian leaders, so they allowed them to keep their dictatorship and promised nonintervention in their internal affairs. But the Soviet commissars to be attached to the Western Ukrainian units would soon make sure that the "revolutionary energies of the people of Western Ukraine, by themselves" and "without the intervention of Soviet Ukraine" would break the back of Petrushevych's dictatorship and replace it with a Western Ukrainian Soviet government federated with Kyiv and Moscow.

The meaning of this offer was clear, and it was equally clear that the Western Ukrainians would have to reject it. The Grekov offensive had created a very strong bond of mutual trust and affection between the officers and men.[374]

The devotion of those troops to their dictatorship was unshakable. Any agitation by Soviet commissars among the Western Ukrainian troops would have led to the rapid demise of those preachers of world revolution and to an uprising against those Bolshevik allies under the banner of Petliura's policy of national independence. This was in fact to happen later, in 1920, among the remnants of the Western Ukrainian army that capitulated to the Bolsheviks. In view of such sentiments, there really was not much for the Western Ukrainian leaders to think about. They would have to join up with Petliura, for they despised the Bolsheviks even more than the Poles.

But these obvious facts were by no means evident to the leadership of Western Ukraine. To the dictator, with his strong sense of justice and fairness, this offer of "nonintervention in internal affairs" was very tempting, for it corresponded exactly to the wish of the Western Ukrainians to keep their own government and army intact. Both the dictator and the military leadership hesitated over whether or not to accept this offer, without really considering the long-term consequences of such a decision. Meanwhile, Petliura's fate hung by a thin thread. The leadership weighed up all the considerations: the true value of the Bolsheviks' "nonintervention"; the views of the Eastern Ukrainian delegation; the personal impression made by Petliura; Western Ukrainian dislike of Bolshevik radicalism; and, above all, the impression this would make on the Entente. Finally the scales tipped in favor of Petliura. On 13–14 July, before the Poles could renew their assault, the northern flank of the Western Ukrainian army north and west of Ternopil retreated in a southeasterly direction with a view to concentrating the whole army west of Kamianets-Podilskyi. They were also concerned to prevent the Poles from pursuing them across the Zbruch. On 14 July Western Ukrainian negotiators were sent to offer a truce to the Poles. Their instructions were: begin with the demand for the Berthélemy line; moderate this to the Delvig line; bring back at least a truce on the Zbruch line. The negotiators, who were received in a very unfriendly manner by the Poles, were taken to Lviv after the Western Ukrainians had already evacuated Eastern Galicia completely, and they achieved nothing. It was not until some days later that a military mission sent by Petliura arranged a truce with the Poles. Meanwhile, on 15 July, the Poles advanced to the Strypa. The Western Ukrainians resisted, giving way only gradually—as, for example, in bitter street fighting in Ternopil—so as to cover the retreat in the rear. But the surrender of Eastern Galicia was a foregone conclusion, and on 16 July the Western Ukrainians crossed the Zbruch west of Kamianets-Podilskyi. The indecisiveness of the Western Ukrainian leadership had only one result: in crossing the Zbruch, the troops abandoned to the Poles many trains with oil and provisions, worth millions, which were badly needed by the Eastern Ukrainians and could easily have been brought across earlier.[375]

With the troops themselves, however, it was a different story. For them Petliura's struggle against the Bolsheviks was as much their own national cause as the struggle against the Poles. No sooner had they crossed the Zbruch than a Western Ukrainian army corps joined the fight against the Bolsheviks and secured Kamianets-Podilskyi. The Eastern Ukrainian troops, in particular the Sich Riflemen, had recovered from the defeat at Proskuriv and, with this significant addition of Western Ukrainian reserves, resumed their advance on 15 July, winning important victories over the Bolsheviks in the next few days. On 29 July, arm in arm with this Western Ukrainian army corps, they finally regained Proskuriv.[376] The united Ukrainian forces thus managed to secure the territory occupied by Petliura and, more importantly, laid the basis for a major offensive against Kyiv, Ukraine's last great military action. The Ukrainian army was now established east of the Zbruch and north of the Dnister, in this "rectangle of death" in which, during the next few months, it would go down to defeat (Map 6).

2. Ukraine and the "All-Russian" Counterrevolution

The recapture of Proskuriv on 29 July was the beginning of a number of important Ukrainian successes against the Bolsheviks. As in the case of the Grekov offensive, it was demonstrated that the forces of Ukraine, though unable to fight on two fronts against both Poland and Russia, probably sufficed to stand up to either of those powers alone. Given the military conditions of this period, the forces that the Ukrainians now (in August 1919) had at their disposal in the fight against the Bolsheviks, especially after the addition of the Western Ukrainians, were by no means insignificant. The best troops were the Western Ukrainians. The victories of the Grekov offensive had filled them with pride and self-confidence. The loss of their homeland had brought them closer together, and unconditional trust between officers and men, iron discipline, and imperviousness to outside propaganda held them together as a united force. Firm in defense, brave in attack, this army was of course less maneuverable than its Eastern Ukrainian counterpart, which was accustomed to more mobile warfare. Without the usual trust from the local population, it was more anxious about covering its flanks and rear and therefore less willing than the Eastern Ukrainian troops to take risks. The Western Ukrainians were friendly in their treatment of the local population,[377] making them almost unique in Eastern Europe of that period, where people had become accustomed to the wild, ruthless and cruel behavior of revolutionaries and counterrevolutionaries alike. It is true that among the Bolsheviks as well as among the counterrevolutionaries, there were many military units that showed greater courage than the Western Ukrainians, and that there were entirely regular individual units among them. But as a full-scale army of some tens of thousands, with an almost immaculate internal organization, a well-behaved reserve, and a friendly attitude to the local population, to which it never applied the laws of war in retaliation for the occasional injustices inflicted on it, the Western Ukrainian army was one whose like had not been seen in Eastern Europe since the German defeat. With all these characteristics, the Western Ukrainian army was much better qualified than any other in Eastern Europe to contribute to the pacification of the turbulent country and the reintroduction of order, public administration and public safety. The people breathed more freely when they got to know this army, a fact that was of immeasurable importance for the troops later, when thousands of them lay weak and hungry because of a typhus epidemic. An important indicator of this relationship between the troops and the local population was the fact that the Jews in Eastern Ukraine, generally hated and persecuted, were sympathetic to the Western Ukrainians and later, in more difficult times, often provided them with assistance. They were not the troops most feared by their enemies, but they were the most respected, by Denikin's troops as well as by the Bolsheviks. That was why those same enemies competed to enlist them later, when they were infected with typhus and it would have been easier to wipe them out than to negotiate with them. For the Eastern Ukrainian state, with such hopeless disarray behind its front lines, the Western Ukrainian army was a gain that could not be too highly prized under prevailing conditions.[378]

The Western Ukrainian army was of the type that could provide the military foundation for a state. The Eastern Ukrainian army, however, like all other counterrevolutionary armies, had more in common with the foolhardy desperados of foreign legions than with a regular army. Led by staff officers of the former Russian service, some of whom were excellent, they were an exceedingly brave frontier guard, but it was not until this Eastern Ukrainian warlike bravado was combined with Western Ukrainian organizational competence in the countryside that the territory under Eastern Ukrainian military occupation was governed in an orderly manner. At no other time was Petliura's Eastern Ukraine so strong or so close to functioning as an independent state as in this period after the arrival of the Western Ukrainians. As an anti-Bolshevik force, Eastern Ukraine now had much greater potential than the Denikin operation, which suffered until its defeat from the same kind of disorder in its territory as had afflicted Petliura's forces before the arrival of the Western Ukrainians.[379]

In purely military terms, the Ukrainians were now a very considerable force. Among the anti-Bolshevik forces of Eastern Europe, they ranked third behind Poland and Denikin's army. They were superior to both Kolchak and Yudenich, as well as to the troops fighting at Archangel. One must recall that in May 1919 the Haller offensive had at its disposal more than 60,000 soldiers, perhaps as many as 65,000—the largest military force in Eastern Europe at the time. In May 1919 General Denikin began his offensive from the Kuban, which took him almost to the gates of Moscow, with a strike force consisting initially of only 40,000 soldiers, 193 cannon and 621 machine guns, and it was only on the march that this force grew in numbers.[380] The Ukrainians, who were cut off from the rest of the world throughout this conflict and received no assistance from abroad, had at their disposal on 12 August 1919 a Western Ukrainian army of 49,795, of whom 18,000 to 19,000 were combat-ready, with 158 field guns and 546 heavy machine guns. The regular Eastern Ukrainian army consisted of about 34,000 to 35,000 men, of whom 15,000 were combat-ready, with 177 light and heavy field guns and more than 550 heavy machine guns. There were, in addition, about 15,000 irregulars. In other words, the Ukrainians had about 100,000 men under arms, of whom 85,000 were regular troops, with 34,000 in combat readiness, not counting the irregulars. They were relatively well armed, with 335 light and heavy field guns and about 1,100 heavy machine guns. This was a force that could stand up to Denikin and perhaps even to Poland.[381] The total Bolshevik forces were of course far superior, but the Eastern Ukrainian peasants, realizing that Petliura, unlike Denikin, was not going to take away the land they had gained as a result of the revolution, were more and more willing to join him against the Bolshevik troops. While Denikin's countryside was very quickly involved in the flames of agrarian revolt, Petliura's countryside became ever more calm, as it was largely occupied by Western Ukrainian reserve troops. The Ukrainians therefore had reasonable grounds to hope that a general mobilization would be successful, bringing the strength of their army to perhaps two or three hundred thousand men; indeed, they reckoned that they could raise an army of half a million. Unlike the Denikin army, which had no roots in the popular masses, the Ukrainians had the prospect of creating a real people's army that might even be able to stand up to all the Soviet forces. This was their last chance.

Two preconditions were essential for this purely military potential to be realized. These were the substantial support of the capitalist world for Ukraine, the kind of support enjoyed by Denikin and the Poles, and the harmonious cooperation of the Western and Eastern Ukrainians so that the territory controlled by Petliura could be politically organized as soon as possible.

Now that the Western Ukrainians had crossed the Zbruch to fight the Bolsheviks in Eastern Ukraine, the situation that Marshal Foch needed for his intervention plans of February 1919 appeared to have been created. The purpose of the Berthélemy plan, after all, was to end hostilities between the Western Ukrainians and the Poles so that the former could fight the Bolsheviks in Eastern Ukraine. Against the will of the Western Ukrainians, this peace had now been imposed on them, and they were now fighting only the Bolsheviks in Eastern Ukraine. Having reached the Zbruch on 17 July, the Poles, apart from a few looting raids across the Zbruch, did not pursue the Western Ukrainians.[382] This de facto truce was soon formalized in a treaty. On 20 July Petliura sent a military mission, headed by his chief of staff, General Petro Lypko, to Lviv, not only to sign a formal truce but also to work out with the Poles some form of cooperation against the Bolsheviks.[383] The Ukrainian mission demanded a truce at the Zbruch and the later evacuation by the Poles of the territory east of the Delvig line of 16 June, including Ternopil. The negotiations were held in Dęblin, with General Karol Trzaska-Durski heading the Polish side. The treaty eventually signed on 1 September established a line of demarcation along the Zbruch that continued from Pidvolochyske to Mazyr on the Prypiat. This was the eastern border demanded by Dmowski, and it lay significantly to the east of the present-day Polish border (Map 6). In any event, the war between Ukraine and Poland was now ended. Within a month of the Zbruch crossing, the united action of the Western and Eastern Ukrainian troops had greatly enlarged the area under Petliura's control. This territory now extended almost to the Prypiat in the north, to the Dnipro in the east, and almost as far as Odesa in the south. There was now no need for them to "go empty-handed to the Peace Conference," as Berthélemy had advised them not to do in February 1919, when he promised them the support of the Entente and the recognition of Ukrainian statehood. There now seemed no reason why Petliura should not get the long-sought protection of France.

In view of the significant victories that the Ukrainian troops were winning against the Bolsheviks on all sides, Petliura and his military leaders saw good reason to hope that the Entente and the Russian counterrevolution, after the bitter experience of the uprising against the Hetman State in November 1918 and after the amazing doggedness with which Ukraine then not only survived on its own resources but even managed to make a comeback, would no longer risk considering the Ukrainian national movement insignificant but would recognize the Ukrainian state as one of the main factors in the struggle against Bolshevism.[384] Another factor that convinced Petliura of this was that as soon as the Western Ukrainian "Bolshevik bands" had evacuated Eastern Galicia, an inter-Allied military mission of French, English and Americans arrived in Kamianets-Podilskyi to take a closer look at those "bands."

On 30 July Petliura presented this mission with his plan for the defeat of the Bolsheviks. He demanded from the Entente the same kind of support, with supplies of war material, that was extended to the other counterrevolutionary armies. If such support were forthcoming, he promised to bring the strength of the Ukrainian army up to between 400,000 and 500,000 men. The Ukrainian army, he said, would be put into the field immediately against the Bolsheviks. After the victory of the counterrevolution, a Ukrainian constituent assembly would decide whether Ukraine would remain in some kind of federation with Russia or become an independent state.

The strategic war plan developed by the Eastern Ukrainians was as follows: the Denikin army was about to advance from the Don with the intention of reaching Moscow via Kharkiv, Kursk and Orel. But there were large Bolshevik forces along the Dnipro as far as the Black Sea and along the coast to Odesa. These forces threatened the left flank and rear of the Denikin army, tying down a large number of his troops. The task of the Ukrainians was to defeat the Bolshevik forces on the Right Bank of the Dnipro and then proceed to capture Kyiv and Odesa. They were then to link up with the left flank of Denikin's army and advance in a northeasterly direction as far as the Nizhyn–Chernihiv line on the Left Bank. They were to stop at this line and at the Prypiat on the other side of the Dnipro. The Polish army would then link up with the Ukrainian left flank on the Prypiat. The Poles would occupy Belarus north of the Prypiat and advance to the Dnipro at Rechytsa, Mahilioŭ and Vitsebsk. The Russian counterrevolutionary armies, especially the forces under Denikin, would then find it relatively easy to defeat the Bolsheviks, who would be forced back to their own Russian territory around Moscow.

However eminently suitable this plan was as a means of defeating the Bolsheviks—although not of restoring a united Russia—it could not have been carried out and was therefore a pure fantasy: although it corresponded well to Ukrainian wishes, it did not correspond at all to the wishes of the Poles or the Russians. As a result, Bolshevism became unconquerable.

Even Romania, which had the greatest natural interest in the erection of a buffer state west of the Dnipro, did not want a rapid stabilization of the situation in Eastern Europe, regardless of the question of Ukrainian independence, because of the continuing uncertainty over its occupation of Bessarabia. Romania wanted to draw out the turmoil and confusion in Eastern Europe as long as possible. At the same time, it was afraid of direct conflict with the Bolsheviks, which made it unwilling to enter into political negotiations with the Eastern Ukrainians. It was all the more willing, however, for this same reason, to supply the Eastern Ukrainian army with a meager amount of munitions[385] that would not suffice for any great expansion of the war effort but would be enough to guarantee that the Ukrainians would continue to protect Romania's borders for some months to come. This support was so ambivalent that when an Eastern Ukrainian army corps, the Zaporozhians, were fighting in the region of Uman in April 1919 and had to retreat into Romanian-occupied Bessarabia because of the evacuation of Odesa by the French and a breakthrough by the Bolsheviks in the north, the Romanians disarmed and interned them. In May 1919 Romania finally allowed them to return to central Volhynia through Galicia, but not before it had taken all their trains, weapons and supplies.* So they could hardly even rely on Romania. In fact, all the "assistance" that Romania now gave derived from what it had previously stolen from the Ukrainians.

With the Poles it was even worse. When Berthélemy made his proposals to the Western Ukrainians in February 1919, Ukraine was a more powerful military force than Poland or the Denikin army, which was only in the organizational stage—this despite the extremely lamentable conditions in Eastern Ukraine under the Directory. Foch's plans for intervention had not yet been rejected in Paris. The possibility existed, therefore, that if the Western Ukrainians accepted the Berthélemy plan and the French military continued to insist on its plan for intervention in Ukraine, then Dmowski's plan of dividing Ukraine between Poland and Russia might not win the upper hand in Poland, but the opinion might triumph that wanted to accept what Berthélemy had to offer and provide direct support for the formation of an independent Ukrainian state that would act as a buffer against Russia in the future. But now the situation had changed completely. France was no longer interested in Ukraine, unless, of course, Poland itself found some reason for wanting to establish an independent Ukrainian state. Foch's plan had been laid to rest for good. Clemenceau's line now carried the day, and he wanted Poland to expand as much as possible against the Germans in the west

* "Not only did Europe not help us," comments Kapustiansky (*Pokhid ukraïns'kykh armii*, 1: 23–24), "and not only did its troops flee from the Bolsheviks [in Odesa], but it actually robbed us of our last supplies of weapons and munitions and left us to fight [the Bolsheviks] with our bare hands." The booty that fell to the Romanians included 80 light and heavy field guns, 700 heavy machine guns, 7,000,000 rifle cartridges, 34,000 grenades, 2,500 hand grenades, and 140 railway cars full of clothing, equipment and food rations (cf. Khrystiuk, *Zamitky i materiialy*, 4: 161).

and against the Bolsheviks in the east. With the Haller offensive in May 1919, Dmowski's policy triumphed completely in Poland. What Dmowski wanted above all else, at least as long as Russia was still in turmoil, was to secure a border for Poland that would be considerably farther east than it is today. For the purpose of keeping down the Ukrainians, they were even willing, in the long term, to have a restoration of a united reactionary Russia.[386] In any case, they had no intention of defeating the Bolsheviks in the near future, as Petliura wanted. Just like the Romanians, the Poles wanted the turmoil in Russia to continue as long as possible so that they could not only secure the Dmowski border militarily but also make it safe for the future. From the viewpoint of the Poles, therefore, including the National Democrats, it was desirable for the Ukrainians east of the Zbruch to drag out their conflict with the Bolsheviks for some time. That is why the Poles did not pursue the Western Ukrainians across the Zbruch, even though no truce was in effect. The Poles were well aware that without the Western Ukrainian hinterland the Eastern Ukrainians could not possibly defeat the Bolsheviks.[387] For the time being, therefore, the Poles postponed their advance across the Zbruch to take Proskuriv and Kamianets-Podilskyi, as demanded by Dmowski, until the Ukrainians had been beaten by the Bolsheviks. While the Bolsheviks were occupied with the war against the Ukrainians, all that the Poles did in the areas north of the Zbruch and in central Volhynia was to reach the proposed Dmowski border with relative ease (Map 6). It was this border that the Poles proposed to Petliura's representatives in Dęblin on 15 August. At the same time, Polish troops moved forward to this line—almost five divisions, including two from the Haller army, with 42,000 men, of whom 24,000 were in combat readiness. The Eastern Ukrainians imagined, because the Poles had not pursued the Western Ukrainians across the Zbruch, that the existence of an Eastern Ukrainian state was "in Poland's interests." They were surprised and even grateful that the Polish troops had not crossed the Dmowski line, except occasionally to plunder Ukrainian trains, even though the treaty with them was not finally settled until 1 September. This confirmed the Eastern Ukrainians in their belief that the Poles were willing to take part in Petliura's plan. Indeed, the Eastern Ukrainian military leaders were happy that "the Polish army was covering the Ukrainian left flank," and in those circles, given the typical political naïveté of military men, there were even stirrings of Polonophilism.[388] Of course, those Polish moves had nothing to do with any inclination to join a coalition, least of all with the Ukrainians, for the purpose of defeating the Bolsheviks. Even more than in the case of the Romanians, Petliura was building on sand when he assumed that he had the support of Poland and failed to realize that Dmowski's plan for the partition of Ukraine between Russia and Poland was already firmly established as Polish policy. As far as Poland was concerned, the only role for Ukraine was to secure Polish occupation of Ukrainian territory until Poland was strong enough to defend itself. Meanwhile, the Ukrainians could go on spilling their blood in this rectangle of death.

Objectively, the withdrawal of Romania and Poland from the decidedly anti-Bolshevik forces meant that the task of fighting the Bolsheviks fell entirely to the Ukrainians and the Russian counterrevolution. This was a fact that the Polonophile Eastern Ukrainians, including Petliura, who was personally evolving in the same direction, failed to recognize either then or later. But the Petliura plan was a failure even from the point of view of the Russian reactionaries, not because it was wrong in itself but because the Russian counterrevolution was too short-sighted.

In this Eastern European struggle against Bolshevism, commonly known as the "Russian Civil War," there were two basic forces at work. The first was the autonomist or separatist movement of the non-Russian nationalities, a new force that arose simultaneously with the defeat of tsarism and the emergence of Muscovite Bolshevism—a movement with great potential for the future that was seeking to break loose from Moscow and St. Petersburg. It included the non-Russian nationalities like the Ukrainians and branches of the Russian family, such as the Siberians and the Don Cossacks, that had retained a certain territorial autonomy vis-à-vis St. Petersburg centralism. The second force, though in decline, was that of the East European counterrevolution. This was the reaction that had supported tsarism and was represented by the upper social strata—the large landowners, the industrial and merchant capitalists, the old officer corps, and the old bureaucracy. From the national point of view this reactionary force considered itself all-Russian and was at home in all the provinces of the old empire.

It is essential, in view of this differentiation, to examine the national question in prerevolutionary tsarist Russia and consider the changes that took place after 1917.

If one were to look at an ethnic map of prerevolutionary tsarist Russia, with its countless peoples and tribes, one might easily be tempted to conclude that this Russia was a multiethnic state. But that conclusion would be wrong, for it would result from a confusion of two distinct things: a nation or a "people" in the ethnic sense and a nation as a historical and political entity. The latter represents a culturally and politically active national force. Within the modern European democratic order, it was the ethnic nations that became the bearers of this activity in the nineteenth century; hence the distinction does not apply to the countries that participated in this development. But Russia, from a cultural and political standpoint, found itself still at the stage of predemocratic Europe. In Russia the idea of nation or "people" still constituted only a passive foundation for territorial differentiation. The nation, in a historical and political sense, was limited to the upper stratum, which stemmed from the people and represented its country as an active cultural and political factor. The ethnic differences within the population of Russia are not in themselves an adequate basis for drawing conclusions about the national composition of this state. The Russian Empire could be regarded as a multiethnic state only if those upper strata not only maintained the language of their passive popular masses but also defended the cultural and political resistance of national elements seeking to maintain an active cultural, social and political life for their country against the empire's central authorities. But in multilingual tsarist Russia, with the exception of Finland and Congress Poland, that was not the case, although there were many examples of unrest among the non-Russian nations, such as Ukraine, that were struggling to regain a lost cultural and political identity. The culturally, socially and politically active upper strata of the non-Russian nationalities—in other words, the nation itself in a historical and political sense—rejected, in their overwhelming majority, any connection with their own national movements and identified themselves completely with the imperial conception of an all-Russian state and culture. They felt no national or political identity with the small numbers of national separatists but adhered completely to the mighty Russians. The basis for such a state of affairs was created over the long period of cultural and political Russification of the tsarist empire. From the viewpoint of such a policy, the ethnic differences among the passive popular masses were a matter of indifference; in any case, the regime had no interest in mass education. Such differences among the masses themselves were not interfered with, but the active strata among the non-Russian nationalities were systematically suppressed as long as they maintained their own national and separatist aspirations. But the world of privilege was open to them as soon as they adopted the all-Russian conception of state and culture, becoming agents of Russian dominance in their own country. By the time the revolution broke out in 1917, this battle had long been won by tsarist Russia. In the non-Russian lands, Russian rule was upheld by those strata of the population that were already Russified. It was in this manner that Russia ruled Ukraine. A separate national consciousness lay dormant in the popular masses, among whom there was no active resistance to Russian rule. The upper strata, however, who prided themselves on their "Little Russian" identity, considered themselves an integral part of the all-Russian nation, of which their "Little Russian" homeland was only a regional subunit.

The tsarist Russian Empire was based not on the power of the dominant nation alone, nor on any compromise between the dominant nation and the national aspirations of the oppressed nations, as is the case in a multiethnic state. It was based rather on the willingness of the representative upper strata of the nationalities to be integrated into the unified political and national culture of Russia. This numerous all-Russian upper stratum, consisting of a bureaucracy in constant flux, as well as of long-established large landowners and bourgeois, gave the empire a unified character that was at once fairly profound and nationally very Russian. It was this stratum that cemented the bond between St. Petersburg and the ethnically non-Russian periphery and knit together the non-Russian masses, with their real but politically inconsequential ethnic differences, into a more or less organic union with the Russian Empire as if this empire were an ethnic unit, an ethnic Russian entity. When the all-Russian representatives of the tsarist empire expressed their contempt for the insignificant separatist activities among the ethnically non-Russian peoples; or when they proclaimed the national unity of the Russians, Ukrainians and Belarusians and described the Ukrainian national movement in Dnipro Ukraine as a fantasy; even when they rejected with indignation the term "multiethnic state" with reference to Russia and preferred to think of it as a united nation-state, then, given the overwhelming dominance of the "all-Russian" idea, they were correct for the time being.

The Revolution of 1917 destroyed this all-Russian unity at one blow. Just as in democratic Europe, it was no longer the upper strata but the people themselves who constituted the nations of the old empire in the historical and political sense. In its final days, this tsarist Russia with its all-Russian culture and politics was reduced to the machinery of the state apparatus. The link between this state and the popular masses had long since been broken. The neglected masses had long been mere subjects of this state. The state itself, consisting of the all-Russian upper strata, had lost all contact with the masses among the various nationalities from which those strata themselves had originated. When this system collapsed in the Revolution of 1917 and the victorious idea of democracy pushed the all-Russian upper stratum to one side, putting power into the hands of the "liberated peoples," imperial Russian unity was suddenly left without any form of practical support. The activation of the popular masses, among whom the tsarist state had cultivated neither a sense of citizenship nor a desire to be part of an all-Russian entity, suddenly brought to the fore two tendencies already present among the masses. These were a general tendency toward social revolution and, especially among the non-Russian peoples, a heightened sense of their own national identity. There was no reason why a democratic sovereign people, in ethnically non-Russian territories such as Ukraine, should allow their state to go on having this all-Russian character, a character that was not only foreign to them but that they regarded with hostility.

During this period of mass popular movements, the non-Russian nations became much more powerful than Russia, although the level of their cultural and political development still lagged behind, since they lacked an upper stratum of their own, this stratum having become part of the all-Russian camp. Intellectually and politically they were at a much lower level than the Russians, but Russia lost all power over them at a blow. The all-Russian movement retained its intellectual superiority, but victory clearly went to the materially more powerful non-Russian nationalities. Whether or not the old unity of the empire would remain now depended not on Russia's ability to maintain this unity either by force or through concessions but on whether the non-Russian nationalities themselves wanted it. Russia as an all-Russian national state, the state of the Russians and the Russified upper strata, was now irretrievably lost. What emerged in 1917 was a multiethnic state in which the democratized and nationally conscious non-Russian peoples regarded themselves as equals of the Russians. The Russians were no longer the people of Russia: they were now simply one of the nationalities of the former Russian Empire.

At the same time as the non-Russian nationalities asserted their self-awareness, other members of the Russian branch, such as the Siberians and the Cossacks, also asserted their independence of the Russian metropolis, Moscow. The whole development of pre-Bolshevik Russia in the year 1917 was decisively in the direction of a decentralization of the old empire and the creation of a federal state or even a confederation. This tendency asserted itself in the first few months of the short-lived Provisional Government of 1917. Ukraine began the process. It was followed by the nations of the Caucasus, the Siberians, the Cossacks, especially the Ukrainian Cossacks of the Kuban and the Russian Don Cossack Army, and, finally, the Ugro-Finnish and Turco-Mongolian peoples in European Russia, as well as in Turkestan and the other Asian parts of the old empire.

The Russian revolutionary and liberal-democratic movements could not stop the disintegration of the old empire without contradicting their own democratic ideology, which gave impetus to that disintegration, unless they were to restore the absolutist all-Russian regime in the name of imperial Russian unity. All that stood in the way of the further development of aspirations to autonomy and independence in the provinces was the political immaturity of the non-Russian peoples themselves, in particular, the internationalist ideology of their small educated strata. These strata were not intellectually independent and came under the influence, ultimately, of Russian ideology. Largely out of inertia, they maintained their solidarity with revolutionary democracy in Russia. In addition to the accustomed feeling of being part of the same state, there were the economic and other advantages to be had from being part of a large world empire. But in the midst of this process of disintegration the old Muscovite-Russian conception of imperial unity emerged again in a new and unexpected form: Bolshevism.

It was their masterly handling of the nationalities question, free from any kind of ethnic prejudice, that enabled the Bolsheviks to confront the massive task of reconstituting the former Russian Empire. Long before 1917, they understood that not only tsarism but also the idea of all-Russian unity had irrevocably played out its historical role in Eastern Europe. They understood, in other words, that Russian national power alone would not be enough to overcome the nationalism and separatism of the non-Russian nations. From the very beginning they recognized in principle the equality of the Russian and non-Russian nationalities and regarded the empire no longer as a unit but as a system embracing different national elements. It was through this insight that Bolshevism demonstrated its superiority as a political and state-building force to the all-Russian reaction. This insight helped the Bolsheviks to victory in the first period of their rise to power, the fight for control of the state in Moscow and St. Petersburg, as well as in the second period, the fight against centrifugal tendencies in the provinces in order to reestablish the authority of the new Soviet Moscow–St. Petersburg central power. Both struggles were won as a result of a careful assessment of the strengths and weaknesses of the non-Russian national movements. What enabled the Bolsheviks to capture central state power in the first period was the recognition that they could win this battle in Moscow and St. Petersburg only if they had the support of the emerging national and separatist movements of the non-Russian nationalities. On the other hand, what enabled them to restore the old imperial unity was the recognition that such unity could only reassert itself if it took a supranational form, one that reckoned with the national sensitivities of the non-Russian nationalities.

Accordingly, in their struggle against the Provisional Government for control of the central apparatus, the Bolsheviks proclaimed the "right of self-determination for the nationalities of Russia, including their right to separate." By this means they won the support of the non-Russian nationalities and achieved their first goal. On 24 October 1917 (O.S.) the Bolsheviks seized power in St. Petersburg and Moscow. The all-Russian reaction later complained that the Bolsheviks, with their proclamation of the "right of self-determination," had created the separatist movements among the non-Russian nationalities. This is just one more proof of the inability of the reactionary movement in Russia to understand the political situation created by 1917. For the Bolsheviks had created nothing new with this proclamation. They simply made use of an already existing powerful movement that had come into existence with the democratization of Russia, without any help from the Bolsheviks. This was a lesson that the reactionaries should have learned when they later attempted to overthrow this Bolshevik government.

Only after the Bolsheviks had established themselves in power in Russia itself could they proceed to the realization of the second part of their plan: the restoration of the old imperial unity. This order of doing things was a conscious strategy, and here also was a lesson that the reactionaries should have learned.

The guiding idea under which this plan managed to succeed was a translation of the now ineffective national categories of the old all-Russian ideology into social categories. Tsarist Russia welded together its different nationalities into a single political nation by winning over the upper strata of the various nationalities to the all-Russian idea, leaving the ordinary masses undisturbed—existing, as it were, in their own merely ethnic, regional, "Little Russian" but politically ineffective particularity. This all-Russian conception was by no means purely nationalist. It also had strong supranational aspects. This all-Russian polity claimed to be the legitimate representative of the whole Greco-Slavic world vis-à-vis the Occident. It also had a social dimension: to the Western inability to resolve the social question it counterposed the Russian solution of this problem—the abolition of individual self-determination and the binding of the individual by means of service to the collective. This all-Russian polity proclaimed the "liberation" of the nations of southeastern and east central Europe. It condemned the "falsehood" and "dishonesty" of Occidental religiosity, morality, law, art and science, counterposing to it the "true" Russian spirit in all spheres of life. Even the nationalist practice of Russification took on a supranational character when Russian spirituality claimed a universal validity for itself and the Russian language was proclaimed as the expression of a supranational community of the whole Slavic world. These were claims and tendencies that reappeared in Bolshevism, although they were given a different intellectual expression and justified in a different manner. In 1917 the old active element among the non-Russian nationalities, the upper strata, became ineffective, and the masses themselves became the active element. The national idea that had previously held the empire together politically now tore it apart, for the old all-Russian unity that this idea justified was now replaced by a concept of national plurality. The nationalities abandoned their "Little Russian" particularities and emerged as full members of the family of nations. In order to stem the centrifugal tendencies of those nationalities and weld them together once more into a united political nation, the Bolsheviks advanced not a political but a social program. Unlike in the old regime, the all-Russian idea would now penetrate to the lower strata. While leaving their ethnic, regional and linguistic particularities untouched, as was the practice under tsarism, the Bolsheviks spoke to the political aspirations of the nationalities, calling on them to create the closest possible bond with the Russian state and, in the name of the international social-revolutionary solidarity of the non-Russian and Russian peoples, to defend Soviet Russia against the whole capitalist world. These nationalities would then be restricted in the process of their development toward nationhood and kept politically at the level of their "Little Russian" regional particularity not by the power of the Russified upper strata but by means of the free will of the non-Russified lower strata. Thus, with the decline of the democratic revolution, an even greater despotism than the tsarist one would emerge: world-revolutionary Soviet Russia.

To reinforce these new bonds of imperial unity, after November-December 1917 the Russian proletarian armies streamed out of Moscow in all directions across the whole former empire to put down non-Russian autonomism and separatism and to secure the borders of old Russia. This campaign for the reconstitution of the old Muscovite state in a new supranational form led to internal divisions in the provinces. The proletarians in the cities, already strongly Russified, and the peasantry supported the Bolsheviks and, giving up their national-separatist cause, joined the ever-growing ranks of the Russian proletarian movement, which grew rapidly in size, like an avalanche, the farther it advanced from Moscow into the non-Russian lands. But the middle strata, which had little or no enthusiasm for social revolution, and those circles among the non-Russian nationalities that, although favorable to social revolution, insisted on maintaining their own national independence, were now forced to give up their international democratic conception of unity with Russia and, somewhat against their will, proclaimed their complete independence from Russia as sovereign states. In this case as well, it was Ukraine that began the process on 22 January 1918, and all the other nationalities that had achieved a higher level of development soon followed suit. Thus Bolshevism did not succeed entirely in eliminating the non-Russian national question and replacing it with a purely social question. The non-Russian national movements that opposed everything coming out of Russia were somewhat weakened by this Bolshevik internationalism but, at the same time, they became an anti-Bolshevik force. The longer this struggle against the Bolsheviks continued, the more strongly counterrevolutionary these nationalist movements became.

This same movement from separatism to counterrevolution took place among the autonomous Russian branches. Whether as a result of the influx of centralizing and leveling Bolsheviks, the drop in living standards or the threat to their old privileges, the Don Cossacks, led by General Petr Krasnov and supported by the German army of occupation, followed Ukraine's lead and proclaimed their independence on 28 April 1918.[389] On 4 July Siberia proclaimed its independence.[390] In the Kuban Cossack region this movement did not lead to a formal declaration of independence. This was partly because much of the fighting against the Bolsheviks took place here; moreover, there was a large migration of Russian reactionaries to the region. But despite the absence of any formal declaration, the separatist tendency here, suppressed by outsiders, was even stronger than among the Don Cossacks or in Siberia.[391]

The first impetuous advance of the Russian Bolshevik armies at the turn of the year 1917–18 to occupy the whole territory of the former Russian Empire on the ruins of the Provisional Government took place at a time when the provinces were in complete internal turmoil. This advance was so unexpected that before the regional forces could consolidate themselves, they were overrun by the Bolsheviks. It was only in the first half of 1918 that certain regions, such as Siberia, managed to fight off this invasion. The situation was more favorable in lands occupied by the Germans, such as Ukraine and the Don region. The latter made use of the German army of occupation in Ukraine to defeat the Bolshevik invasion. In the orderly situation created by the German occupation, the autonomist and separatist movements in Ukraine and on the Don greatly increased their strength, and it was in the Hetman State that the counterrevolution discovered the form in which, if at all, it could defeat the Bolsheviks.

Bolshevism was an incredible mass movement, and this made it impossible to suppress the Bolshevik Revolution of 1917–18 with the forces of the now destroyed Russian state machinery, as had happened in 1905. The Bolshevik idea had to be countered with another idea, equally capable of winning the support of the masses. Tsarist Russia had no such idea. But the development of the revolution in Russia in the course of 1917, before the Bolshevik seizure of power, provided such a means of combating the Bolsheviks. This was the self-determination of the nations and provinces of the old empire and their liberation from Muscovite centralism. If this tendency had been victorious in particular lands of the old empire, such as Ukraine, the Don region, and Siberia, then Bolshevism, unable to expand, would have been mortally wounded. Its whole ideological justification, namely, that it was a force to liberate the whole world from social servitude, would have been exposed as mere phraseology. Its sphere of effectiveness would have been limited to Moscow and St. Petersburg, where it could easily have been destroyed.

The all-Russian counterrevolution, therefore, should not have interfered with the exercise of the right of self-determination by the individual nationalities and branches of the old empire. On the contrary, it should have welcomed the fact that self-determination would allow the provinces to adopt whatever form of government was most appropriate for them. In one case, as in Ukraine, this might take the form of loosely linked but independent nation-states. In another case it might take the form of a provisional federation of states that could exist until the Bolsheviks had been defeated and the federative principle was extended to the whole of the former empire. This was what the Kuban Cossacks wanted when they proposed a provisional federation of the Kuban and Don Cossacks with the Caucasian peoples in a "Southeastern Federation of Cossack States (Kuban, Don and Terek) with the mountain peoples of the Caucasus and the peoples of the free steppe." This proposal met with a favorable response in all those provinces.[392]

All these autonomous movements, including the Ukrainian movement, which was the most powerful, lacked the intellectual and state-building forces that would have made it possible for them to withstand the Bolsheviks. The requisite training and routine were, however, to be found in the camp of the all-Russian reaction. Had this camp, with all its political and cultural advantages, identified itself with the separatist movement of the non-Russian nationalities and the Russian autonomists, it would have given them a firm structure and enabled them to stand up to the Bolsheviks. But the all-Russian reaction did not support the national movements. On the contrary, it opposed them and the Bolsheviks as well. It was inevitable, therefore, that the Bolsheviks would triumph over a divided opposition, subjugating not only the nationalities but also the all-Russian reaction itself. Thus the attempt to reestablish all-Russian imperial unity directly undermined the struggle against the Bolsheviks. Only after a united struggle of the nationalities and the counterrevolution against the Bolsheviks would it be possible, if at all, to reestablish some form of unity among the non-Russian nationalities and the independent regions under a central Russian state. There could be no question, however, of reestablishing the kind of firm imperial unity that had existed in tsarist Russia. This was now a thing of the past. If, out of the ruins of the old empire, a federation of states or even a loose military and foreign-political pact were to emerge, even this would have to be regarded as a great victory for the idea of imperial unity.

From May 1918, three countries manifested the possible forms that the counterrevolution might take. The first was Ukraine under the hetman. From the national viewpoint, this was a Ukrainian state; socially and politically, it was conservative. The second was the Don region under the leadership of General Krasnov. This was a reactionary state based on an estate system that preserved traditional Cossack privileges. The third was Siberia, a democratic state. This multiplicity of constitutional forms in which the struggle against the Bolsheviks had to be waged if it was to be victorious shows how inadequate any "all-Russian" project was for the "salvation of Russia." It also shows what kind of adaptability was required on the part of the all-Russian reaction if it was to lead this struggle and carry it through to victory.

But the reactionary movement was incapable of change. It was intellectually and politically moribund when it began. It was no match for a genius like Lenin. In 1918 this movement had two options. One was the restoration of the Russian Empire as an immediate goal, in which case it would have to place itself at the service of the Bolsheviks. The other was to attempt to save the social and cultural tradition of the empire from destruction by the Bolsheviks. This would mean placing the movement at the service of the non-Russian nationalities and the autonomous territories, forming a united front with them to defeat the Bolsheviks, and postponing to some more favorable conjuncture the task of transforming this united front into some kind of imperial Russian unity. But apart from a small number of senior officers who allied themselves with the Bolsheviks, they chose neither of those options. It was in Ukraine that the choice was made. The intellectual forces of the all-Russian reaction had no real possibility of becoming part of the Ukrainian national movement as long as that movement was permeated by a mixture of Ukrainian nationalism and social-revolutionary ideology, a mixture whose dubious values were well represented by the Central Rada. The Rada had, after all, got rid not only of its conservative elements but even of its moderate ones. But when the hetman took over the leadership of the state on 29 April 1918, the door was open for the all-Russian reactionary movement to place itself at the service of the Ukrainian state. The all-Russian reaction, in fact, took full advantage of this opportunity, but not in order to save this hospitable state, which had accepted reactionary refugees from all parts of Russia, from being swamped by the Bolsheviks. They proceeded from the illusory assumption that the Bolsheviks would not be able to hold out very long in Moscow. Their defeat would also bring down the liberal and democratic movements. The time was therefore ripe, they believed, to prepare an immediate restoration of tsarist Russia with the forces of the all-Russian reactionary movement alone. The successful restoration would also finish, once and for all, separatist movements such as that in Ukraine. They considered themselves, with justice, to be intellectually superior to the Ukrainian nationalists. After the various restorative legal acts of the hetman, they were also secure in their economic power. They forgot, unfortunately, that in this situation they were "generals without soldiers" and had no support among the popular masses, whereas the Eastern Ukrainian pediocracy had at its disposal a politically active human reservoir of millions. Instead of doing the Ukrainians a service such as General Grekov did for the Western Ukrainians, the all-Russian reaction took advantage of the Hetman State in order to destroy its sovereignty as soon as possible. The reactionaries used the Hetman State not only to restore, under a Ukrainian banner, the legal and social relations and administrative practices of old tsarist Russia but even to bring the Ukrainian national movement itself to a halt and reverse the very considerable Ukrainization of the state apparatus that had taken place after the Revolution of 1917. They reintroduced systematic Russification, for instance, the use of Russian as an official language alongside Ukrainian, a practice that was highly offensive to Ukrainian national sensitivities. Ukrainian national revolutionary opposition to the hetman would never have been so great had it not been for the provocative and tactless activities of this all-Russian reaction. The Hetman State proved to the Ukrainians in a thousand ways that the all-Russian officials in its service were engaged in treasonous activity and were preparing a reactionary Russian counterrevolution that would return Ukraine to the status of "Little Russian," "Southwest Russian," "South Russian," and "New Russian" gubernias of the empire.

This happened not only in Ukraine but also in the Russian provinces on the Don and in Siberia. Although there was no reason to suspect that these provinces would not reunite with Russia as soon as the Bolsheviks in Moscow and St. Petersburg were defeated, the all-Russian reaction was not willing to tolerate any kind of separate development. Its dogma of imperial Russian unity had to be put into effect immediately and everywhere. Its goal was the complete restoration of the decadent conditions of old tsarist Russia. A large-scale reactionary all-Russian coup was attempted simultaneously in Ukraine and Siberia. On 14 November 1918 the Ukrainian hetman, Skoropadsky, was persuaded to proclaim the union of Ukraine with Russia in a future Russian federation. An anti-Bolshevik Provisional Russian Government formed on 23 September in Ufa, the "Directory," was dispersed on 17 or 19 November because of its democratic-socialist tendencies. At the same time, Siberia was forced to relinquish its independence. In place of the Directory and the separate Siberian government, a military dictatorship was established under Admiral Aleksandr Kolchak. The Don Cossacks under General Krasnov kept their independence the longest, but when their army was defeated by the Bolsheviks in January 1919, General Denikin took advantage of the situation and forced them to dismiss General Krasnov on 15 February in return for military assistance from the Kuban. They were then forced to submit to Denikin's command as leader of the all-Russian counterrevolution in "South Russia."[393]

The all-Russian reaction thereby destroyed any possible foundation for a successful counterrevolution in Eastern Europe. This not only brought about the mass Eastern Ukrainian uprising against the hetman in November 1918, leading to the destruction of this powerful base that had brought the counterrevolution almost to the gates of Moscow; it also produced total chaos in the country, forcing the remnants of the all-Russian forces to retreat to the Kuban and into the Caucasus. As a result, at the turn of the year 1918–19, the Bolsheviks were able to overrun almost all of Ukraine and the whole Don region. The short-sighted actions of the all-Russian movement in Ukraine also made it possible for the Bolsheviks to use the essentially anti-Bolshevik non-Russian national movements against the all-Russian reactionary forces, just as they had used them previously against the Provisional Government. Whenever the non-Russian national movements were faced with the choice between a reactionary united Russia with its threat of Russification and the creation of national Soviet republics at the cost of the old social order, it was clear that they would choose the latter as the lesser evil.

The basis of the counterrevolution in Hetman Ukraine was not destroyed simply by the weakening of the German army of occupation as a result of the November Revolution in the German Reich. The consolidation on the Don during 1918 showed that such a process was also possible in Ukraine. It was through the activity of the all-Russian reaction that this was prevented from happening. The power of Ukraine's strike force was demonstrated by the fact that despite the terrible upheaval caused by the overthrow of the hetman, the Directory and Petliura were still able to resist the Bolsheviks. How much stronger, then, would Eastern Ukraine have been if the all-Russian movement had allied itself with the Hetman State?

The defeat of the hetman in Ukraine destroyed the hopes of the all-Russian counterrevolutionaries that they would soon march into Moscow and St. Petersburg. Their base was now essentially reduced to the Kuban region, which Denikin had taken in June 1918 as a result of a successful campaign with 10,000 troops from the Don that defeated a Bolshevik force of 80,000 to 100,000. At the end of 1918 these counterrevolutionary troops were preparing to move north again to restore "Russia, one and indivisible." The troops began their advance in May 1919. By the end of July they had taken the Don region, as well as the eastern part of Eastern Ukraine, including Kharkiv, had reached Kursk in the north and had increased their strength, with the aid of volunteers, to about 200,000 men. Their strategic plan was to advance on Moscow by way of Kursk and Tula.[394] But this plan made no provision for the establishment of order in the countryside behind the advancing armies and was quite the opposite of what was required to defeat the Bolsheviks. This was the establishment and consolidation of an anti-Bolshevik state order among the various nationalities surrounding Great Russia, which would have deprived the Bolsheviks of their mightiest weapon, namely, the social disorder and turmoil in the countryside behind the lines of the counterrevolutionary armies.

When Petliura presented his plan for a military alliance between Ukraine and General Denikin's forces to the inter-Allied mission in Kamianets-Podilskyi, he had every reason to believe that this mission would be convinced of the inevitability of the defeat of the all-Russian counterrevolution if the latter did not have the support of the non-Russian national movements, especially the Ukrainian movement. It was not only the costly lesson of the fall of the Hetman State that pointed in this direction. There were also purely strategic reasons. The Bolshevik armies on the lower Dnipro were a threat to the Denikin forces advancing via Kursk, Tula and Orel to Moscow, and without the support of the Ukrainians it would be difficult to deal with that threat. These two facts supported the Petliura plan, but there were other factors in its favor as well. One look at the composition of the counterrevolutionary armies that encircled Bolshevik Russia in July-August 1919 made it clear that even now, with the all-Russian reactionary movement in complete control of the East European counterrevolution, except for Petliura's Ukraine, those forces were made up not of Russian but of non-Russian troops and troops from the autonomous provinces. Everything seemed to indicate that the all-Russian reaction, on purely rational grounds, would have to make political concessions to the forces on which its existence depended and that were absolutely necessary to ensure its victory over the Bolsheviks.

At that time, in July-August 1919, when the Ukrainians, with their 100,000 troops concentrated in Podilia, were one of the major anti-Bolshevik forces, the core of the other anti-Bolshevik forces was the Denikin army. In return for his tacit concession of the oil fields of Baku and Transcaucasia, he was supplied with arms by the English.[395] His army, in the meantime, had grown to a force of more than 200,000 men. Only the original core and leadership of this army were all-Russian reactionaries. Most of the soldiers were Cossacks from the Don and the Kuban and fighters from the peoples of the Caucasus who had by no means given up their autonomist aspirations. A great part of the energy of Denikin's army was wasted on the political suppression of the Cossacks, particularly the Ukrainian Cossacks from the Kuban.

A small Cossack army under General Aleksandr Dutov, which had advanced from the Transcaucasian steppe to the lower Volga, linked Denikin's army with the second major counterrevolutionary force, Kolchak's army in Western Siberia and in the Urals.[396] The core of this army was the Czechoslovak Legion. Among those troops as well, the all-Russians provided only the organizational framework. The troops themselves came from various autonomous movements on the eastern edge of the former Russian Empire. The most important of these were the Siberians. Just as the all-Russian volunteers in Denikin's army ranked second after the Cossacks, in this army the Russian troops from Outer Siberia that had rebelled against the Bolsheviks in July 1918 and established a "Volga People's Army" in Samara ranked second after the Siberians. Next in importance were the Ugro-Finnish and Turco-Mongolian fighters. These were the Kirghiz, the Bashkirs, the Turco-Tatars of Western Siberia, and the Buriats of Eastern Siberia. All of these had established their own national governments under the banner of self-determination, and their fighters were now supporting Kolchak's army.[397] This army had less than 100,000 men; in other words, it was smaller than the Ukrainian army. After a number of defeats suffered by the Volga People's Army in the second half of 1918, this front of the Russian counterrevolution, richly supplied from Japan and America, had a number of successes after December 1918. On 14 March they took Ufa and soon afterwards recaptured Samara on the Volga. In June 1919, however, this army suffered a number of serious defeats and, while Denikin advanced victoriously, this army of Kolchak's retreated in disarray to the east. It finally collapsed in central Siberia in January-February 1920.

Many hundreds of kilometers from the retreating Kolchak front, across the thinly populated northern lands, the third, numerically small, army of the Russian counterrevolution under General Gurko was operating out of Russia's only ice-free port, Murmansk, on the northern coast of the Kola Peninsula, and from Archangel.[398] But even here the Russians were not the only ones to bear the brunt of the fighting. The core of this undertaking was made up of Allied troops: English, Americans and Italians.

The fourth and last of the counterrevolutionary armies was that of General Nikolai Yudenich. This small army of 30,000 to 40,000 men was based in Estonia. In such a small country, where it is relatively easy to have a good overview of social relations and conditions, it becomes even clearer that the essential forces of the counterrevolution were those of the non-Russian national movements for self-determination. Yudenich was unable to come to an understanding with the Estonians, and this crippled his undertaking. In spite of the proximity of St. Petersburg and his occasional victories, he never managed to take the capital: his success consisted in mere survival.[399]

Thus in July-August 1919 the counterrevolutionary Russian forces disposed of somewhat fewer than 400,000 men. The Bolsheviks had about a million. As far as the military value of the troops was concerned, the counterrevolutionaries were superior to the Bolsheviks. As for their military command, they were equal.[400] But what was fatal for the counterrevolution, which thought it could defeat the Bolsheviks by purely military means, was the unity of purpose, strength of will and clear political vision of the Bolsheviks: in a word, Lenin. It is this ingenuity of the Bolshevik leadership and the lack of talent on the side of the counterrevolution that makes the victory of the Bolsheviks in Eastern Europe comprehensible. For the overwhelming majority of the population of the former Russian Empire certainly did not want Bolshevism. But they hated the all-Russian reaction even more, and Bolshevism was preferable to restoration. They suffered from the civil war but did not participate in it. The fight was between two minorities: the Bolsheviks and the all-Russian reactionary movement. The latter, being smaller, was defeated, although it had many opportunities, of which it did not take advantage, to win the majority of the population over to the struggle against the Bolsheviks.

In overestimating its own potential, the all-Russian counterrevolution completely failed to realize that the driving force that could be turned against the Bolsheviks was not its own desire for restoration but the regional desire to separate. The composition of the counterrevolutionary armies proved this. How did the all-Russian reactionary leaders prove their ability to restore the fallen empire? After all, they did assume that the Bolsheviks and the non-Russian nationalities were wholly incapable of doing so and considered themselves the only competent holders of state power. Respect for justice and legality, in contrast to the wild Bolshevik terror, could have won the population, weary of confusion and uncertainty, to the side of the counterrevolution. But the all-Russian counterrevolution was in fact only the representative of an Oriental concept of a "strong state." A sociopolitical order in the European sense exists when the organs of the state, the military and administrative apparatus, are kept in check and the people are ruled by law, not by the arbitrary decisions of soldiers and bureaucrats. But the Oriental "strong state" is an order in which the military and bureaucratic satraps are responsible for nothing and are bound by no higher law. The population, in this system, is subject to an oppressive and arrogant arbitrariness that renders it dumb and submissive. The struggle between the all-Russian reactionaries and the Bolsheviks was therefore simply a struggle between the White and the Red terror. Both were equally cruel and arbitrary. Both of them equally battered the unhappy population. Along with their failure to realize the potential of the regional and national movements, this complete lack of discipline was the second major error of the counterrevolution. It simply turned the counterrevolutionary resistance into a senseless chaos. This White terror was directed not only against actual Bolsheviks but also against the entire working class and peasantry. It took no account of the experience of the Hetman State, which showed that if peasants were allowed to keep their agrarian booty—the land—even temporarily, they would act as allies against the urban, proletarian Bolshevik dictatorship; on the other hand, mistreating them by means of punitive expeditions would only drive them into the Bolshevik camp. The terror was directed against socialist and merely democratic intellectuals—against all those intellectuals, in fact, who were not reactionaries. It was a terror against the non-Russian separatists and even against the autonomy-seeking Kuban Cossacks. It was a terror that simply attempted to cover over the absence of intelligent leadership and real strength. Just as in 1905, the reactionaries believed that they could defeat this incomparably greater revolution by drowning it in blood. This arbitrary and brutal terror from both left and right provoked the population, which was essentially neither reactionary nor Bolshevik, to revolt, sometimes against the counterrevolutionaries, sometimes against the Bolsheviks, but always against the power of the terrorists that was wreaking havoc on its territory. In this to and fro of revolutionary and counterrevolutionary violence, the strength of the whole empire was gradually sapped. Eventually the only one left on the field was the one capable not only of terror but also of political insight, of firm inner discipline, of distinguishing between the essential and the inessential: Bolshevism.

In the Russian counterrevolution there were of course many examples of heroism, self-sacrifice and devotion to duty. The best fell in the heroic battles at the beginning. Any judgment about the character of a historical process must rest, however, not on the noble acts of individuals but on the extent to which this nobility characterized the movement as a whole. What characterized the Russian counterrevolution? Lack of discipline and an absence of sanctions; a poor administration; unbridled greed of bankrupt landlords; arbitrariness, thieving and cruelty among its fighters, who degenerated into mercenaries; bribery and corruption in the reserves; arrogance and barbaric hedonism. These were the chief characteristics of the counterrevolutionary army as a whole. It was as if nothing of the former greatness of the Russian Empire were to be found in this all-Russian reaction. In its final century, the decaying tsarist regime had corrupted not only the political thinking of the upper strata, so that they were no longer capable of understanding the new situation, much less of creating a new social order, but even their civilized character.

This was the army, then, that General Denikin had at his disposal. A personally noble character, motivated by the best intentions, General Denikin belonged in the ranks of men like General Lavr Kornilov, who fell as a hero in battle, and General Aleksei Kaledin, the Don Cossack general who committed suicide in order to spur on his troops against the Bolsheviks when his own words and appeals were no longer adequate.[401] The character of this army was already firmly established by the summer of 1919. It was no longer capable of being reformed. Committed to the dogma of "Russia, one and indivisible," there was no chance that it would make an exception for Ukraine. Its whole character prevented it from joining in an alliance with Petliura, whom it detested as a contemptible adventurer. The Denikinites stormed against Moscow in the belief that victory awaited them. But, dragged down by the weight of their own mistakes and failures, they were in fact rushing to their doom.

The situation in which the Ukrainians found themselves now, in July-August 1919, differed from the one that had faced them in February, at the time of the Berthélemy proposals, in that Denikin's all-Russian counterrevolutionary army had become a powerful military force capable of contemplating an imminent assault on Moscow. At that time, in February 1919, Denikin was only beginning to extend his power beyond the Kuban. Assuming that the Western Ukrainians had been as patriotic in February 1919 as they were now, and assuming that the political leaders and population of Eastern Ukraine could have become as disenchanted with their social radicalism in February as they were now, the Ukrainians, with a large territorial base in Eastern Galicia, could have constituted a much more important anti-Bolshevik force than Denikin at that time. With such strength behind them, they could well have laid down conditions to Denikin for an alliance against the Bolsheviks. Denikin, pressured by the Entente, would perhaps have been forced to accept those conditions.[402] But now, in July-August 1919, with Denikin's troops advancing and growing day by day from the influx of volunteers, and with the capture of Moscow in sight, the counterrevolution could do without Ukraine. Indeed, from the viewpoint of the counterrevolution, the Ukrainian national movement was something that, like Bolshevism, had to be destroyed if a powerful Russia were to reemerge, just as, in Dmowski's case, Ukraine had to be destroyed if Poland were to be great.

As far as the Russian counterrevolution was concerned, then, Petliura's plan had no chance of success. In its external relations Ukraine had now forfeited everything. There was no possibility of an alliance with the Bolsheviks because of its inconsistency after the fall of the hetman. French support was excluded by the Western Ukrainian rejection of the Berthélemy proposals. A united front with the other Eastern European counterrevolutionary forces was made impossible by the overthrow of the hetman. Ukraine did not belong to any political system in Europe and was without any possible allies. Only by giving up their national aspirations and becoming the "Little Russian" branch of the all-Russian nation under General Denikin could the Ukrainians hope for support from the Entente, which was now placing all its hopes in Denikin. The Entente was not prepared to bother him with complications in Ukraine resulting from the growing strength of the Ukrainians. In international politics, Ukraine had been condemned to death. It was not just the fact that the Ukrainians were militarily surrounded by enemies but the fact that they were unable to form an alliance with any of those enemies that brought about their downfall in this rectangle of death.

3. *The End of Ukrainian Statehood*

The tragedy of the Ukrainian situation was even greater now, inasmuch as the Eastern Ukrainian state, after the incorporation of the Western Ukrainians, actually ruled its own territory for the first time since its founding. This territory grew steadily after July 1919 as more and more of it was recaptured from the Bolsheviks. Unrest in the countryside had been brought to an end by the presence of the Western Ukrainian troops, which, although initially distrusted by the local population, were later accepted and highly regarded. Even the Eastern Ukrainian administration, which had been quite useless until then, now carried out its tasks and duties reasonably well, especially as many of the officials were Western Ukrainian. The situation was by no means perfect, but it was incomparably better than anything that had existed in Eastern Ukraine since the fall of the hetman or in the territories controlled by the Russian counterrevolutionary armies. The weary population trusted Petliura and responded willingly to the government's dictates and mobilization orders. But there was not much point in enlisting in the army, or in being willing to enlist, if there were no clothes for the soldiers and no ammunition. Most of the recruits had to be let go.[403]

One would have thought that, given the clarity of the tragic situation in which they found themselves, Eastern and Western Ukraine would close ranks and make one final attempt to survive, relying on their own forces alone. If they could hold out, perhaps the situation would improve. But that did not happen.

Petliura was not a man of any great political talent, and he never really understood the need for proper organization of the army and the country. However, when he heard that the Western Ukrainians had decided to cross the Zbruch, he had enough common sense to begin preparations for the winding up of the Western Ukrainian government in exile and for the formal unification of both armies under a single command. On 4 July the Eastern Ukrainian government created a special Ministry for Western Ukrainian Affairs, thereby pointedly questioning the need for the Western Ukrainian dictatorship.

Although public opinion in both Eastern and Western Ukraine favored a single government, the matter was not so simple as it appeared. There was the question of who would exercise power and of what direction the united government would take. Would it be socialist, as Eastern Ukrainian domestic politics had been until then, or would it be, as the Western Ukrainians would prefer to have it, liberal-democratic or even conservative? Petliura's government was in left-wing hands—the Social Democrats and Socialist Revolutionaries. The Western Ukrainian left, the Social Democrats and the disreputable Peasant-Worker League, had always wanted to have Petliura at the head of a united Ukrainian government. The Western Ukrainian dictatorship, however, was supported by the right-wing and moderate Western Ukrainian parties, as well as by the right-wing Eastern Ukrainian groups that had always wanted the Western Ukrainians to occupy Eastern Ukraine. At this moment the Western Ukrainian dictatorship was in an even stronger position because it had the unshakable loyalty of the whole Western Ukrainian army, and the best troops in Eastern Ukraine wanted it to take power there as well. Since the dictator had no intention of resigning voluntarily, Petliura was unable to resolve this problem. He could not unseat the dictator by force. Similarly, he could not resign in the dictator's favor, even if he had wanted to do so. As noted above, the dictator was firmly committed to the separate legal existence of Western and Eastern Ukraine. Consequently, it made no difference that Petrushevych had enough troops at his disposal to unseat Petliura and at last establish order in Eastern Ukraine. Nor did it make any difference that numerous delegations from both Eastern and Western Ukraine begged him to bring about a united Ukraine. The dictator rejected all arguments and stubbornly held on to his separate government. Moreover, he was not really familiar with the situation in Eastern Ukraine, whose forever seething political caldron made him shudder. The unification of the Ukrainian governments was therefore impossible because Eastern Ukraine was unable to bring it about, and Western Ukraine was unwilling to do so. The link between both was even further weakened when the dictator formally withdrew from the Directory.[404]

The Western Ukrainian dictatorship became a bone of contention for Ukraine. What could Petliura do with this disciplined Western Ukrainian force that had marched into his country not only to fight but also to veto his foreign policy and tie him down militarily? He could do little more than leave them with their naïve leadership to come to grief in the harsh conditions of Eastern Ukraine and hope that the time would come when he would be able to get rid of the Western Ukrainian dictatorship by force.

He flooded the Western Ukrainian army with appeals to the troops to join the Eastern Ukrainian units; he gave refuge to all kinds of adventurers and rebels fleeing the dictator; he welcomed with open arms any Western Ukrainian who wished to join the Eastern Ukrainian civil or military service; and he systematically created disadvantages for the Western Ukrainian troops in such things as rations, supplies and pay.

The Western Ukrainian dictatorship responded by increasing its political pressure. Before the Western Ukrainians would help him, Petliura was forced to abandon his Ministry for Western Ukrainian Affairs. In domestic politics, he was compelled to abandon some of his more socialist policies in favor of what was seen as greater moderation and had to accept Western Ukrainian nominees into his government. The supreme command of both armies, however, was kept separate, and it was not until 11 August, after long-drawn-out negotiations, that agreement was reached to create a joint operational leadership over both commands. The composition of this joint military staff was not determined by merit or as a result of rational consideration of needs but on the basis of a purely mechanical reckoning of the strength of each army and the origin of each officer. Petty considerations of this kind were characteristic of relations between the Western and Eastern Ukrainians in Kamianets-Podilskyi. In view of the superior strength of the Western Ukrainian army, on whose support Eastern Ukraine depended, Petliura had to recognize the sovereign jurisdiction of the Western Ukrainian dictatorship, however unwillingly. The Ministry for Western Ukrainian Affairs was formally dissolved on 29 September.

The Western Ukrainians had a low opinion of the Eastern Ukrainian army and bureaucracy. They were rightly proud of the fact that in organizational matters they were far superior to the Eastern Ukrainians and that on their own side there was no corruption or lack of discipline. They would have earned not only this right to be proud but also the gratitude of the Eastern Ukrainians and their adherence to Western Ukrainian standards of efficiency if only the precise machinery that they brought with them had been more intelligently led; if they had taken over the Eastern Ukrainian government and unified the political and military apparatus in order to clean up the mess in Eastern Ukraine. But while they fought the Bolsheviks, in Kamianets-Podilskyi the intrigue between both governments made the situation worse from day to day. The Western Ukrainians made no secret of their contempt for the Eastern Ukrainians, and the latter, well aware of the damage being caused by the separate existence of the Western Ukrainian dictatorship, developed their own hatred for the Western Ukrainians. In one and the same city, Kamianets-Podilskyi, both governments made their own plans in complete isolation from each other. But because they were dependent on each other, they were obliged to engage in long and tedious negotiations over every issue. In these negotiations each side maneuvered to its own advantage and for the sake of its own prestige. The two armies and bureaucracies developed a strong distrust of each other. There was a constant threat of violent armed conflict between both governments in the city.[405]

In spite of all this, the Ukrainian troops carried out their military duties honorably. On 29 July Proskuriv was taken by a joint action of both armies. East and southeast of Proskuriv the Western Ukrainian troops advanced on their own, winning hard-fought battles to create a space in which their whole army could be positioned for a general offensive. Petliura, now disposing of considerable Ukrainian forces, decided to take Kyiv as soon as possible and make use of this achievement to influence negotiations with the Entente and with Denikin. He also reckoned that with the Dnipro as a natural protective barrier in the east he could devote himself to the task of organizing the population of the Right Bank to continue the war against the Bolsheviks. But the Western Ukrainian military leaders were opposed to this plan. They thought it would be better to capture Odesa than Kyiv, believing that with this port city in their possession they would receive support from the Entente. The Western Ukrainians were so convinced of this that they later blamed the Ukrainian defeat exclusively on the fact that Petliura had taken Kyiv instead of Odesa. In this, as in all other things, the Western Ukrainians hung on to the inessential. From the viewpoint of the Entente it did not matter whether the Ukrainians had a port or not, as supplies could be sent via Romania if the Entente so wished. Entente support depended much more on whether Denikin would come to some agreement with Ukraine. Ukrainian control of Odesa was irrelevant in that regard, for such an agreement was excluded by the very nature of the all-Russian reaction. If the Ukrainians had captured Odesa and moved the government there, as the Western Ukrainians wanted, in order to "open a window on Europe," they would have delivered themselves into the hands of the all-Russian reactionaries. The government residence in Kamianets-Podilskyi was at least safe from being wiped out by the Russians. The successful capture of Kyiv was also bound to do more for their prestige than the capture of Odesa.[406]

Petliura finally got his way, and by 2–5 August 1919 the whole Western Ukrainian army was fighting arm in arm with the Eastern Ukrainians in a hard struggle against the Bolsheviks. Tactically, this assault was arranged in such a way as to capture as much military equipment as possible from the Bolsheviks. In fact, their offensive was almost completely dependent on taking arms and ammunition from the enemy. The strategic goal of this action was to force the Bolshevik Fourteenth Army, which had been fighting from the Odesa region against both Denikin and Petliura, back to Odesa, where it could be surrounded and forced to capitulate, yielding all its military equipment to the Ukrainians. The strongest Ukrainian troops marched on Kyiv to prevent any relief for the Fourteenth Army from that quarter. The next strongest group marched toward the Prypiat to secure the Kyiv operation from any surprise attack from the north. The weakest group, made up mostly of Eastern Ukrainians, marched on Odesa to prevent the Bolsheviks from breaking out of the city (Map 6).[407]

The fighting was extremely hard. The Bolsheviks had fewer troops than the Ukrainians but concentrated their best forces against them, since the Ukrainians were a greater threat than Denikin. The Bolsheviks were fully aware that this battle was decisive; that its outcome would determine whether victory went to Soviet Russia or to the counterrevolution, and they fought heroically. Every foot of territory was defended, and the outcome was decided in bitter hand-to-hand fighting.

Under the slogan "Through Kyiv to Lviv" the Western Ukrainians advanced and fought, with every day bringing new victories. On 29 July, after particularly bloody fighting, the outstanding Eastern Ukrainian military leader Colonel Oleksander Udovychenko captured Vapniarka, an important junction on the railway line to Odesa. On 9 August the Ukrainians took the Kyiv railway junction at Zhmerynka, and on 10 August they captured Vinnytsia, the capital of Podilia. From this position, the general offensive against Kyiv began on 11 August. In this direction, as well as toward the north, the Ukrainian forces were superior to those of the enemy, while in the south they were covered by a force less than half the strength of the Bolsheviks. But the Ukrainian troops were supported by a widespread peasant uprising behind the Bolshevik lines. On 14 August they captured Starokostiantyniv in Volhynia, and on 17 August they crossed the railway line between Shepetivka and Polonne. On 21 August they took the Volhynian capital, Zhytomyr, as well as the town of Novohrad-Volynskyi. On 31 August the fighting reached Korosten in northern Ukraine. If they could make an agreement with Denikin, this would take them as far as the Prypiat. Meanwhile, in the direction of Kyiv, Koziatyn was taken on 18 August and Berdychiv on the following day. On 24 August the Ukrainians captured Fastiv and Bila Tserkva, and on 26 August they were in possession of Vasylkiv, just outside Kyiv (Map 6).[408]

The whole Bolshevik front west of the Volga was now in a catastrophic situation. Between Kharkiv and the Volga the Bolsheviks had been defeated by Denikin's troops, which were now advancing northward under the leadership of General Vladimir Mai-Maevsky. On 5 August Konstantin Mamontov's audacious cavalry took Tambov, then Kozlov on the 10th and Lebediansk on the 15th. On 18 August they captured

Elets and linked up with Denikin's main forces west of Voronezh on 22 August. Troops under General Nikolai Bredov pushed westward from Kharkiv via Poltava in the direction of Kyiv, reaching Cherkasy on the Dnipro on 16 August. Meanwhile, Kuban Cossack troops under Andrei Shkuro had crossed the Dnipro south of there between Katerynoslav and Oleksandrivske (Zaporizhia) and were marching toward Kryvyi Rih in the direction of Odesa. A division of Terek and Kuban Cossacks captured the last railway junction between Kyiv and Odesa at Tsvitkove on 21 August and advanced west toward Khrystynivka and north toward Bila Tserkva. Further west, the Eastern Ukrainians held Uman, Khrystynivka and Vapniarka. The Bolshevik Fourteenth Army in the region of Kryvyi Rih, Kherson, Mykolaiv, Odesa, and Birzula (Kotovske)—a region seething with peasant revolts—lost all railway links with the north and was surrounded, with Denikin's troops on one side and Ukrainian troops on the other. Leaving Odesa to Denikin's troops, the Bolsheviks concentrated all their forces against the Ukrainians between Vapniarka and Khrystynivka, hoping to break through to their troops in the north around Korosten, south of the Prypiat. In a very bloody battle near Vapniarka, a Bolshevik division was almost completely wiped out by the Ukrainians. The survivors regrouped near Khrystynivka to make another attempt at a breakthrough (Map 6).[409]

The Denikin army was now face to face with the Ukrainian forces in a very tense situation. The Bolshevik front separating the two armies had collapsed in the region between Uman and Tsvitkove. On 23 August the Ukrainian troops were cautioned that under no circumstances should they engage Denikin's forces: on the contrary, they should attempt to coordinate their efforts. The advance guards of both armies had already met near Tsvitkove on 21 August under friendly circumstances. On the Denikin side there was a division of Kuban and Terek Cossacks who sympathized with the Ukrainians because they were also seeking autonomy, and some of them were of Ukrainian descent. The Cossack general readily agreed on a demarcation line with the Ukrainians and expressed the wish that they should fight together, albeit under Denikin's command (Map 6).[410]

Relations in this southern sector were harmonious, and negotiations continued. The Ukrainian army in the north continued its advance on Kyiv, in pursuit of the Bolsheviks, hoping to prevent them from moving their military supplies and equipment out of the city. On 30 August the Ukrainians finally broke through the Bolshevik defenses, and on the night of 30–31 August they occupied the city and the bridges across the Dnipro to the east. Kyiv, the goal that had inspired this spirited advance, was now theirs (Map 6).[411]

This was a great blow to the pride of Denikin's troops. General Bredov's troops had marched with great speed from the east in order to take Kyiv before the Ukrainians, but they arrived too late and had to stop at the Dnipro. However, on 31 August, just as the Ukrainian troops were holding a victory parade through the center of town, Denikin's troops managed to surprise the Ukrainian guards (who did not regard them as enemies) on the bridges, disarming them and entering the city. The Ukrainian military parade was now attacked with a hail of fire from the side streets by Denikin's troops. Taken aback by this underhanded assault, the Ukrainian soldiers scattered and were defeated in a brief but intense battle, after which some of them were disarmed and others forced to leave the city. This was the beginning of the war between Denikin and the Ukrainians, exactly as the Bolsheviks had foreseen in the course of their retreat: "Petliura and Denikin will soon attack each other, and we will be back in two months at the latest."[412]

This hit the Ukrainians like a thunderbolt. They had placed all their hopes in the occupation of Kyiv and never doubted that an understanding would be reached with Denikin. This sudden outbreak of hostilities with the all-Russian reaction was such a clear indication of their isolation and of the inevitability of their defeat that their moral resolve began to weaken. In spite of the shame they felt at having lost Kyiv, they continued to seek an agreement with Denikin. In keeping with General Bredov's demands, they vacated the territory as far as Fastiv, about seventy km from Kyiv, and sent a military mission to Bredov headed by General Omelianovych-Pavlenko. This mission demanded: 1) that Denikin's troops evacuate the whole Right Bank, including Kyiv; 2) the recognition of the right of a future constituent assembly to decide the relation of Ukraine to Russia; 3) the signing of a military agreement against the Bolsheviks. Denikin's representatives rejected these demands with rough arrogance and gave the Ukrainians an ultimatum: either submit unconditionally to "Russia, one and indivisible" or be prepared to continue fighting. For Denikin's army, this was madness. They had not settled with the Bolsheviks to the extent that they could afford to take on the Ukrainians as well. The Bolsheviks were marshaling all their forces for a counterattack, yet General Denikin not only refused to take advantage of the 30,000 Ukrainian troops that would have doubled or tripled the strength of his front and established a reserve army in the rear but even committed 15,000 to 20,000 of his own troops to fighting the Ukrainians. A loss of this kind, from an army of about 50,000 combat soldiers, could only end in catastrophe. Nothing obliged Denikin to fight the Ukrainians at this time. Having taken Moscow and destroyed the

Bolsheviks, his forces would have been so much stronger than those of the Ukrainians that he could have thrown out any previous agreements and kept Ukraine as part of Russia by force of arms.

This arrogance of the all-Russian reaction left the Ukrainians with little choice, especially as they were being attacked by Denikin's troops all along their front line. On 24 September Petliura and the Western Ukrainian dictator formally declared war on Denikin, a war that in fact had already broken out.[413] The Entente powers were outraged by this declaration, and their military mission left Kamianets-Podilskyi immediately, giving Denikin a free hand as far as Ukraine was concerned. But for Ukraine those sentiments of the Entente were completely irrelevant: by refusing them any support even as it armed Poland, the Entente had already been fighting against them for some time. The Bolsheviks could now breathe a sigh of relief. The impetus of the earlier victories took Denikin farther north in September 1919, and he captured Orel, just three hundred km from Moscow. But the collapse of Kolchak's army allowed the Bolsheviks to transfer their troops from that front against Denikin. The Bolsheviks gradually scaled down their military operations against the Ukrainians in northern Volhynia in order to concentrate their forces against Denikin's troops in northern Ukraine on the Left Bank of the Dnipro. The Bolshevik Fourteenth Army took advantage of the fact that Denikin and the Ukrainians were fighting each other and executed a brilliant military maneuver in October-November 1919, advancing northward between the enemy fronts past Fastiv into northern Volhynia, where they, too, could fight Denikin. This was in fact a typical result of the situation created by the senseless divisions in the counterrevolution. Gradually more and more Ukrainian troops, unmolested by the Bolsheviks, could be deployed against Denikin's army in the eastern parts of Podilia and Volhynia.[414] Once again the superiority of the Bolshevik strategy over that of the Russian counterrevolution was demonstrated with great clarity. The Bolsheviks could easily have advanced from the north to occupy Ukrainian-held territory in Volhynia and Podilia because the Ukrainians were completely engaged in fighting Denikin. But they did not do so. They preferred to postpone the occupation of Ukraine until Denikin's forces had been finally defeated by the Ukrainians. This was the kind of cleverness that the all-Russian reaction should have shown at the outset.

East and south of the line Yampil–Haisyn–Berdychiv–Zhytomyr, the fighting between the Ukrainians and Denikin's forces was very intense. For the Ukrainians, this was a senseless struggle, and they no longer had the same will to fight as they had previously shown in the war against the Bolsheviks. The troops were exhausted from all the previous fighting, and their ranks were thinning. They lacked weapons and ammunition. Winter was approaching, and the troops were without proper clothing and footwear. Typhus had already appeared during the summer. Now came the cold autumn weather, and within days the ranks of this exhausted and ragged army were plunged into a sudden catastrophe as the disease struck again. Without any means of protection or treatment, there was absolutely nothing they could do. Soon all hospitals, even those newly erected for the purpose, were overflowing. There was no treatment for the sick because of the lack of even the most basic medicines. The doctors and medical personnel were themselves struck down by the disease. Soon it was not even possible to isolate the sick. At every railway station along the front, hundreds of Ukrainian soldiers lay dying, bereft of any assistance. Hundreds more were infected on the march and depended on the mercy of the local population. Within a very short time the Ukrainian resistance was crippled. By the end of October the Western Ukrainian army had only about four thousand combat soldiers left. The Eastern Ukrainians had only two thousand. The rest were suffering from typhus or had succumbed to it. Many could not take this hell any more and tried to save themselves individually as best they could. The Ukrainian lines could no longer offer any real resistance and were easily overpowered by even the weakest of enemy attacks.[415]

But enemy advances became weaker as well. October and November 1919 saw the beginning of the catastrophe for Denikin's army between the Volga and the Dnipro. This army was now retreating in disarray, under assault from Bolshevik infantry and harried by Semen Budenny's cavalry, just as the Bolsheviks themselves had retreated shortly before. Denikin had no reserves, as these had been used up in fighting the Ukrainians—fifty thousand combat-ready men, counting both the Ukrainians and his own troops. Very soon, typhus also became rampant in Denikin's army, causing terrible devastation. Throughout the countryside behind Denikin's lines, the Eastern Ukrainian peasantry, which had had more than enough of his punitive expeditions, rose up against him as it had previously against the Bolsheviks, drowning the all-Russian counterrevolution in a veritable flood of hostility.[416] The end was approaching for both the Ukrainians and the all-Russian counterrevolution. But while the latter found death at the hands of local guerrillas, the Ukrainians were supported and helped by the local population.

The Ukrainian counterrevolution was now in its death agony. But that same death agony had also begun for the Russian counterrevolution, and in November and December 1919 there were battles with the Bolsheviks around Kyiv. True to their promise, the Bolsheviks returned to the city. General Bredov's forces had to withdraw west of the Dnipro and then retreated southward to Odesa and the Crimea.

As was only to be expected because of this catastrophe, conflicts between the two Ukrainian governments became particularly acute. They had different conceptions of how Ukraine could be rescued from the ruins of defeat. Fear of Russia, of the Bolsheviks as well as of the counterrevolution, drove the Eastern Ukrainians to seek help from Poland, even at the cost of Eastern Galicia and the western half of Volhynia. The more precarious the situation became in the war against Denikin, the stronger were the Eastern Ukrainians' hopes of salvation from Poland, although such hopes were pure sentiment and in no way based on rational political considerations. The Eastern Ukrainian press also became strongly Polonophile. Since, for the Western Ukrainians, the hope that Eastern Ukraine would become a base for their struggle against Poland had now disappeared, their representatives in Paris began to negotiate with the representatives of the Russian counterrevolution. Through their reports to the dictator and the military commanders, the representatives urged them to come to some understanding with the all-Russian reaction. As a result, the tone of the Western Ukrainian press became more and more clearly Russophile. Thus each separate government and press was highly offended with the other. Each side accused the other of treason, and the level of accusations exceeded all proportions. It reached the point in Kamianets-Podilskyi that both government residences were guarded by heavily armed troops. The residences had become, in fact, hostile camps.[417] But Eastern Ukrainian Polonophilism and Western Ukrainian Russophilism were a product neither of national treason nor of political error: they were simply an inevitable consequence of dual statehood. They were a product of the fact that until then the whole Ukrainian national movement had been motivated by hatred of the enemy and had not been held together by any reasonable political approach or purposeful self-control. With their strongly felt passions they had run themselves into the ground, blocking all roads for the nation as a whole, incapable, in the end, even of capitulating together. The Eastern Ukrainians wanted to surrender to Poland, the Western Ukrainians to Russia.

In view of the catastrophe among the troops and the hopeless desperation and disunity among the leaders, nothing remained for the Ukrainians but to try to save the lives of their remaining fighters. "For us the war is finished. We have been defeated not by the military strength of our enemy but by disease. Even the most basic needs of the Eastern

Ukrainian troops cannot be satisfied, and they are no longer capable of offering resistance. The Western Ukrainian army is in the same condition. The only task for the government now is to try to rescue what remains." This was the report of the Eastern Ukrainian army commander, General Volodymyr Salsky, on 4 November.

The Western Ukrainian military command was the first to take the initiative. On 20 October it requested the dictator to begin negotiations with General Denikin so that the remnants of the army could recuperate and the sick could be cared for. But in spite of all the conflicts with Petliura, Western Ukrainian national sentiment balked at a separate deal with the enemy—an enemy, moreover, that treated the Eastern Ukrainians as rebels. So the dictator initially rejected the appeal. He still refused to believe that the Ukrainian state was in its death throes. The Western Ukrainian military commander, General Myron Tarnavsky, then acted on his own initiative. On 25 October he secretly dispatched representatives to Denikin's army, officially to negotiate an exchange of prisoners and unofficially to find out Denikin's conditions for a truce. On 1 November, in Ziatkivtsi near Bratslav in Podilia, the Western Ukrainian mission met with General Yakov Slashchev, the commander of Denikin's anti-Ukrainian front. The general's position was as follows:

> We are prepared in principle to negotiate with the Eastern Galician army. Here is General Denikin's telegram to the effect that he is prepared to receive Eastern Galician representatives without difficulty at any time. As far as negotiations with the whole army are concerned, especially the part of it that comes from the Dnipro region, we discussed this before coming into contact with your front, and I can state that such negotiations are entirely out of the question. We consider the Eastern Galician army extraterritorial: it was forced by circumstance to enter southwestern Russia. But the army from the Dnipro region consists of Russian subjects bound by the law of the Russian Empire, which we are reinstating. We will negotiate with you as with any foreign army, but the troops from the Dnipro must surrender their weapons and disband. When we issue a mobilization order for Podilia and Volhynia, they will have to do their military duty like every other Russian citizen. At this moment I am unable to tell you what conditions we shall lay down for the Eastern Galician army. But I can assure you that, compared with the situation in which you find yourselves now, they will be favorable.[418]

A few days earlier, the commander of Denikin's forces in the "Territory of New Russia" (that is, southern Ukraine), General Nikolai Shilling, had issued an "order" to the Eastern Ukrainian troops. They were to assemble in certain areas to surrender their weapons so that the troops could be dispersed and the officers—general staff officers only after legal rehabilitation—integrated into Denikin's army. Sanctions were threatened in the event that the order was not carried out. This order was shown to the Western Ukrainian negotiators so that they would realize how pointless it was to insist on negotiations with the whole Ukrainian army. The Western Ukrainian envoys then presented the following demands: 1) The Western Ukrainian army, as an indivisible whole, should maintain its autonomy; 2) It should not be used against the Eastern Ukrainians; 3) It should be given several months to recuperate; 4) The Western Ukrainian dictator should remain as supreme commander of the army and as the sole representative of Western Ukraine.[419]

Denikin, to whom this was communicated, welcomed the Western Ukrainians and put forward the following counterconditions: 1) The Western Ukrainian army, with all its reserves, supplies and rolling stock, should submit to the Supreme Army Commander of Southern Russia, General Denikin; 2) In view of the loss of its territory, the Western Ukrainian government should cease its activity and move to Odesa under the protection of the Supreme Army Commander of Southern Russia; 3) The Western Ukrainian army would not be used against the Eastern Ukrainians; 4) The Western Ukrainians should assemble in the region of Balta; 5) The Western Ukrainian army would remain an entity, but Russian general staff officers would monitor the Western Ukrainian staff and decide all disputed issues; 6) The Western Ukrainian army command should immediately make contact with General Slashchev, who had led the front operations against it, in order to receive further instructions. The Western Ukrainians were to reply to these conditions by the evening of 3 November.

Meanwhile, on Petliura's initiative, a meeting of the two Ukrainian governments was scheduled for 4 November in Zhmerynka. The Western Ukrainian military command postponed its reply to Denikin until the following day. This meeting, in which both governments and military commands took part, agreed that a continuation of the war was no longer possible but, unaware of Western Ukraine's secret negotiations with Denikin, reached no formal conclusion. Petliura simply declared his agreement in principle that the whole Ukrainian army should enter into negotiations with Denikin for a truce. On 5 November Tarnavsky continued his negotiations with Denikin, and these were concluded on the following day with a formal agreement to a truce. Denikin's representatives had made some concessions. The Western Ukrainian government was allowed to maintain an independent foreign policy and to make appointments and promotions in the Western Ukrainian army, subject to Denikin's approval. There was no mention in the treaty of Russian control over the Western Ukrainian military staff, but Denikin's representatives at the command level would make decisions on all operational, administrative and economic questions. For this purpose, a military mission led by Colonel Zaborsky of the general staff was sent to Vinnytsia.

It was only at this point that the truth about the secret negotiations was made public. On 4 November Tarnavsky had threatened the dictator that he would take independent action if the meeting in Zhmerynka failed to produce results. For this he was dismissed, along with his chief of staff, General Alfred Schamanek, on 6 November. When the Russian military mission arrived in Vinnytsia on 7 November, they found that the Western Ukrainians had a new military leadership. Tarnavsky's place had been taken by General Osyp Mykytka, whose new chief of staff was General Gustav Ziritz.

Among the Eastern Ukrainians there was enormous outrage over what had happened, and the Western Ukrainians were accused of treason in the most extreme and malicious terms. But the Western Ukrainians and the dictator himself were also horrified at what Tarnavsky had done, for he had signed a pact with an enemy who did not even recognize the existence of a separate Ukrainian nationality. On 8 November a second meeting of both governments took place at Derazhnia near Proskuriv. This meeting decided to open negotiations with Denikin immediately on behalf of the whole Ukrainian army. Petliura and Petrushevych jointly signed an arrest warrant for Tarnavsky, for his chief of staff, General Schamanek, and all the Western Ukrainian officers who had taken part in the unauthorized negotiations. On 9 November the new Western Ukrainian military leadership declared the treaty with Denikin invalid, and Tarnavsky and the others were arrested. On 11–13 November the accused were brought before a military tribunal and charged with treason. Even in the midst of defeat, the consciousness of all-Ukrainian unity held greater weight for the Western Ukrainians than any other consideration, and it is vivid proof of their feeling of national unity that they were unwilling to allow any separate political action. In the interest of the Ukrainian state, they were even willing to allow their much-respected supreme commander to face the death penalty. But the military tribunal, taking into account the hopeless situation of the impoverished and disease-ridden army, set the accused free. It was clear that the Ukrainian governments would have to do officially what the defendants had done on their own initiative.

And that was what actually happened. A joint Western and Eastern Ukrainian military mission left for Odesa on 9 November to begin negotiations with Denikin. The supreme commander of the "Territory of New Russia," General Shilling, who had refused to see an Eastern Ukrainian military mission sent to him on 7 November, again refused to speak with the Eastern Ukrainian representatives. Although the defeat and downfall of the all-Russian counterrevolution, like that of Ukraine, was already beyond question, the general refused even now to recognize the existence of Ukraine. The counterrevolution remained true to the death to the very principles that had brought about its own catastrophic defeat. The force of circumstance was now greater than the feeling of Ukrainian national unity and stronger than the desire of the Western Ukrainians not to desert their Eastern Ukrainian comrades. Not wishing to capitulate to the Poles, as did the Eastern Ukrainians, the Western Ukrainians, with the assent of Petrushevych, began separate negotiations with Denikin and, on 17 November, they signed a new and definitive treaty with the all-Russian reaction.

The treaty, like all official documents of the all-Russian counter-revolution, went out of its way to avoid the name "Ukraine." Its main clauses were as follows: 1) The whole "Eastern Galician" army was to go over to the side of the "Russian Volunteer Army," that is, Denikin's army, and submit to the commander of the "Territory of New Russia," that is, southern Ukraine; 2) The army would maintain its organization, officer corps, language, service regulations, and all its property, but its now severely depleted troop units would be reorganized in new tactical formations at 75 percent of their current strength; the Sich Riflemen in the "Army of the Dnipro Region," although made up mostly of "native Eastern Galicians," would not be recognized as "Eastern Galician"; 3) The Russian Volunteer Army would see to the augmentation of the "Eastern Galician" army with native "Eastern Galicians" from abroad*; 4) All "Eastern Galician" staffs, institutions and detachments would be assigned Russian officers, doctors and military officials to maintain liaison with the Russian army and decide all disputed questions; 5) The question of the relationship between the "Eastern Galician" dictatorship and the government of the "Russian Volunteer Army," as well as the question of "Eastern Galicia" itself, would be the subject of future negotiations. Until

* The reference was to the Western Ukrainian brigade interned in Czechoslovakia and to the Western Ukrainian prisoners of war interned in Italy (Lozyns'kyi, *Halychyna*, p. 193).

then, the dictator would remain supreme commander as far as the internal affairs of the "Eastern Galician" army were concerned; 6) This army would not be used against the "Army of the Dnipro Region"; 7) The army was to assemble at Uman and defend that region at Berdychiv against the Bolsheviks in the north; its reserves were to assemble at Olhopil; 8) The sick and wounded "Eastern Galicians" for whom there was no room in their own hospitals would be cared for in Russian hospitals.

This treaty was ratified on the same day by the Russian supreme commander of the "Territory of New Russia," General Shilling, and on 19 November by the Western Ukrainian military leader, General Mykytka. The goals of both parties were clear. The Russians wanted immediately to employ the handful of Western Ukrainian combat troops, now numbering four thousand at most, against the Bolsheviks at Berdychiv. The Western Ukrainians wanted their sick cared for in Russian hospitals. Both parties were well aware they could not carry out those commitments. The Western Ukrainians knew that they were no longer capable of fighting, not even for their own fatherland, to say nothing of "Russia, one and indivisible." The Russians knew that their own hospitals were overcrowded and that they were in no position to help the Western Ukrainians with medical supplies, clothing, and so on. "We knew that the Denikin army was already dead," the Western Ukrainians later explained, "but unfortunately we also knew that this corpse was heavy enough to crush us."

While these negotiations continued in Odesa, both Ukrainian governments in Kamianets-Podilskyi discussed the question of joint capitulation. But these discussions were pointless, for there was no possibility of a shared fate. The Western Ukrainians, pursued to the grave and beyond by the Poles, would inevitably have to make a different capitulation from that of the Eastern Ukrainians, themselves hounded to death by the Russians. The corpse of the all-Russian counterrevolution now had a sudden lease on life, and the remnants of Denikin's army rounded on the Eastern Ukrainian units, ignoring the Western Ukrainian sectors, to wreak vengeance on them before they themselves were swallowed up by the victorious Bolsheviks. There was a strong element of horror in this assault by some hundreds of typhus-stricken all-Russian soldiers against a similar number of diseased Ukrainians. In all cases the Eastern Ukrainian remnants gave up almost without a fight, as the Russians themselves would have done had the Ukrainians been in any condition to "storm" them. In any event, the capture of Kamianets-Podilskyi by these troops of Denikin's seemed inevitable. Petliura decided that he would rather let the Poles take the city, and his decision was communicated to the

Western Ukrainian dictator on 15 November 1919. Petrushevych's troops, which until then had been unshakably loyal to him, now rebelled. It was suddenly recognized that the wretched situation in which Ukraine now found itself was a product of the policy of dual statehood, for which the Western Ukrainian politicians in general and the dictator in particular bore the responsibility. As the walls caved in around the separate Western Ukrainian government, nothing remained but to make its escape. Secretly, on the night of 15–16 November, the government leaders crossed the Dnister into Romania and made their way to Vienna, that city in whose parliament they had been so badly schooled.

On 16 November the Polish cavalry rode into Kamianets-Podilskyi, while the Eastern Ukrainian government hastened toward Starokostiantyniv in central Volhynia. It was a cold day with a frosty wind from the north. As the ragged, barefoot and miserable remnants of the Eastern Ukrainian army marched toward Starokostiantyniv, where they were to assemble, they passed, silently and without any sign of military greeting, the equally ragged, barefoot and miserable remnants of the Western Ukrainian army as they marched eastward into eastern Podilia. One army was on its way to lay down its arms to the Poles, the other to capitulate to the Russians. The path of both was strewn with frozen corpses. On 5 December Petliura crossed the Polish line of demarcation in central Volhynia, and on the same day the remnants of his army laid down their weapons to the Poles north of Starokostiantyniv. Some of those soldiers went over to the side of the Bolsheviks. Others, led by General Omelianovych-Pavlenko, carried out guerrilla actions behind the Bolshevik lines in northern Ukraine. Those who surrendered at Starokostiantyniv were interned by the Poles and gave their hosts typhus, from which thousands of Polish soldiers later died on the eastern front.[420]

The Ukrainian statehood of 1918–19 had now come to its final hour in this rectangle of death.

Chapter 5

The Incorporation of Eastern Galicia into Poland, Nationally and Internationally

1. The Ukrainians in the Emigration

The remaining Western Ukrainian troops did not stay long with the Denikin army. Denikin was soon driven from the Left Bank and the Don by the Bolsheviks and finally defeated in the Caucasus in April 1920. On the Right Bank, from December 1919, the Bolsheviks advanced against what was left of Denikin's forces there, easily overrunning them and driving them, along with the remnants of the Western Ukrainian army, to the Dnister west of Odesa. The Romanians refused them asylum. Since there was no point in defending a bridgehead on the Dnister, which would only be to the advantage of the Romanians, they did the only thing they could do in that situation: on the night of 10–11 February 1920 they sewed a red band on their caps beneath the Ukrainian emblem, arrested Generals Mykytka and Ziritz, whom they hated fiercely for having become tools of the all-Russian reaction, elected soviets in their units and declared themselves Bolsheviks. They were now the "Red Western Ukrainian Army." Among the soldiers themselves very little changed, except that now the officers were officially known as "comrades." The Bolsheviks were pleased with the change, for they had a high opinion of the Western Ukrainian soldiers. Under the circumstances, the Western Ukrainians had little choice but to take advantage of that fact. The battles had been fought and lost and, for better or for worse, they had to come to terms with the new situation in Eastern Europe.[421]

The defeat of the Ukrainian army at the end of 1919 was more than just a severe but transitory catastrophe for the country's military capacity. It was a catastrophe for the Ukrainian national movement itself. An independent national state, as an immediate goal of Ukrainian national policy, would be impossible for an indeterminate period, perhaps many decades. Ukraine was excluded from the East European state system. The Soviet Union and Poland were victors in the field, and the partition of Ukraine in accordance with Dmowski's plan became a basic fact of the situation in Eastern Europe for decades. For the generation that had fought for national independence in 1918–19, there was no longer any possibility of renewing the struggle. This, were it ever to happen, would be a task for future generations. As a result of the battles of 1918–19, the whole length and breadth of Ukraine was laid waste. The most active part of the population, those who had aroused the masses to fight for their national independence, had either fallen or were decimated and dispersed. The population lost its will to fight and, though resenting the alien rule of Bolsheviks and Poles, longed for peace. It was no longer capable of common effort. Even if a popular uprising could have been organized, it would have been pointless, for Bolshevik and Polish rule in Ukraine was based on superior military might. They had at their disposal well-armed and well-organized armies capable of nipping in the bud any attempt at a rising by the population, which had been thoroughly disarmed, especially in Western Ukraine. In the larger territory of Eastern Ukraine guerrilla war was not impossible, as it was in tiny Western Ukraine. But, with the exception of Finland, the Baltic provinces, Poland up to the Dmowski line, Bessarabia, Transcaucasia, and the Crimea, where the remnants of the all-Russian counterrevolution under General Petr Wrangel had temporarily established themselves, the whole of the former Russian Empire was now firmly under Bolshevik control. No military action could dislodge them now. An Eastern Ukrainian guerrilla war would therefore lead to nothing, for the Bolsheviks were capable of overrunning the country and defeating any resistance in a short time. Such uprisings would be no threat to the Soviet rulers and certainly could not lead to the reestablishment of a Ukrainian nation-state. They could only bleed the Ukrainian nation white, which is what happened later, in 1920–23.

But the apparent sovietization of the Western Ukrainian army resulted not only from the fact that it was pointless to continue the armed struggle. There were four different attitudes or policies in Ukrainian national politics. The first policy began from the assumption that the national forces that had inspired cultural and political activity among the Ukrainians in Austria and Russia for decades before 1918 had been exhausted by the conflicts of 1918–19. In a hostile world these forces had not been adequate to establish an independent Ukrainian nation-state in Eastern Europe. If this were to be attempted again at some point in the future, then it was essential now to accept the partition of Ukraine between Poland and the Soviet Union as an accomplished fact that would not change for decades to come. Instead of looking for some solution in the international arena, the main task now should be a rebuilding of the nation from within. For better or for worse, one had to come to terms with the occupying powers. Within a framework established by those powers, the task was, by means of renewed cultural and political activity, gradually to create new national forces that would be socially, culturally, militarily and organizationally stronger than those of 1918 and, at the same time, to make use of these new strengths to compete with the occupying powers for hegemony in the Ukrainian nation. After decades of internal preparation it might again be possible to renew the struggle for Ukrainian independence when either or both of the occupying powers were weakened by war or internal upheaval.

This was one policy. Objectively, as later events were to demonstrate, it was the most correct one. But in 1920 and later only a small number of clear-sighted individuals supported this course. It was therefore quite ineffective.

Two other policies opposed this first one. They were both defended by "yesterday's men," who, also driven from their homeland, were living in emigration and did not want to accept that the historical role played by Ukraine in 1918–19 was already a thing of the past. They could not accept that they themselves, the onetime leaders of their people, had irrevocably departed the political stage along with the Ukrainian armies. The first of those groups, the Western Ukrainian one, set all its hopes on the reunification of Western and Eastern Ukraine under Soviet rule by means of the armed might of the Bolsheviks. They believed that this would lead to such a strengthening of the Ukrainian element within Soviet Ukraine that the country would automatically develop into an independent nation within the Soviet Union. This was a vain hope, for the regime of terror in Moscow soon showed that it was more powerful than Ukrainian separatism.

The second group, the Eastern Ukrainian one, set all its hopes on Poland. "It is in Poland's interest to support a Ukrainian buffer state against Russia," they said, blind to the fact that if an independent Ukraine had been in Poland's interests, then Poland would not have conquered Eastern Galicia and prevented the formation of a Ukrainian state. Fear of Bolshevism led them to believe that it was possible to construct some kind of Eastern Ukrainian frontier guard for Poland by force of Polish arms. They even preferred to see Polish rule extend to the Dnipro rather than see the territory between the Zbruch and the Dnipro remain in Bolshevik hands.

Both these groups believed that the Ukrainian nation itself was incapable of resisting the occupying powers. Fear of Dmowski's plan to Polonize Western Ukraine drove one group into the arms of the Bolsheviks. Fear of the Bolshevik system of extermination drove the other group into the arms of the Poles. Both groups failed to see that the future of Ukraine would be secure only when this security was founded on the nation's own ability to resist and not on the support of one enemy against the other.

The fourth and most disastrous group was made up of the wild anarchists, with their policy of "Balkanizing" Ukraine. A bitter hatred for the enemy and a burning desire for revenge drove many Ukrainians to acts of terror against the Bolshevik and Polish rulers. This rebellious tendency held the greatest danger for Ukraine, for it could prevent the country from ever rising again. It hindered the regrouping of national forces. It made it impossible for national policy to be led by great goals and rational means. Everything was sacrificed to momentary, blind, untamed, disorderly and chaotic passions. This tendency was destroying the nation from within and provoking from the enemy a more determined response that threatened to rob the nation of its last chance of survival. The activities of this group simply pushed the frightened people into even greater apathy.

The Western Ukrainian emigration, meanwhile, still held to the disastrous idea of Entente arbitration in the Polish-Ukrainian conflict. National policy, for this group, was restricted to mere propaganda directed at foreign powers. By shifting the decision about the fate of Western Ukraine onto this international level, it condemned the nation itself to a merely passive role, encouraging it to hope for salvation from abroad and leading it along the path of meaningless protests and demonstrations. This ultimately strengthened the "Balkanization" tendency, for acts of terror were simply a means of impressing on the Entente the urgency of the "Eastern Galician question." This policy lacked all sense of reality and was in fact just a form of madness.

These four political orientations were operative in Ukrainian national politics, both inside the country and in the emigration, for many years. The first two were evident in the Sovietization of the Western Ukrainian army. What was involved here was a desire to adapt to the reality of Soviet Ukraine, to preserve and promote the Ukrainian national cause under Soviet rule. In the orientation on Soviet Ukraine lay the hope that, in the expected battles to come between Poland and the Bolsheviks, Western and Soviet Ukraine would be united.

The emigration had an important influence on events inside the country. The most important Ukrainian leader during 1918–19 had been Petliura, and his role in the emigration had a very important influence, especially on Eastern Ukraine. It was in Petliura's policies that the second two of the previously described orientations made themselves manifest, namely the Polish orientation and the Balkanization policy. Before crossing over to the Polish side in central Volhynia, Petliura seems to have realized that any continuation of the struggle against the Bolsheviks was pointless, and that all that remained for Ukraine was a long, hard effort to survive and rebuild itself under foreign rule. In spite of this, however, when Petliura arrived in Warsaw in December 1919, his anti-Russian sentiments led him to become a tool of Polish policy. The Poles feared at the time that the Bolsheviks, having defeated the all-Russian counterrevolution and Ukraine, would be in a position to overrun Poland itself. Until then the Bolsheviks had had only five divisions on their Polish front, which meant that until the beginning of 1920 the Poles did not have to fight them. But now the Bolsheviks were moving more of their troops to this front.[422] A Bolshevik invasion was expected in the spring of 1920. Piłsudski decided to block it with a general Polish offensive that would enable him to dictate the terms of peace on the Dnipro. It was most important to win Petliura for this undertaking in order to ensure, or so they hoped, the friendliness of the Eastern Ukrainian population. Piłsudski offered him the prospect, in the event of victory, of a Ukrainian state dependent on Poland.

From fighting for your own national cause to serving the interests of a third power that benefits from that fight is a short step, and it was this step that Petliura now took.

The Eastern Ukrainians who had been part of the joint Western and Eastern Ukrainian mission under the Eastern Ukrainian Andrii Livytsky, sent from Kamianets-Podilskyi to Warsaw to negotiate with the Poles on 3 October 1919, had already been won over to this idea of an alliance between Poland and Eastern Ukraine. Despite the protests of the Western Ukrainians, who then withdrew from the mission, the Eastern Ukrainians had signed an agreement on 2 December 1919 recognizing a border with Poland that followed the Zbruch and then a line through central Volhynia to be determined later by the Peace Conference. Petliura, as president of the Directory of the Ukrainian People's Republic, now formally accepted this agreement in a treaty that he signed with Piłsudski on 22 April 1920. The Polish border accepted in this treaty corresponds in general to the present-day eastern border of Poland.[423]

This Eastern Ukrainian action of relinquishing all claims to Western Ukraine led to the breaking of all links between the Eastern and Western Ukrainians. The Western Ukrainians considered that Petliura had betrayed Ukraine.* But Petliura's guilt did not lie in the fact that he had

* In view of the tremendous changes in Eastern Europe, it seems idle to inquire into the formal legal implications of such an act as Symon Petliura's pact of 22 April 1920 with Józef Piłsudski. In this case, however, there is some point in asking such a question. It was this very pact that Poland employed for diplomatic purposes with the Entente in order to obtain its assignment of Eastern Galicia to Poland, pointing out that the "Eastern Galician question" had been resolved and the Polish-Ukrainian struggle ended, as Ukraine had renounced its claims to Eastern Galicia in favor of Poland. One of the authors who cite the pact in this way is Dr.

"relinquished" Western Ukraine. The territories he "relinquished" were in fact already occupied by the Poles and, given that the Ukrainians were in no position to win them back, his "relinquishing" them made no difference whatever. Even if a Ukrainian state had existed east of the Zbruch, it, too, would have had to "relinquish" Western Ukraine in order to make peace with Poland. After all, an eternal state of war could

---

Julius von Twardowski in his article "Ostgalizien" in the *Wörterbuch des Völkerrechts und der Diplomatie*, edited by Professor Julius Hatschek and Dr. Karl Strupp—an article that is also replete with distortions of fact and fanciful assertions. The question here is that of the right of the Ukrainian People's Republic, represented by Symon Petliura, to determine the disposition of Western Ukraine in international law. The Western Ukrainians strongly contested the validity of Petliura's renunciation of their territory, maintaining that the annexation of Western Ukraine to the Ukrainian People's Republic, that is, to Eastern Ukraine, had never been properly completed. The present excursus seeks to clarify this question, and the reader should also recall the discussion of the Ukrainian Acts of Union earlier in the book (pp. 87–92).

Lozynsky (*Halychyna*, pp. 69–71) adopts this Western Ukrainian viewpoint and argues more or less as follows:

> The Ukrainian Acts of Union adopted in December 1918 and January 1919 did not establish a new, united republic consisting of two hitherto independent Ukrainian states but only proclaimed it and indicated the path toward its establishment. The new republic was to be established by an all-Ukrainian constituent assembly, elected on the territory of both states as if they already constituted a single state. The two governments were to come to an understanding on the time and procedure for the convocation of such a constituent assembly. Only at the moment when the assembly's resolution on the establishment of a united Ukrainian state took legal effect would the two states formally cease to exist, becoming a single state. The form of such a future united state is mentioned only once in the acts of union: the preliminary agreement of 1 December 1918 contains a clause on autonomy for Western Ukraine. It follows that the two states did not intend to establish something in the nature of a federal state consisting of two equal governments but a united state within which the former territory of the Western Ukrainian People's Republic would be autonomous. Thus, until the establishment of a united state by the constituent assembly, the two states were to continue to exist independently of each other, with their own governments, according to the provision in the resolution of 3 January 1919 adopted by the Ukrainian National Rada of Western Ukraine. This resolution was also taken under advisement by the Directory and the Congress of Toilers, which also made it binding on Eastern Ukraine, constituted as the Ukrainian People's Republic. Since this resolution excluded any state authority on Western Ukrainian territory other than that of Western Ukraine until the establishment of a united Ukrainian state, it also excluded the authority of the Ukrainian People's Republic, recognizing it as valid only for Eastern Ukraine. By admitting Western Ukrainians to the Congress of Toilers and to the Directory, Eastern Ukraine acted contrary to the principle of its own sovereignty, but this entails no loss of sovereignty on the part of Western Ukraine. Whereas the all-Ukrainian constituent assembly never convened, Western Ukraine remained sovereign, and the Ukrainian People's Republic had no right to impose any legally binding acts on Western Ukraine.

The following objection should be made to this: The Western Ukrainian acts do not deal with the intention of establishing a new state in place of the two existing ones but with the intention of annexing the Western Ukrainian Republic to the already existing Eastern Ukrainian Republic, which bore the name "Ukrainian People's Republic." On 3 January 1919 the Western Ukrainians declared this intention accomplished, thereby acknowledging the sovereignty of the Ukrainian People's Republic in Western Ukraine. The Eastern Ukrainians accepted this acknowledgment on 22 and 23 January 1919, which amounted to Eastern Ukraine's accepting the sovereignty over

not be maintained without actual hostilities, and Poland was strong enough to march into such a Ukrainian state and force it to sign a peace treaty formally relinquishing those territories. Petliura's guilt lay much more in the fact that he invited a foreign power into his country of his own free will, a foreign power that was essentially hostile to Ukraine, in the belief that it would be possible to drive out one occupying power, the Bolsheviks, by bringing in another, the Poles, and establish an independent state with foreign bayonets when the nation's own forces had failed. His guilt lay in his false hope that the Poles, having triumphed over the Bolsheviks in Ukraine, would actually withdraw from the Right Bank, leaving sovereignty in the hands of Petliura.

This Polish-Eastern Ukrainian "alliance" was almost a mockery. The general offensive began on 17 April 1920. A strong body of Polish troops, given the balance of forces at the time, was accompanied, for the sake of appearances, by a handful of Eastern Ukrainian soldiers.[424] The goal of the offensive was the capture of Kyiv and all of Right-Bank Ukraine. The offensive was initially successful, forcing the Bolsheviks to retreat all along the line.

Now, as usual, what remained of the Western Ukrainian army made a fatal error in its judgment of the international situation. It had ten thousand men under arms in three brigades scattered among various Bolshevik divisions. The inhuman cruelty of the Bolsheviks, the vulgarity

Western Ukraine that had been offered to it. Thus Western Ukraine forfeited its independence with regard to foreign policy in favor of Eastern Ukraine, and the Eastern Ukrainian Directory obtained the right to dispose of Western Ukrainian territory in international law. Western Ukraine itself acknowledged this by sending its official representatives to the Directory at the invitation of Eastern Ukraine and changed its name to the "Western Province of the Ukrainian People's Republic." The fact of this annexation was also communicated to the Entente powers by the Ukrainian People's Republic on 25 February 1919 (*Notes présentées*, pp. 16–18), with no protest from Western Ukraine. The exercise of the sovereignty of the Ukrainian People's Republic over Western Ukraine could affect it with regard to international law only insofar as Western Ukraine had a representative in the Directory. By contrast, the autonomy clause in the preliminary agreement of 1 December 1918 and the reservation in the agreement of 3 January 1919 on the implementation of legislation by the Ukrainian National Rada and of civil and military administration in Western Ukraine by its organ, the State Secretariat, until the convocation of the constituent assembly did not pertain to international law and foreign policy but only to national law and the internal independence of Western Ukraine from the Ukrainian People's Republic. There is not a word in the reservation about Western Ukraine's preservation of sovereignty in international law. Thus Eastern Ukraine, or the Ukrainian People's Republic, undoubtedly had the right to relinquish Western Ukraine to the benefit of Poland in 1920. Nevertheless, Petliura's renunciation of 22 April 1920 was invalid. Only the Directory as a whole was authorized to exercise state sovereignty on behalf of the Ukrainian People's Republic, and as this renunciation was carried out by Petliura alone, with no valid authorization from the Directory, the document was merely a private paper of his that claimed the authority of an official document. Thus the Ukrainian People's Republic never issued a valid declaration of disinterest in Western Ukraine, although it was entitled to do so.

of the system, the subversive propaganda among the troops against their officers—all this filled the Western Ukrainians with disgust. Only a few among them had really become communists. Throughout the countryside the peasants were conducting a guerrilla war against the Bolsheviks. As noted earlier, a detachment of soldiers from the old Eastern Ukrainian army, led by General Omelianovych-Pavlenko, was active in this part of the country attacking Bolshevik garrisons. Emotionally, the Western Ukrainians had had enough to make them rebel against the Bolsheviks. Sent to fight on the Polish front, they believed the rumors that the army approaching them was an Eastern Ukrainian one, with only a few Polish units. They failed to realize that it was the Poles who were now invading Ukraine. Given the possibility of winning Ukrainian leadership within a Bolshevik Ukraine, albeit under an internationalist and not a nationalist Ukrainian banner, it was highly doubtful that a Polish advance to the Dnipro was a lesser evil for Ukraine than Bolshevism. But now those feelings erupted in the Western Ukrainian army. The Bolshevik commissars in the Western Ukrainian units were executed or driven out, and the Western Ukrainians, with the exception of a few units that had a better insight into what was happening, went over to Petliura on 23 April 1920. The Poles, however, refused this "outstretched hand" of the Western Ukrainians. Apart from one small unit under General Antin Kravs that was sent to join Petliura's soldiers, the rest were disarmed by the Poles and sent to prisoner-of-war camps. The Bolsheviks repaid this desertion by disbanding the rest of their remaining Western Ukrainian units. Numerous officers were executed and, in this manner, the Western Ukrainian army came to its final end.[425]

On 7 May 1920 the Poles entered Kyiv, but their stay was not to be a long one.[426] Petliura succeeded in getting ten to fifteen thousand Eastern Ukrainians to join his army, but the Eastern Ukrainian population had no love for the Poles. In this war between the Poles and the Bolsheviks the population remained completely passive. After a breakthrough by Budenny's cavalry, the Poles fled from the city in disarray on 11 June, and in the weeks that followed they were forced out of Eastern Ukraine. All that remained from this alliance for Petliura, who had been joined by Omelianovych-Pavlenko's detachment, was the dubious honor of covering the headlong Polish retreat with his small but battle-hardened forces; always quite a distance from the fleeing Polish army, the Eastern Ukrainians had to take the brunt of the enemy's fire. It was the heroic courage of the Eastern Ukrainians that defeated the Bolshevik attempt to take Warsaw and Cracow from the southeast by way of Lviv and Zamość. This, in all likelihood, was what saved Poland, which was on the verge of collapse, and made possible what was later known as the "miracle on the Vistula."

The remaining soldiers of the Eastern Ukrainian army soon became mere mercenaries in the service of Poland. Objectively, Petliura had nothing more to do with any struggle for Ukrainian statehood. His troops were soon defending the Polish occupation of Eastern Galicia on the Zbruch. In the course of further fighting, these troops were driven south of the Dnister. The handful of Western Ukrainians under General Kravs who had joined the Eastern Ukrainians took advantage of the situation and, at the beginning of August 1920, marched from the Kolomyia region to Carpatho-Ruthenia, where they surrendered to the Czechs and were interned in the Sudetenland. They had no interest in defending the Poles against the Bolsheviks, just as, one year earlier, the Poles had had no interest in defending the Ukrainians against those same Bolsheviks. These were the last of the Western Ukrainians to lay down their arms.

In August 1920 the Bolsheviks suffered a devastating defeat just outside Warsaw. The leader of the anti-Bolshevik forces was General Maxime Weygand, Marshal Foch's chief of staff, who arrived in haste to conjure up the famous "miracle on the Vistula." The Poles then reoccupied the eastern territories up to the present border. Although his support had been essential to them before, the Poles now no longer had any use for Petliura.* In September 1920 the Polish-Bolshevik negotiations began in Riga, and the Poles readily accepted the Bolshevik condition that they break their alliance with Petliura. Deserted by his "ally," Petliura, in despair, stormed across the Zbruch on his own initiative, captured Kamianets-Podilskyi and, with arms supplied from Poland, took up once more, in this rectangle of death, the old military struggle for Ukrainian statehood, relying on his own forces. But the massive superiority of the Bolsheviks, who at that time, in October-November 1920, had just taken the Crimea from General Wrangel,[427] meant a very rapid defeat for the courageous Eastern Ukrainians in November-December. They were pushed back across the Zbruch, where they were again disarmed by the Poles and interned, this time for good.

* At the beginning of July 1920 the following proposal was conveyed to Petliura from several officers of the Sich Riflemen who were then living abroad: "If Symon Petliura should ever risk becoming involved in an intervention, then it would be advisable not to cover the Polish retreat now but to withdraw the Eastern Ukrainians south of the Dnister into the Carpathians without giving battle. Then, once Poland collapsed, it would probably come to an all-European intervention, possibly with German participation, and then the Ukrainians could take part in that intervention under far better conditions—specifically, with Eastern Galicia as their military base—than Poland has ever been prepared to offer Symon Petliura." Petliura resolutely rejected this proposal on the grounds that "he did not want to betray his ally." The ally, however, proved less true to him.

Petliura now sank even lower. In alliance with the Polish general staff he began to take part in the "Balkanization" of Ukraine.[428] In the ridiculous belief that a larger insurgent Ukrainian army could be built from such a movement, and that this army could succeed in driving the Bolsheviks from Ukraine and establishing an independent Ukrainian state, he built up a secret network covering the whole of Eastern Ukraine during 1921 and 1922. This secret network then carried out guerrilla actions against the Bolsheviks. Some of the best young men, excellent officers from both Eastern and Western Ukraine, were won over to this project. Instead of attempting to win the leadership of Soviet Ukraine, rejecting all such politics of ostentation and accepting for the time being the banner of international Bolshevism, these men devoted themselves to actions that soon led to their discovery by the Cheka. They died honorably, believing that what they were doing was for the good of the fatherland. In reality, it only served the interests of Poland. This movement soon declined and was finally drowned in blood by the Bolsheviks in 1923. For a few years the Bolsheviks pursued a policy of "Ukrainization," attempting to win Ukraine over to Bolshevism. But then, realizing that the Ukrainian national movement could not be placed entirely at the service of Moscow, the Bolsheviks turned abruptly against any manifestation of Ukrainian independence. What happened to the Ukrainian movement then was something like a natural catastrophe against which man is powerless, for reason, will, prudence and ingenuity are of no avail. The process to which the Ukrainian movement fell victim was a cruel and bloody one, the only purpose or meaning of which was the extermination of the Ukrainian people and the destruction of its regenerative strength forever. The Polish-Bolshevik nonaggression pact of 1933 put the final seal on this national catastrophe. The Bolsheviks, their western borders now secure, lost all inhibitions in their effort to wipe out the national movement in Ukraine. No other province of the former Russian Empire spilled so much of its blood in the struggle against Bolshevism. None resisted so doggedly or suffered so much as Ukraine.

The Bolsheviks then demanded Petliura's expulsion from Poland. Since his network had already been liquidated by the Bolsheviks, the Poles no longer had any use for him personally, and he was expelled. He moved to Paris, where he met his doom. Piłsudski's dictatorship had just been established in Poland, and the Bolsheviks had reason to fear once again that the Poles would make use of Petliura to attack the Soviet Union. But shortly afterwards, on 25 May 1926, Petliura was murdered by one Shalom Schwartzbard, who gave as his motive revenge for the anti-Jewish pogroms allegedly carried out by Petliura in Ukraine.[429]

The Western Ukrainian emigration outside Soviet Ukraine was not so active. When they heard of the Eastern Ukrainian declaration of 2 December in which Petliura "relinquished" Western Ukraine, the Western Ukrainian delegates, Vasyl Paneiko and Stepan Tomashivsky, formally withdrew from the joint Ukrainian delegation in Paris on 19 December (they had actually withdrawn in August) and set up a separate "Delegation of the Western Ukrainian People's Republic" to represent Western Ukraine's interests at the Paris Peace Conference. They had already established links with the all-Russian counterrevolution and wanted the Ukrainians to join with Denikin in the hope that, after the restoration of a federative Russia by the counterrevolution, Western Ukraine would be able to break free from Poland. They now went further in this direction and established the Russophile "Ukrainian National Committee" (Comité national ukrainien) in Paris under their own leadership. This committee would represent the "true voice" of Ukraine. The committee allied itself with the all-Russian representatives of a "federative Russia," but after the defeat of Denikin this "federative Russia" was a meaningless concept. If Russia was to liberate Western Ukraine from Poland, it would not be the all-Russian counterrevolution but the Bolshevik Soviet Union that would have to do this.[430]

The attitude of the Western Ukrainian dictator, Petrushevych, to all this activity was initially one of benevolent neutrality. He had arrived in Vienna at the beginning of December 1919. He immediately traveled to Paris and London to build support for Western Ukraine. Then he settled in Vienna, where, on 25 July 1920, he established a Western Ukrainian government in exile to take charge of the diplomatic efforts to persuade the Entente to end the Polish occupation of Eastern Galicia and permit the reestablishment of an independent Western Ukrainian state. This activity was realistic insofar as the Western Ukrainian population, until 1923, recognized the Petrushevych government as the only legitimate authority in Western Ukraine. Only the Social Democrats did not. The dictator's orders were followed unconditionally, whereas the Polish authorities had to rely on the use of force. The Polish government was rejected by the Western Ukrainian population for years, and quite openly, as illegitimate. Nonetheless, the activity of the Petrushevych government was pointless. It broke with the Russophilism of its Paris representatives and based its legitimacy on formal legal arguments. Article 87 of the Versailles Treaty of 28 June 1919 stated that the borders of Poland, to the extent that they were not laid down in the treaty itself, were to be determined later by the Entente powers. In Article 91 of the Treaty of Saint-Germain-en-Laye, signed on 10 September 1919, Austria relinquished in favor of the Allied and associated powers its sovereignty over all territories of the old Austrian empire whose national status had not already been laid down in the treaty. Since, in the decision of the Supreme Council of 8 May, as well as in the Treaty of Saint-Germain, Western Galicia was explicitly recognized as being part of Poland, Eastern Galicia became a subject of the Allied and associated powers from the viewpoint of international law. According to the Supreme Council's decision of 25 June, Poland was given a mandate by the Entente to militarily occupy Eastern Galicia but was not granted national sovereignty over the territory. The formal legality of the situation was very unclear because Poland refused to sign the Treaty of Saint-Germain, which gave the Entente sovereignty over Eastern Galicia. This question of legal status occupied the Petrushevych government in Vienna for years. This government recognized the sovereignty of the Entente in Eastern Galicia and, in the name of the right of national self-determination, called on the Entente to end Poland's military occupation of the country and transfer sovereignty to the Western Ukrainian government. What Petrushevych wanted was a neutralization of Eastern Galicia guaranteed by the League of Nations.[431] This was of course a complete fantasy, but the Western Ukrainian government, as well as the Western Ukrainian emigration and the population of the country itself, were, with very few exceptions, firmly convinced that the Entente would give in to this demand. The whole of Western Ukrainian diplomatic activity was now devoted to this hopeless campaign, with countless memoranda and notes to the Entente that we need not describe here in detail. For in reality the Western Ukrainians had only one option, at least theoretically, if they wanted to achieve something that would improve their difficult situation under Polish rule, and that was to recognize Polish sovereignty over Eastern Galicia in order to end the legal argument between Poland and the Entente and attempt to win some form of autonomy directly from Poland. Apart from the fact that Petrushevych, as always, would not acknowledge the plain reality of the situation, and the fact that a government that had only recently ruled the country would be unlikely to declare itself subject to Poland, it was in practice extremely unlikely that the Western Ukrainians would have succeeded in winning any kind of autonomy from Poland. Such an agreement is only possible when the ruling nation recognizes the subject nation as an equal. But the Poles were a long way from recognizing the Ukrainian nation or respecting its interests. Poland's aim was to Polonize the Western Ukrainians, and if, from time to time, they tried to lure the Western Ukrainians with some promise of autonomy, this was by no means because they took into account the national interests of the Ukrainians or because they really wanted some agreement between Ukrainians and Poles. Rather, the promise of some agreement, or even sentimental talk about Polish-Ukrainian fraternity, was only meant to facilitate the process of Polonization, first politically, then in the field of national culture and language. Since the Poles shirked their obligations with alacrity whenever these became inconvenient, it is extremely doubtful that they would have carried out this promise of autonomy even if the Western Ukrainians had recognized Polish sovereignty, allowing the Entente finally to settle the Eastern Galician question in Poland's favor. This settlement with the Entente was all that mattered to the Poles. Although a genuine agreement between two nations within a common state system is possible in the case of a supranational monarchy like Austria-Hungary, or in the case of a supranational empire like the British one, it is not possible between democratic nations based on the concepts of the nation-state and popular sovereignty. The Western Ukrainians lost nothing through this activity of the Petrushevych government. In fact, they won a certain amount of international recognition as a result of this propaganda campaign. The achievement of autonomy for Western Ukraine, however, remains a task for the future. Only an extraordinary rise in the cultural, political and socioeconomic level of the Western Ukrainian movement, carried out in a systematic way by the Western Ukrainians themselves in a process of ongoing competition with Polish state power, could force the Poles to concede defeat in this Polish-Ukrainian conflict, put an end to the Dmowski plan for the Polonization of the country, recognize the Ukrainian and Polish nations as equal, and replace the concept of a Polish nation-state with that of a supranational empire in which an agreement between Poles and Ukrainians would be possible, similar to the agreement reached in 1867 between Austria and Hungary that created the Austro-Hungarian union. But in 1923, as in the decade since then, the Ukrainian movement, as a result of the defeat suffered in 1919–20, was still in a state of decline.

2. *The Draft Statutes for Eastern Galicia at the Paris Peace Conference*

Even before the Petrushevych government in Vienna could begin its diplomatic activity, the question of Western Ukraine had ceased to exist as an international problem. Although Western Ukraine had been an active factor in European politics up to the time of the Haller offensive because of its undefeated military capability, the Supreme Council's decision of 25 June 1919 and the retreat of the Western Ukrainian army on 16 July of that year meant that Eastern Galicia became a question to be settled between Poland and the Entente. This was formally recognized by the Paris Peace Conference when it gave the Commission on Polish Affairs the task of drawing up a treaty between the Entente and Poland concerning the statute of Poland's mandate in Eastern Galicia. The commission began its work on 2 July, establishing a subcommission for this purpose under the leadership of General Henri Le Rond. The elimination of Western Ukraine as an active factor was demonstrated in practice by the exclusion of the Western Ukrainian delegation from the work of the subcommission. It was treated merely as representative of one of the "Eastern Galician population groups" alongside the Poles, Jews and Russophiles.[432]

The Western Ukrainian attitude to this process no longer mattered. What mattered was the attitude of the Poles. The latter protested, at first, against any time limit on their annexation of Eastern Galicia and demanded that the Polish government and Diet be given the opportunity to express their opinion. The subcommission declared that it was not within its competence to alter this decision of the Supreme Council and pointed out that the decision was in any case an official secret that could not be publicly discussed. It also declined to give the Poles any additional time so as not to delay its own work.

On 5 July 1919 the Polish delegation presented documentary material to the subcommission dealing with the former autonomy of Galicia under Austrian rule, the Polish constitution, and Polish law with respect to civil liberties. It also presented a draft statute of autonomy for Eastern Galicia that it wished to see accepted. In this document the Poles expressed their willingness to extend to Eastern Galicia all Polish constitutional and minority rights in political, national and religious matters and to provide a constitutional guarantee of autonomy for Eastern Galicia that would not conflict with the unity of the Polish state. A legislative assembly for Eastern Galicia, elected on the basis of universal suffrage and proportional representation, would function autonomously in the following matters: 1) laws concerning public worship; 2) public education; 3) public welfare; 4) public health; 5) public transport at all levels; 6) agriculture, commerce, trades, and industry; 7) all other matters devolved to it by the Warsaw Diet. They declared Ukrainian the second official language of the country alongside Polish and left it to the local population to decide the language of schooling. To ensure the political unity of Eastern Galicia and Poland, the Poles insisted that the Polish head of state have the right to appoint a governor as head of the Eastern Galician administration, that Eastern Galicia elect representatives to the Polish Diet, and that conscription into the Polish military service be extended to Eastern Galicia. They undertook, in turn, a commitment to appoint officials from the local population without regard to nationality or religion, to have Eastern Galicia represented in the Polish cabinet by a minister without portfolio, to create special departments in the Warsaw ministries to deal with the autonomous affairs of Eastern Galicia, and to appoint a high official of Ukrainian nationality who would act as adviser to the Council of Ministers in Warsaw concerning Ukrainian affairs.[433]

Many of the points in the Polish proposal benefited not the Ukrainians but the Eastern Galician Poles, for instance, the appointment of a minister for Eastern Galicia. As amply demonstrated by the subsequent fate of Eastern Galician autonomy, the Poles had no intention of actually implementing their own proposals. By promising a form of autonomy they were only concerned to speed up the process of annexation and restrict as much as possible the statute being drawn up by the Le Rond subcommission. The draft statute drawn up by the subcommission on the basis of the Polish proposals was ready on 5 August.

While the Polish delegation virtually dictated the statute of autonomy to the Le Rond subcommission and the latter listened to representatives of the Polish and Jewish minorities and even to the politically insignificant Russophiles, the Ukrainians remained completely outside this whole process. This was because of intrigue within the Ukrainian delegation and disputes between the Eastern and Western Ukrainians. The Ukrainian delegation as such decided on 3 July not to appear before the Le Rond subcommission, arguing that because Eastern Galicia was an autonomous province of Ukraine, it could not take part in negotiations intended to make the territory an autonomous province of Poland. The Western Ukrainian representative, Paneiko, accepted the invitation in principle on 2 July but asked that the negotiations be postponed so that he could consult with the Western Ukrainian government. Paneiko and Tomashivsky returned to the subcommission on 23 August with the Western Ukrainian demands, but they were told that they were too late, for the statute was already in final form, and no substantial changes could be made.[434]

The Western Ukrainian demands were now drawn up in the form of a declaration that began by protesting against the fact that the Western Ukrainians were the only nationality of Austria-Hungary to be denied their national and political rights. It pointed out that the commitment of the Peace Conference not to let its decisions be determined by any fait accompli had been flagrantly violated in the case of Western Ukraine. Finally, it declared the willingness of the "Ukrainian delegation from Galicia," as an act of self-defense against the Polish terror regime in Eastern Galicia, to take part in the negotiations concerning the statute.

After this introduction, the declaration put forward the following conditions: 1) the explicitly provisional character of the statute; 2) the territorial amalgamation of the Ukrainian parts of Eastern Galicia and Bukovyna; 3) an Eastern Galician indigenate [right of citizenship—Ed.] as applied in the case of Danzig; 4) the establishment in the statute of a firm date for a plebiscite; 5) a formal distinction in international relations between Poland and Eastern Galicia for the duration of the statute; 6) no obligation of military service in the Polish army; 7) an exact description of Poland's powers in Eastern Galicia; 8) the governor to be a Ukrainian nominated by the Eastern Galician assembly; 9) the statute to be published along with a public guarantee that it would be carried out. Not a single one of these demands, to the extent that they went beyond the decision of the Supreme Council of 25 June, was incorporated into the statute.

The proposals of the Le Rond subcommission were examined by the Commission on Polish Affairs. Since these proposals were about to be discussed by the Supreme Council, Poland sent a memorandum to the president of the Peace Conference, Clemenceau, on 25 August, demanding the unconditional incorporation of Eastern Galicia into Poland.[435] As was usual in Polish National Democratic propaganda, the Western Ukrainians were described as an uncultured people with an as yet undeveloped language. The memorandum claimed that Austria had maintained the unity of Galicia and handed it over to Polish administration because the Western Ukrainians were incapable of governing themselves. The centuries-old history of Eastern Galicia as a frontier territory in which Poland fought off the Turks and Tatars had prevented the Western Ukrainians, said the Polish memorandum, from developing any feeling for law and order. On the contrary, it had provided fertile ground for their wilder instincts, which alone explained the success of Austria, Russia and, finally, Germany in stirring up the Western Ukrainians against Poland. A merely provisional solution to the Eastern Galician question would only nourish the primitive instincts of the Ukrainians and encourage permanent unrest and agitation against the authorities. A memorandum handed to the Peace Conference on 24 August by a Polish delegation from Eastern Galicia made the same claims.[436] It added that a merely provisional solution would give Germany the opportunity to stir up the Ukrainian movement in Eastern Galicia in order to weaken Poland and defeat Russia. This latter memorandum also claimed that the recent war between the Poles and the Western Ukrainians was no proof of any hostility to Poland among the Western Ukrainians, for this war had been instigated by the Central Powers. Both memoranda strongly expressed the hope that in spite of their wildness, the Western Ukrainians would soon be reconciled with the Polish state, which was so well disposed to them and so well known for its toleration, democracy and liberalism.

In view of the pro-Denikin sympathies of the Entente, Paneiko and Tomashivsky, who constituted the "Ukrainian Delegation of Galicia," thought that their interests would be better served if Western Ukraine were to break formally with the Ukrainian People's Republic, which they did in the name of Western Ukraine on 28 August.

It was under such conditions that the Supreme Council once again considered the Eastern Galician question. Since France supported Poland, and England wanted to await the outcome of Denikin's military campaign, the council decided to postpone any decision.[437]

Up to that point the Eastern Galician question was part of the larger question of what to do with the territories of the former Austro-Hungarian Empire. Since a peace treaty with Austria was being discussed, the Eastern Galician question had a certain relevance and actuality. But those negotiations soon came to an end, and on 10 September a treaty was signed with Austria at Saint-Germain-en-Laye. Article 91 of this treaty stated that Austria relinquished to the Entente sovereignty over all its former territories, including Eastern Galicia, whose political affiliation was not specified in the treaty. The Eastern Galician question thereby lost its urgency. The Entente was now free to postpone any decision on Eastern Galicia for years.

But at the beginning of November 1919, in view of the defeats being suffered by the Russian counterrevolution, England once again placed Eastern Galicia on the agenda of the Paris Peace Conference. England's plan was for Eastern Galicia to become a mandate territory of the League of Nations under Polish administration. Beginning on 8 November, the Commission on Polish Affairs now reworked the Le Rond proposals according to this plan. The need to protect the millions of Western Ukrainians was so obvious that on 21 November the Supreme Council accepted the new statute of autonomy for Eastern Galicia in spite of Polish objections. The essential point was that the statute took the form of a treaty between Poland on the one side and, on the other side, America, England, France, Italy, and Japan. The statute gave Poland a twenty-five-year mandate to "govern and administer Eastern Galicia" (Art. 1) on condition that the territorial autonomy of the country, spelled out in subsequent articles, be respected. This Polish administration was also under the control of the League of Nations (Art. 2). The western border of the territory was to run in an almost straight north-south direction along a line slightly east of Przemyśl. The eastern border was to include a small part of northwestern Bukovyna (Map 1). At the end of twenty-five years, the League of Nations would have the right to renew the mandate, withdraw it or change it (Art. 2).[438]

Protest actions broke out as soon as the Supreme Council's decision was communicated to Poland on 24 November. The protests came from mass meetings, town and city councils, and the Diet itself.[439] The goal of Polish diplomacy was to have the Supreme Council decision suspended. Whereas previously the Poles had used the Western Ukrainian military successes as an argument for the Polish annexation of Eastern Galicia, since this would enable the Poles to devote all their forces to fighting the Bolsheviks, now the defeat of the Ukrainians was offered as an argument for the same annexation. It was necessary, said the Poles, so that Poland could better defend itself against the Bolsheviks. The tragedy of the situation for the Western Ukrainians was perhaps never more evident than now. It was the Western Ukrainians who had initially shielded Poland from direct contact with the Bolsheviks, making it possible for Poland to organize itself politically and militarily in relative peace. It was the blood of the Ukrainians, spilled in the struggle with the Bolsheviks, that had enabled Poland to grow into a strong power capable of breaking through this Ukrainian shield. On the distant plains of Eastern Ukraine, tens of thousands of Western Ukrainians were dying in indescribable misery, driven out of their homeland, cut off from Europe and denied any assistance. And their very death was now to serve as a means of strengthening their traditional Polish enemy.

On 4 December the Polish Foreign Ministry telegraphed its delegation in Paris: "Describe to the Peace Conference the situation that has arisen on the southeastern front. This situation has changed completely of late. Denikin's forces have been defeated, Kyiv has fallen, and the Bolsheviks are approaching Kharkiv. Petliura's troops are disorganized, and at any moment the whole defense of Europe against the Bolsheviks will depend on our army, the same army that defended Lwów and cleared Galicia of the Ukrainian bands. Under such circumstances the publication of the decision of the Peace Conference as a final solution of the Galician question would have fatal consequences. This is a solution that would rob Poland of Lwów and the whole of Eastern Galicia and deprive the army of the fruits of its victory. The main question for us now is the maintenance of discipline and morale among the troops. Both have been severely shaken today by the announcement of the Peace Conference's decision, which has provoked indignation not only among the population but also among the troops. The Polish Government requests the Peace Conference to reconsider the Galician question, not only because of the justness of our demands and because Poland deserves to be treated in the same manner as our Czechoslovak neighbor but also because Europe needs our troops. It is imperative that the decision be postponed for several months."[440]

Stanisław Patek intervened with Clemenceau to this effect, and on 11 December he sent a memorandum to the Peace Conference.[441] In this memorandum Poland again committed itself to grant the broadest possible autonomy to Eastern Galicia if this territory were handed over to it unconditionally. The memorandum also claimed, as before, that Polish annexation corresponded to the wishes of the Ukrainians. Once again it maintained that "recent unrest has been instigated by German and Austrian intrigue." The memorandum concluded that in the event of a provisional mandate in Eastern Galicia "it would not be difficult, in view of the well-known close links between the Ukrainian leaders and Germany, to establish where unrest would come from in the future."

Now Lloyd George received a visit in London from Clemenceau. The latter convinced him on 22 December to withdraw his resolution of 21 November by formally suspending it until another discussion could be held at some indefinite time in the future. With great satisfaction, Clemenceau announced this turn of events to the Polish delegation in Paris on the same day.[442] Entente guarantees for the protection of Ukrainian national rights under Polish rule were dropped once and for all. On the following day, 23 December, Clemenceau reported to the French parliament that he had "succeeded in settling this question. It may appear a small matter, but in reality it is very important, for we have now established around Germany's borders sufficient forces to guarantee our own peace and security."[443]

3. The Incorporation of Eastern Galicia into Poland

The activities of the Ukrainian emigration marked the end of the Ukrainian liberation struggle of 1918–19, and the Supreme Council's decision of 22 December signaled the end of the international significance of the Eastern Galician question. All that remained was for Eastern Galicia to be integrated into the internal development of Poland, a process interrupted by the aforesaid struggle.

At the time of the Polish conquest of Eastern Galicia by the Haller army, the old Galician rights of autonomy had already been greatly restricted by Warsaw. But even more important was the electoral law imposed by Piłsudski and the Daszyński cabinet on 28 November 1918. As a result of this electoral ordnance, an election was held in Congress Poland, Western Galicia and the Poznań region on 26 January 1919. The legislation declared, however, that the representatives of Eastern Galicia in this "Polish Constituent Diet" were to be the Eastern Galician deputies in the old Austrian parliament—but only those of Polish nationality. This first Diet convened on 10 February. Poland did not even bother to have a token Western Ukrainian presence in its legislative body. The Western Ukrainians had acted quite differently on 1 November 1918, when they immediately invited the Polish minority in Eastern Galicia to send representatives to the Ukrainian National Rada. In spite of the war with Poland, the Western Ukrainian electoral law of 15 April 1919 had guaranteed a presence for the Polish minority in the Western Ukrainian parliament on the basis of proportional representation.[444]

Immediately after the occupation of Eastern Galicia in July 1919, the Poles established a civilian administration for the whole territory except the small southeastern corner still occupied by the Romanians (which they soon vacated in any case). The place of the former viceroy was taken by an appointed Lviv-based delegate of the Warsaw government. He was installed very promptly, the French having accorded the Poles "the opportunity to act without delay." The subordination of the Western Ukrainians to this system was brought about at the cost of tens of thousands interned and imprisoned.[445]

While the Supreme Council discussed Eastern Galician autonomy, Poland eliminated what remained of Galicia's old autonomous rights. The Western Ukrainians did the only thing they could do, which was to protest in vain against all those Polish measures. Although the Supreme Council's decision of 8 December 1919 had stated that the eastern border of Poland, within which it could establish a civilian administration, was the so-called Curzon line, which was identical with the western border of Eastern Galicia proposed in the draft statute of 21 November 1919, the Warsaw Diet passed a law on 30 January 1920 abolishing the old Austrian Diet for Galicia and its executive committee.[446]

This process of incorporating Eastern Galicia suffered a temporary setback as a result of the defeat of Polish forces near Kyiv by the Bolsheviks in June 1920. Poland appealed to the Entente for help, requesting that the Entente mediate between itself and Soviet Russia in order to bring this war to an end. Poland declared itself prepared to sign a peace treaty with Russia on the basis of respect for the right of national self-determination for the nationalities residing between the two countries. This catastrophic defeat came about because Poland had overstretched its forces by pushing too far to the east. That led to a forced treaty with the Entente powers, signed in Spa on 10 July 1920 by Stanisław Grabski. In this treaty Poland agreed to the following conditions: 1) Vilnius would immediately be given back to the Lithuanians and a truce established with the Bolsheviks on the Curzon line of 8 December 1919. The Bolsheviks would withdraw fifty km from this line, and in Eastern Galicia the front line as of the day on which the truce was signed would be regarded as the line of demarcation; 2) Poland would send representatives to London, where a peace conference would be organized between Poland, Soviet Russia, Finland, Lithuania, and Latvia. Representatives of Eastern Galicia would also be present at this conference; 3) Poland would submit to the Supreme Council's decision concerning its border with Lithuania, the future of Eastern Galicia and the Cieszyn region, and its impending treaty with the city of Danzig.

The Western Ukrainian cause had been so decisively defeated that the reestablishment of a Western Ukrainian state was not even seriously considered on this occasion. The English demand for an immediate plebiscite in Eastern Galicia was put aside without too much difficulty. A proposal from Grabski that the Western Ukrainian representatives should not be recognized as delegates but should be allowed to attend the London conference to present their case was accepted without argument. It was clear in any case that Eastern Galicia would remain attached to Poland in some way or other and that Poland was committed only to accepting an Entente statute for the territory.[447]

Nothing came of this agreement, however, because the Bolsheviks, who were aiming for a complete victory over Poland, refused the mediation of the Entente. But the Bolshevik invasion of Poland failed, as the Poles brought off their "miracle on the Vistula" on 16 August 1920, and the Bolsheviks were driven back beyond Poland's present-day borders.

The new situation made it possible for Poland to consider the obligations undertaken at Spa null and void.[448] In the Treaty of Sèvres of 10 August 1920 between the Entente and Austria's successor states, the clause concerning autonomy for Eastern Galicia appeared once more: consequently, Poland refused to sign this treaty.

Negotiations between the Poles and the Bolsheviks began soon afterwards. These led to the signing of a preliminary agreement on 12 October 1920 and the Treaty of Riga on 18 March 1921. In the midst of the negotiations, on 24 September 1920, the Bolsheviks demonstratively demanded that Poland recognize Eastern Galicia's right of self-determination and organize a plebiscite on that territory. When the Poles refused, however, the Bolsheviks dropped this demand. Art. 1 of the preliminary agreement and Art. 2 of the Treaty of Riga explicitly recognized the old Austro-Russian border on the Zbruch as the boundary between Poland and Soviet Russia. Thus the Riga agreements were among the first international legal acts that indirectly recognized Polish sovereignty in Eastern Galicia.[449]

Of course the Western Ukrainians protested against the Riga agreements, but they considerably strengthened Poland's position on the Eastern Galician question at the Supreme Council. One of the reasons why England had supported the Western Ukrainians on this question was its belief that Russia would not be satisfied to see Eastern Galicia go to the Poles. But now the counterrevolution had been defeated, and there was no longer any doubt that it was the Bolsheviks who were the heirs of the Russian Empire. Since the Bolsheviks were willing to recognize Polish sovereignty in Eastern Galicia, England no longer had any objection. The Eastern Galician question lost importance as an international issue, and all further discussions on this question between the Entente and Poland were nothing but a meaningless diplomatic squabble.

It was in this form that the Eastern Galician question made its way to the League of Nations. Among liberal and democratic circles in the Entente countries, especially in the English-speaking world, continuing activity on the part of the Western Ukrainians succeeded in making the Eastern Galician question—the fact that Poland still refused to grant any kind of autonomy in Eastern Galicia in spite of all its promises and the Entente's commitments—into a small international scandal. On numerous occasions both England and the League of Nations expressed the view that the Eastern Galician question was still an unresolved international problem and that Poland had no right to the legal exercise of national sovereignty in that country.[450]

But Poland ignored all this. True to its policy of establishing faits accomplis, Poland continued the process of unifying both countries. In order not only to destroy Western Ukraine nationally and politically but even to wipe out any memory of its separate existence, Poland did away with the name "Galicia" and began to refer to the territory as "Little Poland." This was in spite of the fact that in historical Poland the name for the greater part of Eastern Galicia had been the Rus' palatinate. Pursuant to this policy, on 3 December 1920 the Polish Diet divided Galicia into four provinces (*województwa*): Cracow, Lwów (Lviv), Stanisławów (Stanyslaviv), and Tarnopol (Ternopil). This destroyed the unity of Eastern Galicia, which now existed simply as three "Little Polish" provinces. By incorporating a large part of Western Galician territory into the Lviv province, Poland conveniently turned the Western Ukrainian majority of that region into a minority.

Poland did not proceed immediately to split up the country. At first, on 8 February 1921, it got rid of the autonomous Galician School Board, which had existed since Austrian times, and brought the whole Eastern Galician school system under the direct control of Warsaw. The Polish Constitution of 17 March 1921 left open the question of Eastern Galician autonomy. But once repeated incidents made it clear that the Entente was not going to interfere with what happened in Eastern Galicia, Poland split up the territory into three "Little Polish" provinces in September 1921. A Western Ukrainian terrorist group retaliated with an attempt to assassinate the Lviv provincial governor, Kazimierz Grabowski. The Poles justified their action with reference to a fraudulent census that they had organized in Eastern Galicia. The Western Ukrainians had boycotted this census as an act of the Polish state. The census established that the Poles of Eastern Galicia were close to forming a majority! Not only administrative but also economic measures were used against the Western Ukrainians. A one-time property levy, enacted on 16 December 1921, was carried out in Eastern Galicia in such a way that a large part of the Western Ukrainian population was driven to the brink of economic ruin. Polish peasants from Western Galicia were now settled in Eastern Galicia on land expropriated from large estates. The purpose of this was to Polonize the country and simultaneously to reduce the Western Ukrainian peasants to poverty. The peasants held insufficient land of their own and were generally forced to work as laborers on the large estates.

To prove that Eastern Galicia was now truly Polish, the government bestowed Polish civil rights on its citizens. According to Piłsudski's decree of 18 August 1922, elections to the Diet and Senate were to be held not only in central Poland but also in Eastern Galicia. These elections, also boycotted by the whole Western Ukrainian population as an act of the Polish state, took place on 5 and 12 November 1922. They were accompanied by a wave of terrorist actions throughout the country. Although in Volhynia not a single Pole was elected, but only Ukrainians and Jews, in Eastern Galicia, as a result of the Western Ukrainian boycott, only Jews and four or five native Western Ukrainians working for the Polish secret service were elected to the Diet with the votes of Polish administrators. Their role was to testify, ostensibly in the name of the Ukrainian population, to Eastern Galicia's wish to be integrated into Poland. At the end of 1922, Western Ukrainians were forced into the Polish military service. Eastern Galicia had ceased to exist as a separate entity.

These Polish faits accomplis were extremely embarrassing to the Entente powers. For the sake of their own prestige, they could not hand over Eastern Galicia to Poland as long as the latter gave no appearance of wanting to carry out its promise concerning autonomy for the territory. As they were unable to force Poland to honor its commitment, there was little they could do but advise the Poles that it was in their own interest to do so, since international recognition of Poland's legal rights in Eastern Galicia depended on it. The Polish National Democrats firmly rejected this advice, although shortly before, when their situation was still uncertain, they had committed themselves to the most thoroughgoing autonomy for the Western Ukrainians. The uncertainty about the status of Eastern Galicia in international law had its drawbacks for Poland. The formally unresolved Eastern Galician question made Poland a state without internationally recognized borders, and this was both economically and politically a very great disadvantage. In April 1922 Poland asked the Entente to recognize the Treaty of Riga, which had been registered at the League of Nations on 12 August 1921, but the unresolved Eastern Galician question stood in the way. It was also clear from the discussions at the League of Nations that the issue of Eastern Galicia was damaging to Poland's reputation, as it put the spotlight on Polish domestic conditions that would not otherwise have come to public attention abroad.[451]

All these problems, as well as the pressure of the Polish representative at the League of Nations, Szymon Askenazy, finally convinced the National Democrats that they should give in and create some appearance of autonomy for the Western Ukrainians. This would be useful for Polish diplomacy, and there was of course no question of ever carrying it out in practice. The question of autonomy was actually resolved by a Polish National Democrat, Stanisław Głąbiński, who proposed that all the provinces of Poland should be made autonomous. Supreme power would remain with the Diet in Warsaw, but the manner in which its laws were implemented could be left to the provinces in those matters that the statute of 21 November 1919 designated as within the competence of the Eastern Galician assembly. This was known as "provincial autonomy." It was quite meaningless, for if the Diet decided to leave nothing to the discretion of the province, this autonomy would have no practical effect. Provincial assemblies (*sejmiki wojewódzkie*) were to be elected to implement this autonomy. In the three "Eastern Little Polish"—that is, Eastern Galician Ukrainian—provinces, there were to be separate chambers for Poles and Ukrainians. Issues of concern to each of the nationalities would be decided in the separate chambers, not in the assembly as a whole. Such was the decision of the Diet on 26 September 1922. The Diet promised to implement this autonomy within two years. It never happened.[452]

The Polish foreign minister, Count Aleksander Skrzyński, informed the Entente powers immediately of the new legislation. There was now no formal objection, from the viewpoint of international law, to the

Polish annexation of Eastern Galicia. Skrzyński described Poland as one of the powers guaranteeing peace in Eastern Europe and described himself as a man who unreservedly supported minority rights. Since the Entente powers, especially England, were incapable of imposing a solution on Poland against the latter's will, they were quite happy to allow themselves to be deceived in this matter. On 15 February 1923, on the occasion of renewed conflicts with Lithuania, Poland insisted that the Entente come to a final decision on the question of its eastern borders. The Entente seized the opportunity and, by decision of the Council of Allied Ambassadors in Paris on 14 March 1923, formally recognized the Polish borders as laid down in the Treaty of Riga. With respect to the autonomy of Eastern Galicia and Polish commitments in the Minorities Treaty of 28 June 1919, the decision stated that the Peace Conference recognized Polish sovereignty over all territories located between Russia and Poland's western borders.[453] Both materially and formally, Eastern Galicia had now become an integral part of the Polish Republic.

The Western Ukrainians protested unanimously against this decision, those in the emigration as well as those inside the country. They refused to recognize the validity of this international agreement or to consider themselves Polish citizens. They continued to uphold the right of Ukrainians to self-determination and proclaimed their intention of taking up the struggle for independence at the first opportunity. The Polish response was another series of blows. Almost the whole Ukrainian school system in Eastern Galicia was abolished. The Ukrainians were also denied their own national name, as the Poles introduced into the administrative and educational system the name "Ruthenians," rejected by the Ukrainians.[454] This, however, was mere shadowboxing. The essential question was whether, as Dmowski and the National Democrats hoped, the Polish nation would succeed in Polonizing the six million Ukrainians in Eastern Galicia and Volhynia. The ten years since 1923 have seen a breakdown of Western Ukrainian national life, an unrestrained civil war of all against all. The old national organizations are no longer capable of stopping the decline, and the new national forces are not yet strong enough. This is a result not only of the deliberate attack on the Ukrainian movement by the Polish state but also of the despair and the feeling of hopelessness among the Western Ukrainians themselves. This feeling of hopelessness is exacerbated by the chaotic Balkanization of Western Ukraine. But in Poland itself one also finds the same breakdown of national life beneath the surface, a frighteningly rapid decline in the spiritual and political life of the nation and a mutual hatred among all the various factions. The deadly poison of Polish-Ukrainian relations is slowly killing the Polish national organism itself. The Polonization of the Western Ukrainians, so confidently awaited by the Poles, has made not the slightest progress. The Ukrainian question in Poland, from the Polish as well as from the Western Ukrainian point of view, remains unresolved. It seems now, with the passage of time, that the Polish conquest of Eastern Galicia was not one of those creative conquests that are capable of giving rise to political and spiritual renewal. It was, rather, a destructive conquest, a curse for the victor as well as for the vanquished. Both peoples now, it seems, are caught up in a wild and vicious conflict in their slide toward dissolution and internal collapse—the fate that has already overtaken the Russian nation.[455]

Endnotes

1. Srokowski, *Zarys historji*, pp. 120–24, 158–91, 268–350.
2. Seyda, *Polska na przełomie dziejów*, pp. 72–117.
3. Srokowski, *Zarys historji*, pp. 191–267.
4. Ibid., pp. 1–14, 59–65, 76–78, 337–38, 348–50.
5. Bobrzyński, *Wskrzeszenie Państwa Polskiego*, 1: 163.
6. Ibid., pp. 204–7, 211, 222–27.
7. Ibid., p. 211; Kutrzeba, *Polska odrodzona 1914–1922*, p. 84.
8. Cf. Lozyns'kyi, *Halychyna*, p. 22.
9. Levyts'kyi, *Velykyi zryv*, pp. 52–54, 92–94; Lozyns'kyi, *Halychyna*, pp. 22, 25.
10. Cf. Bobrzyński, *Wskrzeszenie Państwa Polskiego*, 1: 211, 223, 232.
11. Lozyns'kyi, *Halychyna*, pp. 25–28; Levyts'kyi, *Velykyi zryv*, pp. 103–5; Biliński, *Wspomnienia i dokumenty*, 2: 181.
12. Lozyns'kyi, *Halychyna*, pp. 27–29; Levyts'kyi, *Velykyi zryv*, pp. 105–11.
13. Lozyns'kyi, *Halychyna*, pp. 29–32; Levyts'kyi, *Velykyi zryv*, pp. 111–18.
14. Lozyns'kyi, *Halychyna*, pp. 33–36, 38; Levyts'kyi, *Velykyi zryv*, pp. 120–22, 132–35.
15. Kumaniecki, *Odbudowa Państwowości Polskiej*, pp. 120–23, 126; Bobrzyński, *Wskrzeszenie Państwa Polskiego*, 2: 11; Lozyns'kyi, *Halychyna*, pp. 36–37.
16. Bobrzyński, *Wskrzeszenie Państwa Polskiego*, 2: 14; Daszyński, *Pamiętniki*, 2: 310–19; Kutrzeba, *Polska odrodzona 1914–1922*, pp. 91–93; Kumaniecki, *Odbudowa Państwowości Polskiej*, p. 127; Lozyns'kyi, *Halychyna*, p. 37.
17. Kumaniecki, *Odbudowa Państwowości Polskiej*, p. 127; Kutrzeba, *Polska odrodzona 1914–1922*, p. 93; Bobrzyński, *Wskrzeszenie Państwa Polskiego*, 2: 14; Lozyns'kyi, *Halychyna*, p. 37.
18. Lozyns'kyi, *Halychyna*, p. 35.
19. Biliński, *Wspomnienia i dokumenty*, 2: 184.
20. Lozyns'kyi, *Halychyna*, pp. 32, 35–39; Lipiński, *Wśród lwowskich orląt*, pp. 8, 10.
21. Lipiński, *Wśród lwowskich orląt*, pp. 6, 9; Lozyns'kyi, *Halychyna*, p. 49n.
22. Lipiński, *Wśród lwowskich orląt*, pp. 9–10; Lozyns'kyi, *Halychyna*, p. 48; Daszyński, *Pamiętniki*, 2: 317.
23. Levyts'kyi, *Velykyi zryv*, pp. 124–25; Lozyns'kyi, *Halychyna*, pp. 38, 41.
24. Lozyns'kyi, *Halychyna*, pp. 38–40.
25. Ibid., p. 41.
26. Cf. *Litopys Chervonoï Kalyny*, 1930, no. 1.
27. Cf. Bobrzyński, *Wskrzeszenie Państwa Polskiego*, 2: 29–30, 1: 232. See also J. von Twardowski, "Ostgalizien."
28. Shukhevych, *Spomyny*, 1: 10, 20, 85–86.

29. Lipiński, *Wśród lwowskich orląt*, pp. 12–13; Lozyns'kyi, *Halychyna*, p. 50.
30. Lipiński, *Wśród lwowskich orląt*, pp. 13–14, 18 ff.; Lozyns'kyi, *Halychyna*, pp. 32–33, 36–38, 40–44, 50.
31. Lozyns'kyi, *Halychyna*, p. 43.
32. Cf. Bobrzyński, *Wskrzeszenie Państwa Polskiego*, 2: 27–28; Shukhevych, *Spomyny*, 1: 22–24.
33. Lozyns'kyi, *Halychyna*, pp. 43–44, 48, 55–56.
34. Ibid., pp. 31, 44–45.
35. Lozyns'kyi, *Halychyna*, pp. 45–46; Khrystiuk, *Zamitky i materiialy*, 3: 3 ff.
36. Lozyns'kyi, *Halychyna*, pp. 46–47.
37. Cf. the legal substantiation of de facto Polish sovereignty immediately upon the collapse of the Central Powers in Roth, *Die Entstehung des polnischen Staates*, p. 30.
38. Lipiński, *Wśród lwowskich orląt*, pp. 16–25, 27–31; Mączyński, *Boje lwowskie*, vol. 1.
39. Cf. Lozyns'kyi, *Halychyna*, p. 50.
40. Cf. Mączyński, *Boje lwowskie*, vol. 1; Lozyns'kyi, *Halychyna*, p. 49; Vityk, "Do desiatyrichchia Zakhidn'o-Ukraïns'koï Narodn'oï Respubliky," *Bil'shovyk Ukraïny* (Kharkiv), 1928, no. 20: 63–76.
41. Cf. Antonovych, *Pol's'ko-ukraïns'ki vidnosyny*.
42. Cf. Lipiński, *Wśród lwowskich orląt*, pp. 23, 90.
43. Ibid., pp. 12–17.
44. Lozyns'kyi, *Halychyna*, p. 56.
45. Cf. ibid., pp. 48–49, 52.
46. Cf. the formula of the insurgents' oath in Lipiński, *Wśród lwowskich orląt*, p. 59.
47. Lozyns'kyi, *Halychyna*, p. 56.
48. Ibid., pp. 47, 53, 55.
49. Ibid., p. 52.
50. Ibid., pp. 48–49, 55–56.
51. Ibid., pp. 51–52; Lipiński, *Wśród lwowskich orląt*, pp. 20–21, 27–28, 32–33.
52. Shukhevych, *Spomyny*, 1: 9–10, 13–14, 17–18; Lozyns'kyi, *Halychyna*, pp. 48–49; Hupert, *Zajęcie Małopolski Wschodniej*, p. 25.
53. Shukhevych, *Spomyny*, 1: 25; Lozyns'kyi, *Halychyna*, pp. 48–49; V. K., *Sichovi Stril'tsi*, pp. 10–11, 25; Davnyi, *Pro Sichovykh Stril'tsiv*, pp. 23–24, 42.
54. Lozyns'kyi, *Halychyna*, pp. 49, 52, 56; Lipiński, *Wśród lwowskich orląt*, pp. 32–35; cf. Mączyński, *Boje lwowskie*.
55. Lozyns'kyi, *Halychyna*, pp. 52–54; Lipiński, *Wśród lwowskich orląt*, pp. 56–61.
56. Lozyns'kyi, *Halychyna*, p. 49n; Hupert, *Zajęcie Małopolski Wschodniej*, p. 25; Lipiński, *Wśród lwowskich orląt*, pp. 62–64.
57. Lozyns'kyi, *Halychyna*, pp. 50–51.

58. Ibid., p. 58.

59. Ibid., pp. 53–54.

60. Lozyns'kyi, *Halychyna*, p. 55; Lipiński, *Wśród lwowskich orląt*, pp. 64–67.

61. Lipiński, *Wśród lwowskich orląt*, pp. 67–69; Bobrzyński, *Wskrzeszenie Państwa Polskiego*, 2: 31–32; cf. Lozyns'kyi, *Halychyna*, p. 55.

62. Shukhevych, *Spomyny*, 1: 19–22, 45–47, 67–68.

63. Ibid., pp. 19, 25, 89–90; *Republyka*, no. 24 (1 March 1919).

64. Shukhevych, *Spomyny*, 1: 27–42, 47, 50–57, 63, 68–69.

65. Ibid., 2: 48–50, 78.

66. Lozyns'kyi, *Halychyna*, pp. 57–59; Baker, *Woodrow Wilson*, 1: 54 (U.S. ed. 1: 55–56); *Notes présentées par la Délégation de la République Ukrainienne à la Conférence de la Paix à Paris* (hereafter *Notes*), pp. 16–18, 21–22.

67. Lozyns'kyi, *Halychyna*, pp. 59–61; *Notes*, pp. 19–20.

68. Lozyns'kyi, *Halychyna*, p. 57; *L'Ukraine Occidentale*, pp. 10–58.

69. Lozyns'kyi, *Halychyna*, pp. 42, 62; cf. Tryliovsky's programmatic speech of 5 February 1919 in *Republyka*, no. 5 (7 February 1919).

70. Lozyns'kyi, *Halychyna*, pp. 63–73, 89–91; cf. Wielopolska, *Gontowszczyzna*, p. 32.

71. Lozyns'kyi, *Halychyna*, pp. 92–95.

72. Bobrzyński, *Wskrzeszenie Państwa Polskiego*, 2: 10.

73. Kutrzeba, *Polska odrodzona 1914–1922*, p. 95.

74. Bobrzyński, *Wskrzeszenie Państwa Polskiego*, 2: 9–10.

75. Kutrzeba, *Polska odrodzona 1914–1922*, pp. 95–96; Daszyński, *Pamiętniki*, 2: 310–11; Bobrzyński, *Wskrzeszenie Państwa Polskiego*, 2: 12–14, 16, 23–24; Hupert, *Zajęcie Małopolski Wschodniej*, p. 9.

76. Bobrzyński, *Wskrzeszenie Państwa Polskiego*, 2: 14–15; Daszyński, *Pamiętniki*, 2: 311, 316.

77. Daszyński, *Pamiętniki*, 2: 310; Kumaniecki, *Odbudowa Państwowości Polskiej*, pp. 128–29; Bobrzyński, *Wskrzeszenie Państwa Polskiego*, 2: 15–16; Kutrzeba, *Polska odrodzona 1914–1922*, p. 96.

78. Bobrzyński, *Wskrzeszenie Państwa Polskiego*, 2: 17; Daszyński, *Pamiętniki*, 2: 320–26; Kutrzeba, *Polska odrodzona 1914–1922*, pp. 96–97; Kumaniecki, *Odbudowa Państwowości Polskiej*, pp. 130–32.

79. Bobrzyński, *Wskrzeszenie Państwa Polskiego*, 2: 27–29.

80. Cf. ibid., pp. 10, 18.

81. Ibid., pp. 18–23; Kumaniecki, *Odbudowa Państwowości Polskiej*, pp. 135–37; Kutrzeba, *Polska odrodzona 1914–1922*, pp. 97–98; Daszyński, *Pamiętniki*, 2: 325, 328–30.

82. Daszyński, *Pamiętniki*, 2: 329–30.

83. Hupert, *Zajęcie Małopolski Wschodniej*, pp. 9–13.

84. For a general description of the Hetman government from the "revolutionary-

democratic" viewpoint, see Khrystiuk, *Zamitky i materiialy*, vol. 3, and Vynnychenko, *Vidrodzhennia natsiï*, vol. 3. For a favorable account of the Hetman government, see the articles and memoirs in the collection *Khliborobs'ka Ukraïna*, vols. 1–5, and Doroshenko, *Istoriia Ukraïny 1918–1923 rr.*, vol. 2, *Ukraïns'ka Het'mans'ka Derzhava 1918 roku.*

85. Vynnychenko, *Vidrodzhennia natsiï*, 3: 158–61; Khrystiuk, *Zamitky i materiialy*, 4: 29.

86. Cf. V. K., *Sichovi Stril'tsi*, and Davnyi, *Pro Sichovykh Stril'tsiv*.

87. Lozyns'kyi, *Halychyna*, pp. 67, 73–74. Twardowski's claims in "Ostgalizien" are not based on any factual evidence.

88. Cf. Khrystiuk, *Zamitky i materiialy*, 4: 3–31.

89. Lozyns'kyi, *Halychyna*, pp. 67–68.

90. Margolin, *Ukraina i politika Antanty*, pp. 101–2; Khrystiuk, *Zamitky i materiialy*, 4: 3–91.

91. Lozyns'kyi, *Halychyna*, p. 69; Khrystiuk, *Zamitky i materiialy*, 4: 57–60.

92. Lozyns'kyi, *Halychyna*, pp. 69–70.

93. Khrystiuk, *Zamitky i materiialy*, 4: 81, 91–128; Kapustians'kyi, *Pokhid ukraïns'kykh armii*, 1: 14–40; Lozyns'kyi, *Halychyna*, p. 70.

94. Khrystiuk, *Zamitky i materiialy*, 4: 90 ff.; Gol'del'man, *Lysty zhydivs'koho sotsiial-demokrata pro Ukraïnu*, p. 7.

95. Kapustians'kyi, *Pokhid ukraïns'kykh armii*, 1: 16, 22–23, 25, 37–40; Lozyns'kyi, *Halychyna*, p. 72; Omelianovych-Pavlenko, *Ukraïns'ko-pol's'ka viina 1918–1919*, pp. 14–16.

96. Khrystiuk, *Zamitky i materiialy*, 4: 124–27; Kapustians'kyi, *Pokhid ukraïns'kykh armii*, 1: 23.

97. Lozyns'kyi, *Halychyna*, pp. 71–73.

98. Cf. Vynnychenko, *Vidrodzhennia natsiï*, 3: 394–404.

99. Lozyns'kyi, *Halychyna*, pp. 71–72; Hupert, *Zajęcie Małopolski Wschodniej*, p. 21.

100. Cf. Dillon, *The Peace Conference*, pp. 21–37.

101. Lozyns'kyi, *Halychyna*, pp. 95–96.

102. Cf. Mazepa, *Bol'shevyzm i okupatsiia Ukraïny*.

103. Lozyns'kyi, *Halychyna*, pp. 96–97.

104. Ibid., pp. 99, 101; Vynnychenko, *Vidrodzhennia natsiï*, 3: 321.

105. Lozyns'kyi, *Halychyna*, pp. 97–100.

106. *Republyka*, no. 30 (8 March 1919).

107. Lozyns'kyi, *Halychyna*, p. 101.

108. *Republyka*, no. 1 (2 February 1919).

109. Lozyns'kyi, *Halychyna*, pp. 98–99, 101, 103.

110. Temperley, *Peace Conference*, 4: 159–61; 1: 353–57.

111. Vynnychenko, *Vidrodzhennia natsiï*, 3: 322–28; Lozyns'kyi, *Halychyna*, p. 102.

112. Vynnychenko, *Vidrodzhennia natsiï*, 3: 323; Lozyns'kyi, *Halychyna*, pp. 102–3.

113. Lozyns'kyi, *Halychyna*, p. 103.

114. Dmowski, *Polityka polska*, passim, e.g., pp. 120, 170. Cf. also the opinion on the value of the grand prince's appeal in Dmowski's article "Zagadnienia środkowo- i wschodnio-europejskie" (ibid., p. 486) and the observations on Russian policy with regard to the Polish question in all of Dmowski's other memoranda. See also Seyda, *Polska na przełomie dziejów*, pp. 49–71, 118–65.

115. Dmowski, *Polityka polska*, passim, e.g., p. 167. Cf. Seyda, *Polska na przełomie dziejów*, pp. 166–79.

116. Dmowski, *Polityka polska*, passim, e.g., p. 166.

117. Ibid., p. 167.

118. Cf. Recke, *Die polnische Frage*, p. 282.

119. Cf. Dmowski, *Polityka polska*, p. 186; Seyda, *Polska na przełomie dziejów*, pp. 397–410.

120. Dmowski, *Polityka polska*, p. 200.

121. Kozicki, *Sprawa granic Polski*, p. 10; Dmowski, *Polityka polska*, pp. 168–69; Seyda, *Polska na przełomie dziejów*, pp. 295–96.

122. Dmowski, *Polityka polska*, p. 193; Recke, *Die polnische Frage*, pp. 297–98; Roth, *Die Entstehung des polnischen Staates*, pp. 36–37.

123. Dmowski, *Polityka polska*, p. 193.

124. Cf. *Akty i dokumenty, dotyczące sprawy granic Polski na Konferencji Pokojowej w Paryżu 1918–1919* (hereafter *Akty i dokumenty*), 1: 73.

125. Seyda, *Polska na przełomie dziejów*, pp. 297–98.

126. Kumaniecki, *Odbudowa Państwowości Polskiej*, p. 106.

127. Cited in Roth, *Die Entstehung des polnischen Staates*, p. 40.

128. Kumaniecki, *Odbudowa Państwowości Polskiej*, pp. 103–6; Roth, *Die Entstehung des polnischen Staates*, pp. 131–33.

129. Kumaniecki, *Odbudowa Państwowości Polskiej*, pp. 107–8.

130. Dmowski, *Polityka polska*, p. 324.

131. See Sosnowski, *Prawda dziejowa 1914–1917*, passim.

132. Dmowski, *Polityka polska*, p. 335.

133. Sosnowski, *Prawda dziejowa 1914–1917*, viii–ix, 577–93.

134. Dmowski, *Polityka polska*, p. 342.

135. Ibid., p. 336.

136. Ibid., p. 334.

137. Cf. Recke, *Die polnische Frage*, p. 330.

138. Dmowski, *Polityka polska*, p. 387; cf. Recke, *Die polnische Frage*, p. 343.

139. Cf. Recke, *Die polnische Frage*, pp. 306–7.

140. Kozicki, *Sprawa granic Polski*, pp. 48–49.

141. Dmowski, *Polityka polska*, p. 387.

142. Bobrzyński, *Wskrzeszenie Państwa Polskiego*, 2: 41–46.
143. Ibid., pp. 38, 47.
144. Ibid., p. 48; Kutrzeba, *Polska odrodzona 1914–1922*, pp. 103–4.
145. Kutrzeba, *Polska odrodzona 1914–1922*, p. 109 ff.; Kozicki, *Sprawa granic Polski*, p. 129.
146. Temperley, *Peace Conference*, 4: 131; 5: 133 n; Kutrzeba, *Polska odrodzona 1914–1922*, p. 31.
147. Dmowski, *Polityka polska*, p. 202.
148. Ibid., p. 273.
149. Ibid., pp. 220–25.
150. *Akty i dokumenty*, 1: 75–77.
151. For a complete German translation of this memorandum, see Roth, *Die Entstehung des polnischen Staates*, pp. 133–51.
152. Temperley, *Peace Conference*, 6: 238.
153. Kozicki, *Sprawa granic Polski*, p. 61; Dmowski, *Polityka polska*, pp. 364–67.
154. *Akty i dokumenty*, 1: 32 ff.
155. This was Stanisław Kozicki: see *Akty i dokumenty*, 1: 98.
156. Ibid., pp. 86–87.
157. Ibid., p. 89.
158. Temperley, *Peace Conference*, 1: 249, 263–64.
159. See the chronology ibid., 3: 11.
160. Dmowski, *Polityka polska*, pp. 369, 372–73.
161. Temperley, *Peace Conference*, 6: 238.
162. Ibid., p. 277.
163. Haskins and Lord, *Some Problems of the Peace Conference*, pp. 190–91.
164. Temperley, *Peace Conference*, 6: 269–70; cf. Lozyns'kyi, *Halychyna*, p. 142.
165. Haskins and Lord, *Some Problems of the Peace Conference*, p. 193.
166. Ibid., pp. 191–92.
167. Ibid., p. 193.
168. Ibid., p. 194.
169. Ibid., pp. 193–94.
170. Mermeix, *Le combat des Trois*, p. 279.
171. Baker, *Woodrow Wilson*, 3: 193–94 (U.S. ed. 3: 220–21).
172. Shukhevych, *Spomyny*, 1: 138–39.
173. Cf. Dmowski, *Polityka polska*, p. 397.
174. Haskins and Lord, *Some Problems of the Peace Conference*, p. 210.
175. Cf. Baker, *Woodrow Wilson*, 1: 289 (U.S. ed. 1: 361).
176. Ibid., 1: 304; 2: 215 (U.S. ed. 1: 381–82, 2: 283–84).

177. Ibid., 1: 306; 2: 217, 37, 41 (U.S. ed. 1: 383–84, 2: 286–87, 47, 52–53).
178. Ibid., 2: 213 (U.S. ed. 2: 281–82).
179. Ibid., 1: 240 (U.S. ed. 1: 296–97).
180. Margolin, *Ukraina i politika Antanty*, pp. 155–56.
181. Ibid., p. 155.
182. Ibid.
183. Cf. Temperley's general remarks (*Peace Conference*, 6: 239) on reservations concerning Western Ukraine out of consideration for Russia. However strongly this author reflects reactionary Russian influences, these reservations may well have been taken as the opinions of the Conservative members of the English peace delegation. Cf. also Dillon's extremely hostile attitude toward the Western Ukrainians as an example of the extent to which the Conservatives simply left the provisional decision on Western Ukraine up to Polish and Ukrainian arms.
184. Baker, *Woodrow Wilson*, 2: 215 (U.S. ed. 2: 284).
185. Ibid., 1: 312 (U.S. ed. 1: 391).
186. Ibid., 2: 215 (U.S. ed. 2: 285).
187. Ibid., 1: 318 (U.S. ed. 1: 398–99).
188. Cf. Hoffmann, *Erdölpolitik*, although his information is incorrect in certain details.
189. Baker, *Woodrow Wilson*, 2: 22 (U.S. ed. 2: 27–28).
190. Temperley, *Peace Conference*, 6: 267.
191. Cf. Baker, *Woodrow Wilson*, 2: 38 (U.S. ed. 2: 48–50).
192. Ibid., pp. 225–26 (U.S. ed. 298–99).
193. Cf. Mermeix, *Le combat des Trois*, pp. 268–99; Temperley, *Peace Conference*, 6: 311–17.
194. Mermeix, *Le combat des Trois*, p. 281.
195. Temperley, *Peace Conference*, 6: 312.
196. Ibid., p. 316.
197. Cf. Baker, *Woodrow Wilson*, 2: 22, 11 (U.S. ed. 2: 27, 12–13).
198. Cf. ibid., p. 25 (U.S. ed. 30–31); Margolin, *Ukraina i politika Antanty*, p. 152.
199. Cf. Baker, *Woodrow Wilson*, 2: 25, 1: 317–18 (U.S. ed. 2: 30–31, 1: 397–99).
200. Cf. Margolin, *Ukraina i politika Antanty*, pp. 151–52.
201. Khrystiuk, *Zamitky i materiialy*, 4: 28–29.
202. Cf. Margolin, *Ukraina i politika Antanty*, pp. 150–51.
203. Lozyns'kyi, *Halychyna*, p. 117.
204. Khrystiuk, *Zamitky i materiialy*, 4: 29; cf. Margolin, *Ukraina i politika Antanty*, pp. 102, 111 ff.
205. Cf. Khrystiuk, *Zamitky i materiialy*, 4: 28.
206. Baker, *Woodrow Wilson*, 2: 23, 25 (U.S. ed. 2: 28–29, 30–31).

207. Khrystiuk, *Zamitky i materiialy*, 4: 42–44, 92 ff.

208. Ibid., p. 29; cf. Margolin, *Ukraina i politika Antanty*, pp. 102, 111 ff.

209. Margolin, *Ukraina i politika Antanty*, pp. 109–12; Khrystiuk, *Zamitky i materiialy*, 4: 29, 42–44, 92 ff.

210. Khrystiuk, *Zamitky i materiialy*, 4: 92; Notes, p. 34.

211. Cf. Khrystiuk, *Zamitky i materiialy*, 4: 102, 92–93.

212. Ibid., p. 92; Margolin, *Ukraina i politika Antanty*, p. 123.

213. Margolin's formulation (p. 123) that France was prepared to recognize the Directory as the de facto government of Ukraine is wrong. Cf. *Notes*, p. 23. Some of Margolin's other statements (pp. 121–24) are also incomplete, to say the least. Cf. Khrystiuk, *Zamitky i materiialy*, 4: 27–29, 40–44, 68 n, 91–108; *Notes*, pp. 32–37.

214. Cf. Khrystiuk, *Zamitky i materiialy*, 4: 31, 124.

215. Ibid., pp. 97–8.

216. Ibid., pp. 102–3.

217. Ibid., p. 103.

218. Cf. ibid., p. 104.

219. Temperley, *Peace Conference*, 6: 311.

220. Baker, *Woodrow Wilson*, 2: 23 (U.S. ed. 2: 28–29).

221. Ibid., 3: 212 (U.S. ed. 3: 242).

222. Ibid., 2: 23n (U.S. ed. 2: 28–29).

223. Ibid., 1: 240 (U.S. ed. 1: 296–97).

224. Ibid., 3: 213 (U.S. ed. 3: 243).

225. Ibid., 2: 36 (U.S. ed. 2: 46).

226. Dmowski, *Polityka polska*, pp. 351 ff., 397 ff., 360 ff.

227. Lozyns'kyi, *Halychyna*, pp. 74–75.

228. Ibid., pp. 74–82.

229. Cf. Baker, *Woodrow Wilson*, 2: 21–23 (U.S. ed. 2: 26–29).

230. Khrystiuk, *Zamitky i materiialy*, 4: 91–128.

231. Margolin, *Ukraina i politika Antanty*, p. 124; Baker, *Woodrow Wilson*, 2: 25, 3: 213 (U.S. ed. 2: 31, 3: 243).

232. Baker, *Woodrow Wilson*, 2: 22, 3: 213 (U.S. ed. 2: 27–28, 3: 243).

233. Ibid., 2: 23–24, 3: 213 (U.S. ed. 2: 28–30, 3: 243).

234. Ibid., 2: 22 (U.S. ed. 2: 27–28).

235. Ibid., 3: 213 (U.S. ed. 3: 243).

236. Ibid., 2: 43 (U.S. ed. 2: 55).

237. Temperley, *Peace Conference*, 6: 238.

238. Cf. Dmowski, *Polityka polska*, pp. 342, 362, 383, 371; Temperley, *Peace Conference*, 6: 238.

239. Margolin, *Ukraina i politika Antanty*, p. 161; Lozyns'kyi, *Halychyna*, pp. 117–18.

240. Temperley, *Peace Conference*, 6: 238–39.
241. Bobrzyński, *Wskrzeszenie Państwa Polskiego*, 2: 86–90.
242. Lozyns'kyi, *Halychyna*, pp. 113–14.
243. Ibid., p. 114; *Notes*, pp. 5–11.
244. The complete text of this document has been published in Margolin, *Ukraina i politika Antanty*, pp. 114–18.
245. Ibid., pp. 109–21.
246. Lozyns'kyi, *Halychyna*, pp. 115–16, 118–19.
247. Ibid., p. 114–16, 118.
248. Temperley, *Peace Conference*, 6: 266.
249. Ibid., pp. 239–40.
250. Ibid., p. 242.
251. Ibid., p. 246.
252. Cf. ibid., p. 270.
253. Cf. ibid., p. 246.
254. Cf. ibid., p. 245.
255. Cf. ibid., p. 246.
256. Ibid., pp. 270–72.
257. Bobrzyński, *Wskrzeszenie Państwa Polskiego*, 2: 34, 87–88; Hupert, *Zajęcie Małopolski Wschodniej*, pp. 25–28.
258. Bobrzyński, *Wskrzeszenie Państwa Polskiego*, 2: 69–70; Hupert, *Zajęcie Małopolski Wschodniej*, pp. 9 ff., 29.
259. Hupert, *Zajęcie Małopolski Wschodniej*, p. 23.
260. Shukhevych, *Spomyny*, 1: 24; *Republyka*, no. 12 (15 February 1919).
261. Hupert, *Zajęcie Małopolski Wschodniej*, pp. 20, 25–26.
262. Lozyns'kyi, *Halychyna*, p. 66; Shukhevych, *Spomyny*, 1: 25.
263. Cf. Hupert, *Zajęcie Małopolski Wschodniej*, pp. 10–11.
264. Ibid., p. 35.
265. Data on the possibility of forming a Ukrainian legionary army in Italy (letter from Lieutenant Yevhen Bachynsky to Dr. Vasyl Paneiko, 4 March 1919, in the private collection of Dr. Stepan Tomashivsky).
266. Hupert, *Zajęcie Małopolski Wschodniej*, p. 23; Shukhevych, *Spomyny*, 2: 5 ff., 16–17, 20; 1: 25–26, 105, 96.
267. Shukhevych, *Spomyny*, 1: 19–20, 85–86, 69, 105–6, 118. Cf. rosters of the Sich Riflemen in the author's possession dating from December 1918 and various subsequent months.
268. Lipiński, *Wśród lwowskich orląt*, pp. 83, 85 ff., 120–24; Shukhevych, *Spomyny*, 1: 23–24, 84–85, 99–114, 148–49, 138, 123–24, 175; 2: 5–20, 37–47, 99, 132; Hupert, *Zajęcie Małopolski Wschodniej*, pp. 18, 23.

269. Shukhevych, *Spomyny,* 1: 113, 122, 152, 161–64; 2: 51–56, 101 ff., 114, 124–26, 138 ff.

270. The general's own memoirs are particularly informative about his character. Cf. also Shukhevych, *Spomyny,* 1: 150–51, 69 ff., 107 ff., 110, 112–13, 94–95, 119–22; Lozyns'kyi, *Halychyna,* p. 66.

271. Shukhevych, *Spomyny,* 2: 50, 53–61, 77; Hupert, *Zajęcie Małopolski Wschodniej,* p. 23.

272. Shukhevych, *Spomyny,* 1: 85 ff., 95, 104, 92 ff., 96, 112, 114, 153.

273. Shukhevych, *Spomyny,* 1: 111; Omelianovych-Pavlenko, *Ukraïns'ko-pol's'ka viina 1918–1919,* pp. 14–19; cf. Sopotnicki, *Kampanja polsko-ukraińska.*

274. Lipiński, *Wśród lwowskich orląt,* pp. 76–81, 110–11; Shukhevych, *Spomyny,* 1: 128; Hupert, *Zajęcie Małopolski Wschodniej,* p. 26; Omelianovych-Pavlenko, *Ukraïns'ko-pol's'ka viina 1918–1919,* p. 19; cf. Sopotnicki, *Kampanja polsko-ukraińska.*

275. Cf. Hupert, *Zajęcie Małopolski Wschodniej,* p. 18; *Republyka,* nos. 3–24 (3 February–1 March 1919); cf. also letters to Baron Mykola Vasylko from Dr. Lev Hankevych (22 February 1919) and from Metropolitan Andrei Sheptytsky (17 January 1919) in the private collection of Dr. Stepan Tomashivsky; cf. Shukhevych, *Spomyny,* 1: 109, 154 ff.

276. Shukhevych, *Spomyny,* 1: 30, 32–33, 50, 61–63, 68–69, 82, 99, 78 ff., 81, 91 ff., 96, 97 ff., 150–60, 130 ff., 108–19, 129–30, 166; 2: 46–50; Kapustians'kyi, *Pokhid ukraïns'kykh armii,* 3: 19 n; Omelianovych-Pavlenko, *Ukraïns'ko-pol's'ka viina 1918–1919,* pp. 14–23; cf. proceedings of the Ukrainian National Rada on 4–5 February 1919 in *Republyka,* nos. 4–5 (6–7 February 1919).

277. Shukhevych, *Spomyny,* 2: 104 ff., 114 ff., 124 ff., 122.

278. Hupert, *Zajęcie Małopolski Wschodniej,* pp. 23, 25.

279. Lipiński, *Wśród lwowskich orląt,* p. 110; Hupert, *Zajęcie Małopolski Wschodniej,* p. 27.

280. Hupert, *Zajęcie Małopolski Wschodniej,* p. 27.

281. *Republyka,* no. 1 (2 February 1919).

282. Lozyns'kyi, *Halychyna,* p. 83.

283. Shukhevych, *Spomyny,* 1: 122 ff., 128; Hupert, *Zajęcie Małopolski Wschodniej,* pp. 27–28; Omelianovych-Pavlenko, *Ukraïns'ko-pol's'ka viina 1918–1919,* pp. 24–44; cf. *Republyka,* no. 18 (22 February 1919) for a radio report of 15 February to the American mission in Paris on Poland's military situation and on Berthélemy's statements before the Warsaw Inter-Allied Commission concerning the situation in Lviv.

284. *Republyka,* no. 20 (25 February 1919); Shukhevych, *Spomyny,* 1: 130–32; Lozyns'kyi, *Halychyna,* pp. 75–81; Omelianovych-Pavlenko, *Ukraïns'ko-pol's'ka viina 1918–1919,* pp. 45–47.

285. Lozyns'kyi, *Halychyna,* pp. 76–78; Omelianovych-Pavlenko, *Ukraïns'ko-pol's'ka viina 1918–1919,* p. 47 ff.

286. Cf. Lozyns'kyi, *Halychyna,* p. 84.

287. Hurwicz, *Geschichte des russischen Bürgerkrieges*, pp. 144–201.

288. Shukhevych, *Spomyny*, 1: 140 ff.; Lozyns'kyi, *Halychyna*, pp. 81–84.

289. *Republyka*, nos. 30–33 (8–13 March 1919) and 39–40 (19–20 March 1919); Shukhevych, *Spomyny*, 1: 146–70; Hupert, *Zajęcie Małopolski Wschodniej*, p. 30; Omelianovych-Pavlenko, *Ukraïns'ko-pol's'ka viina 1918–1919*, pp. 49–61; Sopotnicki, *Kampanja polsko-ukraińska*, p. 115 ff.

290. Lozyns'kyi, *Halychyna*, p. 86.

291. Baker, *Woodrow Wilson*, 2: 22 (U.S. ed. 2: 28).

292. Lozyns'kyi, *Halychyna*, p. 85.

293. Ibid.

294. Shukhevych, *Spomyny*, 1: 168; Lozyns'kyi, *Halychyna*, p. 86; cf. Temperley, *Peace Conference*, 1: 336.

295. Lozyns'kyi, *Halychyna*, p. 86.

296. Hupert, *Zajęcie Małopolski Wschodniej*, p. 30 ff.

297. Temperley, *Peace Conference*, 1: 336; report of F. J. Kernan to Wilson, dated 11 April 1919, in Baker, *Woodrow Wilson*, 3: 191–96 (U.S. ed. 3: 218–24); cf. Dillon, *The Peace Conference*, p. 130.

298. Lozyns'kyi, *Halychyna*, pp. 86–88.

299. Ibid., pp. 87–88.

300. Temperley, *Peace Conference*, 1: 336; Lozyns'kyi, *Halychyna*, p. 120; Baker, *Woodrow Wilson*, 3: 191–96 (U.S. ed. 3: 218–24).

301. Kumaniecki, *Odbudowa Państwowości Polskiej*, p. 172; Temperley, *Peace Conference*, 3: 17 (chronology); Hupert, *Zajęcie Małopolski Wschodniej*, p. 40.

302. Hupert, *Zajęcie Małopolski Wschodniej*, pp. 31–36.

303. Lozyns'kyi, *Halychyna*, p. 87.

304. Ibid., p. 119.

305. Hupert, *Zajęcie Małopolski Wschodniej*, p. 40; Dmowski, *Polityka polska*, p. 398; Lozyns'kyi, *Halychyna*, pp. 104–5; Dillon, *The Peace Conference*, pp. 212–13.

306. Letter from Isaiah Bowman to Mr. Joseph C. Grew in the private collection of Stepan Tomashivsky.

307. Shukhevych, *Spomyny*, 1: 166 ff., 175 ff., 2: 11 ff.; Wielopolska, *Gontowszczyzna*, passim.

308. Kapustians'kyi, *Pokhid ukraïns'kykh armii*, 1: 23–24.

309. Shukhevych, *Spomyny*, 1: 169–72.

310. *V zashchitu Sovetskoi Ukrainy*, p. 33 ff.

311. Shukhevych, *Spomyny*, 2: 22 ff.; Hupert, *Zajęcie Małopolski Wschodniej*, pp. 49–50; Omelianovych-Pavlenko, *Ukraïns'ko-pol's'ka viina 1918–1919*, p. 61 ff.

312. Lozyns'kyi, *Halychyna*, p. 87.

313. Hupert, *Zajęcie Małopolski Wschodniej*, p. 32; Shukhevych, *Spomyny*, 2: 14–38; Lozyns'kyi, *Halychyna*, p. 104; Omelianovych-Pavlenko, *Ukraïns'ko-pol's'ka viina*

1918–1919, pp. 65–66.

314. Lozyns'kyi, *Halychyna*, pp. 104–5.

315. Dillon, *The Peace Conference*, pp. 207–8, 210.

316. Lozyns'kyi, *Halychyna*, pp. 120–32; Dillon, *The Peace Conference*, p. 208; Dmowski, *Polityka polska*, pp. 400–401.

317. Dillon, *The Peace Conference*, p. 213; Lozyns'kyi, *Halychyna*, pp. 105, 138–42; Bobrzyński, *Wskrzeszenie Państwa Polskiego*, 2: 69, 71, 73; Hupert, *Zajęcie Małopolski Wschodniej*, p. 28; Baker, *Woodrow Wilson*, 3: 191–96, 2: 236, 225–26; 1: 317–18 (U.S. ed. 3: 218–24, 2: 311, 298–99, 1: 397–99).

318. Cf. the data—not always reliable, by the way (for example, the Western Ukrainians never had a "Volhynian reserve")—in Hupert, *Zajęcie Małopolski Wschodniej*, pp. 40–41, also 32–39, 42–57.

319. Hupert, *Zajęcie Małopolski Wschodniej*, pp. 40–67; Shukhevych, *Spomyny*, 2: 63–69; Omelianovych-Pavlenko, *Ukraïns'ko-pol's'ka viina 1918–1919*, pp. 67–69.

320. Shukhevych, *Spomyny*, 2: 65–66, 70–71; Lozyns'kyi, *Halychyna*, pp. 105–6; Hupert, *Zajęcie Małopolski Wschodniej*, pp. 67–72.

321. Shukhevych, *Spomyny*, pp. 67–68, 91.

322. Hupert, *Zajęcie Małopolski Wschodniej*, pp. 72–75; Lozyns'kyi, *Halychyna*, p. 106.

323. Temperley, *Peace Conference*, 1: 337; Hupert, *Zajęcie Małopolski Wschodniej*, p. 47.

324. Lozyns'kyi, *Halychyna*, pp. 134–42; Temperley, *Peace Conference*, 1: 337; Dmowski, *Polityka polska*, pp. 401–2.

325. Cf. Dillon, *The Peace Conference*, pp. 212–13; Hupert, *Zajęcie Małopolski Wschodniej*, pp. 40–85.

326. Hupert, *Zajęcie Małopolski Wschodniej*, pp. 63, 68, 71, 74–75, 77. Piłsudski's reply was kept secret; it is mentioned in Temperley, *Peace Conference*, 1: 337. On 5 June 1919 the Paris press reported, on the other hand, that Poland had answered that it was only waging a defensive war (Lozyns'kyi, *Halychyna*, p. 140).

327. Kapustians'kyi, *Pokhid ukraïns'kykh armii*, 1: 25.

328. Hupert, *Zajęcie Małopolski Wschodniej*, p. 86.

329. Shukhevych, *Spomyny*, 2: 80 ff.

330. Ibid., 2: 75–82, 105 n; Lozyns'kyi, *Halychyna*, pp. 106–7; Kapustians'kyi, *Pokhid ukraïns'kykh armii*, 1: 25, 2: 42–45; Hupert, *Zajęcie Małopolski Wschodniej*, pp. 75–84.

331. Kapustians'kyi, *Pokhid ukraïns'kykh armii*, 2: 42–83; Shukhevych, *Spomyny*, 2: 83.

332. Shukhevych, *Spomyny*, 2: 80–84; Lozyns'kyi, *Halychyna*, p. 107; Omelianovych-Pavlenko, *Ukraïns'ko-pol's'ka viina 1918–1919*, pp. 67–71.

333. Hupert, *Zajęcie Małopolski Wschodniej*, pp. 82, 84–85.

334. Kapustians'kyi, *Pokhid ukraïns'kykh armii*, 2: 42–43; cf. Hupert, *Zajęcie Małopolski Wschodniej*, pp. 42, 49, 57 ff.

335. Omelianovych-Pavlenko, *Ukraïns'ko-pol's'ka viina 1918–1919*, pp. 69–70.

336. Hupert, *Zajęcie Małopolski Wschodniej*, pp. 85–87; Shukhevych, *Spomyny*, 2: 86–88.

337. Shukhevych, *Spomyny*, 2: 86–100, 129.

338. Ibid., 2: 89, 91, 107, 129, 130–32.

339. Ibid., 2: 100, 115; Hupert, *Zajęcie Małopolski Wschodniej*, p. 87.

340. Shukhevych, *Spomyny*, 2: 90–92, 101 ff., 112 ff., 133.

341. Ibid., 2: 110 ff.

342. Kapustians'kyi, *Pokhid ukraïns'kykh armii*, 3: 10–11; Lozyns'kyi, *Halychyna*, p. 109.

343. Kapustians'kyi, *Pokhid ukraïns'kykh armii*, 3: 8–12; Lozyns'kyi, *Halychyna*, p. 108.

344. Hupert, *Zajęcie Małopolski Wschodniej*, p. 92; Shukhevych, *Spomyny*, 2: 115–16; Lozyns'kyi, *Halychyna*, p. 108.

345. Kapustians'kyi, *Pokhid ukraïns'kykh armii*, 3: 11–12; Shukhevych, *Spomyny*, 2: 145–46.

346. Cf. Hupert, *Zajęcie Małopolski Wschodniej*, p. 92; Shukhevych, *Spomyny*, 2: 128.

347. Hupert, *Zajęcie Małopolski Wschodniej*, pp. 85–96; Shukhevych, *Spomyny*, 2: 86, 89–90, 94–95, 108 ff., 128–29, 131; Kapustians'kyi, *Pokhid ukraïns'kykh armii*, 2: 58, 3: 7–12.

348. Shukhevych, *Spomyny*, 2: 104 ff.

349. Margolin, *Ukraina i politika Antanty*, pp. 144–46.

350. Ibid., pp. 146–48.

351. Lozyns'kyi, *Halychyna*, pp. 133–34, 134 n.

352. Temperley, *Peace Conference*, 6: 246.

353. Lozyns'kyi, *Halychyna*, p. 142.

354. Cf. Temperley's brief mentions in *Peace Conference*, 1: 337.

355. Cf. Hupert, *Zajęcie Małopolski Wschodniej*, pp. 85–97.

356. Lozyns'kyi, *Halychyna*, p. 108 n.

357. Cf. Temperley, *Peace Conference*, 1: 335–37, 6: 272–73.

358. Ibid., 6: 273; *Akty i dokumenty*, 3: 20.

358. *Akty i dokumenty*, 3: 3–4; *L'Ukraine Occidentale*, app. 14; Lozyns'kyi, *Halychyna*, pp. 152, 150, 143–48, 110–12.

360. Cf. Hupert, *Zajęcie Małopolski Wschodniej*, p. 97.

361. Ibid., pp. 96–104; Shukhevych, *Spomyny*, 2: 131 ff., 149 ff., 150 ff.; Lozyns'kyi, *Halychyna*, p. 110.

362. Lozyns'kyi, *Halychyna*, p. 112.

363. Nazaruk, *Rik na Velykii Ukraïni*, pp. 182–84, cited in Lozyns'kyi, *Halychyna*, p. 112.

364. Kapustians'kyi, *Pokhid ukraïns'kykh armii*, 3: 41.

365. Ibid., 75–77; Hurwicz, *Geschichte des russischen Bürgerkrieges*, pp. 144–53.

366. Kapustians'kyi, *Pokhid ukraïns'kykh armii*, 2: 75–83, 3: 6–7.

367. Ibid., 3: 6–7.

368. Ibid., 2: 80, 3: 13–14; Shukhevych, *Spomyny*, pp. 138–46.

369. Kapustians'kyi, *Pokhid ukraïns'kykh armii*, 2: 77–83, 3: 24–33.

370. Cf. Shukhevych, *Spomyny*, 2: 91, 130–31, 142–45, 174–75; 3: 8–10; Margolin, *Ukraina i politika Antanty*, p. 188 ff., 192f.

371. Nazaruk, *Rik na Velykii Ukraïni*, pp. 178–81, quoted in Lozyns'kyi, *Halychyna*, pp. 109–10.

372. Kapustians'kyi, *Pokhid ukraïns'kykh armii*, 3: 31–4.

373. Nazaruk, *Rik na Velykii Ukraïni*, pp. 178–81, quoted in Lozyns'kyi, *Halychyna*, pp. 109–10. The date can be established on the basis of Kapustians'kyi, *Pokhid ukraïns'kykh armii*, 3: 31–34, 20, 38. It was between 11 and 13 July 1919.

374. Shukhevych, *Spomyny*, 2:. 132–33.

375. Kapustians'kyi, *Pokhid ukraïns'kykh armii*, 3: 31–34, 36, 38, 40; Nazaruk, *Rik na Velykii Ukraïni*, pp. 178–81, quoted in Lozyns'kyi, *Halychyna*, pp. 109–10; Hupert, *Zajęcie Małopolski Wschodniej*, pp. 103–4.

376. Kapustians'kyi, *Pokhid ukraïns'kykh armii*, 3: 38–51.

377. Ibid., p. 51.

378. Ibid., pp. 16–17; Shukhevych, *Spomyny*, vol. 3 passim.

379. Kapustians'kyi, *Pokhid ukraïns'kykh armii*, 3: 17–19; cf. the description of a battle (ibid., p. 115); Hurwicz, *Geschichte des russischen Bürgerkrieges*, pp. 154–201.

380. Hurwicz, *Geschichte des russischen Bürgerkrieges*, p. 144.

381. Kapustians'kyi, *Pokhid ukraïns'kykh armii*, 3: 90–91.

382. Ibid., pp. 96–97, 112; Shukhevych, *Spomyny*, 3: 18 ff.

383. Kapustians'kyi, *Pokhid ukraïns'kykh armii*, 3: 92–95.

384. Ibid., pp. 62–64.

385. Ibid., pp. 7, 41, 87, 87 n.

386. Bobrzyński, *Wskrzeszenie Państwa Polskiego*, 2: 147.

387. Cf. Shukhevych, *Spomyny*, 2: 164–65.

388. Hupert, *Zajęcie Małopolski Wschodniej*, pp. 104–7; Kapustians'kyi, *Pokhid ukraïns'kykh armii*, 3: 94, 95, 96–97, 112.

389. Hurwicz, *Geschichte des russischen Bürgerkrieges*, pp. 76–93.

390. Hurwicz, *Geschichte der jüngsten russischen Revolution*, pp. 166–67.

391. Hurwicz, *Geschichte des russischen Bürgerkrieges*, pp. 33–57, 94–121.

392. Ibid., pp. 39–43, 102–21, 213–19.

393. Hurwicz, *Geschichte der jüngsten russischen Revolution*, pp. 175–83; idem, *Geschichte des russischen Bürgerkrieges*, pp. 141–43.

394. Hurwicz, *Geschichte des russischen Bürgerkrieges*, pp. 94–121, 202–3; idem, *Geschichte der jüngsten russischen Revolution*, pp. 161–62; Kapustians'kyi, *Pokhid ukraïns'kykh armii*, 3: 57–58, 60.

395. Hurwicz, *Geschichte des russischen Bürgerkrieges*, pp. 122–43.

396. Hurwicz, *Geschichte der jüngsten russischen Revolution*, pp. 163–208.
397. Ibid.
398. Kapustians'kyi, *Pokhid ukraïns'kykh armii*, 3: 58; Temperley, *Peace Conference*, 6: 311.
399. Kapustians'kyi, *Pokhid ukraïns'kykh armii*, 3: 58; Temperley, *Peace Conference*, 6: 311; Hurwicz, *Geschichte der jüngsten russischen Revolution*, p. 196 n.
400. Kapustians'kyi, *Pokhid ukraïns'kykh armii*, 1: 38–40.
401. Hurwicz, *Geschichte des russischen Bürgerkrieges*, pp. 18–32, 46–57.
402. Cf. Lozyns'kyi, *Halychyna*, p. 179; Margolin, *Ukraina i politika Antanty*, pp. 155–59.
403. V. K., *Sichovi Stril'tsi*, p. 38.
404. Lozyns'kyi, *Halychyna*, pp. 169–70.
405. Shukhevych, *Spomyny*, 2: 83, 174–76; 3: 5–6, 8, 10, 13 ff.; Kapustians'kyi, *Pokhid ukraïns'kykh armii*, 3: 85–89; Lozyns'kyi, *Halychyna*, pp. 171, 188.
406. Kapustians'kyi, *Pokhid ukraïns'kykh armii*, 3: 46–55, 56, 62–68.
407. Ibid., pp. 68–71.
408. Ibid., pp. 72–85, 89–92, 95–99, 110–14.
409. Ibid., pp. 100–107, 114–19.
410. Ibid., pp. 107–10; cf. Lozyns'kyi, *Halychyna*, p. 184.
411. Kapustians'kyi, *Pokhid ukraïns'kykh armii*, 3: 120.
412. Lozyns'kyi, *Halychyna*, pp. 184–86.
413. Ibid., pp. 178–80.
414. V. K., *Sichovi Stril'tsi*, p. 38; Davnyi, *Pro Sichovykh Stril'tsiv*, p. 67.
415. Davnyi, *Pro Sichovykh Stril'tsiv*, pp. 67–68; V. K., *Sichovi Stril'tsi*, pp. 38–39; Lozyns'kyi, *Halychyna*, p. 188.
416. Hurwicz, *Geschichte des russischen Bürgerkrieges*, pp. 204–42.
417. Lozyns'kyi, *Halychyna*, pp. 174–79, 195–97, 182–83.
418. Ibid., pp. 189–90, 199.
419. Ibid., p. 191.
420. Ibid., pp. 192–201.
421. Kuz'ma, "Na rozputti. Prychynok do istoriï UHA," pp. 182–84.
422. Stachiewicz, *Działania zaczepne 3 armji na Ukrainie*, 1: 1–5.
423. Lozyns'kyi, *Halychyna*, pp. 187–88, 200–201.
424. Stachiewicz, *Działania zaczepne 3 armji na Ukrainie*, 1: 9–29, 33 ff.
425. Kuz'ma, "Na rozputti. Prychynok do istoriï UHA," pp. 184–98; cf. R. S., "Reflieksiï," *Litopys Chervonoï Kalyny*, 1930, no. 2.
426. Stachiewicz, *Działania zaczepne 3 armji na Ukrainie*, 1: 75–107.
427. Hurwicz, *Geschichte des russischen Bürgerkrieges*, pp. 243–300.
428. Cf. *Sovetskaia Ukraina i Pol'sha*, passim.

429. Cf. *Osteuropäische Korrespondenz*, no. 11 (12 June 1926).
430. Lozyns'kyi, *Halychyna*, pp. 118–19, 204–10.
431. Ibid., pp. 203–4, 209–17.
432. *Akty i dokumenty*, 3: 3; cf. Lozyns'kyi, *Halychyna*, p. 151n.
433. *Akty i dokumenty*, 3: 3–4, 23–32.
434. Lozyns'kyi, *Halychyna*, pp. 115–18, 150–54; *L'Ukraine Occidentale*, pp. 60–61.
435. *Akty i dokumenty*, 3: 5, 40–45.
436. Ibid., pp. 6, 48–51.
437. Ibid., p. 6; Lozyns'kyi, *Halychyna*, p. 118; Temperley, *Peace Conference*, 1: 335n.
438. *Akty i dokumenty*, 3: 6, 62–63, 66, 67. Cf. the telegrams (10, 12 and 14 November 1919) from the Polish delegation in Paris to the Warsaw foreign ministry in *Akty i dokumenty*, 3: 67–68. See also the delegation's note to the president of the Peace Conference, dated 9 November 1919, in *Akty i dokumenty*, 3: 54–55. Cf. also the reply of the General Secretariat of the Peace Conference, dated 12 November 1919, in *Akty i dokumenty*, 3: 58–59.
439. *Akty i dokumenty*, 3: 6; Lozyns'kyi, *Halychyna*, p. 166.
440. *Akty i dokumenty*, 3: 92.
441. Ibid., pp. 7, 94–97.
442. Ibid., pp. 7, 106–7.
443. Ibid., pp. 100–102.
444. Cf. Bobrzyński, *Wskrzeszenie Państwa Polskiego*, 2: 24, 51, 97–99; Lozyns'kyi, *Halychyna*, pp. 89–91.
445. Bobrzyński, *Wskrzeszenie Państwa Polskiego*, 2: 135–36; Twardowski, "Ostgalizien."
446. Bobrzyński, *Wskrzeszenie Państwa Polskiego*, 2: 96, 136–37.
447. Ibid., 2: 159–61; cf. Lozyns'kyi, *Halychyna*, p. 213.
448. Bobrzyński, *Wskrzeszenie Państwa Polskiego*, 2: 187–88.
449. Lozyns'kyi, *Halychyna*, pp. 213–15.
450. Lozyns'kyi, *Halychyna*, pp. 215–17; Bobrzyński, *Wskrzeszenie Państwa Polskiego*, 2: 259.
451. Bobrzyński, *Wskrzeszenie Państwa Polskiego*, 2: 137, 187, 217, 257, 266–69.
452. Ibid., pp. 246–47, 263–65.
453. Ibid., 2: 280–83.
454. *Propamiatne pys'mo*, passim.
455. Cf. Kuchabs'kyi, *Ukraïna i Pol'shcha*.

Bibliography

Documentary Sources

Akty i dokumenty, dotyczące sprawy granic Polski na Konferencji Pokojowej w Paryżu 1918–1919 zebrane i wydane przez Sekretarjat Jeneralny Delegacji Polskiej. Part 1, *Program terytorjalny Delegacji* (Paris, 1920); Part 3, *Sprawa Galicji* (Paris, 1926).

Khrystiuk, Pavlo. *Zamitky i materiialy do istorii ukraïns'koï revoliutsiï 1917–1920 rr.* 4 vols. Vienna, 1921–22.

Kumaniecki, Kazimierz Władysław. *Odbudowa Państwowości Polskiej. Najważniejsze dokumenty 1912–styczeń 1924.* Warsaw and Cracow, 1924.

Levyts'kyi, Kost'. *Velykyi zryv. Do istoriï ukraïns'koï derzhavnosty vid bereznia do lystopada 1918 r.* Lviv, 1931.

Lozyns'kyi, Mykhailo. *Halychyna v rr. 1918–1920. Ukraïns'ka revoliutsiia. Rozvidky i materiialy. Knyha p'iata.* Vienna, 1920.

Narodnyi Komissariat po inostrannym delam USSR. *Sovetskaia Ukraina i Pol'sha. Sbornik diplomaticheskikh dokumentov i istoricheskikh materialov.* Krasnye knigi 3. Kharkiv, 1921.

Narodnyi Komissariat po inostrannym delam USSR. *V zashchitu Sovetskoi Ukrainy. Sbornik diplomaticheskikh dokumentov i istoricheskikh materialov.* Krasnye knigi 1. Kharkiv, 1921.

Notes présentées par la délégation de la République Ukrainienne à la Conférence de la Paix à Paris. Paris, 1919.

Republyka (Stanyslaviv). Vol. 1 (1919).

Sosnowski, Jerzy Jan. *Prawda dziejowa 1914–1917.* Warsaw, 1925.

L'Ukraine Occidentale. Vienna, 1920.

Memoirs, Letters, etc.

Baker, R. S. *Woodrow Wilson. Memoiren und Dokumente über den Vertrag zu Versailles.* Trans. Curt Thesing. 3 vols. Leipzig, 1922–24.

Biliński, Leon. *Wspomnienia i dokumenty.* Vol. 1, *1846–1914*; Vol. 2, *1915–1922.* Warsaw, 1924–25.

Daszyński, Ignacy. *Pamiętniki.* 2 vols. Cracow, 1925–26.

Dillon, E. J. *The Peace Conference.* London, 1920.

Dmowski, Roman. *Polityka polska i odbudowanie Państwa. Z dodaniem memorjału "Zagadnienia środkowo- i wschodnio-europejskie" i innych dokumentów polityki polskiej z lat 1914–1919.* 2d ed. Warsaw, 1926.

Gol'del'man, Solomon. *Lysty zhydivs'koho sotsiial-demokrata pro Ukraïnu. Materiialy do istoriï ukraïns'ko-zhydivs'kykh vidnosyn za chas revoliutsiï.* Vienna, 1921.

Khliborobs'ka Ukraïna. 5 vols. Vienna, 1920–25.

Kossak, Tadeusz. *Wspomnienia wojenne (1918–1920).* Cracow, 1925.

Kuz'ma, Oleksa. "Na rozputti. Prychynok do istorii UHA." In *Iuvileinyi Kaliendar Tovarystva "Prosvita" na perestupnyi rik 1928*, pp. 182–99. Lviv, 1928.

Lipiński, Wacław. *Wśród lwowskich orląt.* Warsaw, 1927.

Litopys Chervonoï Kalyny (Lviv), 1930.

Margolin, Arnold. *Ukraina i politika Antanty. Zapiski evreia i grazhdanina.* Berlin, 1921.

Omelianovych-Pavlenko, Mykhailo. *Ukraïns'ko-pol's'ka viina 1918–1919.* Prague, 1929.

Shukhevych, Stepan. *Spomyny z ukraïns'ko-halyts'koï armiï (1918–1920).* 3 vols. Lviv, 1928–29.

Vynnychenko, Volodymyr. *Vidrodzhennia natsiï.* Vols. 2 and 3. Kyiv and Vienna, 1920.

Monographs

Davnyi, R. *Pro Sichovych Stril'tsiv.* Vienna, 1921.

Haskins, Charles Homer, and Robert Howard Lord. *Some Problems of the Peace Conference.* Cambridge, Mass., 1920.

Hupert, Witold. *Zajęcie Małopolski Wschodniej i Wołynia w roku 1919.* Lviv and Warsaw, 1928.

K., V. [Vasyl' Kuchabs'kyi]. *Sichovi Stril'tsi.* Lviv, 1920.

Kapustians'kyi, Mykola. *Pokhid ukraïns'kykh armii na Kyïv-Odesu v 1919 rotsi.* 3 vols. Lviv, 1921–22.

Kozicki, Stanisław. *Sprawa granic Polski na konferencji pokojowej w Paryżu.* Warsaw, 1921.

Mączyński, Czesław. *Boje lwowskie.* 3 vols. Warsaw, 1921.

Mazepa, Isaak. *Bol'shevyzm i okupatsiia Ukraïny. Sotsiial'no-ekonomichni prychyny nedozrilosty syl ukraïns'koï revoliutsiï.* Lviv and Kyiv, 1922.

Mermeix. *Le Combat des Trois. Notes et documents sur la Conférence de la Paix. Fragments d'histoire 1914–1919.* Vol. 6. Paris, 1923.

Sopotnicki, Józef. *Kampanja polsko-ukraińska.* Lviv, 1921.

Srokowski, Konstanty. *Zarys historji Naczelnego Komitetu Narodowego.* Cracow, 1923.

Stachiewicz, Juljan. *Działania zaczepne 3 armji na Ukrainie. Studja operacyjne z historji wojen polskich 1918–21.* Vol. 1. Warsaw, 1925.

General Works

Bobrzyński, Michał. *Wskrzeszenie Państwa Polskiego.* Vol. 1, 1914–1918; Vol. 2, 1919–1923. Cracow, 1925.

Doroshenko, Dmytro. *Istoriia Ukraïny 1917–1923 rr.* Vol. 2, *Ukraïns'ka Het'mans'ka Derzhava 1918 roku.* Uzhhorod, 1930.

Hurwicz, Elias. *Geschichte der jüngsten russischen Revolution.* Berlin, 1922.

———. *Geschichte des russischen Bürgerkrieges.* Berlin, 1927.

Kutrzeba, Stanisław. *Polska odrodzona 1919–1922.* 2d augmented ed. Cracow, 1922.

Recke, Walter. *Die polnische Frage als Problem der europäischen Politik*. Berlin, 1927.

Roth, Paul. *Die Entstehung des polnischen Staates. Eine völkerrechtlich-politische Untersuchung*. Öffentlich-rechtliche Abhandlungen, vol. 7. Ed. Heinrich Triepel, Erich Kaufmann, and Rudolf Smend. Berlin, 1926.

Seyda, Marjan. *Polska na przełomie dziejów. Fakty i dokumenty. Od wybuchu wojny do zbrojnego wystąpienia Stanów Zjednoczonych*. Poznań, Warsaw, Vilnius, and Lublin, 1927.

Temperley, H. W. V., ed. *A History of the Peace Conference of Paris*. 6 vols. London, 1920–24.

Other Writings

Antonovych, Volodymyr. *Pol's'ko-ukraïns'ki vidnosyny XVII st. v suchasnii pol's'kii pryzmi. Z nahody povisty H. Sienkevycha "Ohnem i mechem."* Lviv, 1904.

Hoffmann, Karl. *Erdölpolitik*. Berlin, 1925.

Kuchabs'kyi, Vasyl'. *Ukraïna i Pol'shcha. Otverta vidpovid' pol's'komu konservatystovi*. Lviv, 1933.

Osteuropäische Korrespondenz (Berlin) 3, no. 11 (12 June 1926).

Propamiatne pys'mo Naukovoho Tovarystva imeny Shevchenka u L'vovi z pryvodu zaborony pol's'koiu Kuratoriieiu L'vivs'koho Shkil'noho Okruha natsional'noho imeny ukraïns'koho narodu. Lviv, 1923.

S., R. "Reflieksiï na 'Spomyny' D-ra S. Shukhevycha." *Litopys Chervonoï Kalyny* (Lviv), 1930, no. 1: 20–22; no. 2: 19–22.

Twardowski, Jul. von. "Ostgalizien." In *Wörterbuch des Völkerrechts und der Diplomatie*. Ed. Julius Hatschek and Karl Strupp. Berlin and Leipzig, 1924–25.

Vityk, Semen. "Do desiatyrichchia Zakhidn'o-Ukraïns'koï Narodn'oï Respubliky." In *Bil'shovyk Ukraïny* (Kharkiv), 1928, no. 20: 63–76.

Wielopolska (Janowska), Marya Jehanne. *Gontowszczyzna. Wspomnienia z rebelji ukraińskiej w Małopolsce Wschodniej*. Poznań, 1925.

Maps

Map 1: Galicia and the Polish-Ukrainian Military Situation at the End of 1918–

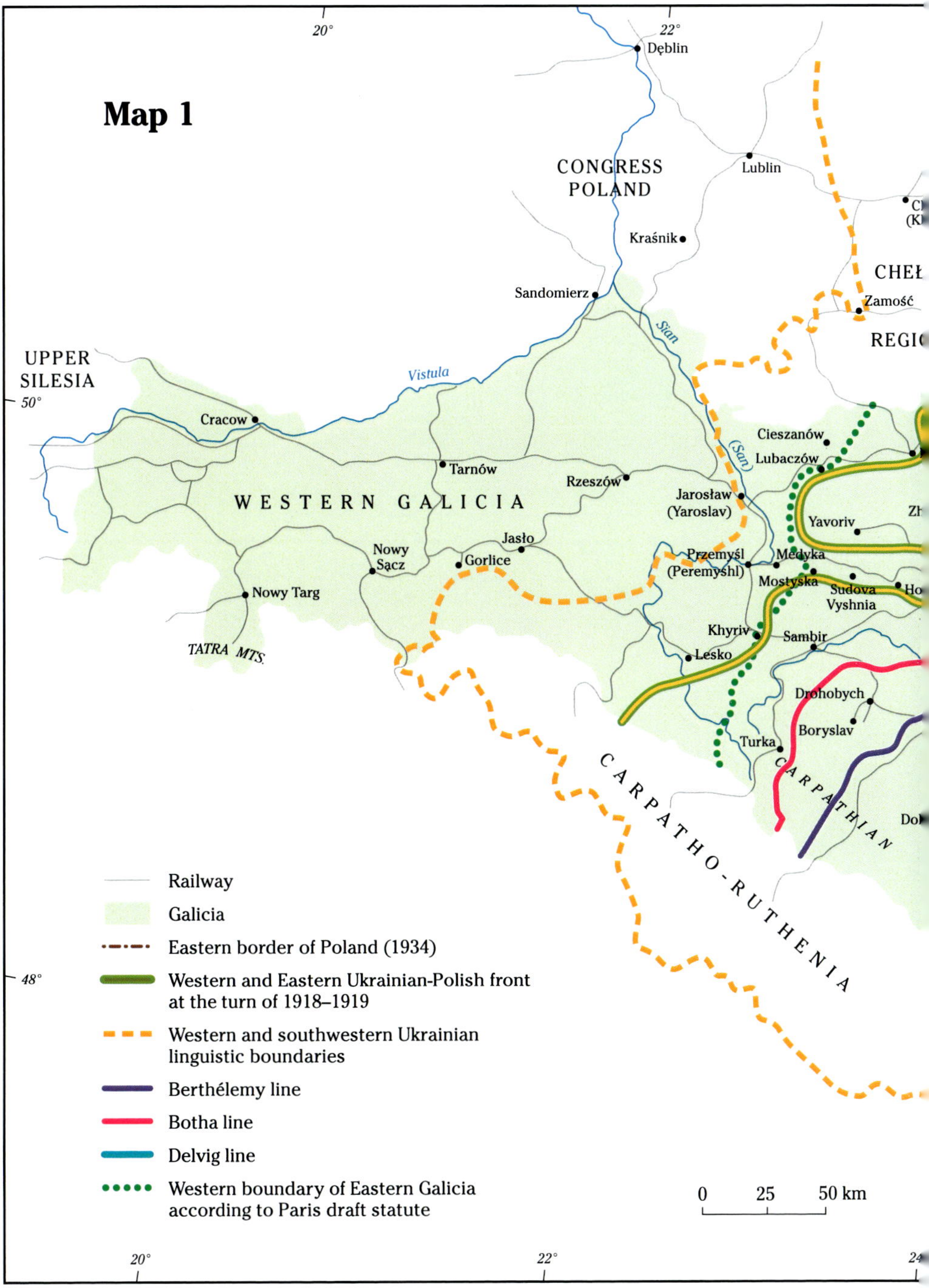

eginning of 1919

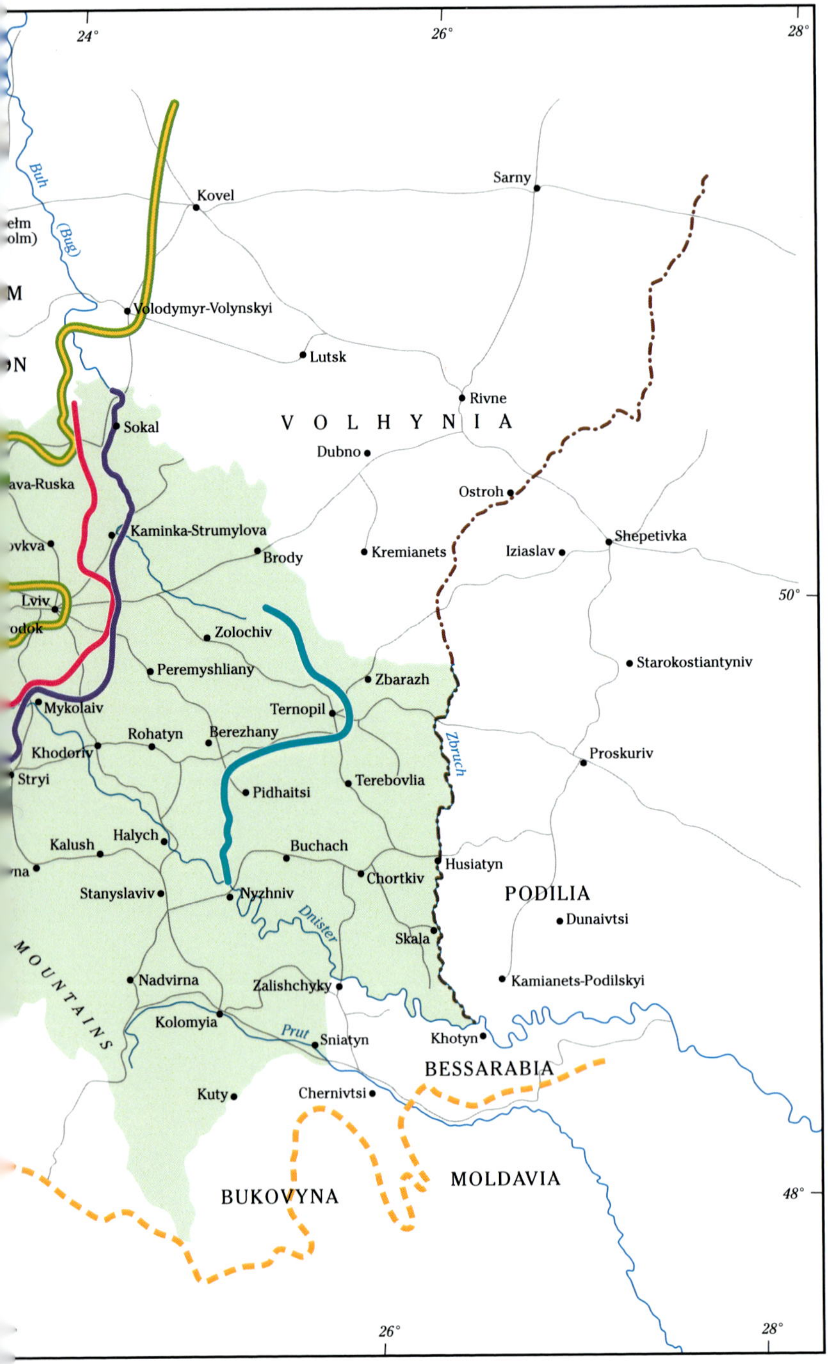

Map 2: The Military Situation in Western and Eastern Ukraine at the Beginning

of March 1919

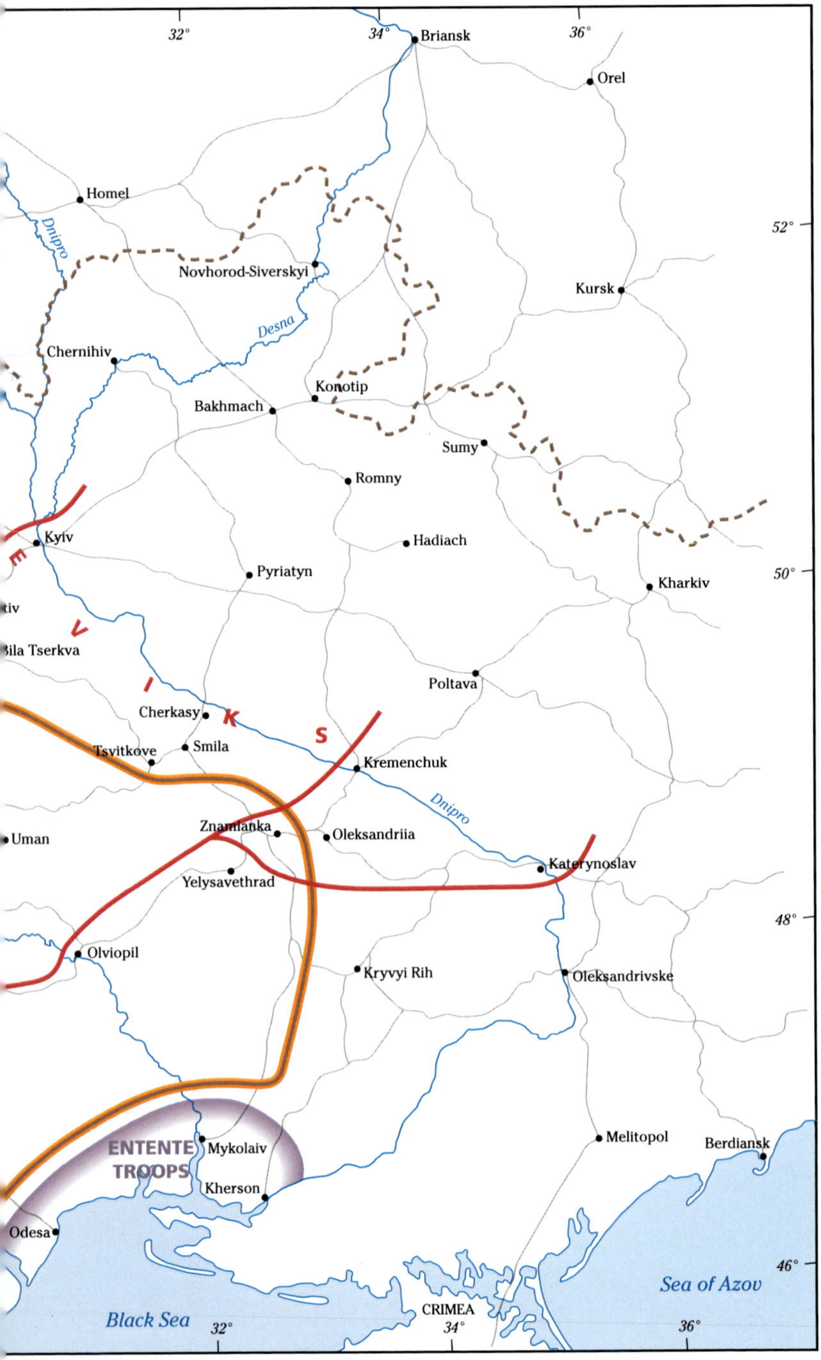

Map 3: The Haller and Bolshevik Offensives against Western and Eastern Ukraine in May 1919

Map 4: The Ukrainian Counteroffensives against the Poles and the Bolsheviks

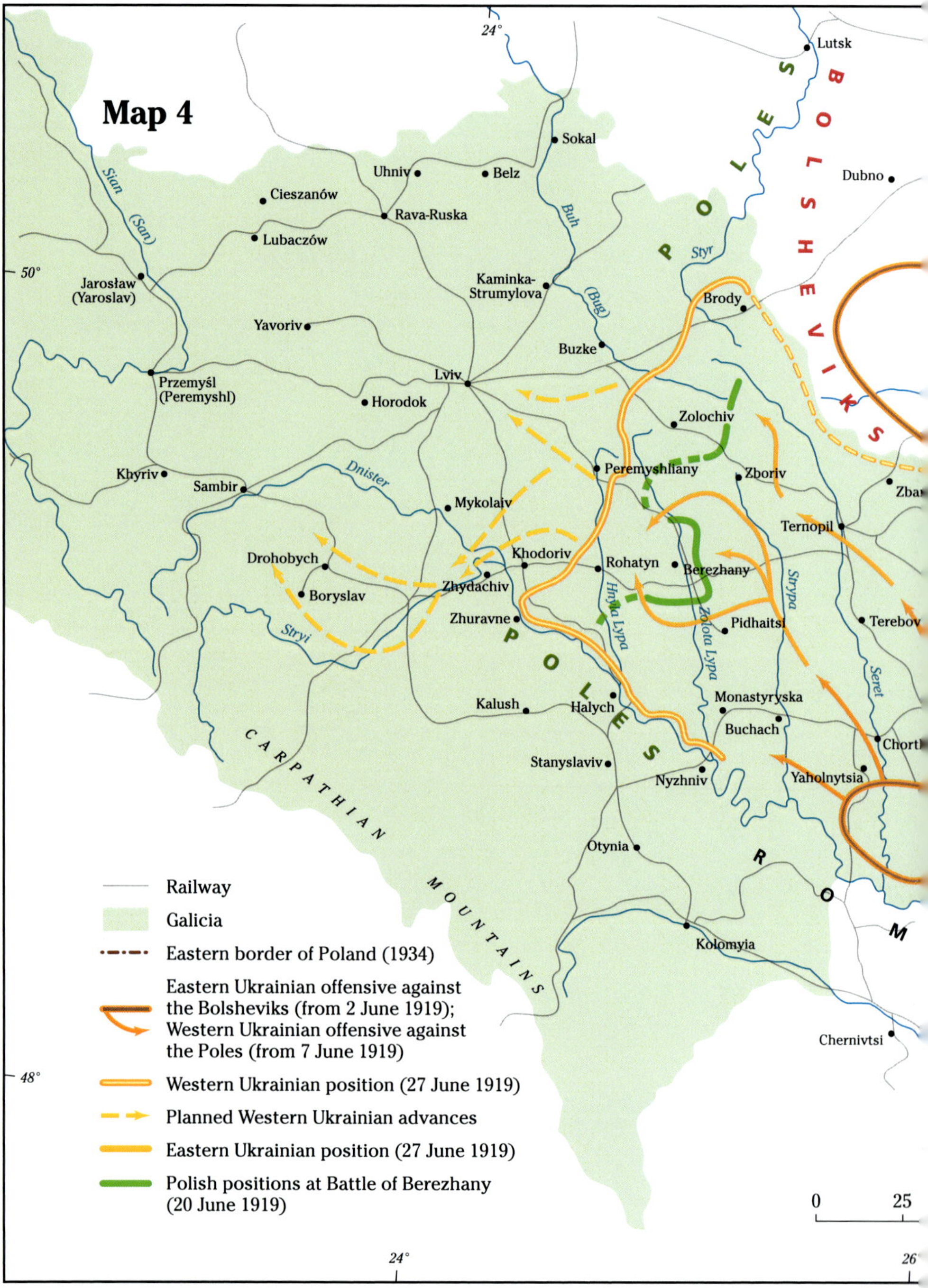

n June 1919

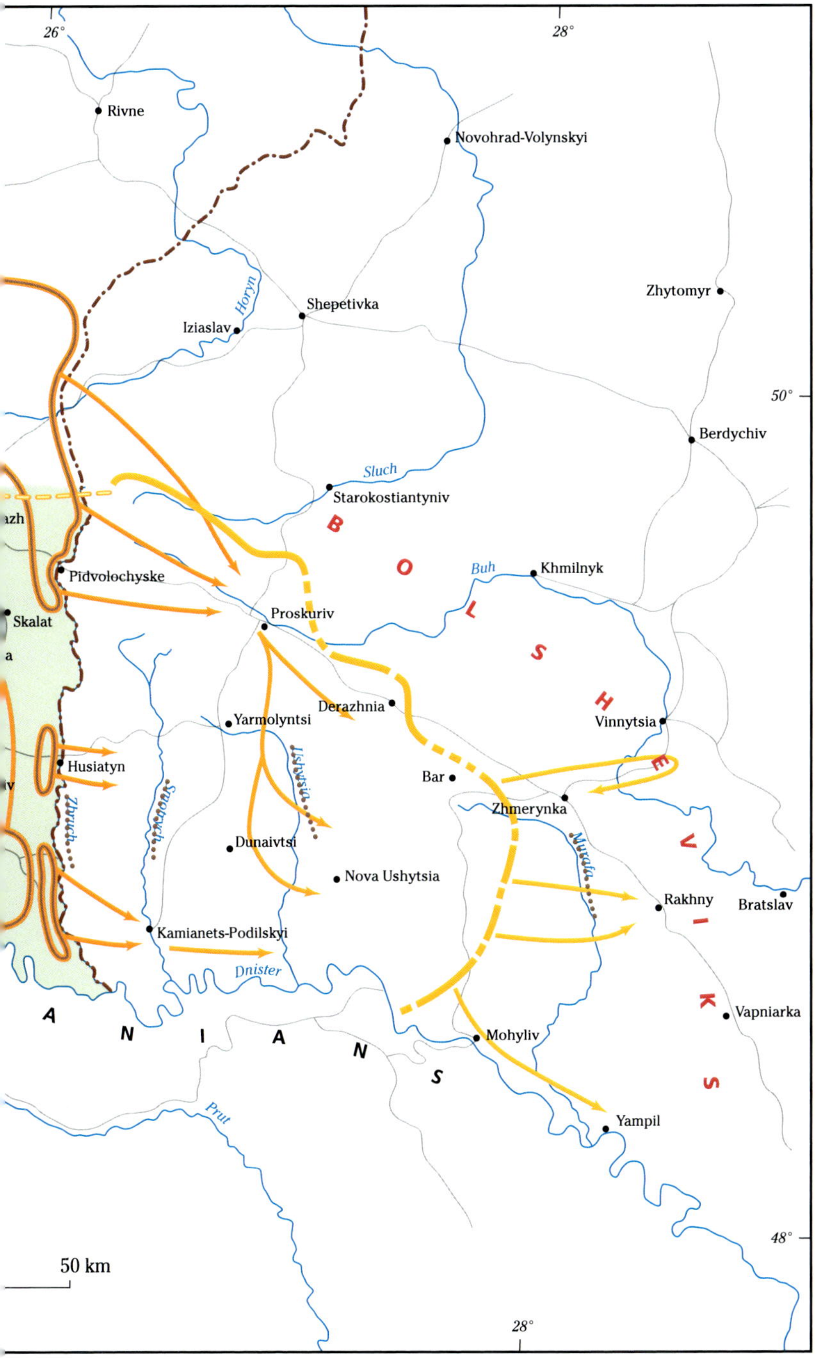

26°
28°
Rivne
Novohrad-Volynskyi
Zhytomyr
Horyn
Iziaslav
Shepetivka
50°
Berdychiv
Sluch
Starokostiantyniv
B O L S H E V I K S
Pidvolochyske
Buh
Khmilnyk
Skalat
Proskuriv
Derazhnia
Yarmolyntsi
Vinnytsia
Husiatyn
Zbruch
Smotrych
Ushytsia
Bar
Zhmerynka
Murafa
Dunaivtsi
Nova Ushytsia
Rakhny
Bratslav
Kamianets-Podilskyi
Dnister
A N I A N S
Mohyliv
Vapniarka
Yampil
Prut
48°
50 km
28°

Map 5: The Second Polish and Bolshevik Offensives against the Western and E

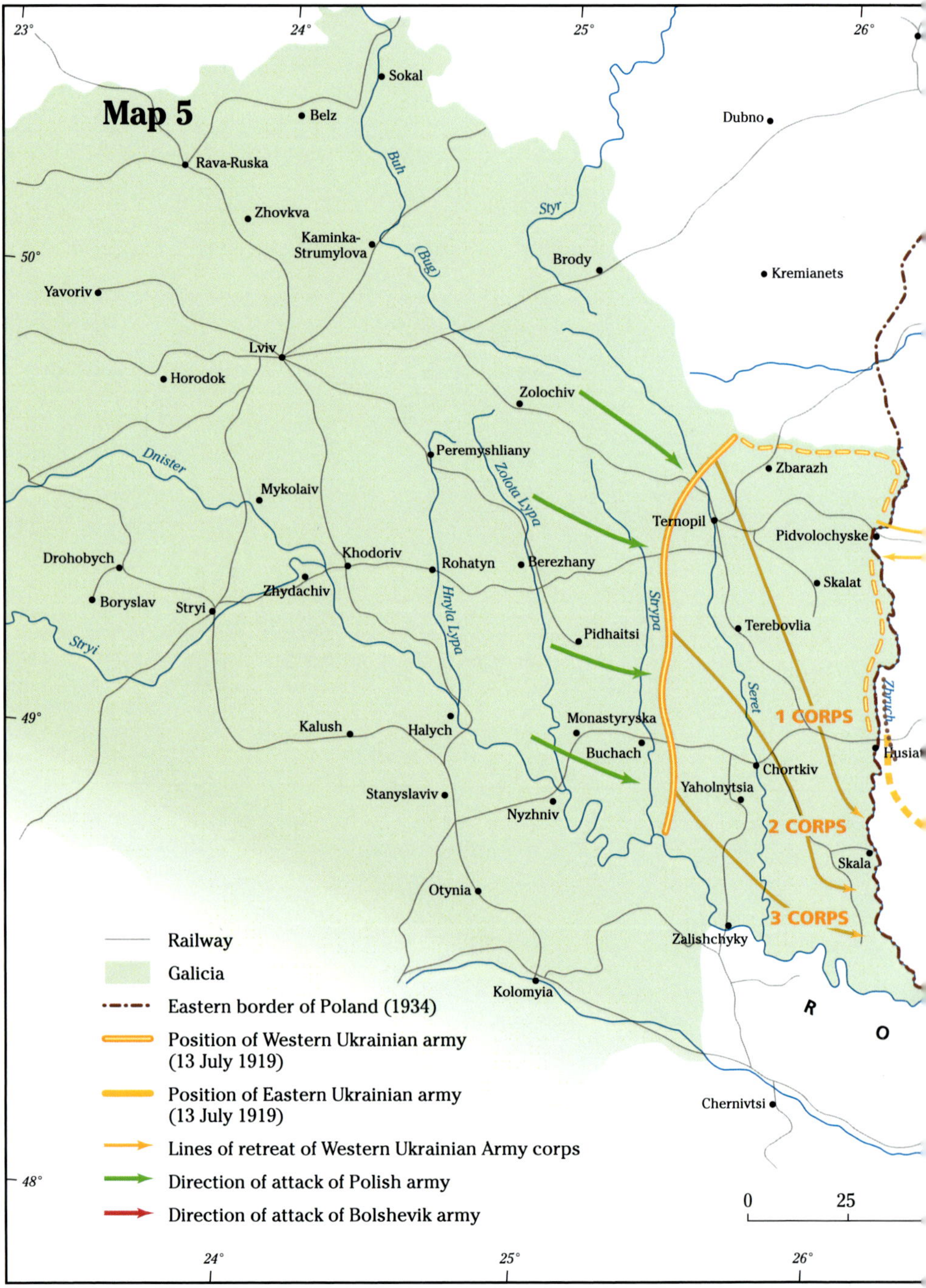

stern Ukrainians in July 1919

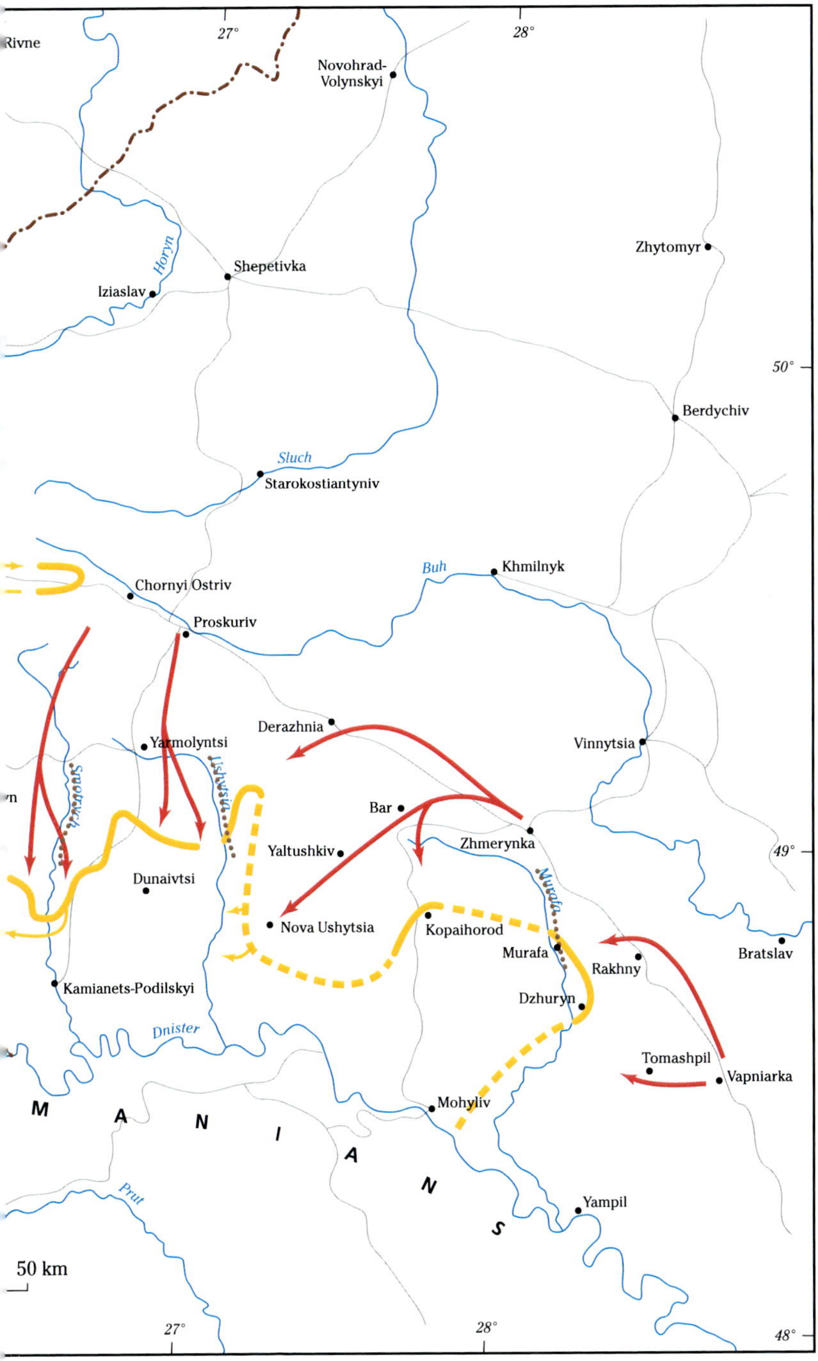

Map 6: The "Rectangle of Death" and the Advance of the United Ukrainian Ar

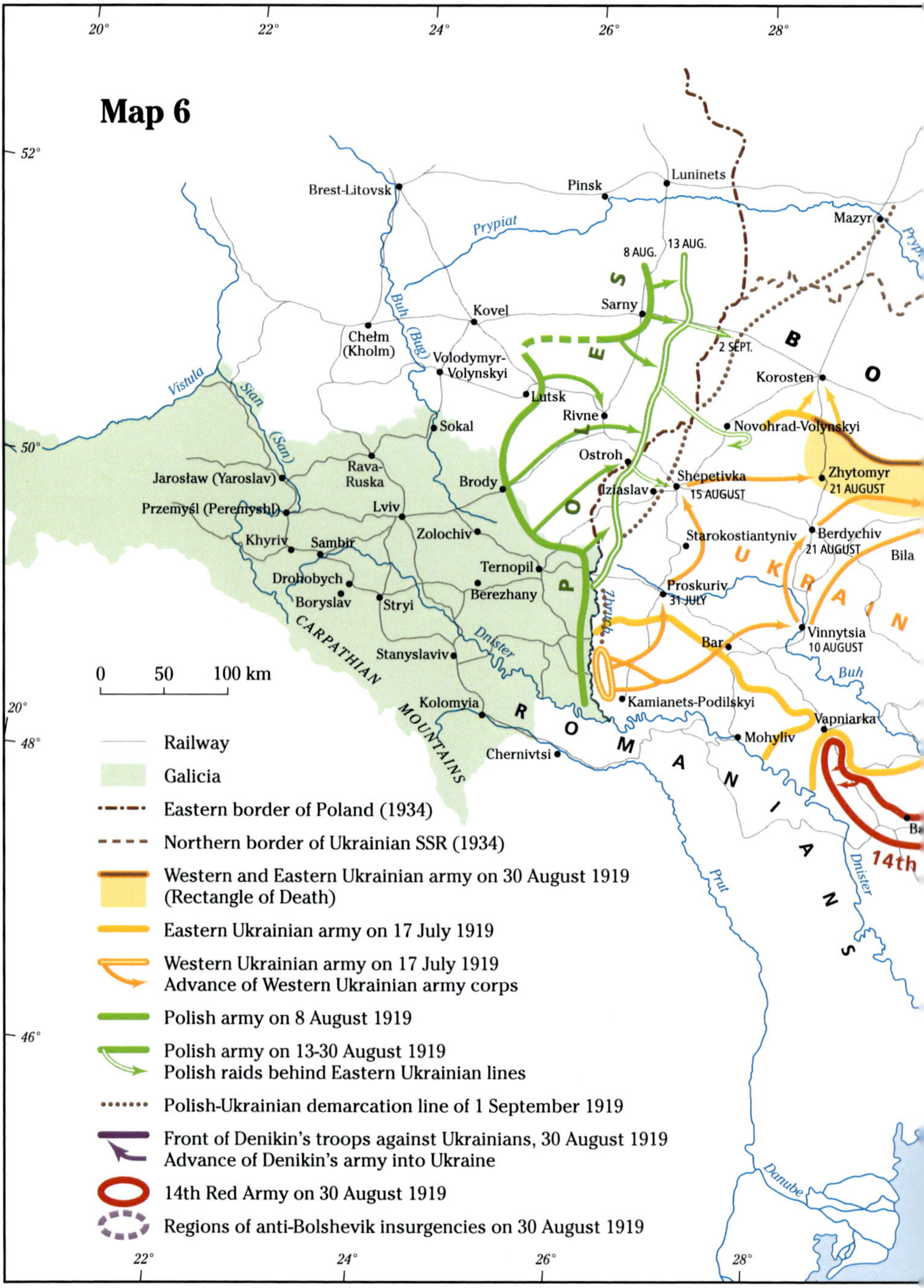

nies on Kyiv in August 1919

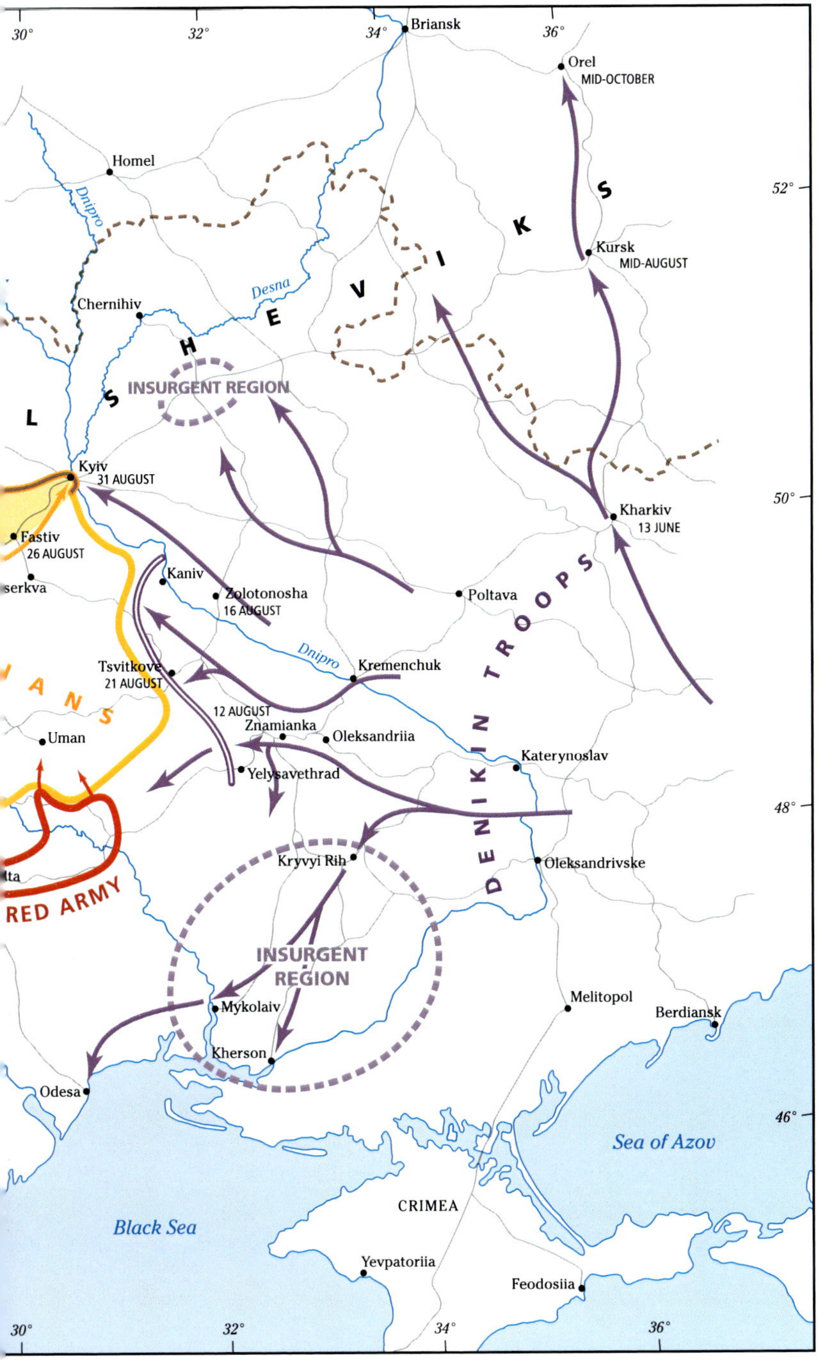

Index